LUTHER:
EARLY THEOLOGICAL WORKS

THE LIBRARY OF CHRISTIAN CLASSICS

ICHTHUS EDITION

LUTHER:
EARLY THEOLOGICAL
WORKS

Edited and translated by

JAMES ATKINSON, M.A.,
M.Litt., Dr. Theol.

Philadelphia
THE WESTMINSTER PRESS

Published simultaneously in the United States of America and in Great Britain by The Westminster Press, Philadelphia, and the S.C.M. Press, Ltd., London.

Library of Congress Catalog Card No. 62-12358

9   8   7   6   5   4   3   2   1

TYPESET IN GREAT BRITAIN
PRINTED IN THE UNITED STATES OF AMERICA

GENERAL EDITORS' PREFACE

The Christian Church possesses in its literature an abundant and incomparable treasure. But it is an inheritance that must be reclaimed by each generation. THE LIBRARY OF CHRISTIAN CLASSICS is designed to present in the English language, and in twenty-six volumes of convenient size, a selection of the most indispensable Christian treatises written prior to the end of the sixteenth century.

The practice of giving circulation to writings selected for superior worth or special interest was adopted at the beginning of Christian history. The canonical Scriptures were themselves a selection from a much wider literature. In the patristic era there began to appear a class of works of compilation (often designed for ready reference in controversy) of the opinions of well-reputed predecessors, and in the Middle Ages many such works were produced. These medieval anthologies actually preserve some noteworthy materials from works otherwise lost.

In modern times, with the increasing inability even of those trained in universities and theological colleges to read Latin and Greek texts with ease and familiarity, the translation of selected portions of earlier Christian literature into modern languages has become more necessary than ever; while the wide range of distinguished books written in vernaculars such as English makes selection there also needful. The efforts that have been made to meet this need are too numerous to be noted here, but none of these collections serves the purpose of the reader who desires a library of representative treatises spanning the Christian centuries as a whole. Most of them embrace only the age of the Church fathers, and some of them have long been out of print. A fresh translation of a work already translated may shed much new light upon its meaning. This is true even of Bible translations despite the work of many experts through the centuries. In some instances old translations have been adopted in this series, but wherever

9

necessary or desirable, new ones have been made. Notes have been supplied where these were needed to explain the author's meaning. The introductions provided for the several treatises and extracts will, we believe, furnish welcome guidance.

JOHN BAILLIE
JOHN T. McNEILL
HENRY P. VAN DUSEN

CONTENTS

General Introduction

Four distinctive writings from the early formative period of Luther's career (1517–21) have been selected for this volume. The writings are:

1. *The Commentary on the Epistle to the Hebrews.* March 1517–March 1518.
2. *The Disputation against Scholastic Theology.* September 4th, 1517.
3. *The Heidelberg Disputation.* April 21st, 1518.
4. *Answer to Latomus.* June 20th, 1521.

The purpose of the selection has been to show the young Luther at work in those vital formative years between 1517 and 1521, and to make available to English readers for the first time a representative selection of Luther's theological output during those years apart from the widely known Theses of 1517 and the Reformation Treatises of 1520. The selection embraces a complete commentary on a book of the New Testament given to undergraduates; a learned disputation against the scholasticism of his day for his academic colleagues; a long and sustained argument given before his fellow Augustinians of what his new theology meant long before any break with Rome; and finally, a full-scale learned justification of his position in controversy with the brilliant Latomus of reactionary Louvain, a controversy engaged on before Luther's appearance at Worms but completed during his enforced exile at the Wartburg. The last-named work is second only to Luther's *Bondage of the Will* in theological importance.

In reading these four books a man may see the death of the old medieval world and the birth of the new, and keep company for a few short hours with that shy monk who more than any other shattered the former and founded the latter. Readers should note carefully that in the first work of this volume, his commentary on the Epistle to the Hebrews, there can be clearly seen the young university scholar, an unknown monk teaching theology in a university backwater using the traditional medieval technique of gloss and scholion for the last time. Within the four short years which saw the publication of the four writings of this volume he had successfully challenged the Aristotelian scholasticism of his day, broken the revolting traffic in Indulgences (for Catholicism as well as Protestantism), and given a defence of his new theology to his fellow Augustinians at Heidelberg; he had faced John Eck at Leipzig and there launched the ship of the Reformation on the high seas with himself at the helm by showing to Eck and the world that the issue was not a matter of academic, scholastic theology but rather a matter of the priesthood of all believers, freedom in Christ, the authority of Scripture and the right and duty of private judgment; he had written his crucial Reformation Treatises of 1520 by first appealing to the intelligent and responsible laity, to the theologians with his Babylonish Captivity of the Church, and to all spiritual men by his Freedom of a Christian Man; and he had faced the organized authority of Church and State combined at Worms. At the end of those four years he stood a protected prisoner with neither pulpit nor lecture room, alone, with nothing but a Bible, a pen—and God. It was then that he wrote the *Contra Latomum*, the fourth work selected for this volume, which was a defence of his theology against the attack which emanated from the reactionary University of Louvain. (Louvain had sided against Erasmus and had blamed Erasmus for creating an intellectual climate in which Luther could flourish. It eventually goaded Erasmus into an attack on Luther some three years later, but at this period it was known that Louvain was preparing a theological attack on Luther.)

Such a period of theological turmoil and development played against a background of intense sociological, ideological, political and cultural change, could not but fascinate any thoughtful Christian man, and the four writings selected for this volume are determinative documents of those momentous years.

Translator's Preface

There are four very different types of work in this volume each one couched in its own technical linguistic and literary form. There is a commentary in traditional medieval form with glosses on the text, scholia and notes. Secondly, there is a terse disputation of ninety-seven theses which purports to attack the scholastic theology. There is thirdly a full-dress disputation called to make clear the meaning of the new evangelical theology. And lastly there is a full-length argument in normal continuous Latin prose written in defence of his position against a learned and informed criticism emanating from the conservative University of Louvain.

This diversity of writing, coupled with the fact that many of the terms Luther uses are re-charged or are being re-charged in an interaction with a momentous background of change and event, has made the translator's task difficult. I have sought therefore in the first place to make Luther's theological meaning clear, but at the same time I have tried to preserve some measure of formal dignity to the language as befits a man of Luther's historical significance as well as not to lose the touch of strong and forceful language of which he was master.

Notes and comments I have kept to a minimum, and where they were necessary, I have put them not in introductions nor appendices but rather as footnotes and insertions, so that the reader may be able to read the argument and have the help he might need on the page that is open in front of him without having to refer to introductory notes at the front or explanatory notes at the back of the book. I have always sought to be faithful to the text, but on those rare occasions where they have conflicted I have not allowed fidelity to the letter to take precedence over clarity of thought. Luther had a very great command over the Latin language, and though never careless in his use of the language could write that occasional false agreement or other *lapsus calami*. To such minor defects I have drawn no attention, and stick

15

resolutely to the task of making Luther write and talk in plain English. The scholar will neither read nor need this translation: he will always consult the original sources. This translation is made for the man or woman serious enough to want to know what Luther wrote and thought in those crucial years of 1517–1521, who feels he cannot avail himself of the sources, and even if he could, he still might not feel able to read the Latin with any ease or certainty. (In any case the material is available only in a few university and private libraries and not readily available for borrowing.) I hope simply that the general reader will be helped to a knowledge of these writings, as little known as they are available but of great importance none the less, and that the scholar may judge the translation as a reliable guide to Luther's thought and not too unworthy of the literary and theological worth of the originals.

The Bible text which Luther quotes I have translated as it stands with all its differences and variations. I have sought neither to correct nor amend it, for often Luther's comments take their point from the version of the scriptural text he is using. Further, many of his quotations seem to be made from memory. These again I have translated as quoted and not as found in the Vulgate. In the Luther text, particularly those texts like the Commentary on the Epistle to the Hebrews which were dictated by Luther, there is often found the opening words of a biblical quotation followed by an "etc." sign. In these cases I have completed the quotation to the extent I deem necessary in the context, and for this purpose translated from the text of the Vulgate. This practice was shown necessary by his frequently referring in the subsequent exposition to portions of the text embraced in the "etc." sign. In the case of the Psalms I thought it wise to adopt the number and verse of our English versions so that the English reader could the more readily read the reference in its context. On those occasions Luther remembers chapters (and sometimes even books wrongly!), though the Weimar editors consistently and properly give these as Luther wrote or dictated them, I have taken the liberty of correcting them, but make no reference to the original error.

To the massive and monumental scholarship of the Weimar editors every scholar is heavily indebted, not least myself. I am obliged to them for every one of their learned notes, comments and references. I have drawn heavily and fully upon them, as these scholars would have wished. In addition, I am also indebted to the fuller and more valuable critical apparatus of the Latin text of the Commentary on the Hebrews with annotations which Hirsch and

Rückert edited and published in 1929, and also to the German translation of the Scholia of that text by Vogelsang in 1930. In the case of the *Contra Latomum* I received welcome help from America. At the beginning of my labours Professor George Lindbeck sent me a typescript copy of the translation he was making for the Muhlenberg Press, but it was his copy which he had worked over several times and was therefore heavily corrected and almost illegible. At the end of my labours I received the final translation in the shape of Vol. 32 of the Philadelphia translation. I found his work as interesting as it was helpful and I am grateful both to him and to his publishers for their kind help. In the end I decided to go my own way and make my own translation. I have a secret admiration for the verve and freshness which characterize the American use of English, but I thought it better to make my own translation and keep the language in line with my three other translations. But it was not an easy decision, and I gratefully acknowledge the opportunity of reading Professor Lindbeck's prior translation.

Lectures on the Epistle to the Hebrews
(1517—1518)

INTRODUCTION

1. Form and Manner of Delivery

Luther's total exposition falls into two separate parts, that is, the Glosses and the Scholia. A gloss on a text is a brief linguistic explanation of a word or clause or even a whole sentence whereby the author seeks to elucidate the meaning of the word or clause or sentence. The writer may use merely one word and insert it in or around the text, or he may use whole phrases, sentences, parallel passages and even marginal comments and footnotes. Here is an example taken at random and is Luther's gloss on Hebrews 2:10:

> "DECEBAT dignum erat opus misericordia sua ENIM EUM, Deum patrem PROPTER QUEM OMNIA ad quem seu ad cuius gloriam sunt et fiunt ET PER QUEM[1] OMNIA[2], QUI per adoptionem gratiae i.e. adoptionis gratiam MULTOS FILIOS IN GLORIAM ADDUX-ERAT[3] praeparaverat adducere ab aeterno AUCTOREM ducem, caput SALUTIS EORUM PER PASSIONEM CONSUMARE, i.e. ut consumaret et perfectum redderet Christum.

The notes [1, 2, 3] are additional comment in the form of footnotes of five, one and one line length respectively. A scholion is a continuous prose comment on a word, or phrase or sentence of the biblical text, and may be as long as a paragraph or even several pages. This second part is what we would tend to call Luther's commentary proper.

The glosses were not necessarily written at the same time as the

19

scholia, nor were glosses and scholia given on one occasion. But it will be obvious that both the gloss and the scholion ought to be studied together if the reader is to know what Luther said or thought on a particular passage. Luther's normal method of delivery was to dictate both his glosses and his scholia, and it is generally believed that his normal practice was to gloss the text in its entirety first of all, and after this linguistic discipline had been done to turn to the text again and explain as fully as he deemed necessary the meaning and significance of the passage under examination.

For the benefit of his students Luther persuaded the printers to print a large, clear text of the Vulgate, with plenty of space for the students to write in, on and around the text, as well as in the margin, the glosses he felt necessary. In addition there were fuller notes of a scholarly nature, more often than not relating the passage to the rest of Scripture. Still further, there are occasionally *obiter dicta* which are not infrequently the most interesting as well as the most instructive of all his comments. With the exception of these last comments the material was dictated by Luther to his students.

All this material the Weimar editors have collated in a manner both simple and comprehensive. They have printed the Vulgate text bold and Luther's glosses in normal type to run on with the text. His further explanatory notes are included on the same page in the form of numbered footnotes. Footnotes exist in three forms which are preserved in three distinctive types. There is the series of numbered explanatory notes just mentioned which is printed in the normal type as the glosses. The second series of footnotes in small type is reserved for variant readings. The third printed in italics is the massively learned footnotes of the Weimar editors themselves which are of quite inestimable value containing biblical, patristic and other references. Luther's *obiter dicta* are contained within the text and marked with a pair of parallel lines at the beginning and end in the pattern of brackets thus: ‖*obiter dictum*‖. Immediately following the ninety-one pages of glosses there follow the one hundred and forty-one pages of scholia which present none of the above difficulties either to the editors or translator for they are straightforward Latin prose, although there is another difficulty in that the scholia cease with Hebrews 11:8.

The reader will have begun to realize already the complexity of rendering Luther's comments on the text of the Epistle to the Hebrews into normal English form. A Latin text glossed in the Latin language is readable as it is to "perfect Latin men," but once it has gone through this process the outcome has lost the perfect grammatical shape of the original text having been lengthened with modifying, qualifying and explanatory adjectives, nouns, verbs, adverbs and every type of clause conceivable, sometimes even a whole sentence or sentences, together with footnotes, and is therefore no longer a sentence as such. To put this amount of thinking into a normal English sentence was impossible. To put it into several sentences demanded a paraphrase with too much of the translator's own material to relate the points into a flowing idea.

I adopted the following technique with a view to giving the reader all this material in a form as near to normal English continuous prose as was possible. I have made the basis of the commentary the scholia, for these already exist in good continuous Latin prose. Where the glosses contain important theological material I have incorporated them *ad loc.*, together with any footnotes I judged as specially worth while. All glosses, and all notes from the glosses I have set in from the margin. The scholia alone take the full page. In certain instances where there is a change from one to another, or where there might be confusion, I have indicated the glosses by the sign "Gl." followed by page and line and the scholia by the sign "Sch." followed likewise by page and line. See for example pages 153, 169.

This practice was sound up to Heb. 11:8 when Luther had to break off to go to Heidelberg. After this point I incorporated all the glosses and notes in order to complete the commentary. It is interesting to note that after this point the glosses seem more detailed and more valuable than the earlier ones. In effect what we have in this volume is a complete translation of the scholia, which exist as far as Heb. 11:8 supplemented by any points in the glosses which are not included in the scholia, and completed by all the glosses and notes from Heb. 11:8–end.

The final problem was how to present a glossed text with notes where there was no scholion on which to base it. I adopted the simple form of setting down the Vulgate text in column form on the left half of the page in bold type with Luther's relevant glosses running parallel immediately opposite on the right hand of the page in column form. This may prove the most frustrating part of the book to the reader, but the translator could devise no better method if this material were to be contained within the translation (See the glosses from Heb. 11: 9–end pp. 215–250.)

By this stage I realized why this valuable text had never been Englished before today! Nevertheless, I offer it in good heart knowing the worth of the text if not the translation.

I have followed the Weimar text throughout, but grammatical errors and wrongly remembered texts and references (astonishingly many, considering Luther's phenomenal grasp of Scripture!) I have corrected without drawing attention to them. In one or two instances where the text was incomplete, or too briefly noted, or difficult, or where variant readings exist, I took the liberty of deciding for myself the reading which best suited the context, or even of offering the meaning in the form of a looser paraphrase. This was rare, and I have not drawn attention to these occasions, as such practice in a volume of this sort would serve pedantry rather than sound learning. A scholar will always use the original text: a translator can but offer a faithful and readable version and hope for the scholar's approval and the reader's gratitude.

2. CONTENT

It is not the intention to summarize the teaching of Luther's commentary on this Epistle, but to let Luther's work speak for itself after making a few preliminary remarks to guide the reader.

These lectures lasted a full year, and it is not only interesting to consider the historical events through which the lecturer was going (and which he was largely shaping), but such knowledge is of first importance in showing the reader a more sensitive appraisement of the content of the lectures. When he embarked on them all was quiet and uneventful. He was an unknown university don. Young and brilliant, true, but known only to his superiors and his students. Intense, earnest, scholarly; deeply concerned for and wholly committed to the life and work of his Church in society in general and in the university in particular. That is also true. But all this could be said of many another of his contemporaries. What could not be said of them is the ominous involvement in history and event Luther seemed destined to take. Within a few months he is involved in the Indulgences controversy and has nailed up his Ninety-Five Theses in the vain hope that men would discuss with him an issue of the gravest pastoral, theological and ecclesiastical concern long since grown utterly out of hand. The Archbishop of Mainz has lodged proceedings against him at Rome on a charge of heresy. The Dominicans are clamouring to have his blood. By the time he has reached Chapter 11, where he brings his lectures to an end, he is summoned to Heidelberg to give an account of his newly fashioned theology to his critical though interested fellow Augustinians. Every word of the lectures seems doubly charged. First, there is the plain meaning of his words, but secondly, there is the significant undertone of what the words meant in relation to the events which all sensed but whose outcome few could see. The former we can all see, and that meaning the translator is about to offer. The latter the reader himself can perhaps provide if he tried to put himself in the desks of those young men at Wittenberg in the spring of 1517 and listen to Father Martin. Young men who saw the Theses nailed up and were the first to discuss them; who heard of official proceedings of heresy against Martin; who heard his disputation against Scholastic Theology; who saw him walk away on a spring day in 1518 to Heidelberg to give a proper account of himself; who wondered if he would ever return. If the reader can put this into his reading he will be twice blessed. Against the pregnancy of this tumultuous background, whilst outwardly adhering both to the outward medieval form of gloss and scholion as well as to the medieval vocabulary in that stubborn conservatism which characterized him all his life, the thoughtful reader may sense him wresting his new theology under the divine necessity of event. The old garment is bursting at every seam. Already, to change the metaphor, he is sloughing off the old skin and the new body is working its way out to its new life newly clothed and fitted. It could be said and largely justified that already in this commentary the whole of Luther's theology appears to view even if not fully worked out and developed. The major themes of his theology are clearly discernible; for example, the centrality of Christ, atonement, faith and works, law and gospel, the Word of God, the theology of the cross.

In the matter of the theological content of this commentary, the editor draws the attention of the reader to the following emphases, not as a summary but as indicative of his thought. First, Luther's fresh formulation of the person and work of Christ. It was Luther's Christology that set him apart from contemporary theology and eventually shaped the new evangelical theology. Examples in the commentary may be found in his comments on Chapter 1. Note for instance his terse comments on 1:3 (p. 33f) where he sets Christ's work over against man's ideas of how he may approach God with his notions of penances and works-righteousness. Or again, 1:9 (p. 40f) on his teaching on righteousness in Christ. Or further, his comments on 2:10 (p 56f) and 2:14 (p. 58f) on Christ as the author of our salvation and Christ as the victor in the flesh over the dominion of death. Or again, his teaching on Christ, the great High Priest, bringing and effecting forgiveness for men on 5:1 (p. 102). Or further on 7:1 (p. 132), where the theme is righteousness in Christ (an equivalent term for justification by faith alone), and the difference between the Old Testament of Moses and the New Testament of Christ. See here especially the Corollary (p. 138).

Secondly, sin in this Epistle seems to be considered as that love of self which is the great enemy of a love of Christ and therefore prevents faith in Christ. Sin works for a kind of works-righteousness and militates against a true faith in Christ. Attention is drawn to his note on 13:15 (p. 257) and his glosses on 12:1 and 12:4 (pp. 227, 230). See further his long treatment of 1:8 and 1:9 on the theme of righteousness and note the tension between the law and the gospel and the consequences of a legalist religion (p. 38ff). Note, too, in these passages that the righteousness by the law is interpreted as a self-righteousness, but the righteousness in Christ is a new creation in man. There is a fine passage on 3:7 (p. 74ff) on the destruction of the self under the power of the Word of God.

Thirdly, there is present in this commentary Luther's mature distinction between the law and the gospel, woven through the texture of every doctrine. See his comments on 2:3 on salvation in Christ (p. 45f) and especially his long treatment of the theme on 7:12 (p. 137) followed by the Corollary (p. 138). Note also his chapter headings to each chapter of the Epistle where he keeps recapitulating the argument of the epistle and summing up its meaning. He identifies the work of the law as God's *opus alienum* and the work of the gospel as God's *opus proprium* (See 2:14, p. 58ff). Righteousness plays the same part as it does in his commentary on Romans, and central to it all is the expression of righteousness and grace in terms of Jesus Christ. As in the Heidelberg Disputation this incarnation theology is integrated into his newly developing theology of the cross. In other words Luther was emphasizing that it is not by our own powers of thought that we learn to know God and serve him rightly. Such thinking is to dwell with merely human concepts, and no matter how lofty they might on occasion be, they are nevertheless human, and therefore idolatrous in a religious sense. It is to make God in our own image. The only non-idolatrous image of God is the image God himself made for us in the humanity of Jesus and that humanity as it eventually faced the cross and was raised by God. Not only do we know God in this way as an empirical fact, but it is the only way the Church may know God in a fallen world, and the way intended. Note also the authority of the law on 2:1 (p. 44f) and the careful discussion of law and gospel in the long Chapter 9 (pp. 157–188).

Fourthly, never far from Luther is his primacy of the Word of God. This he sees as the divine activity expressed in its most articulate form as gospel. It is the divine instrument through which he intended and intends to address man. See especially his comments on 3:1 and 3:7 (pp. 67f, 73ff). He stresses the importance of reading it not in the light of one's own study and understanding but in the light of the internal testimony of the Holy

Ghost, 3:12 and 10:5 (pp. 8of, 193). On 4:12 he discusses the Word of God and its meaning under six headings (p. 94f), and then under his second exposition (p. 95) its present and ultimate authority.

Fifthly, faith, too, receives its due proportion of emphasis. Note particularly the glosses on faith and unfaith on 3:12; 4:2; 11:29; and 11:32 (pp. 81f, 86f, 222, 223). The reader should note his long exposition of 5:1 on Christ as the High Priest appointed by God. Especially interesting is his treatment of faith in relation to works throughout the Epistle, as are the passages on faith and works in his comments on 3:12 and 9:24 (pp. 8of, 183) and his discussion of the meaning of the story of Cain and Abel in 11:4 as the difference between a religion of faith and a religion of works. Luther emphasizes faith as the work of God and not man's own, in for instance his gloss on 10:38 where, in a footnote he further discusses justification by faith. He removes it out of the realm of psychological subjectivism altogether and sets · in its happy healthful sphere of divine activity and initiation. Luther's teaching on faith at this early and non-polemical stage of his career has a precious and peculiar value. His emphases here, if remembered, would have safeguarded against much of the later misunderstandings of Protestantism on faith, and particularly how its opponents have tended to think of it. Luther keeps faith closely linked to the mercy of God and to the grace of God. See his scholion on 2:16 (p. 65) as well as both his glosses and scholia on the chapter on faith, chapter eleven pp. 202, 226). It is on the climax of faith that the scholia end. Protestantism sometimes tends to make of justification by faith an article of faith, or in certain circumstances a party cry. But with Luther it was the sole, only and full basis of a man's total salvation in Christ. The value of the phrase is most clearly seen in a polemical situation; or perhaps as a safeguard against the inclination of the natural man to believe that he must be acceptable to a good God by virtue of his fundamental decency or his honest moral effort (the worth of both of which nobody either denies or disapproves). But the fundamental meaning of justification by faith alone, which Luther safeguards in this epistle by relating it to the grace of God and his mercy, and by keeping the centre of gravity within God never within man, is salvation in Christ only—no more, no less.

Lectures on the Epistle to the Hebrews
1517–1518

(*WA*, 57, Pt 3. pp. 1–238)

(Gl. followed by chapter and verse means a gloss on that text, or sometimes a gloss with a footnote, or the footnote itself, or an introductory note to a gloss.

Sch. followed by chapter and verse means a scholion on that text. Ed.)

THE TEXT

CHAPTER ONE

Gl. 1:1 (5:10). The reader must bear in mind that in this Epistle Paul is commending trust in the grace of God as opposed to any confidence in a humanistic and legalistic righteousness. He set out to prove that apart from Christ neither the law nor the priesthood, neither prophecy nor even the ministry of angels in the last resort, are sufficient unto salvation. On the contrary, all these were instituted and effected to find their fulfilment in the Christ who was to come. There is no shadow of doubt that Paul laid down that what needed to be taught was Christ, and Christ alone.

1:1. In olden days God spoke to our fathers through the prophets in many different ways and by many different means. Now at last in these days he has spoken to us in a Son, whom he has appointed to inherit all things.

There would appear to be this difference between the two words **in many ways**[1] (*multifariam*) and **by many means**[2] (*multis modis*). *Multifariam* refers to the distribution of the prophetic gifts among the many, as we read in Num. 11:17: "I will take some of the spirit which rests on you and give it to them instead." We also read of it in Acts 2:17: "I will pour out my spirit upon all flesh." *Multimodus* on the other hand, refers to the varied and repeated use every prophet whoever he may be makes of this one and the same gift. Consequently, every prophet is hammering away as often as not at the same prophetic message. Or, it is the same prophetic message he produces in different thought forms for different people.

It amounts to this: in times past God apportioned to many the spirit of prophecy, and through such apportionment caused Christ to be preached in many different ways. As a result, it is not so much

---

1 *Polymeros* = consisting of many parts.
2 *Polytropos* = in various modes.

a matter of there being one preacher of Christ but many. And not only are there many of them but in fact everyone of them prophesied in different ways. On the strength of this Paul adduces for his argument many a prophet, and also uses one and the same prophet, whether it be an Isaiah or a David, in many a different way. This distinction the Greek text seems to approve. It reads *polymeros* and *polytropos*. *"Poly"* means many, and *"Meros"* a part, therefore the word as an adverb means multipartite so to speak, which in Latin is translated *multifariam*.[1] *Tropos*, on the other hand, means mode or manner, and therefore *Polytropos* really signifies in many ways or in many forms.[2, 3]

In this way the Apostle established the most powerful argument (from the smaller to the greater as it is usually described). It amounts to this in fact: if the word of the prophets is accepted, how much more ought we to seize the Gospel of Christ, since it is not a prophet speaking to us but the Lord of the prophets, not a servant but a son, not an angel but God. And further, it is not our forefathers he is addressing, but us. Quite clearly the Apostle argues in this way so that every excuse of unbelief is excluded. Such an excuse our fathers understandably had, for they were given the Word by angels, by Moses and by prophets. They themselves used the same argument: "We are disciples of Moses: but we do not know this man, nor where he comes from" in 9:2 f. The Apostle lays the coping stone to this argument in chapter two where he says: "Therefore, we ought to give the more earnest heed to the things that we heard, lest happily we drift away from them" (Heb. 2:1).

1:2. Through whom he created the worlds also.

He describes the one and the same Christ both as Son of Man and Son of God. When he speaks of Christ in the phrase "appointed to inherit all things" it properly applies to him in respect of his humanity. However, when he says, "through whom he created the worlds also" it properly applies to him with regard to his divinity. With these and the following words, right down to the end of the chapter, he furthers his argument, which he substantiated with a wealth of biblical quotation. It is the same argument which he

---

1 "at sundry times" in the Authorized Version.
2 "in divers manners" in the Authorized Version.
3 It was a cardinal principle of Luther's biblical exegesis not merely that the Old Testament was fulfilled in the New Testament but more strongly that the Bible could only be understood backwards. The long story of man's salvation can only be understood when the last act, i.e. the birth, death and resurrection of Christ is understood.

lightly touched upon in his prologue to the Epistle to the Romans,[1] where he said, "Declared[2] to be the son of God in power" (Rom. 1:4). In this passage from the Epistle to the Romans, the Apostle merely states but does not develop the idea that Christ was "declared Son of God." In the text from the Epistle to the Hebrews which we are discussing, he states the very same idea and makes it perfectly plain not only in his own words but by quotations from Scripture.[3] Of these he aptly introduces six of the most important.

To revert to the text, "through whom he made the worlds also," he refers to "the worlds also" in the plural (secula), although there is by all appearances only one world (seculum). Presumably he does this to show that Christ is the Author of all the worlds, that is of this world and the world to come. It is true seculum can be taken quite literally to mean a century, but it is better understood in this context as meaning two worlds, viz., this present world and the world to come. Christ referred to these two worlds in the words, "Whosoever shall speak a word against the Holy Spirit, it shall not be forgiven him neither in this world, nor the world to come" (Matt. 12:32). The Apostle also said: "Above every name that is named, not only in this world but even in the world to come" (Eph. 1:21). There are, however, in the world to come the angels who have been created, and man therefore as far as his body (corpus seculorum) matters is in this world, but as far as his soul is concerned, is in the world to come. In short, man knows of two worlds, and partakes of two worlds.

Now the Apostle's procedure must be very carefully noted. First he declares the humanity of Christ and then proceeds to his divinity. As a consequence, he establishes that principle by which true knowledge of God may be found. For the humanity of Christ is that holy ladder set for us. It is on the rungs of this ladder we rise to a knowledge of God. Cf. Gen. 28:12. See also John 14:6: "No man cometh to the Father but by me." And again "I am the door" (John 10:7). Therefore, whoever wishes to rise to a true love of God and knowledge of God, let him put away all the human and metaphysical rules on how to attain to the knowledge of God,

---

[1] Luther does not raise the question here whether or not the Epistle to the Hebrews is of Pauline authorship.

[2] The text of Luther's version has "praedestinatus". This word was later to have a stronger meaning for Luther, but here it is clear he takes the word in the sense of declared or decreed rather than predestined or foreordained. Support for this view can be found in his exposition of the actual text in Rom. 1:4. See WA, 57, 7.10 ff.

[3] Here Luther expresses another of his cardinal principles of biblical exposition, viz., Scripture is its own interpreter. It was his invariable practice to elucidate Scripture by other passages of Scripture and not by speculation.

and as his first task let him seek to understand the humanity of Christ. After all, when God himself humbled himself to make himself known to us, it is the most impious rashness for man, by the exercise of his own wisdom, to plan for himself some other way of salvation[1].

1:2 Who, being the brightness of his glory and the express image of his person

The Apostle says the same thing as this to the Colossians, "Who (i.e., Christ) is the image of the invisible God" (Col. 1:15), i.e., of this God who is not seen. And it is written in the Book of Wisdom: "Wisdom is the glow that radiates from eternal light, she is the untarnished mirror of God's majesty, she is the likeness of his goodness" (7:26). For the brightness or the reflection of God (in Christ) is described as the likeness of the glory of God. It is so described because it is not to us but to God that the simile "the glory of God" applies. In this description the Father sees himself and it is he who is reflected back. There then follows the phrase, "the express image of his person." This statement is tautologous and merely repeats the same thing. The expression "the brightness of his glory" does not necessarily affirm a distinction of persons in the Trinity as some expositors would have it. Neither does the expression "the express image of his person" necessarily affirm the unity of the divine essence. For both ideas are meant in both expressions. It should also be observed that in this passage the Greek text does not have "*typos*" i.e., "*schema*" which properly connotes "*figura*," nor "*ousia*" which signifies essence or substance, but the text has: *charakter tes hypostaseos autou* i.e., the sign, the mark, the pattern of his substance or essence. Not that the nature of the essence of God belongs to us. No! That belongs only to God alone. Hence only God perceives his own form in himself (i.e., in Christ). For this reason the Apostle did not say simply "his glory and his image,"

---

1 In this section Luther gives expression to a view that was later to thrust him into a life-long polemic, and was also to be determinative for his own theology. The view should be carefully noted. Luther denies the validity of all efforts to climb up to a knowledge of God, be they moral, mystical or rational. All true knowledge of God he taught began in the incarnation whose end is the cross. There could be for Luther no *theologia gloriae*, only a *theologia crucis*. This set Luther against the generally accepted ecclesiastical technique, and he abandoned all anthropocentric efforts to earn salvation or to seek a knowledge of God whether it was the road of speculation, the path of mysticism or the way of works. This was all but a part of Luther's total view of salvation as justification in Christ alone.

Readers will recall the emphasis Anders Nygren places on this argument in his *Agape and Eros*. Regin Prenter makes frequent reference to Luther's incarnational approach. Vide *Creator Spiritus*. See particularly in this volume the Heidelberg Disputation, p. 274.

for both angels and men are the images of the splendour of God and the signs of his Majesty. The Apostle does in fact say "the brightness of his glory and the image of his person," so that by means of this image we may understand the unique, innermost nature of God. That we are made in the image of God is for our own sakes rather than God's. It is not that God recognizes himself in us but that we recognize God in ourselves.

1:3. Upholding all things by the word of his power

The participle "upholding" is charged with a special significance. It is a Hebrew idiom for which there is no adequate Latin or Greek equivalent. The Apostle has Hebraicized the word. Thus what we describe as "keeping," the Hebrews more appropriately describe as "carrying." This word captures the idea of a certain delightful care in cherishing the things he created, even a motherly care we might say. The idea is found in Deut. 32:11: "He spread out his wings and took him up, and carried him on his back." Or again in Isa. 46:3 f.: "Listen to me, O house of Jacob, and all the remnant of the house of Israel, who have been borne by me from birth, and carried from the womb. Even to your old age, I am he; and even to hoar hairs will I carry you: I have made and I will bear; even I will carry you, and I will save you." The same thought is expressed in Num. 11:12: "Have I conceived all this multitude? (have I begotton them) that thou shouldst say unto me, Carry them in thy bosom, as a nursing mother beareth the sucking child, (unto the land which thou swarest unto their fathers)?"

Gl. 6.2 ff.: "Upholding all things." might have been better expressed in terms of purpose, *viz.*, "that he might uphold all things . . . ," i.e., that he might gently rule all things by the word of his power. This he performs of his own gracious will and by the order of his own authority and power. The purging of our sins, which neither law nor priest effected, he performed.

This he did by means of his passion, and now sits at the right hand of God. . . .

1:3. When he had purged our sins

By these words he forthwith makes short work of all notions of righteousness and every idea of penances which the natural man holds. It is the supreme mercy of God he commends. This means that it was he who purged our sins and not we ourselves, and that it is our own sins he has purged, and not the sins of somebody else. Therefore we must despair of our own penances and our own purging of our sins, because before we even begin to confess, our sins have already been forgiven. I would even go on to say, that it is not till then (i.e., until we despair of our own penance and purging), that Christ's own purging becomes operative, and produces true penitence in us. It is in this way that his righteousness works our righteousness. This is just what Isaiah meant when he said: "All we like sheep have gone astray. Each of us has gone off on his own way, and God laid on his shoulder our guilt, the guilt of us all" (Isa. 53:6).

1:5. Did God ever say to one of the angels, Thou art my Son, I have begotten thee this day?

The words "I have begotten thee this day" may be understood as referring either to the human or to the divine generation of Christ. Augustine[1] took it as referring to the divine generation, wherefore he interpreted the word "today" as meaning "in eternity." So also did ·Peter Lombard.[2] Yet it could be taken not inappropriately as referring to the human generation of Christ for the following three reasons. First, because divine generation is never described anywhere else in Scripture as having taken place in time, nor is it associated with such a temporal phrase as the word "today." On the contrary, it is understood as having taken place before time began, as it says in Ps. 72:17, "His name abides before the sun." This Paul of Burgos explains, "Before the sun was created his name was begotten." Or, as other Hebraists expound it, The Son's generation or name was known before the sun. And again in Prov. 8:25, "Before any hill was made was I born."

Secondly, (a second reason for taking the text as referring to human generation), the Hebrew idiom expresses a precise and clear time by the word "today," of such a kind that it requires its own article in the Greek. It was in the Hebrew thus: Today, or on the first day (that is on some precise and accountable day), I begat thee. This day was in fact the day of Christ's birth.

Thirdly, it is consonant with the passage of Scripture in Isa. 8:2 f.: "And I took to myself faithful witnesses, Uriah the priest and Zachariah, the son of Baruch, and I went in to the prophetess, and she conceived and brought forth a son." That these words were spoken not as applying to the person Isaiah but of God himself, Nicholas Lyra proves learnedly enough at least. His proof is based on the fact that Zachariah and Uriah whom he names as witnesses lived long after Isaiah. Therefore it was the Lord who went in to the prophetess and the prophetess was the Virgin Mary. For she

1 Aug., *Enarratio in Ps.* 2:6; Migne, 36.71.
2 *Peter Lombard, Sent.* I. dist. 2, 6; Migne, 192.528.

submitted herself to no man, only to God. And God did this not in the flesh which he does not possess, but in the Holy Spirit, through whom "he went in unto her," and through whom "she conceived and brought forth a son," the Son of God. It is of him God now speaks when he says, "It is I who have today begotten thee." As if to say, "Even as man thou art my Son—but a Son born of the Virgin."

1:5. **And again, he shall find in me a Father, and I in him a Son?**

We do not deny that in a literal sense this text could be understood as referring both to Solomon and to Christ. Nevertheless, it can be very convincingly shown that it refers only to Christ. The words were spoken of Christ and have been thus understood. This may be proved from the text itself and then from the prophets who sing his praises most diligently and time and again are constantly found saying the same thing. This is especially true of the psalms. He says to David: "... and this too the Lord promises thee, that the Lord will grant thy line continuance. So, when thy days are ended and thou sleepest with thy fathers, I will set up thy seed after thee which shall proceed from thine own body, and I will establish the throne of his kingdom for ever" (II Sam. 7:12). This is sung in Ps. 132:11, "The fruit of thy loins will I set upon thy throne." But it is clear that Solomon was born before the end of David's days. He had not only been delivered from the womb, but set upon the throne. *Therefore it is Christ who is meant here, the fruit of the loins of David, i.e., The womb of the Virgin Mary, who was born of the seed of David. For that reason her womb is called the loins of David.* This mode of speech is not unusual in the Scriptures, since both "belly" and "loins" of men are attributed to the devil: His strength (Behemoth) is in his loins and his power in the navel of his belly (Job 40:16). Therefore it is right that with David and the other prophets we understand this promise as referring to Christ. We find the same thing in Isa. 55:3: "I will give to you the faithful mercies of David," or as Luke renders it in Acts 13:34: "I will give to you the privileges I have promised to David." These promised privileges mean sanctifying grace, grace eternal promised to David from the mercy of God. The same thought is to be found in Ps. 89:1: "I will sing unto eternity of the mercy of the Lord," or better still, "I will sing of the eternal mercy of the Lord."

1:6. **And let all the angels of God worship him**

It is never recorded that angels worshipped another angel or that angels worshipped a man. But what we do read is that angels were worshipped by Moses as well as by Lot and Abraham, and by

Joshua and the other prophets as well. We even read that kings were worshipped, as David was by Nathan and Bathsheba in I Kings 1:16, 23.

On these grounds, therefore, it stands an incontrovertible argument that the man Christ was very God, because it is written that he was worshipped by the angels, and what is more, not only by some of them but by all of them. The authority of the Apostle in this passage is sufficient proof that the psalm under discussion (Psalm 97) should be interpreted as referring to Christ the God incarnate, as our ruling King in the present-day Church.

If we were to demand further proof, then almost every single word of the psalm supports this argument. For when the psalmist writes: "The Lord reigns as King: let the whole earth be glad about it, let the remotest isles rejoice," he doubtless means by the words "the whole earth" and "the remotest isles" mankind now living on this earth and in these islands, because had he meant God's Kingdom as distinct from Christ's present Kingdom on this earth, he would have said: "Let the heavens rejoice, let the angels be glad."

Further, there is another reason. The Kingdom of Heaven does not have "cloud and darkness round about." There there is the purest brightness, for there we shall see him as he is. On the other hand, it is Christ's Kingdom which is in the cloudy enigma of faith, as Ezekiel says, I will cover the sun with cloud (Ezek. 32:7). That means, I will take captive the wisdom of men by faith. Moreover, in the Kingdom of Christ his throne is maintained by righteousness and justice, but in heaven there will be no place for correction, nor judgement, nor any cross. It will be a place of peace and complete salvation. Neither do the other words of the Psalm apply, ". . . a fire goeth before him to burn up his enemies round about him," since only his friends are there. Nor the words, "the heavens will declare his righteousness" because there "tongues will cease." Nor will there be any need of exhortation as "Ye who love the Lord will hate evil," because in heaven there is nothing but good.

1:7. **Who makes his angels spirits**

Even if the Master of the Sentences, and many others with him, construe and understand this verse by hypallage[1], we disagree. With this technique they interpret the text as meaning that God

---

1 The phrase is *"per hipallagen"*, from the Greek. It means a rhetorical figure of speech in which the parts of a proposition seem to be mutually interchanged to draw out a paradoxical meaning, by means of interchange of cases or attraction of adjectives to nouns to which they do not properly belong.

made the spirits angels, and not that God made the angels spirits. They seek to describe in this verse not the nature of angels but their work. It is possible to disagree with them, and not without considerable justification.

In the first place, it is certain that the Apostle understands the word "makes" as applied to the creation of angels: he uses the word in this sense throughout the passage. It is as if he intended to say, God makes, i.e., God creates angels to exist as spiritual beings.

Secondly, their view is not acceptable, because it is plain to see that the name "angel" describes not the nature but the office[1]. Of course, the word also means the nature of the being, though it is derived from the office and assignment. In the same way we find in the Scriptures many things are called by the names of events that have not yet happened. For example, the tree of the knowledge of good and evil becomes the tree of life, and other examples.

The third ground of disagreement is that it would be difficult to change round the other half of the verse by this same trick of hypallage, and read, "who makes flames of fire into his ministers."

Finally the Holy Spirit if he wished could say quite clearly, "who makes spirits into his angels and a flame of fire into his ministers."

Wherefore, in the light of these arguments, and offering no headstrong unconsidered opinion, we understand this verse to mean the following, viz., those who are angels and are called angels God makes into spirits; those who minister to him he makes into flames of fire. By these words he glorifies their nature in a metaphor: he means quite plainly that they are not in the form of flesh and blood, but are "spirit," that is nature at its finest and fastest.

For this reason it is said of them in Ps. 104:3, "Who walketh upon the wings of the winds," i.e., the wings of the spirits or angels. Moreover, they are of the clearest and brightest nature like fire burning and resplendent, as in the case of the angel sitting by the sepulchre of Christ "whose countenance was like the lightning." For when we have here, "a flame of fire," in the Hebrew it has, according to Jerome, "a burning fire." As Johannes Reuchlin[2] describes it "fire quivering and scintillating" like a polished sword in the sun, or like a concave mirror gleams and scintillates. Be that as it may, the angels are described as fiery and fleet as the stars which shine, because they rejoice and exult in the praise and worship of God, as it says in Job 38:7:

[1] Luther is obviously referring to the etymology of the word angel, viz., angelos, messenger.
[2] Johannes Reuchlin (1455–1522) the distinguished Hebraist. Note how Luther looks up the Hebrew text in Old Testament quotations, here and elsewhere.

"The stars of the morning sang with me,
And all the sons of God shouted for joy."

1:8. Thy throne, O God, is an everlasting throne

It is common knowledge that the Greek word for throne *thronos* is the same as the Latin *sedes*. This throne, however, means heaven itself, that is the spiritual populace "whose conversation is in heaven." As we find in Isa. 66:1: "Heaven is my throne." And also in Ps. 19:4: "He set up a tabernacle for the sun among them," as it says in the Hebrew[1]. Or again, in Ps. 114:1 f.: "When Israel came out of Egypt, the house of Jacob from a strange people, Judah was made his sanctuary and Israel his dominion." In other words, Judah was consecrated to priesthood for God, and Israel to lordship and kingship. All this was done that God himself might be King and Priest, and his people the priestly kingdom or royal priesthood. As it says in I Peter 2:9: "But ye are an elect people, a royal priesthood, a holy nation." And also as Moses says in Ex. 19:6: "All the earth is mine, and ye shall be to me a priestly kingdom, a holy nation . . ." Truly, all the things described in this verse, run counter to all human reason. The reason for this is that those who want to grasp the truth of these matters need a faith as tough as oak. For nothing is more unlike a throne, especially God's throne, than the people of Christ, if we have regard to the outward appearance. For these people look like no kingdom, but rather like a people in exile; a people not living but always a-dying; a people not in glory but in shame; a people living not in wealth but in the direst poverty. And just exactly the same, whoever wishes to be a partaker in this kingdom, must experience the same ignominies and sufferings in his own person. The insignia of Christians are poverty, tribulation, sorrow. This is how God's throne should be distinguished. And God's throne is man[2].

1:8. A sceptre of righteousness

According to the Hebrew idiom the sceptre (*virga*) signifies the royal sceptre, as in Gen. 47:31 and Heb. 11:21, Israel worshipped "leaning on the top of his staff (*virga*)," which Jerome translated "bowed himself on the head of the bed." The Greek word sceptre (*sceptron*) is called in Latin a virge (*virga*). Thus in Esther 5:2: "He held out the golden sceptre (virge), which he was holding in his

---

1 The Hebrew text reads literally:
"For the sun is set a tabernacle in them." In the context the passage probably means that the sun after running his daily course sinks into his tabernacle, but Luther's version seems acceptable.
2 The last three sentences were made as *ex tempore* comment by Luther on his original MS.

hand, and drawing near Esther kissed the tip of the sceptre (virge)." This means the "iron sceptre" by which Christ rules us, and by which in the long run he breaks the carnal old man as a "potter's vase" (Ps. 2:9). As also Ps. 110:2: "The Lord will send from Zion the sceptre of thy strength, to rule in the midst of thine enemies." Isa. 2:3 and Micah. 4:2 are interpreted in the same way: "The law will go forth out of Zion, and the Word of the Lord from Jerusalem." And so is the Apostle in Rom. 1:16: "For I am not ashamed of the Gospel. For it is the power of God unto salvation to everybody who believes." Although others[1] interpret this sceptre as meaning unyielding power, as indeed it certainly is, yet in the real nature of the case it is nothing else of course than the Gospel of Christ or the Word of God. For by no power other than the Word does Christ rule the Church, as it is written, "By the word of the Lord were the heavens made . . ." (Ps. 33:6). According to the Hebrew, however, it says "sceptre of equity." That means righteousness, or, what amounts to the same thing, uprightness. In Latin this would be expressed as a just sceptre, or a righteous sceptre, or a true sceptre, just as in Ps. 21:3 we read, "with blessings of delight," which we would express in Latin, with delightful blessings. Therefore, unlike all other kingdoms, including even the synagogue though possessing the law of God, it is called the "sceptre of thy kingdom." It is not like other kingdoms whose sceptre is a sceptre of crookedness and wickedness. Of thee alone is the sceptre a sceptre of righteousness. For there is no doctrine whatever, be it secular or spiritual, philosophical or indeed of any kind at all devised by man, which is able to direct man in the right path and make him righteous. If indeed it brings him so far as to establish good habits, it yet leaves him a man in bondage to the old Adam. Therefore of necessity such doctrine makes nothing but dissemblers and hypocrites, for the dregs and filthy bilge water still remain in the unredeemed old man: this is, of course, the love of self. On that account it is rightly called a wicked doctrine, since it has not the power to make a man righteous. But the gospel, on the other hand, says: "Unless a man be born again of water and the spirit, he cannot enter the kingdom of heaven" (John 3:5). Thus the gospel retains nothing of the old man but destroys him in his entirety, and goes on making the new man until the stage is reached where a man so hates himself that he roots out self-love from the very depths of his being through faith in Christ. Therefore, vain is all boasting of learning, wisdom and knowledge, no matter how good and praiseworthy gifts of God they are, for

---

[1] *Glossa Ordinaria* on Heb. 1:8, Augustine, Migne, 36.504, and Nicholas Lyra in Ps. 44:17. See notes by Hirsch-Rückert, p. 111.

nobody is made any the better by them. Further, apart from the fact that these things do not make a man good they become rather a shield to his wickedness and a veil over his diseased nature. The result is that those who flatter themselves on the possession of these, and seem righteous and redeemed in their own eyes, put themselves beyond redemption.

1:9. **Thou hast loved righteousness and hated iniquity**

This text follows aptly on the phrase, "the sceptre of righteousness," for it is that sceptre which makes real this love of righteousness and this hatred of iniquity. Therefore this text refers to none other than Christ, because no one except Christ alone has loved righteousness. All others love money, or pleasure, or honour, or if they despise these things, at all events they love glory: or even, be they the best of people, they still love themselves more than they love righteousness. For the same reason Micah says: "The good man has perished from the earth and there is not a righteous man among men; the best of them is as a briar, and the righteous as a thorn hedge" (Micah 7:2, 4). And the reason follows at once, because "they describe the evil work of their hands as good." Therefore, as long as the love of self is there, a man is unable to reach the stage where he can love righteousness, speak righteousness and work righteousness, though he may appear to do all these. It follows that the virtues of all philosophers, indeed of all men whether canonists or theologians, though they have the appearance of virtues are in reality vices.

Therefore, it has to be realized that this righteousness must be understood as the righteousness of God and not the righteousness of men (i.e., the righteousness acceptable to God and not a righteousness acceptable to men). For the righteousness of men always remains piecemeal and particularist (*particularis*): it gives to a particular person what is his, be it money, possessions, honour and so on, nevertheless, it does not give its own things to other people. Worse still, it lusts after the things of others for itself. Last and most important, the righteousness of men never gives the glory to God, while the righteousness of God gives and returns to God and man his own self and all that he has. Therefore, it is of the nature of Christ alone to love righteousness and hate iniquity; on the other hand, it is of the nature of man to love iniquity and hate righteousness. But, it is of the nature of a Christian man to begin to hate iniquity and love righteousness, nor does he manifest any love except the love he manifests through Christ. This statement of showing love through Christ means that Christ, the lover of righteousness, fills up with his own love our love as it begins to form in us. The following texts may be adduced in support of this view: "Abominable and filthy is man who drinks iniquity like water" (Job 15:16). "Every man is a liar . . ." (Ps. 116:11). But concerning the Christian man James says: "That we might be a kind of first fruits of his creation" (James 1:18).

1:12. [And, Thou, Lord, in the beginning hast laid the foundation of the earth, and the heavens are the works of thy hands. They shall perish; but thou continuest: And they all shall wax old as doth a garment; And as a mantle shalt thou roll them up, And as a garment,] they shall be changed.

Gl. (8:18). The preceding verses of the above quotation, (Ps. 102:25 ff.), compel us to interpret the passage as referring to Christ, i.e., from verse 13, "Thou shalt arise and have mercy on Zion . . .", right down to the passage quoted by the Apostle beginning at verse 25, "Of old hast thou laid the foundation of the earth. . . ." In this Psalm the incarnation of the Divine Majesty and the rule of the Incarnate Son is promised, and we are forced to understand the passage as referring to nobody but the Person of the Son.

He says quite precisely "they will be changed" and not "they will perish," and means that they will be changed as a man changes his clothes. The same reference occurs in the Scriptures elsewhere to changes of clothing[1]. For instance, Naaman gave to the servant of Elisha two changes of raiment (II Kings 5:22 f.). Or, again in Zech. 3:4, "Behold, I will clothe thee with new garments." For the same reason Christ did not say "heaven and earth will perish . . ." but "heaven and earth will pass away" (Matt. 24:35), that is, they will pass over from the old form of the present into a new and better form, or they will be changed and each will experience in its own way its own transition (or passover—*phase*).

1:13. [To which of the angels hath he said at any time,] Sit at my right hand [till I make thine enemies the footstool of thy feet]?

Many expositors interpret the phrase "at the right hand of God" as meaning the experience of the "more preferable bles-

---

[1] Luther seems to interpret the putting on of new clothing or festive raiment as analogous to the emergence of the new man. He may have had Rom. 13:14 in mind, "Put ye on the Lord Jesus Christ". . . . If so, his second reference to Zechariah is valid, but hardly the first to Gehazi.

sings" (i.e., true, spiritual experiences)[1]. If we accept this interpretation it would seem that this phrase means universal dominion, and that means of such a kind as equal to God's. Just as the Apostle says in I Cor. 15:27 quoting Psalm 8:6, he put all things under his feet, except naturally, "him who put all things under him." The sense therefore seems: "Sit at my right hand," i.e., rule over so many and so totally, as far and as wide, as I do, except thou be subject to me alone. Herein is commanded a charming admonition to meekness when he says: "While I make thine enemies a footstool under thy feet," and does not say: "While thou makest thine enemies a footstool under thy feet." Herein we may learn to leave vengeance to God, since even Christ who was the Lord of all, left vengeance to God. As it says in Deut. 32:35, "Vengeance is mine": therefore it belongs to nobody else.

1:14. **[Are they not all ministering spirits], sent forth to do service for the sake of them that shall inherit salvation?**

It is a widely discussed controversy, whether or no all the angels are sent. The saintly Dionysius (the Areopagite) says that the superior hosts are never sent (*De Coelesti Hierarchia*, 6.2.) Here, however, the text is perfectly clear, and says, "all are sent out to minister." Dionysius is certainly supported by Daniel who distinguishes between angels who stand by and angels who serve: "A thousand thousands ministered to him and a thousand millions stood before him" (Dan. 7:10). Therefore, only the merest fraction of the angels is on active service (i.e., on behalf of mankind to bring them redemption). But, on the other hand, Luke seems to agree with the Apostle: "And when this was done there was with the angel a multitude of the heavenly host" (Luke 2:13), when all the angels are seen to be present with the angelic spokesman.

1 Luther is seeking here to exclude the Church's claim to rule the world. As is clear from his exposition of this Epistle, Luther has by now discovered his *theologia crucis*, which he sets over against the prevalent *theologia gloriae*. This distinction he was to define more precisely at the Heidelberg Disputation 1518 (page 274). By it Luther taught that the only true knowledge of God is to be found in Christ crucified, and that the prevalent theology of God, *theologia gloriae*, based as it was on speculation on the attributes of the deity, was false and anthroponomous. This being so, Luther saw that a Church seizing for itself the right to rule and govern, was in a false position. It was later when scholars like Valla disclosed that the Papal Decretals and the Donation of Constantine were but forgeries, that Luther repudiated *de facto et de jure* the theology of the Papists, and taught that the role of the Church was as its Master's—service and sacrifice. It will be remembered that Gibbon characteristically described the Decretals and the Donation as ". . . the two magic pillars of the spiritual and temporal monarchy of the Popes."

There is a further reference just mentioned in verse 6: "Adore him, all ye his angels."

Therefore, the answer to the question raised is, that Dionysius is referring to the visible mission and to that extent, therefore, not all are sent. The Apostle on the other hand, is referring to the invisible mission and to that extent, therefore, all are sent[1].

Bonaventure writes on this subject at greater length in Book 2, quest. 2, dis. 10[2].

[1] Luther is seeking to point out that whatever differences of rank and dignity there might be, all are one in this that they are all ministering spirits sent forth to a ministry as each occasion arises. Luther shows no interest in the controversy on angels as such, but seeks to draw out what the text actually says about them.

[2] Hirsch and Rückert point out in a footnote (p. 16) that Bonaventure in *Sent.* II, dist. 10, art. 1, quest. 2 does not speak of a visible and an invisible sending, but of an external sending (to us), and of an internal sending (to other angels, but on our behalf).

Chapter Two

2:1. **Therefore we ought to give the more earnest heed to the things that were heard, lest haply we drift away from them. For if the old law, which only had angels for spokesmen, was none the less valid, and every transgression and disobedience incurred its just retribution how shall we escape if we neglect so great salvation?**

> Gl. 9:10. After the Apostle has set off the dignity and majesty of Christ the Teacher with advantage, he now starts off with the teaching itself, and induces in the reader the reverence necessary to understand it.

Scripture has an idiom all its own when it describes a law or precept as being established or not established. It is this: when the Scriptures want to say that the law is established and proved, they say it has been fulfilled. On the other hand, when they want to say that the law has been rendered inoperative and of none effect, they say that it has not been fulfilled. An example of this occurs in Rom. 8:3 where Paul writes: "For what the law could not effect, in that its dependence on flesh and blood kept rendering it of none effect, God, sending his own Son in the likeness of sinful flesh, did effect." In other words, the law was not being fulfilled, but in fact was being brought into disrepute. In the same way the law is said to be confirmed and ratified, or, on the contrary, to be made void or of none effect. It is used in this sense further on in the Epistle, where it says: "A man who sets at nought the law of Moses dies without any hope of mercy . . ." (10:28). A further instance is in Rom. 3:21: "Do we then make the law of none effect through faith? God forbid! Nay, we establish the law."

It will now be asked, however, what truth is there in the statement that the old law which had had angels as its spokesmen was none the less valid, because Paul teaches throughout his writings both that the law had become of none effect (as has been already said in reference to Rom. 8:3), and also that through this very

44

same law sin had been made to abound more and more, as he
argues at great length in the Epistle to the Romans (Rom. 5:20).
The answer is: for the simple reason that he himself might be
allowed to explain what he wants to be understood by the term
"the fulfilling of the law." He does so by completing his statement
that the old law had been fulfilled by saying **and every transgression and disobedience incurred its just retribution.**
From which it is clear that he is speaking of the external punishments which the law imposed, as he does later in the Epistle when
he says: "A man who sets at nought the law of Moses dies without
any hope of mercy" (10:28). Therefore, if he is talking about
penalties which are external, it is clear that he is referring to
transgressions that are also external, which means that he is
referring to a fulfilling or establishing that is equally external.
Wherefore, as they used to be punished externally for an external
transgression of the law, in like manner they were rewarded
externally for the external observance of the law. By which it came
about that the law was established by nothing other than the fear
of punishment or the love of reward. To establish law in this way
is to make for naked hypocrisy and much rather to make the law
of none effect. This really means that the heart is set on something
far removed from the law: it pays regard either to punishment or
reward. For this reason Elijah charges the Israelites with wavering between two opinions (I Kings 18:21) and of pursuing one
thing inwardly and feigning something else outwardly. So is every
man who lives apart from Christ. That is what the Psalmist means
when he says, "every man is a liar" (Ps. 116:11), "and every man
living is altogether false" (Ps. 39:5). In the unique glory of man's
mind lies his destruction.

2:3. (How shall we escape) if we neglect so great salvation?

Law and Gospel differ in this further respect, that in the Law
many works are enjoined, and all external, but in the Gospel
there is one only, an internal work, and that is faith. For that
reason the works of the law make a righteousness which is external, but faith makes a righteousness hidden with God. That
is why, when the Jews asked Christ, "What must we do, that
we may work the works of God" (John 6:28 f.), he drew them
away from the idea of a plurality of works to the one and only
requirement, saying: "This is the work of God, that ye may believe in him whom he sent." Therefore, the whole essence of the
new law and its righteousness is first and foremost faith in Christ.
But such a faith is not like a human idea, which always remains
solitary and unproductive, for Christ lives. He not only lives but

works: he not only works but reigns. Therefore it cannot possibly come about that faith in Christ becomes dead, for it is lively, and of itself works and triumphs. In this way works issue forth spontaneously from faith. Thus our patience comes from Christ's patience, our humility from his humility, and his other gifts issue from him in the same way, if only we firmly believe that he has done all these things on our behalf. Yea, and not only on our behalf (*pro nobis*) but before our eyes as an example to us (*coram nobis*). As Augustine used to express it, "not only for a sign (*sacramentum*) but also as an example (*exemplum*) 1." Wherefore Peter said: "Christ has suffered for us (this with respect to the sign), and left us an example" (I Peter 2:21). The sign (*sacramentum*) of the passion of Christ is his death and the remission of sins, and the example (*exemplum*) is the imitation of his sufferings in us. Therefore, if any man wants to follow Christ as an example, he must first firmly believe in the divine sign (the *sacramentum*) that Christ suffered and died for him. Consequently, those who contrive to blot out their sins by good works and penitential disciplines do err very greatly, for they begin by trying to follow the example set by Christ when they ought to begin with the sacrament wrought by Christ (i.e., the passion of Christ). It may be briefly summed up in this way: the gospel is neglected because of unbelief, the law through disobedience.

2:4. . . . which, having at first been spoken through the Lord, was confirmed unto us by them that heard, God also bearing witness with them by signs and wonders, and by manifold powers, and by gifts of the Holy Ghost. . . .

Gl. 10:20. This statement that salvation was confirmed unto us by them that heard is a very strong argument against Pauline authorship, for Paul both says and proves in the Epistle to the Galatians (Gal. 1:1, 17) that he had received nothing from the apostles. In the same way there is a further argument against the Pauline authorship when the Author quotes the Gospel of Mark as his authority (Mark 16:20, *infra*). He says these things, however, that is, that God was bearing witness to the preaching of the apostles by signs and wonders, lest the word of salvation be condemned on the grounds that it was handed down by men. This word is the same word which God himself spoke. Furthermore, God co-operates with those who teach his word, and confirms by signs that their word is his Word (Mark 16:20).

1 *De Trin.*, IV, 3, 6. Quoted frequently by Luther.

It is difficult to give precise differences of meaning to these words ("signs," "wonders," "manifold powers," and "distributions of the Holy Spirit") since Scripture uses them all without distinction. For Scripture calls the things which God once wrought in Egypt at one time signs, another time wonders and sometimes prodigies or portents, terrible deeds or merciful deeds. For instance: "As he wrought in Egypt his signs and wonders" (Ps. 78:43). Or again: "He performed great wonders before the face of their fathers" (Ps. 78:12). Or, again: "The great temptations and the great portents which thine eyes have seen" (Deut. 29:3). Or again: "And men will speak of the might of thy terrible acts" (Ps. 145:6).

In the light of all these examples it may be assumed that just as the Word of God, though one and the same thing is called many different names, such as law, proclamation, discourse, precept, command, testimony and so on (as is quite clear in the one hundred and nineteenth Psalm) so also the Work of God, even though it amount to the same thing, may justly bear many different names. It may be called a miracle, because it happens with power and might. It may be called a sign, because it manifests divine power, wisdom and the like. It may be called a portent from its effect. It may even be described as the terrible deeds of God or the wonderful works of God, and many other examples could be quoted.

But Paul does not think in these terms. He distinguishes between the diversities of gifts, diversities of ministrations and diversities of workings; between gifts of healings and workings of miracles (I Cor. 12:4 ff.) saying: "Are all apostles? Are all prophets? Are all teachers? Are all workers of miracles? Have all gifts of healing?" Wherefore, if we follow Paul, we must interpret "manifold powers" in this context (Heb. 2:4) as those workings of miracles which pertain not to healings and making whole, but to those which move mountains and trees, miracles which exercise power over water and air, fire and rain, and the like. By the word signs we must understand healings and making whole, such as Mark refers to in his final chapter, "These signs shall follow them that believe: in my name they shall cast out devils . . . they shall lay their hands on the sick," etc. . . (Mark 16:17 f.). And similarly we may interpret "portents": they may be either the same signs and miracles just described, or those which excite wonder and the greatest admiration, such as the resurrection of the dead and victory over the evil hosts of the firmament[1].

[1] Interpreting *terrores celestium corporum* with Eph. 6:12 in mind, and supplying the implied idea of victory.

2:4. (God also bearing witness with them, both by signs and wonders, and by manifold powers, and by gifts of the Holy Ghost), according to his own will.

Gl. 11:10. He says "according to his own will," and not "in accordance with our will," lest our free will should boast, for a man can receive nothing unless it be given him from above (John 3:27).

It would seem that Christ teaches a contrary doctrine. He seems to imply that we receive grace in relation to our willing it, for he says, "Ask, and it shall be given you; seek and ye shall find; knock, and it shall be opened unto you. For everyone that asketh receiveth; and he that seeketh findeth; and to him that knocketh it shall be opened" (Matt. 7:7 f.). But this contradiction is easily explained, because this wanting and seeking, this searching and knocking, is the gift of prevenient grace and is not consequent on our will seeking to elicit it[1]. Therefore, God disposes petitions as well "according to his own will." Or to put it in this way, He disposes our wishes according to his, as is expressed in John 3:27, "A man can receive nothing, unless it is given him from above."

2:5. For not unto angels did he subject the world to come of which we speak. But one hath somewhere testified (Ps. 8:6) saying, What is man that thou art mindful of him? Or the son of man that thou visitest him? Thou madest him a little lower than the angels, Thou crownest him with glory and honour, And didst set him over the works of thy hands.

Many are the expositors who have worked on the meaning of this verse.

1. A great number of Church Fathers, particularly Jerome[2], and to a certain extent Augustine[3], Ambrose[4] and Chrysostom[5] seem to understand the passage as referring to man pure and simple. But briefly my interpretation is as follows. It is not permissible for the text ("Thou madest him a little lower than the angels, or thou madest him for a little while lower than the angels") to be interpreted as referring to man. It is as if one were to interpret the text "He will rule from sea to sea" (Ps. 72:8) as referring to the emperor, when it should be understood as referring only to Christ. Or again, as if one were to interpret the text, "Thy children will

---

1 Vogelsang (p. 22) notes that *actus elicitus* is a scholastic technical term, and is still in use in Roman Catholic moral theology.
2 *Brev. in Ps.* 8; Migne, 26.838. 3 *Enarr.;* Migne, 36.115.
4 *Opera*, Basle, 1555, V, 429. 5 *ad loc.*

be as the olive branches" (Ps. 128:3), as applying to the children of some particular family when in fact it refers to the children of the Church. Yet the text cannot properly be understood unless it is taken as referring to Christ. If this interpretation is not followed, then the words which precede and follow the passage in question must be made to fit the other interpretation by dint of tortuous twistings and turnings. Therefore, those who think that in this instance the text refers to the dignity of human nature as being very near to that of the angels[1] pursue a false meaning which destroys the true meaning.

2. Other expositors understand the verse as referring to Christ, that he is lower than the angels[2] not as far as his soul is concerned but as far as the frailty of the body is concerned. But even this interpretation will not do, since it is less a matter of his being made lower than the angels, but rather that he was made lower even than man, since he himself said, "I am a worm and no man" (Ps. 22:7).

3. Lefèvre d'Etaples says that in Hebrew it would say "Thou hast made him a little lower than *Elohim*," which means God, and not "Thou hast made him a littler lower than *malachim*" which means angels. But Erasmus disagrees with Lefèvre. In the first place, because Christ was made not so much lower than God but lower even than the lowliest of men, as was said above. Therefore, it would be more correct to say not "a little lower," but the lowest possible differentiation from God. And secondly, because *Elohim* in Hebrew means not only God but angels, indeed judges and men set in special positions of responsibility. For instance, in the matter of permanent slavery it says in Ex. 21:6: "Let his master bring him before God" (*Elohim*). In this context it means "before the judges and priests."

There is a further point. Lefèvre d'Etaples, though motivated by the highest ideals, yet failed to establish what he purposed. He tried to prove that the Apostle (Paul) wrote this epistle in Hebrew and that a Greek translator had not rendered the word *Elohim*

---

[1] Nicholas of Lyra expounds: "Thou madest him to have dominion over the works of thy hand; thou hast put all things under his feet" (Ps. 8:6), that though man is weak by reason of his body, yet by reason of his soul made in the image of God, he is not far removed from the nature of angels. This is the precise interpretation to which Luther is referring.

[2] Gl. interl. glosses *minuisti* by the phrase "by reason of his nature which was capable of suffering". Nicholas of Lyra remarks that angels are not capable of suffering. Erasmus in his *Annotations* interprets the text as referring to the humanity of Jesus, who was made lower than the angels not in consequence of his soul but in consequence of the body he assumed, through which he became mortal and more liable to suffering. See notes, *WA*, 57, 116.

faithfully. The two points following may be adduced in disproof of this. First, the Apostle rarely if ever quotes the Hebrew text of the Bible, as is clear from Rom. 3:10 ff. and many other places. Secondly, because it is perfectly clear that this epistle was written not in Hebrew but in Greek, since the author is writing to those converts of Christ dispersed among the Gentiles who used the LXX.

4. Fourth and last, Erasmus is of the opinion that the phrase "a little lower" refers not to the measure of the diminished dignity, but to the short time during which he was made lower. The Glossa Ordinaria interprets the passage in this way, and so does Chrysostom.

Yet the difficulty remains: though Christ was made lower for that short space of time, yet there is still the further idea that he was made a good deal lower than the angels. In any case, speaking without any presumption, it seems that this verse says nothing of the dignity of our human nature, but is in explanation of the preceding verse. The text refers to the wondrous mindfulness of God and of the visitation of God, who is then most mindful when he forgets, and who most truly visits when he forsakes. For when God exalted Christ above all things, it was then he subjected him to all things. For his very passion was his Passover, a passing over to his hour of glory.

The root cause of the misunderstanding is the translation of this word *"minuisti,"* thou hast made smaller. In Hebrew the word *hasar* means "to be defective," "to be wanting" and so on. The meaning is therefore, thou hast so made him that he would be deserted and forsaken by God, or by angels. Not for a long time but for a short time, even less than a short time, for the shortest time possible, namely three days, because thou gavest him up into the hands of sinners. Whether, therefore, *Elohim* signifies in this context God, angels, judges, or any kind of exalted personage, has really nothing to do with the passage, though it would be more suitable to translate "God," for God did cause Christ to be forsaken not only by the divinity, but by the protecting power of angels and all earthly might.

It may be concluded, therefore, that the verse, "Thou hast made him a little lower than the angels, thou crownedst him with glory and honour" has the same meaning as Isa. 54:7f.: "For a small moment have I forsaken thee; but with great mercies will I gather thee. In a little wrath I hid my face from thee for a moment; but with everlasting kindness will I have mercy on thee."

It amounts to this, that in the verse "What is man . . .?" the word "what?" seems more to strike the note of how entirely unworthy man is that God should seek him. The text may be translated literally, "What is man that thou thinkest of him?" Or still better with a sense of awe and wonder, "How wonderful for man that thou visitest him!" Paul of Burgos says on Isa. 38 that the Hebrew word *mah* may be taken sometimes as a question, and sometimes as an interjection expressing wonder, as in Ps. 84:2, "How wonderful are thy dwellings. . . ." He argues that our translation, "And Hezekiah said, What will the sign be, that I shall go up into the house of the Lord?" is parallel. He says it ought to be rendered, "What a wonderful sign it is, that I shall ascend unto the house of the Lord!" Therefore it would seem that in this context instead of "What is man . . .?" should be said, "How is man . . .?" This means how wonderful is man, for the reason that thou art mindful of him when thou seemed most forgetful of him. The meaning is then similar to Ps. 118:22: "The stone which thou hast rejected, has become the lintel. This has been done by the Lord, and it is wonderful in our eyes."

In Hebrew there are three words for human nature, *'ish*, *'enosh* and *'adam*. It says in the text under discussion, "What is man (*'enosh*) that thou art mindful of him, and the son of man (*'adam*) that thou visitest him?" Eusebius says in his *Praeparatio Evangelica*[1] that man is called *'enosh* from the root meaning *'anash* "forgetting," but in my opinion a better interpretation is "affliction." For *'anash* according to Reuchlin means to go about in sorrow or weakness and the like. Therefore *'enosh* means man in that he is heir to corruption and weakness, as Solomon said, "whose life is nothing but an affliction of the spirit (Eccl. 1:13).

The word *'adam* is spoken of man in regard to his body, because he was made from the ground. *'Adamah* means earth, especially in the sense of red earth. For *'adam* means red-haired or ruddy, whence we have the word Edom and Edomites. That is probably the origin of the common phrase, "Adam was created in a Damascene field," Damascene meaning not a field near Damacus the Syrian town, but rather figuratively, Damascene red, from *'adam*, or *dam* meaning blood. Josephus also writes that Adam was made from red earth, for, as he says, virgin earth is of such a kind in its true and real condition. For that reason the masculine body inclines to red more than the woman's which inclines to white, as if every body represents its own nature by its colour, for the woman was made from bone of man but the man from red earth.

The word *'ish* (as *vir* in Latin) is spoken of man in two ways. First, with regard to sex (Gen. 2:23), She shall be called *'ishah* (woman) because she was taken from *'ish* (man). Or if one may

[1] Migne, 21,856 ft. (Greek series).

express it Latin-wise, "She shall be called *vira* because she was taken from *vir*." Or, secondly, it may be spoken of man with reference to power and dominion, as in Judg. 7:14, "This is nothing other than the sword of Gideon, the man of Israel," i.e., man, in the sense of the hero or the leader of Israel.

2:8. (Gl. 12:4). Thou didst put all things in subjection under his feet

As it says in Phil. 2:9 f.: "God gave unto him the name that is above every name, that in the name of Jesus every knee should bow, of things in heaven, and things on earth, and things under the earth, and that every tongue should confess that Jesus Christ is Lord, to the glory of God the Father"—**For in that he subjected all things unto him, he left nothing that is not subjected to him. Now we see not yet all things subjected to him** but they will be in the future: in the eyes of the faithful all things have already been subjected to him.

Gl. 12:19. He applies himself to the meaning of these things by interpreting Scripture (Ps. 8 in this case), for he is not talking about things tangible, he is preaching faith. For all things do not as yet appear subjected to Christ. On the contrary, it is he who is under subjection together with all that are his. As it says in Isa. 10:6, "He will tread them down like the mud of the streets." Therefore we need faith before we can enter into the meaning of these words.

2:9. But we behold him who hath been made a little lower than the angels, even Jesus, because of the suffering of death, crowned with glory and honour. . .

This text has been corrupted by an interpreter or scribe. It does not produce one iota of sense to say that Christ has been made a little lower than the angels. In addition, this same form of words is found in the Greek text, "thou hast made him a little lower than the angels." It is possible to take the words in this way: "Thou crownedst him, he who was made lower than the angels for a time shorter even than a short time" (for this is what *paulominus* means). By which truth the Holy Ghost comforts us, that in time of suffering we should have patience and hope, because tribulation is limited and consolation eternal, as it says in I Peter 5:10: "The God of all grace, who called you unto his eternal glory in Christ, after that ye have suffered a little while, shall himself perfect, stablish, strengthen you." Again in Ps. 2:12: "For his wrath will endure but a short time: blessed are they who put their trust in him."

The same Hebrew expression of Ps. 2:12 "but a short time" is in the Latin translation of Heb. 2:9 rendered *paulominus* "a little less." In fact, literally rendered the verse reads: "Since he is angered a little, blessed are those who trust in him." This means that it necessarily follows that when God is angry and scourges, blessed are they who endure, "lest (as the Psalmist expresses it) when he is thus angered, ye perish from the way" (Ps. 2:12).

The wrath of God is needful because of "the body of sin" (Rom. 6:2) and "the law of our members" (Rom. 7:23). For "the body of sin must be destroyed," since it is impossible for "anything impure to enter the Kingdom of Heaven." Such destroying of the body of sin takes place through the cross, through suffering, through death and ignominy. God kills in order to make alive, humiliates in order to exalt, and the like. This is what the Apostle glories in when he says that he knows nothing save Jesus Christ, and him not glorified but crucified (I Cor. 2:2), bearing in his own body the marks of his Lord (Gal. 6:17). For to have Christ crucified in oneself is to live a life full of trial and suffering. Christ then becomes for the natural man, "a sign which is spoken against" (Luke 2:34).

Therefore it is wise to accept all trials with open arms, yes even death, just as we would receive Christ himself thankfully and gladly. For Christ invariably comes in the same form he assumed when he laid aside the form of God. This is what James means when he says: "Count it all joy my brethren when you fall into many trials" (James 1:2). Or again: "I will fill thy mouth with my praise, lest thou perishest" (Isa. 48:9). And again: "I will praise and call upon the Lord, so will I be saved from my enemies" (Ps. 17:4).

2:9. . . . that by the grace of God he should taste death for every man

The word *ut* (so that) affirms a consequence. It should be related to the participle "made lower" and not to the participle "crowned" so as to avoid the meaning that he was crowned in order to taste death, which is absurd, when it means, much rather, that he tasted death in order to be crowned. Still better, it should be related both to all that has gone before as well as to the entire context. It is like the passage in Gal. 2:2 when Paul says: "I discussed with them the Gospel . . . lest by any means I should be running, or had run, in vain." Jerome expounds this very passage in the same manner[1]. The same applies to Rom. 4:18, Abraham believed God "to the end that he might become a father of many nations." Not that he strove to become a father by dint of believ-

---

[1] Jerome, *Comment. in ep. ad Gal.*, I, chap. 2, on Gal. 2:9, Migne, 26.333.

ing, but that the fatherhood followed as a consequence of his faith[1].

The text under discussion, "He was made lower and crowned with glory," must be understood in the same way, to show that Christ tasted death not by the compulsion of circumstances but by the grace of God. Other exegetes mean the same when they say that the word *ut* is to be taken in a consecutive sense and not a causal, as is frequently the case in Scripture.

The word *gustare* (to taste) has a special force. He does not say "that he might die" but "that he might taste death." In fact, as Chrysostom says, one who only tastes death spends but a brief interlude in death, and forthwith rises again. It is like the case of a doctor who, though not needing to taste the food prepared for the invalid, yet tastes the food first for the patient's sake to persuade him the more readily to accept the food. In the same way, because all men fear death, the Lord though under no compulsion to do so tasted death himself to persuade men to face death in confidence. "The prince of this world cometh," he said, "and he has nothing in me" (John 14:30).

2:10. **For it became him, for whom are all things and through whom are all things, in bringing many sons to glory, to make the author of their salvation perfect through sufferings.**

| Gl. (12:17). **It was meet** | a work becoming God's mercy |
| **that he** | God the Father |

| **for whom and through whom are all things** | for whose sake or to whose glory all things exist and are made |

through whom: The words "through whom" do not seem characteristic of Paul. When he speaks of the Father in his other epistles, Paul does not say "through whom" but rather "out of whom" or "from whom," but when he speaks of Christ he usually says "through whom" as happens for

---

1 It is interesting to compare Luther's gloss on Rom. 4:18—he writes: It was not because he was to be a father of many nations that he believed, but rather for the sake of God. Even if he were never to be a father of many nations, he would still have believed the future. Therefore when Paul says "that he might become . . ." he indicates the consequence rather than the cause. This is clearer if it is expressed negatively: Had he not believed, there would not have been this result, that he became a father of many nations. Therefore, in order that this should follow that he should become a father, he had to believe, *WA*, 57, 47.26 ff.

example, in St. John's Gospel,"All things were made through him" (John 1:3). There is a similar example in Heb. 1:3 also where he writes, ".... through whom he made the world ... and was upholding all things by the word of his power." In Pauline language this phrase "through whom" is more appropriately used of the Father than the Son.

all things: God who is the only God, and for whose sake alone he made all things.

who through the adoption of grace, in other words, the grace of adoption.

had led

The Greek participle "in leading" is better than the Latin "had led"

many sons into glory
should make the author the leader, the head
of their salvation
perfect through suffering God had foreordained to send the author of their salvation from heaven to earth. In other words, that he might make Christ perfect and restore him perfected.

Ambrose interprets **"the author of their salvation"** as the "leader of their salvation" which is better than the author of their salvation, and others have "the chief and head of their salvation." They interpret the word in this way so that it might be clearly understood as spoken of Christ the man who, on the authority of the Father, had been instituted leader in the redemption of his sons. For authority is more appropriate to God, whilst obedience is more appropriate to Christ the man.

Chrysostom, however, understands "the captain of our salvation" to mean the same as "the cause of our salvation," as it means later on in the Epistle where it says: "He has become to all who are obedient to him, the cause of their eternal salvation" (Heb. 5:9). By which is beautifully shown the manner in which we are saved, that is through Christ as archetype and example, to whose image are conformed all who are saved. For God the Father made Christ that he might be the image and the archetype, that those who cleave to him through faith might be transformed into that same image, and thus be drawn away from the images of this world. This is the meaning of Isa. 11:9: "The Lord will raise a sign

among the nations, and will gather together the outcasts of Israel."
And again in the same place: "The root of Jesse, which stands for
a sign among the peoples, him shall the nations seek" (Isa.
11:10).

This gathering together of the sons of God may be likened to a
ruler who has put on a play and the people flock to see it; they
leave their work and their homes and direct all their attention to
this one thing. In like manner Christ has drawn all men to him by
the Gospel as by a mighty drama performed before all the world.
He captured everybody by getting to know them and caring for
them, and lured them away from the things by which they cling
to the world. It is in this manner he describes Christ as the cause
and captain of salvation, because through him God draws away
his sons and leads them into glory, which is widely interpreted to
mean that Christ is the instrument and means by which God
draws his sons to himself. When he therefore planned to draw to
himself his sons through Christ, he rightly said, "it was meet for
him to consummate Christ through his passion," which means to
make the most perfect and complete example by which he would
inspire his sons and draw them to him. For God does not compel
men to be saved by force and fear. In this mighty drama of the
enacted gospel, he inspires all those he has pre-determined to save
and draws them to him by love.

2:10. ... to make the author of their salvation perfect through suffering

The text of those authorities which read "to be made perfect
through suffering" ought to be corrected. In most cases the Greek
texts have "sufferings" in the plural and "to make perfect" in the
active mood. Therefore the phrase "through sufferings," or as the
Hebrew expresses it "in sufferings," should be replaced by the
phrase "to make perfect by means of sufferings," using the Latin
construction of the ablative of instrument which needs no preposition. There is an instance of this in Ps. 32:6, "By the word of the
Lord (ablative of instrument) were the heavens made," where in
the Hebrew text it says "in the word of the Lord." So in this passage the meaning is, "It seemed good to God to make (Christ)
perfect through sufferings," i.e., by means of suffering, taking
"sufferings" as an ablative of instrument. Thus the meaning would
be, It pleased God to make Christ the perfect author of salvation,
and he used suffering as a means of fulfilling this work. For if there
had been no suffering we would never have had a perfect example
by which he could inspire us and draw us even to the point of
loving death and suffering.

2:11 ff. **For both he that sanctifieth and they that are sanctified are all of one: for which cause he is not ashamed to call them brethren, saying, "I will declare thy name unto my brethren, in the midst of the congregation will I sing thy praise" (Ps. 22:22). And again, "I will put my trust in him" (Isa. 8:17). And again, "Behold, I and the children which God hath given me" (Isa. 8:18).**

It is not certain what force the Apostle attaches to these two quotations, unless the meaning be taken from the preceding passage, which would then mean that he was wanting to prove that "he that sanctifieth and they who are sanctified are from one" (i.e. God). For this reason Chrysostom also says that with the last words the Apostle refers to the Father, but with the words "I will declare thy name . . ." he points to the brethren. And thus the two texts prove that the sanctifier has come from God. The text, "I will declare thy name unto my brethren," and more clearly still the text, "I and the children which God hath given me" further prove that those who have been sanctified also come from God.

It would appear that both texts are taken from Isa. 8:17 f. where it reads: "I will wait for the Lord (this means to trust in God) who hides his face from the house of Jacob, and I will look for him. Behold, I and the children whom the Lord hath given me are for signs and wonders in Israel from the Lord of Hosts. . . ." Over and above the authority of the Apostle's interpretation of this passage, it is clear from the words preceding that the words are spoken of the person of Christ: "Bind up the testimony, seal the law among my disciples. And I will wait for the Lord, who hides his face from the house of Jacob, and I will look for him. Behold, I and the children whom the Lord hath given me are for signs and wonders in Israel from the Lord of Hosts" (Isa. 8:16).

> Gl. 14:17. It is not sufficiently clear what the Apostle is seeking either to prove or to effect by these quotations, unless it is perhaps to emphasize that Christ the sanctifier both comes from the same God and is also of the number of those who trust in God, i.e., that he is truly man, partaker of flesh and blood with us. In fact he immediately goes on to say this in the next verse: "Since then the children are sharers in flesh and blood, he also in like manner partook of the same. . ."

2:14. **Since then the children are sharers in flesh and blood, he also himself in like manner partook of the same. . .**

Here the Apostle distinguishes between the brotherhood on the one hand between the angels and ourselves, and on the other hand

between Christ and ourselves. He praises the exceeding love of God
who in his mercy made Christ not only our brother in the spirit
but also even our brother in the flesh. Consequently, the one and
the same Christ is at once both higher than the angels and also like
unto us. Indeed he is more closely related to us than the angels are.
It is for this reason that he alone is called our neighbour in the
parable of the Good Samaritan (Luke 10)[1].

The phrase "flesh and blood," however, is a Scriptural idiom
for "man," particularly after the fall, as it says in Genesis, "My
spirit shall not abide in man forever, for he is flesh" (Gen. 6:3) In
fact the Apostle himself calls the apostles "flesh and blood," saying, "I conferred not with flesh and blood" (Gal. 1:16), i.e., he
did not discuss his interpretation of the gospel with the other
apostles.

Sometimes, however, the phrase is taken in a bad sense for the
depravities of human nature or for corrupted human nature, as in
I Cor. 15:50, "Flesh and blood cannot inherit the kingdom of
God." Also in Eph. 6:12, "We wrestle not against flesh and blood."

The reason for this twofold meaning is that a man is called both
that which he is, and also that which he loves. For truly he both is
flesh and blood, and also loves flesh and blood. In the same way a
man who loves righteousness, wisdom and goodness is rightly
called righteous, wise and good. Therefore in this passage the
Apostle does not merely want to say quite neutrally, "The children were flesh and blood," but quite emphatically, "The children partook of flesh and blood." He did this to show that through
Christ partaking of flesh and blood with them they were no longer
mere flesh and blood but were partakers of flesh and blood like
Christ.

**2:14. . . . that through death he might bring to nought him
that had the power of death, that is, the devil.**

CONCERNING THE DESPISING OF DEATH

Scripture attributes death to the devil. It is recorded: "Through
envy of the devil death came into the world" (Wisdom 2:24), and
also: "God did not make death neither has he pleasure in the
destruction of the living. For he created all things that they might
have their being" (Wisdom 1:13 f.). It is not recorded in the first
chapters of Genesis that death is one of the works of God. Similarly in Ezekiel, "I have no pleasure in the death of him that dieth,
saith the Lord" (Ezek. 18:32), or again, "As I live, saith the Lord,
I have no pleasure in the death of the wicked" (Ezek. 33:11). Or

---

[1] In his commentary on Rom. 4:8, Luther refers to ". . . our Samaritan Christ
picked up the man who was half-dead to save him . . .", *WA*, 57, 165.10 f.

again in the Psalms, "In his indignation is wrath, and in his favour life" (Ps. 30:6), i.e., death and wrath displease him but life gives him pleasure. Or again in Hosea, "I will be thy death, O death" (Hos. 13:14). Were death the work of God, he would not destroy it.

Now in the first Epistle St. John says, "For this purpose the son of God appeared, that he might destroy the works of the devil" (1 John 3:8), and in the Gospel, "I came that they might have life and have it abundantly" (John 10:10). Therefore, death and sin as well are necessarily the works of the devil. For the same reason in the Apocalypse the devil is called "the angel of the bottomless pit" whose name in the Hebrew tongue is *Abaddon* and in the Greek tongue *Appolyon*, or in Latin "the destroyer."

God's proper work, however, is "life, joy, peace" and all the other fruits of the Spirit enumerated in Gal. 5:22. The fact that God destroyed the devil not by the work of God but by the very own work of the devil himself lends truth to the texts (Vulg.) that "the Lord has exalted his holy ones" (Ps. 4:4) and "the Lord is wonderful among his saints" (Ps. 68:36). For this is the most glorious kind of victory, to strike down the enemy with his own weapon and slaughter him with his own sword, as we sing in the hymn,

"By his own javelin prostrate stricken"

In this way God promotes and perfects his proper work by means of his alien work, and by a marvellous wisdom compels the devil to work through death nothing else than life itself, with the consequence that as the devil is working his damnedest against the work of God, he is by dint of his own work but working against himself and forwarding God's work. In this way he worked death in Christ, which Christ swallowed up into himself and rose again in glory. This is referred to as "the mighty hand of God." This happy victory God promised in Job: "He will capture him before his eyes with a hook, and will bore his nostrils with a spike (to lead him captive)" (Job. 40:24). Job is asked,

"Canst thou draw out leviathan with a hook?
and wilt thou bind his tongue with a cord?
Canst thou put a ring in his nose
or bore his jaw to take an iron hoop? . . .

Wilt thou play with him as with a pet bird,
or tie him up for thy maidservants?

Canst thou fill the net with his skin
and the fishook with his head?

Shall his enemies cut him up for a meal
Shall the merchants traffic his carcase?"

(Job 41:1–7)

Concerning this passage of Job see Gregory the Great (*Moralium*
Bk. XXXIII, 7:14–8:34; Migne, 76, 680–696)[1].

As therefore death is destroyed and with it all the works of the
devil in "the author of our salvation" (or in the holy of holies, in
Christ our head, however expressed), it has to happen in the same
way in each and every member. For Christ, though subject to
death in that he was human, was yet at one and the same time a
person both mortal and immortal. Just because his whole person
could not die entirely, death failed. The devil was slain by his
dying. And so death was devoured and swallowed up in life. The
curse was transformed into a blessing and sorrow turned into joy.
All that was evil was overcome by all that was good, and utterly
vanquished. And so now through Christ, it is God's will to destroy
in us death and the works of the devil. We Christians ought so to
learn these things that we face death joyfully. For just as it is
impossible for Christ, the victor of death, to die any more, so it is
impossible for the person believing in him to die. As Christ said:
"Whosoever believeth in me shall not die eternally. Though he
dies, yet shall he live" (John 11:26, 25). Whatever is made alive
in God is immortal. And again in Ps. 23: "If I walk in the valley,
i.e., in the midst of the shadow of death, I will fear no evil, for
thou art with me." For as Christ by the union of his flesh with his
immortal divinity conquered death by dying, so the Christian,
through his unity with the undying Christ, which comes through
faith in him, also overcomes death by dying. And thus God destroys the devil by the devil himself, and fulfils his "proper work"
by his "strange work."

This is just the theology the world does not understand. This is
what is meant in Hab. 1:5: "Behold I shall work a work in your
days which no one will believe when it is told them." For this
reason Chrysostom says on this point: "This writer shows us
something marvellous:—that the very power the devil once
wielded, by this same power was he overcome: the weapon of
death by which he threatened the world, by this same weapon
Christ defeated him. Do you see, therefore, how much good death
has worked? Why be afraid, why fear it? It is terrifying no longer:
it has been trodden under foot, it is despised" (Migne, *loc. cit.*,

---

[1] An exegesis of the book of Job in the threefold literal, mystical and moral
sense with emphasis on the latter.

63.266). And further on he says: "For no longer now is death a bitter thing, it is little more than a sleep."

For this reason also the Apostle Paul preaches everywhere with great joy the resurrection of Christ, because through it law and sin, death and hell, the devil, the world and the flesh have all been conquered by all who believe in him and call upon him. The same in I Cor. 15:57: "To God however be the thanks, who has given us the victory through Jesus Christ, our Lord." "Has given us," he says, not "has kept" so great a victory for himself. And in I Thess. 4:13: "We do not wish you to be ignorant concerning those who are asleep; that you sorrow not even as the rest who have no hope. For if we believe that Jesus died and rose again, even so them also that have fallen asleep God will bring with him through Jesus." Hos. 13:14 also: "From the hand of death I will free them, from death I will redeem them; O death, I will be thy death; O hell, I shall be thy sting!" And there follows a description of how he will do it: "The Lord shall bring a burning wind from the desert, and will dry up his water springs and desert his fountains." For Hosea is alluding to Ex. 14:21 when the Lord brought in a strong and burning wind the whole night and dried up the Red Sea. In that incident is figured the drying up of the pains of death, i.e., sin, because death rules by sin. This wind brought in from and caused by the desert, is the wind of the Holy Spirit, and the desert, Christ crucified.

COROLLARY

He who fears death or is not willing to die, is not sufficiently Christian. As yet such people lack faith in the resurrection, and love this life more than the life to come. These people are just like those about whom the psalmist writes; "They despised the pleasant land" (Ps. 106:24). *Whosoever does not gladly die, ought not to be called a Christian*[1]. *For the same reason when Chrysostom comments on this text he reproves those who bewail the departed: "Such deserve their grief who still fear death and are terrified in the face of it, and who still do not believe the resurrection."* Therefore, when such folk pray, "Thy Kingdom come," either they are offering no prayer at all or they are praying against themselves, that is they are mocking both God and themselves. They have been baptized in vain, since according to the Apostle (Rom. 6:3 ff.) "as many of us as were baptized into the death of Christ were baptized that we might accept death for ourselves readily, and follow the example of Christ more gladly."

But in reply to this you will say: It is not mere death I fear but

1 This sentence is an *ex tempore* comment.

an evil death, because "the death of sinners is the worst kind of death" (Ps. 33:22, Vulg.) and "evil things shall take the unrighteous man in death" (Ps. 140:11). A man who speaks in this vein, however, clearly proves that he lacks faith in Christ, because he does not believe that Christ is "the lamb of God taking away his own sins." For the more casually this is believed the more death is feared, and the more firmly it is believed the more confidently death is despised. It is indeed true that *it is only the sense of sin which makes death horrible, as Paul says, "The sting of death is sin"* (I Cor. 15:56). *However, nothing takes away the sense of sin save faith in Christ, because: "The victory has been given to us through Jesus Christ"* (I Cor. 15:57, as above).

That is why God makes death, judgment and hell plain that he might make known the strength of faith in Christ, that through faith a Christian might overcome these tyrants. For these tyrants we ought to fear are nothing more than exercises through which faith becomes "strong as death and hard as hell" (Cant. 8:6). They batter and assault us and try to separate the heart from faith in Christ. Therefore, when Jesus preached the signs men ought to fear (Luke 21:28) he at once added the following words for the strengthening of faith, "When these things begin to come to pass look up and lift up your heads," so that these things would be overcome by faith. If therefore death is feared on account of sin how much more ought it to be desired on account of sins, because it is death alone which brings sin to an end and kills it. Therefore death, the destroyer of sin, is to be loved as much as sin is feared.

Therefore, as Cyprian writes in his "De Mortalitate" [1]*: "For us the battle is against avarice, unchastity, wrath and ambition: it is an unremitting and difficult struggle against the sins of the flesh and the allurements of the world. The mind of man is beset. It is beleaguered on all sides by the attacks of the Devil. He can hardly meet these attacks singly. It is with difficulty he resists at all."* And Cyprian concludes that death comes as a help and succour to us [2]. *And later on he writes, "Every day the soul endures so many persecutions, and the heart is oppressed by so many dangers. And yet, it delights to tarry a long time here in the midst of the darts of the Devil, when rather it should desire and even hope for the speeding hand of death to hasten its journey to Christ."* That is what Cyprian says. The consolation of death! [2]

Nevertheless, we must not despair of those who are afraid of death. They must be cherished and exhorted as those who are weak in faith whom the Apostle commands us to receive (Rom. 14:1). For this contempt of death and the grace derived from this

[1] *De Mortalitate*, Migne, 4.606 f.
[2] Both these sentences are *obiter dicta*.

contempt, preached by the Apostle and the saints, is that goal and perfection towards which the whole life of Christians ought to endeavour, although very few indeed attain to such perfection. For in the same way Paul in the Epistle to the Romans calls Christians righteous and holy and free from sin, not because they are such already but because they have begun to be, and by constantly advancing, ought to become such. For holy men, too, are terrified by death and the judgments of God. The text of the psalm speaks of them: "The fear of death took hold of me," and again, "Fear and trembling came upon me" (Ps. 55:5). And elsewhere, "By the power of thine hand am I consumed in chidings" (Ps. 39:11). And again, "The sorrows of death compassed me and the pains of hell came over me" (Ps. 116:3). And yet again, "My soul is full of troubles, and my life has drawn near to the grave" (Ps. 88:4).

Therefore people like this must be consoled and encouraged. First, by Christ himself, who not only underwent death on our behalf to make death for us an enemy defeated and despised, but also took even the fear of death unto himself for the sake of the weak in faith. He conquered this fear and sanctified it, that it need not be rejected by us as likely to bring us to damnation. Otherwise it is pure sin to wish not to die and to fear death. He did all this that nothing be left undone, a virtue desired of the best priest. See then, what more ought our most merciful saviour to have done which he has not already done! Sin he bore to the full. Death he left us, though he left it conquered. And however much death had been conquered and was no longer to be feared, he rendered the fear of death incapable of hurting our soul.

The second way in which people who have a fear of death may be consoled and encouraged is by the words with which Christ himself consoles us in the text: "Fear not those who kill the body" (Matt. 10:28). Or again, by the text from Isaiah: "O my people be not afraid of the Assyrian" (Isa. 10:24). For the Lord does not will death, and though he uses the devil and evil in the death and suffering of his saints (as it says in Job 40:19: "He who made him shall use his sword against him" and in Isa. 10:5; "Woe Assyrian! who is the rod and instrument of my wrath, and in whose hand is my indignation"), yet, nevertheless, he performs that work from a heart serene and kind. As he says in Job 41:1: (Vulg.) "Not as unmerciful shall I raise him." After all, he rebukes and reproves those who have done more than he actually commanded. As he says in Zech. 1:14: "I am jealous for Zion with a great jealousy, and I am very sore displeased with the heathen that are at ease; for I was angry only a little (with the Jews) but they (the heathen God used as instruments to punish his people) actually made it worse."

And yet it is surely still more marvellous that God smites and pounds his saints to move outsiders to mercy, so that heathen should intercede to God on behalf of the saints. For instance in Ezek. 13:5: "You have not gone up over against the wall (i.e., to fill up its breaches), neither have you made up the wall for the house of Israel, to stand in the battle in the day of the Lord." And the same further on: "And I sought for a man among them who should make up the hedge and stand in the gap before me for the land that I should not destroy it; but I found none" (Ezek. 22:30). For that very reason we have the cry of Job: "Have pity on me, have pity on me, at least ye my friends, for the hand of God has touched me" (Job. 19:21). And for the same reason also, the praise of Moses in Ps. 106:23, that "he stood in the breach in the sight of the Lord lest he should destroy Israel." And yet (as mentioned in the last paragraph), he seriously rebukes those who added to the pain of the wounds: "For they persecute him whom thou hast smitten" (Ps. 69:26).

2:15. ... who through fear of death were all their life subject to bondage.

Chrysostom understands this in three ways: "First, he who fears death is a slave, and submits to anything rather than die. Or secondly, all were slaves of death, and as long as they were not redeemed, were held in bondage to it. Or thirdly, men were living in perpetual fear, always expecting to die, and could take no pleasure in life as long as this fear remained in them" (Migne, *loc. cit.*, 63.266). All three senses seem to run into one another in one exposition of the words of Paul. For he himself draws the contrast. He said that the devil was the ruler of death, and therefore such people must have been subjected to his dominion. Thus the second sense is true, that all were slaves of death and subject to the prince of death. Then the first and third express the miseries accompanying such subjection. The first meaning shows that when people are enslaved to a subjection of such a kind they are driven to and fro in fear and uncertainty and never possess the true peace of mind referred to by Isaiah: "There is no peace for the wicked, saith the Lord" (Isa. 48:22). Or again in Deuteronomy: "The Lord will give thee a trembling heart, and thy life shall hang in doubt before thee. In the morning thou wilt say, who will give me evening? And in the evening thou wilt say, who will give me morning?" (Deut. 28:65 ff.). The third meaning shows that the fear of death makes men slaves of sin. This is the spirit of servitude, which always makes men worse, and makes them hate the law and righteousness the more.

Therefore Christ, when he took away the fear of death, freed us from bondage to sin, and by means of sin (for we were in bondage to sin because of the fear of death) destroyed the fear of death. He did not however destroy it in such a way that it no longer existed, but in that same manner as we are freed from the law by the spirit: i.e., not that law no longer exists, but that it need not be feared. In the same way we are freed from dominion of the devil: not that he no longer exists, but that he need not be feared. Similarly, we are freed from death as well: not that death no longer exists, but that it need not be feared. Further examples could be instanced.

I conclude, therefore, that for a Christian there is nothing more to be dreaded either in this life or the life to come, seeing that death and all evil have been turned into salvation and blessing.

2:16. For he never seized on the nature of angels: it was the seed of Abraham he seized.

Chrysostom (Migne, *loc. cit.*, 63.271) notes the emphasis in the use of the word *apprehendere* which means "to seize." He points out that the writer did not use the word *suscipere* "to take up," but *apprehendere* "to seize." This word applies to persecutors striving their utmost to seize those in flight and lay hold on them, as Christ pursued after human nature and overtook it when it was fleeing far from him. He shows by this choice of word that the power which effected this was his mercy alone, his grace, and the love he has towards us. So much for Chrysostom.

This same point is clearly shown in the gospel narrative in the parables of the lost sheep and the lost coin. These were sought and found quite obviously not by their own efforts but by the mercy of the seeker[1].

2:17. [Wherefore it behoved him in all things to be made like unto his brethren], that he might be a merciful and

---

[1] Readers should note how clearly Luther's evangelical theology is already formed at this early stage. Luther is here opposing any and every idea of works or merit, and is at pains to show that man's salvation is the free undeserved gift of God. It was not that God was far from man and that man must make every effort to draw near. The contrary is true. Man is far from God, and God himself made the effort to draw nearer. This was Luther's gospel. There is no other.

It should also be observed how Luther drew this truth out of an ancient and acceptable Church Father. It was not merely a clever move to draw this out of the patristic tradition. It was more. Luther always believed that he stood in the genuine line of Catholic doctrine and tradition, and that it was those who later turned out to be his enemies who were in fact fighting for innovations rather than catholic tradition. Luther was a reformer and never an innovator.

faithful high priest [in things pertaining to God, to make propitiation for the sins of the people].

He commends two virtues in Christ, which ought also to illuminate every priest by Christ's example; *viz.*, that a priest should be merciful to the people he is set over, and also faithful to God on behalf of his people. In that he is merciful, he ought to empty himself and make all the evils of those set under him into his own and to feel them in no other way than as if he himself were actually involved in them. In that he is faithful, he ought to share all his goods among them. For in this way Christ "emptied himself of the form of God and took on the form of a servant" (Phil. 2:6 f.): i.e., he did not consider the things which pertained to himself but those which pertained to us. For the things that were his own were righteousness, wisdom, salvation, glory, peace, joy and so on: the things that were ours were sin, folly, perdition, ignominy, the cross, sorrow and the like. In these circumstances he took unto himself the things that were ours and pursued his course as if he had never known the things pertaining to himself. For this reason it says likewise in the law: "And Aaron will carry their sins which the children of Israel brought" (Ex. 28:38), and also: "And the Lord spoke to Aaron: Thou and thy sons with thee, and thy father's house with thee shall bear the iniquity of the sanctuary, and thou and thy sons together shall bear the iniquity of the priesthood" (Num. 18:1).

CHAPTER THREE

3:1. Wherefore, holy brethren, partakers of the heavenly calling, consider the Apostle and High Priest of our confession, Jesus.

The Apostle draws them to Christ gently and pleasantly, calling them "holy brethren," as though he were courting them. By which he teaches us that it is not by passion or storm of words we ought to preach Christ. Indeed, Christ cannot be preached except peacefully and tranquilly. For the thundering sermon pertains rather to the law, as it is portrayed in Ex. 19:16; 20:18, where the heavens were terrified by the voice of the trumpet, the thick cloud upon the mountain, and the flashing lightning. Or again in I Kings 19:11 when after the wind, and after the earthquake and after the fire there came "a still, small voice," and the Lord was in it. Therefore, the law has to be revealed to the hard-hearted and the stiff-necked with fulminations, but, when they have been frightened and humbled, the gospel must be introduced with gentleness. For this reason Isaiah 42 speaks of Christ: "Behold my servant, a bruised reed shall he not break, and the smoking flax shall he not quench" (Isa. 42:1 f.), i.e., rather will he comfort the fainthearted and afflicted.

3:1. [The High Priest] of our confession

A new phrase makes its appearance! But it is a Hebrew idiom, and expresses the vital issue in a wonderfully appropriate way, for our whole life's work is but a confession. As it is expressed in Ps. 96:6, "Confession and beauty are before him" (i.e., in his church), "sacredness and majesty in his sanctuary." Ps. 111:3 gives expression to the same thought: "Confession and honour are his work. . . ." Ps. 145:5 has the same meaning: "They will speak of the glorious magnificence of thy sanctuary, and will tell of thy wonderful works." As if he meant to say that the whole of what they say and do is praise, confession, honour and sanctification, by which they praise, confess, magnify and sanctify thee. Nevertheless, all

67

this work is the work thou doest in them. The same thought is found in Ps. 8:2: "Out of the mouths of babes and sucklings thou hast perfected praise . . .", as well as in Isa. 43:21: "This people have I formed for myself, they will show forth my praise."

For the same reason in the inscription on the cross Christ is called "The King of the Jews" in other words "The King of the Confessors[1]." Confession is understood here not so much as a confession of sin as a confession of praise. Indeed, the confession of sin and the confession of praise is one and the same thing. (An exception to this would be the confession of those faithless Jews called after Judas Iscariot. Iscariot or Scharioth is from *sachar*, which means in Latin *merces*[2].) The real confession is that whereby a man gives to God the glory for his righteousness, his wisdom, his power and for all his good deeds; but credits himself with nothing save his sin, his folly and his weakness. Such a confession must be expressed from the heart by word and deed.

Further, the Apostle distinguishes between confessions and possessions in this text. For in the world it is said, quite rightly, that a person is a lord or a king of lands, rivers, cities, herds and the like. Such possessions are not a matter of words or confessions, but have their actual existence in things material. Now the synagogue also had its own confession, that of Moses, which was based on physical wonders, by which she was redeemed from her weakness, her poverty and her bondage in Egypt. This is why the Apostle speaks of "our" confession, i.e., of a new confession, because we believe and confess wonders of a different sort, *viz.*, redemption from the weakness of the spirit, from bondage of the spirit, from poverty of the spirit. For that reason Moses is the apostle of their confession, but on the other hand Christ is the Apostle of our confession. Therefore, Chrysostom interprets "our confession" as meaning "our faith." Chrysostom, however, expresses a metanomy or a transference of terms, *viz.*, faith is substituted for its own work which is confession, just as grammarians accept the word Mars as a term for war, and Minerva as a term for the arts.

Wherefore . . . (3:1).

1 The reference is to the birth of Judah when Leah says, "This time will I praise ['*odeh* (Reuchlin, *hōd*)] the Lord: therefore she called his name Judah" (Gen. 29:35). In the Middle Ages the word Judah or Jude was widely taken as etymologically rooted in the word "to praise" or "to confess", thence Luther's substitution of the word "confessors" for the Jews.
2 There were many interpretations and explanations of the significance of the meaning of the name Iscariot, but Luther, using Reuchlin's Lexicon goes back to the Hebrew root *sachar* meaning hire, wages or reward, and translates with the Latin word *merces* meaning goods or merchandize. Lewis and Short give instances of the word meaning "a bad lot" when applied to persons.

Gl. (15:13 ff.) After the author has praised the excellency of
Christ in that he was made higher than the angels, he turns
in the passage following to teach that Christ must be preferred
to Moses whom the Jews hold in the very highest esteem next
after the angels. He does this to take from the Jews their faith
in Moses and to convert them to faith in Christ alone.

(3:1).

wherefore,	for that reason
holy brethren,	sanctified in Christ.
partakers	
of a heavenly calling,	that is, an evangelical calling, which came from heaven by the word of God, as it is written in Ps. 18:3: "The Lord thundered from heaven and the most high uttered his voice."
consider	give heed to the sharing out of grace to all who follow after
the Apostle	because he was sent into the world by the Father
and High Priest	because he intercedes with the Father on our behalf
of our confession	i.e., of faith and of the new testament
even Jesus.	

(3:2).

who was faithful to him	God the Father
who made him	apostle and priest
as also Moses was	i.e., not less than Moses, but rather more than Moses
in all his house	in the whole Church of God.

In this passage he is referring to Num. 12:7: "My servant
Moses is not so; he is faithful in all my house: with him will I
speak mouth to mouth, even manifestly, and not in dark
speeches; and the form of the Lord shall he behold: where-

fore then were you not afraid to speak against my servant, against Moses?" Because of this passage Moses was regarded as approved by God and obtained the highest authority over the people. For the very same reason the Jews set this very man in opposition to Christ, and said, "We know, because it was God himself who spoke to Moses." But on the contrary, this Apostle, in answer to such people, sets Christ, who is indeed not less but more faithful to God. And so Moses and Christ contend with one another as to who is "faithful in the house of God." Still, Moses is but a part of the whole house, namely the head; Christ, however, is not only the head but even its Lord and Founder—as God. Therefore, Christ has an honour greater than Moses in proportion as we regard the house (Christ) as greater than its part (Moses).

(3:3).

For he has been counted worthy of more glory than Moses by so much as he that built the house has more honour than the house

he is held more worthy and is more worthy by a greater grace

the house is the house of Israel.

(3:4).

For every house is built by somebody

the glory of the builder is greater than the building.

This means that it is not we who built this house, because, if we agree that we are the house, the glory of the builder of the house is greater than our glory, the glory of the house. In other words, Christ is like us and yet was made greater than us; he is with us and yet he it is who is creating us.

3:5. And Moses was indeed faithful in all God's house as a servant, for a testimony of those things which were afterward to be spoken.

Here again there seems to be an Hebraic manner of speech. For thus in Ps. 81:8 God calls both his Word and his preachers his witnesses: "Hear, my people, and I will testify unto thee." This word "testify" the Latin language is not able adequately to express by one single word. The meaning is: in time to come I will speak a word in the midst of you or among you. (The Hebrew has "I will testify *in* thee.") Now this word will not be a manifestation of things already at hand but is a testimony of things not yet seen. For that reason you have to give hearing to what you can neither see nor understand. Christ expresses the same thing in John 3:11: "Verily I say unto thee, we speak what we know, and testify what we have seen, and yet you do not accept our testimony." Both words are placed here deliberately, "hear" and "I will testify." It is as if he wished to say, "Be thou the hearer and I will be the preacher." For what Christ has said about heaven and about the future life can be understood in no way except by hearing. Because not only do Christ's words outsoar the highest to which the human mind can aspire, but also all that the human heart could desire. Therefore, the testimony of the Lord is a word of faith, it is a hidden wisdom, it is open only to the perception of the meek. It is described in Isa. 53 as something which has to be heard[1]: "Lord, who hath believed our report?" "Our report" means our voice, which we cause men to hear by preaching the gospel.

Further, it is most appropriate that the Word of God is called "a testimony." For just as in legal disputes whatever is judged on the testimony of witnesses is assessed by hearing alone and believed in by faith, and is established in no other way at all, not even by the powers of intellect or reason, so is the gospel received by no other way than by hearing. Therefore the apostles are called witnesses of Christ as in Isa. 43:10: "*Ye are my witnesses, saith the Lord, and my servant whom I have chosen: that ye may know and believe me, and understand that I am he.*" Also in Ps. 122:4: "For thither the tribes went up, the tribes of the Lord, the testimony of Israel," which in my judgment ought to be rendered thus: For thither the tribes went up, the tribes of the Lord, for a testimony to Israel[2]. For, since the Hebrew has "to Israel" or "for Israel" in the dative case, and "testimony" in the ablative case, according to our texts it ought to be taken as "for a testimony" in the same way as Christ says in Matt. 10:18: "And ye shall be brought before kings and governors for my sake, for a testimony to them and to the Gentiles." It has the same meaning in the text under discussion when the writer says that Moses was a servant "for a testimony of those things which were yet to be spoken." It means that Moses was a witness of God in those things which were to be spoken by the angels.

3:6. **But Christ was faithful as a son over his house; whose**

---

[1] *etiam audibile*. P has *auditus* (as the text of Isa. 53 has in the line following) and is followed by H-R. *Auditus* is translated in the German Bible by *Predigt* (sermon).

[2] The German Bible translates "for a testimony to Israel" by "to preach to the children of Israel."

house are we if we hold fast unto the end the confidence and glory of our hope.

Chrysostom writes: "The man who sorrows in the midst of tribulations and collapses, does not glory: the man who is ashamed, and hides himself, has no faith[1]." From which it is clear that in this text the word "glory" is put for glorying or boasting, which the Greek text also has, *viz.*, *kauchema*. For "glory" in Greek is *doxa*, which for us means esteem, reputation, glory. (Whence *cenodoxia* means "empty fame.") So in Hebrew *"cabod"* means glory, *"pe'er"* glorying, as in Ps. 24:8 ff.: "Who is the king of glory?" (*cabod*), and Ps. 89:17: "Since thou art the glory (i.e., *pe'er*, or *gloratio*) of their strength . . ." i.e., thou art their strength, and they glory in it.

But these two words are wonderfully inter-related, since in the topic under discussion there is no small difference at stake. For boasting (*gloratio*) is to be taken rather in an active sense, glory (*gloria*), on the other hand, in a passive sense. For "glory" (*gloria*) is the opinion about us, the opinion others hold about us, but glorying (*gloratio*) is our own opinion of ourselves. Now if, this glorying is a glorying in ourselves it is hollow; if, however, it is a glorying in Christ by us, it is solid ground indeed. As the Apostle says in II Cor. 10:17: "Whoever glories, let him glory in the Lord."

Therefore we accept Chrysostom's interpretation, that "the confidence" and "the glory of our hope" may be differentiated in the following manner. Confidence characterizes him who ventures the cross of Christ and begins to take it upon himself, just as on the contrary lack of faith is to flee the cross of Christ and be ashamed of it. On the other hand, glory assuredly characterizes him who is advancing and triumphing while complaints and sadness characterize him who is failing and falling. As it is written in Rom. 5:3: "We glory in our tribulation." The Apostle says this in this place, because he had said we were the house which Christ "builds." A building, however, is nothing else than tension and pressure. Put into other words, we are built by experiencing the cross and sufferings which we go through in Christ. In this way, therefore, he wants us to know that it is necessary for us to be raised and fashioned by a firm faith and glorious hope in him, lest we fail, and in the course of building are the more ruined.

Gl. 17:14. This is a necessary process, for the building is accomplished through many sufferings.

---

[1] Chrys., *Homil.*, 5. f. 30. Migne, *loc. cit.*, 63.273.

3:7. **Wherefore, even as the Holy Ghost says, Today if you will hear his voice**

Wherefore. Gl. 17:15. After he has commended Christ as the Apostle and the glory that is his, he now begins to urge faith in him. Up to this point he has done nothing other than praise Christ as the apostle, as if he were writing some sort of prologue, just as he normally commends his own apostleship in other epistles. And this is perhaps the reason why this epistle alone is without a title, because he knew that Christ was the Apostle and Minister of the circumcision, as he says here and also in Rom. 15:8 that he is the apostle and minister to the Gentiles (Cf. Rom. 15:16). On that account he had in this epistle to commend not his own name but Christ's.

The literal rendering of the text from the Hebrew is: "For God himself is our God and we are the people of his pasture and the sheep of his hand. On that day when you hear his voice, do not harden your hearts as in the provocation, as in the day of temptation in the wilderness, when your fathers tempted me, proved me, and even saw my works for the space of forty years. I have spurned this generation and said, it is a people who err in their very heart, who have not known my ways. Unto whom I swore in my wrath: if they enter into my rest" (Ps. 95:7 ff.) [See comments on 3:11, for the meaning of word "if."]

Now in the first place it is clear from this text that the prophets knew the future pattern of the affairs of the children of Israel. For notice that the writer speaks in a manner of comparison [comparing the former history with future events] when he says, Harden not your hearts when you hear his voice on that day in the future, as your fathers hardened their hearts when they heard his voice on that day in the past. He understood the phrase "the land of promise" as signifying another kind of possession, and he indicates this his own interpretation by a remarkable distinction. He says, "If they enter into my *rest*." He does not say, "If they enter into that *land*," as it says in the Book of Numbers: "Ye shall not enter into the land concerning which I lifted up my hand" (Num. 14:30). At the same time he reminds us of that peace in which God is said to have rested from his labours (Gen. 2:2).

Secondly, he clearly discerns by means of the phrase "today" or "on that day" another day from that referred to further on in chapter four, verse eight: For if Jesus (Joshua) had given them rest he would not afterward have spoken of another day. This other day, therefore, is the day concerning which the prophets were wont to speak when they used to say, "On that day. . . ." They meant without doubt the time of fulfilment. This is the method of synecdoche, a figure of speech by which the part is put for the whole. The phrase "on the day of temptation" is a similar representation. The phrase "when you will hear his voice" is a literal semitism. For the verb "you will hear" is to be taken as a neuter, that means that the noun is to be understood in the place of the verb. Or in other words the verb is to be replaced by the noun. That means we should understand by the phrase "when you will hear his voice" the meaning "when you will be hearers" or "when you have heard the word spoken." And note it says: a hearer *in* his voice, which means a hearer by means of his voice. As it says in Rom. 10:17: "For hearing comes through the word of Christ." Further, it is more significantly expressed in the Hebrew than it is in our translation (the Vulgate). For in the Hebrew text it sounds as a promise of future hearing through the voice of Christ, as if he said: "When he himself speaks and makes you hear, you will not harden your heart" [as your fathers did when they heard my voice but hardened their hearts]. In our translation it reads as if the outcome were uncertain [and not a promise].

It is of the utmost importance to notice that the one and greatest demand which God makes upon the Jews (and indeed upon every man) is that they hear his voice. Whence Moses continually forces upon the Jews in Deuteronomy the necessity of hearing. Thus: Hear, O Israel; and: If you will hear the voice of the Lord thy God. . . . In the same vein Jeremiah writes; "Add your burnt offerings to your sacrifices, and eat flesh. For I did not speak to your fathers nor gave them any commandments about burnt offerings and sacrifices on the day I led them out of the land of Egypt. But I did give them this command: Hear my voice, and I shall be a God to you and you will be a people for me" (Jer. 7:21 ff.). In fact nothing resounds throughout the prophets more frequently than the phrases "hear thou," "hear ye," "they did not hear," "they did not want to hear." And rightly so, because without faith it is impossible for God either to be with us or to effect any work, since he himself works all things only by the Word. In like manner, no one can co-operate with him unless he holds fast to the Word, which takes place through faith, as a tool can effect nothing for the workman until it is held in his hand. On that account it is the height of perversity to hasten to perform good works before God has worked in us, i.e., before we believe.

Of course, the natural man shrinks violently from hearing understood in this way, for he must first be reduced to nothing and stand in total darkness before he can hear this Word. As it says in Psalm 27: "I was reduced to nothing and did not understand," i.e., I knew nothing. [Actually Ps. 73:22. H-R suggest Ps. 38:10:

"As for the light of my eyes even that is not with me."] Or again in Ps. 116:11: "I said in my haste: all men are liars." Just as it is impossible for the potter when he is making a pot out of clay to preserve the former shape of the clay and at the same time mould a pot. For the former shape is contrary to the new, and the mass of unworked clay is the opposite of a finished pot. The philosophers have a saying for it: the making of the one necessitates the destruction of the other, or evolution is dialectical[1]. And thus natural man with his own inner light is inclined towards the light of grace, as darkness to light and formlessness to form. Whence Jeremiah says, making a most beautiful parable concerning the potter and the clay: "Behold, as clay in the hand of the potter, so art thou, house of Israel, in my hand" (18:6). Therefore, for that man with whom and in whom God is at work, it is quite impossible for his natural innate conversation, his resolution or his wisdom, his purpose or his good intentions either to remain as they were or to develop any further. For all these are as raw material, the shapeless clay, which, as soon as God sets to work on it, dies in its original form and gives place to its opposite.

Those, therefore, who do not wait upon the counsel of the Lord but shine bright in the light of their own wisdom, harden their hearts to their own unspeakable harm, and impede the work of God in themselves, for God works far and away above all human potentialities and all human feelings, and above all the plans and thoughts of man. Isaiah expresses it thus: As the heavens are higher than the earth, so are my ways higher than your ways, saith the Lord (Isa. 55:9). For he is the most high and therefore his work is the very highest. This is clear if we take single instances such as the flight of the children of Israel from Egypt.

From this argument it is now clearly understood who are the provokers, the instigators, the murmurers and the wranglers to whom Scripture so often refers. Clearly these are they who do not believe the word of God, and are impatient with the work of God. They are like the horse or mule which follow their master only so long as they enjoy the visible things by which they are nourished. If these supports should go, then they go under too. On that account, faith in Christ is the most difficult thing imaginable, because it is torn away and removed from all those things which can be experienced inwardly by the spirit or outwardly by the body and is founded on those things which can be known neither

---

[1] These ideas were common parlance in the Aristotelian world of scholasticism. In Latin they ran, *generatio unius est corruptio alterius*, and *motus est a contrario in contrarium*.

inwardly nor outwardly. Faith is founded on the most high God, the invisible, the incomprehensible.

3:9. When your fathers tempted me

This is meant to censure unbelief of so gross a kind. Granted indeed that faith in God is the most difficult of all things, yet still, through the words and works of God that have happened in the past, it is greatly strengthened and comes more easily. On that account they are convicted of not believing the promise of God when he was offering the land of Canaan, although they had already experienced from the hand of God similar nay even greater things so many times already. It was no less an impossibility to escape the Egyptians through the Red Sea than it was to conquer the Canaanites, and yet they had seen the escape effected, as he actually says here, "they have seen my work." It is as if he meant to say, I would be less angry if they were compelled to believe so much on the strength of my word alone, as if they had never seen anything like it before: just as he was not angry on that occasion when they crossed the sea, even though they doubted his word then.

From all this the prophets and saints derive sound doctrine which comforts them and strengthens their faith. As in Ps. 143:4 ff.: "My spirit is anxious within me; and my heart within me is thrown into confusion." What shall I do? Shall I cease believing? Away with such talk. Then these words follow: "I remember the former days, I have meditated on all thy works, and will meditate in the deeds of thine hands. I stretched forth my hands to thee. I thirst after thee as a land without water." Similarly in Ps. 77:12, where, having lamented his own similar affliction, the Psalmist says: "I was mindful of the works of the Lord. I will be mindful of thy wonders from the beginning, and will meditate in all thy works and occupy myself with thy doings." Or again, the words from I Maccabees 4:9: "Think on how our fathers were saved," viz., in faith. As Psalm 44 shows more beautifully than anywhere else: "God, we have heard with our ears, our fathers have told us, what work thou didst in their days, in the days of old . . .," right through to the end of the psalm. ["For they got not the land in possession by their own sword, neither did their own arm save them: but thy right hand, and thine arm, and the light of thy countenance, because thou hadst a favour unto them. . . . For I will not trust in my bow, neither shall my sword save me. But thou hast saved us from our adversaries, and hast put them to shame that hate us. In God have we made our boast all the day long, and we will give thanks unto thy name for ever. . . . But now thou hast cast us off, and brought us to dishonour. . . . Awake, why sleepest thou, O Lord? Arise, cast us not off forever. Wherefore hidest thou thy face, and forgettest our affliction and our oppression? For our soul is bowed down to the dust: our belly cleaveth unto the earth. Rise up for our help. And redeem us for thy lovingkindness sake[1]."]

So it happens, that the faith of our fathers who have gone before us becomes a source of gain and strength to the faith of those following after. In fact the faith of our forefathers was the more praiseworthy in that it grew strong by the help of fewer examples than we have, and the unbelief of their descendants all the more blameworthy in that having so many more examples than they had it has not grown strong. The unbelief of Christians standing in the tradition of so many martyrs and saints is utterly deplorable when they take fright at the sorrowful road of faith and reject it in anger.

Gl. 18:8 ff.

When your fathers tempted me

They did so because they had no faith in God. That is why they said, "Is the Lord among us or not?" (Ex. 17:7).
[And Moses called the name of the place Massah (tempting, or proving), and Meribah (chiding, or strife), because of the striving of the children of Israel, and because they tempted the Lord, saying, Is the Lord among us or not?]
This question means, "Who knows whether God wills these things, or whether Moses is rightly representing these things?"

they have proved

They have experienced my works and know them for a certainty.

---

1 Luther writes after his quotation of the first verse of the psalm *"per totum,"* the whole lot. Only a few selected verses are here quoted to keep the argument clear, though doubtless Luther would read the whole psalm in this place.

and have seen my works	They did not believe in works that never happened but saw them with their own eyes.
forty years. Wherefore I was displeased	I was hostile, I was disgusted
with this generation	because of their unbelief
and said, these people err in their heart always	Admittedly, they make an exemplary show of outward works.
but these people did not know	because they presumed on their own strength and had no faith in the help of God, though they had experienced that help so many times
my ways	the ways of righteousness and goodness, in which God walks with us and within us, and in which he makes us walk.

3:10. Forty years long was I near to this generation and said they do always err in their heart.

This reading "Forty years long was I *near*," which is used in the hymnody of the Church, is taken from the Roman Psalter, which alone has this reading. All the other versions, the Greek, Hebrew and Latin are different, and have "being hostile," or "grieved" instead of "near." If one wanted to harmonize the contradiction, one could do so by saying that God was near to them in chiding them. For God draws near to man in two ways—in anger and in mercy. As it says in Ecclesiasticus 5:7: "His mercy and wrath come suddenly near us." In this way "being hostile" could mean the same thing as "being near."

It is rather interesting, however, to ask where the adverb "always" comes from, since every schoolboy knows that in Hebrew "*'am*" signifies not "always" but "people." The word "*tamid*" stands for "always." It would seem that the error has crept in from the Greek: "*laoi*" means people in the plural, "*aei*" means "always." Therefore, perhaps the letter "*l*" was omitted and the letters remaining "*aoi*" began to be read for "*aei*." And so perhaps the words "the people err" was written for "they always err."

It is certain that this semitic expression "displeasure towards a generation" refers to a future time for the Hebrews, though admittedly it may refer to a time past for the Greek and Latin peoples. It seems, therefore, that either the future is put for the past, which often happens in the Old Testament, or rather that the prophet meant that the people yet to come would be the same, and displease God as the older generation had displeased God. For that phrase "displeasure towards a generation" without the demonstrative adjective "this" or "that" is a figure of speech which expresses the displeasure of the speaker, as if he scorned to indicate such people openly. People usually act like this when they have to talk about something very distasteful.

3:11. Unto whom I sware in my wrath: if they enter my rest

This phrase "if they will enter" (literally) is also a Hebrew idiom. For thus God was wont to sware by means of this rhetorical pause (*aposiopesis* in Greek), in which the completion of the thought has to be supplied. For instance: "I am a liar . . ." or "I shall not live, if they will enter" (literally). Because it cannot be conceived that God can be a liar, or could die, much more put into words, it is very properly suppressed, and the meaning of the if-clause then completed by being negatived, i.e., "they will *not* enter." The same occurs in Ps. 89:35: "Once have I sworn by my holiness, if I will lie to David," meaning, of course, I will *not* lie to David. Men, however, usually swore to one another without using this rhetorical device, as for instance, when Saul and David swore to one another in I and II Samuel. "And Saul said, God do so and more also: for thou shalt surely die, Jonathan" (I Sam. 14:44). "God do so unto the enemies of David, and more also, if I leave of all that pertain to him by the morning light so much as one man child" (I Sam. 25:22). "God do so to Abner, and more also, if, as the Lord hath sworn to David, I do not even so to him" (II Sam. 3:9).

Gl. 18:17
**Unto whom I sware
in my wrath**

Num. 14:28. "As I live, saith the Lord, as you have spoken, so shall I do to you." For they had said

in the same chapter:
"Would God that we had
died in the land of Egypt!
or would God that we had
died in this wilderness!
And wherefore doth the
Lord bring us unto this
land, to fall by the sword?"
(*loc. cit.*, 2).

**if they will enter
into my rest**

For the same reason we find
in Deut. 9:7: "Remember,
forget thou not, how thou
provokedst the Lord thy God
to wrath in the wilderness,
from the day thou wentest
forth out of Egypt until ye
came into this place, ye
have been rebellious
against the Lord." And
Ps. 78:37, too: "For their
heart was not right with him
neither were they faithful to
God." The rest may be
read in Num. 14 from which
all this passage and the
prophecies are taken.

**3:12. Take heed, brethren, lest haply there shall be in any
one of you an evil heart of unbelief, in falling away from
the living God[1].**

The whole force of this sentence is placed in the single word
"heart." For the writer does not say, Take heed lest there be in
any one of you a grasping hand, a shifty eye, a sensuous ear. For
before everything else one must see to it that the heart is good,
pure and holy, as it says in Ps. 51:12: "Create in me a clean heart,
O God, and renew a right spirit within me." As if to say, the purity
of the works of the flesh is nothing, unless the purity of the spirit be
there first. For this impurity of the heart is so deep that no man
understands it fully, much less is he able to purge it by his own
strength. As Jeremiah says, "The heart of man is vicious and

1 To appreciate fully the following passage the reader must bear in mind that
whenever Luther talks about the Word of God he always has Christ in mind at
the same time. There is a double allusion both to the Bible as containing the
Word and Christ who is the Word.

inscrutable: who can understand it? I the Lord search the hearts and reins (of men)" (Jer. 17:9 f.).

In fact, the heart does not become clean and good except through faith in Christ, as it says in Acts 15:9, "God made no distinction between us and them, cleansing their hearts by faith." For faith in the Word purifies, because as the Word of God is the purest and best, it makes him who cleaves to it similar, i.e. pure and good. Whatever virtue it has, whatever power it possesses, it shares to the full with him who adheres to it and believes in it. It says in Ps. 19:8: "The Law of the Lord is perfect and converts souls." And Christ also said: "Ye are clean because of the word which I have spoken to you" (John 15:3). Accordingly, Ps. 51:6 says in the Hebrew: "Against thee only have I sinned [and done this evil in thy sight], therefore shalt thou justify in thy word, and wilt make clean when thou judgest." (It is he who believes in the Word of God, who is righteous, wise, true, good and the like.) And contrariwise, too, he who has been separated from the Word of God, or has departed from it, will necessarily abide in malice, uncleanness and in all those things which are contrary to the Word of God. (The saying, "He is a fool who trusts in his own heart" is spoken against trust in oneself.) The Apostle says to Titus: "To the impure nothing is pure, (to the pure all things are pure): but to them that are defiled and unbelieving nothing is pure; but both their mind and conscience are defiled" (Titus 1:15). This is exactly what is meant when the Apostle uses here the phrase "departing from the living God." A man may be said to depart from the living God when he departs from his Word, which is living and makes all things live. In fact the Word is God himself. Therefore, when men depart from the Word, they die. (He who does not believe is dead.) Departing from God comes to pass through unbelief. Accordingly, it becomes clear in what way the heart is evil, *viz.*, through unbelief. In short, there is nothing good in it, it is entirely evil, because it turns back from everything that is good.

Gl. 19:2. Take heed, brethren, lest there be in any one of you

i.e., each sees into the depths of his own heart; lest he be of the number of those having

an evil heart of unbelief

an obdurate heart for unbelief alone separates from God, as faith alone unites with God. For

unbelief has no fear of God,
and on the other hand, faith
effects the fear of God. As
it says in Job 41:16
(Vulgate): "When he (the
devil) raises himself up, the
very angels (the elect) shall
fear and being terrified
shall purify themselves."

in falling away

the unbeliever will most
certainly go to his death
and to the god of the dead

from the Living God

This is what the Apostle
says to the Romans: "The
just man lives by his faith."
And the reverse is true: the
wicked man dies from
unbelief.

3:13. Exhort one another day by day, so long as it is called today.

Since we live in the midst of enemies and are enticed continually by allurements without end, are harassed by cares and burdened by labours, through all of which we are led away from purity of heart, there is therefore only one course left open to us. We must exhort ourselves and stir up our indolent spirit by the Word of God with all the zeal that we can muster. We must meditate on it, read it, and hear it assiduously, just as the Apostle advises us to do here. We should be like Cecilia "who used to cherish the gospel of Christ in her heart continually and ceased neither day nor night from prayer and conversation with God[1]." Otherwise, if we do not do this, we shall be completely destroyed in the long run by the multitude of these things, and overwhelmed by indolence and lukewarmness of spirit. This last is the worst of all possible dangers, for the Jews suffered from this in the wilderness, when they sickened of the manna. As it says in Ps. 107:18: "Their soul loathed all meat, and they drew near to the gates of death." Indeed, the psalmist spoke from his own experience when he said, "My soul fell asleep for heaviness, strengthen me again in thy words." (Ps. 119:28), and again in Ps. 102:4: "I am smitten and am like withered grass, for I have forgotten to eat my bread." For as the body cannot exist without its daily bread, otherwise it would grow weak, so the heart of man is not made strong except

[1] Petrus de Natalibus, *Catalogus Sanctorum*, l.x.c. 96; *WA*, 57, 148.

by that bread which is the Word of God. For as often as we forget the Word of God, we fall back into a materialist frame of mind and are corrupted. We are not purified of this corruption unless we turn back again to the Word. The Scriptures often capture this idea by means of the imagery of ear-rings. For this reason: just as ear-rings hang in the ears all the time, so ought the Word of God continually to sound in our heart[1]. The Word of God must be understood as meant by the articles "ear-rings," as it is in Ex. 35:22[2]. Finally, that is why Christ commanded us to preach his word with all diligence.

3:13. Lest any one of you be hardened by the deceitfulness of sin.

Again, how aptly and appropriately expressed, "the deceitfulness of sin." Now here is a description of how unbelief arises. First, man finds joy in created things. Next, the Creator gets forgotten. Then, a man becomes attached to material things as constituting what is good in life. Every man wants to experience the world of created being, but he sets about it in the wrong way. From this there comes the habit of mind of loving it, and consequently the heart of man is hardened against the word of the Creator who calls man the creature back from the natural tendency of the creature. Then unbelief comes as a consequence. Indeed, it is rightly called the deceitfulness of sin, because it deceives under the appearance of good.

This phrase "the deceitfulness of sin" ought to be understood in a much wider sense, so that the term includes even one's own righteousness and wisdom. For more than ought else one's own righteousness and wisdom deceives one and works against faith in Christ, since we love the flesh and the sensations of the flesh and also riches and possessions, but we love nothing more ardently than our own feelings, judgment, purpose and will, especially when they seem to be good. For the same reason Christ said, when he healed the paralytic at the Pool of Bethesda, that it was impossible for such people to be able to believe: "How can you believe who receive glory from one another?" (John 5:44). Why are they not able to believe? Because the "deceitfulness of sin," i.e., the love of their own righteousness blinds them and hardens their heart. Yet at the same time they think it a good thing to glory in their own righteousness and be pleased with it, though that indeed is the very

1 Presumably Luther means that just as a wearer of ear-rings must be continually aware of them by the tinkling sound of the metal as they dangle, so must the believer ever have the Word of God sounding in his ears.
2 This sentence was spoken as an *obiter dictum*. In the Gl. interl. of this passage ear-rings are interpreted as meaning obedience of subjects, good hearing.

worst of all vices, the extreme antithesis of faith. Faith rejoices and glories in the righteousness of God alone, i.e., in Christ himself.

It should be noted that *obduratio* (hardness of heart) is to be understood in this passage simply as difficulty in believing. The Hebrew language has the most beautiful metaphors, and thus *obduratio* signifies something hard or unimpressionable, a simile taken from the use of wax, which, as long as it is hard will not take the imprint of the seal, but when it is soft is easily formed into any shape. And so man stands at the cross-roads. When the heart cleaves to God, its nature melts through his word. It softens towards God and hardens towards things. When it cleaves to things, it hardens towards God and softens towards things. All the time, therefore, the human heart is now hard now soft, with respect to these two different allegiances. This cleaving to God is nothing but faith in the Word, the betrothal Hosea describes: "I will betroth me unto thee in faith" (Hos. 2:20). Paul also describes it: "He who is joined to the Lord is one Spirit" (I Cor. 6:17). (The captive follows him who loves him.)

This corollary follows: Faith in Christ is all virtue and unbelief all sin, as is clear enough from what has been said. For through faith a man becomes like the Word of God. But the Word is the Son of God. Thus it follows, that every son of God is he who believes in him (John 1:12), and because of this the believer is without sin and full of all virtue. The contrary necessarily holds. The unbeliever is full of all sin and evil: he is in fact a son of the devil, a son of iniquity.

3:14. For we are become partakers of Christ, if we hold fast the beginning of our confidence firm unto the end.

It is certain that in this place the shoes of philosophy ought to be removed from the feet of the faithful, because *substantia* [literally— substance, but here, as in many other Greek writers, meaning "resolute confidence"] cannot be taken here as having the same meaning as in previous passages (Heb. 1:3), especially as the Greek has *hypostasis* and not *ousia*. In this place, therefore, *substantia* signifies, according to the general usage of Scripture, potentialities, or the possession of things, as in Prov. 3:9: "Honour the Lord with the substance. . . ." Also in Luke 8:43: "A woman . . . who had spent all her substance on doctors." And in I John 3:17: "If any man has this world's substance (or goods), and sees his brother have need, how does the love of God abide in him?" In this passage John the Apostle clearly shows two kinds of substance, the one of this world, the other of the future life. And the same thing is shown again later in this epistle. . . . "You accepted joyfully the spoiling of your goods, knowing that you have a better substance that endures" (Heb. 10:34). And faith begins this, or rather is its beginning, because through faith we begin to possess what in eternity we shall possess fully. We find the same in chapter eleven further on: "Now faith is the substance of things hoped for," i.e., the possession now of things which will be fully possessed in the future. Jerome expounded the word "*faith*" in the same way in Gal. 5:23. Chrysostom, however, expounded "substance" otherwise than Jerome: he took it for "essence" (*essentia*) or "reality" (*subsistentia*). For he writes in this place: "The beginning of substance[1] [reading substance here in the sense of real or true existence] invokes faith, through which we are born, through which we exist, and through which we are made truly alive (*essentiales*), if I may be allowed to use such a word[2]." This is not to be understood as referring to natural existence but to a spiritual existence in Christ, just as it says in Ephesians: "For we are his workmanship, created [in Jesus Christ] unto good works" (Eph. 2:10); and in John 3:5 "Except a man be born again of water and the spirit, he cannot enter into the kingdom of heaven"; and in Galatians: "In Christ neither circumcision availeth anything, nor uncircumcision, but a new creature" (Gal. 5:6; 6:15); and in James 1:18: "Of his own will he begat us by the word of truth, that we might be a kind of first-fruits of his creatures." Whence we pray, Give us our daily bread. . . . The word in the Greek is *epiousion*, translated in the Latin by *supersubstantialem*, "necessary to support life": that means bread which transfers us into a new creation in the spirit. (Praying is speaking well, handsomely and beautifully.) Even if the taking of *substantia* in the second meaning of "being" does not seem appropriate to the laudation of faith which follows in chapter eleven, (because in that context is added "the substance of things hoped for" in the way that sounds very like the first meaning, i.e., the possession of things), yet it is possible and not inappropriate to take the word in this context in this second meaning of "being." Then let us join in one, for on the one hand Christ becomes our substance (our possession) through faith, i.e., he is called our riches, whilst on the other hand, we, through that same faith and at the same time, are made into his "substance" (his essence) or being, i.e., we become a new creation.

Gl. 20:16. It is characteristic of the Apostle to take the word "substance" in the sense of "faith," especially in this epistle.

---

[1] This must be the only way to take *substantia* in this context. Chrysostom would seem to approach a modern existentialist position here!

[2] Chrys., *Hom.*, 6, f. 31; Migne, *loc. cit.*, 63.279.4. *Cf.* Migne, 26.448.

3:15. While it is said, Today, if you will hear his voice, harden not your hearts as in the provocation.

Gl. 20:4.

Harden not your hearts
as in the provocation   when they followed their
                               own desires and resisted the
                               Word of God.

Chrysostom wants a hyperbaton here, i.e., a transposition or rearrangement of the text. He suggests that from the words: "For who, when they heard, did provoke?" (3:16) down to, "For we which have believed do enter into that rest, even as he saith" (4:3) is an interpolation and interrupts the order, and that the following should be the order of the words: "Let us fear therefore . . ." (4:1) down to, "For we which have believed do enter into that rest" (4:3). Then should follow: "For who, when they heard . . ." (3:16) down to: "Let us fear, therefore . . ." (4:1). Then should follow: ". . . While it is said, Today, if you will hear his voice," etc. . . . (3:15). And this is the end of the change. Then follows, "For we which have believed do enter into that rest . . .," etc. (4:3). And it is right to have faith in such a learned Greek doctor.

3:16 f. For which of them, when they heard, did provoke? Did not all who came out of Egypt by Moses? And with whom was he displeased forty years? Was it not with them that sinned, whose carcases fell in the wilderness?

The Exodus of the children of Israel from Egypt should be considered not so much as an historical event but also at the same time as a spiritual event. The Apostle clearly says: "I would not have you ignorant, brethren, how all our fathers were under the cloud, all crossed the sea, and all were baptized in Moses in the cloud and in the sea, and all ate the same spiritual meat and all drank the same spiritual drink," and so on (I. Cor. 10:1 f.). How, therefore, can these statements be reconciled, that in the one place (I. Cor. 10) he says "all," and in the other (Heb. 3:16) he says "some"? In fact, in the first instance he immediately added, "But with many of them God was not well pleased, for they were overthrown in the wilderness." (loc. cit. 5). The answer is: The Apostle speaks there (I Cor.) as here (Heb.) to those who have followed "the beginning of their substance [faith] in Christ." [See exposition of 3:14 for this interpretation of substantia.] In order to persuade them to persevere, he sets before them the terrible example of those Israelites who had all begun well but had never persevered and of course had never won through [to God's Rest]. Wherefore, in that very place, after the Apostle had said that all had been baptized and eventually some of them were overthrown, he concluded the matter by saying, Let him therefore who thinks he stands take heed lest he fall (I Cor. 10:12). It is as if he wished to say, When you see what happened to these people, preserve in fear what you have entered upon, lest you fall in the same manner. He makes a like exhortation everywhere. Since we have been made partakers in Christ and have the beginning of his substance [see exposition of "substance" at 3:14], (i.e., since we have begun happily just as they did), let us fear lest by defecting we lose "the beginning of the substance," as they lost it and defected. The text, "Some when they had heard, did provoke, howbeit not all . . ." (Heb. 3:16) and so on, I rather suspect should be understood thus: Not all were provoked when they left Egypt, but all of them had faith, as it is said in Ex. 12:50 and above in I Cor. 10:2, "All were baptized . . ." and so forth. Therefore, all of them made a good beginning at the Exodus under Moses, but afterwards defected in the course of events. Therefore God said, "Forty years long was I grieved with this generation," and so on. In a much higher sense, however, they did not win through. That is why he says that God had sworn to them as defectors, that they would never enter into his rest.

CHAPTER FOUR

4:1. What we have to be afraid of when we have been left a promise of entering into his rest is that one of you should be found wanting.

Gl. 21:13. The apostle exhorts his readers to perseverance, because it is easy to make a start but much harder to make progress and grow more perfect. More people fall in the course of a journey than at its start. At the outset, not one of the children of Israel remained in Egypt, but in the course of the journey they all lagged behind eventually and fell in the wilderness. All except two—Caleb and Joshua.

Chrysostom has the reading "lest any of you." Lefèvre d'Etaples thinks it should read "lest any of us," because at the beginning of the sentence it has "let us fear" in the first person and not "fear ye" in the second person. The same thing happens in the next verse where it says, "For unto *us* was the Gospel preached," i.e., in the first person and not "unto you" in the second person. But his reason is not sufficiently compelling, since it is an acceptable procedure in the Scriptures to change the persons, times, numbers and modes in various ways. A brief final example: "Christ suffered for us [leaving us an example], that *ye* should follow his steps" (I Peter 2:21). He did not write ". . . that *we* should follow. . . ."

Chrysostom interprets the word "to have come short of" (*deesse*) in the sense of "having been alienated" (*alienatus esse*); Lefèvre d'Etaples as "having been disregarded or put aside" (*postponi*); Erasmus as "of no effect" (*frustratus esse*), "not having attained to" (*non assecutus esse*), meaning, that while others go forward and go in, they remain behind. For thus it happened to those who fell in the desert. He also says in a beautiful antithesis, that the words "being left" (*relicta*) and "to come short of" (*deesse*) mean: Let us fear lest we ourselves through unbelief lose the promise, and the peace of God depart from us also through the wrath of God. (This

88

is the argument from contradictory propositions: if one proposition be true the contradictory is false, and conversely.)

4:2. For indeed we have had good tidings preached to us as they also had.

The Greek text has literally, We also have been evangelized as they have, just as in Latin it says "we are taught" or "we have been taught." Wherefore, as the interpreter in this place (i.e., in the Latin construction) has quite legitimately changed the case and the verb, *viz.*, the nominative into the dative and the passive verb into the impersonal verb (i.e., it has been preached unto us, *nobis nunciatum est*) so ought he to make Matt. 11:5 "the poor are evangelized" into "the gospel was (or is) preached to the poor."

...But the word of hearing did not profit them ...

Chrysostom has "The Word of the sermon did not profit those who had not been restrained by the faith of those who had heard" (*loc. cit.*). Lefèvre d'Etaples follows him and translates thus, But the word of hearing did not profit them, when those who heard had not been made into one by faith. For with Chrysostom he does not read "united" in the singular (*admixtus*) and therefore agreeing with the word "word" (*sermo*), but in the plural (*admixtis*) and agreeing with the pronoun "those" (*illis*), i.e., those hearers who would be united with the Word by faith. Erasmus, however, has "united" in the singular (*admixtus*), and translates like this: It did not profit them to have heard the sermon, because it was not united with faith in those who had heard it. That, however, amounts to the same thing, for the uniting of the Word with the heart, the making of the Word and the heart into one, are reciprocal terms. These three things, faith, Word and heart become one thing. Faith is the glue or the link. The Word and the heart lie furthest apart, but through faith these two become one spirit, as man and wife become one flesh. Therefore, it is true to say, that the heart becomes cemented to the Word by faith, and the Word cemented to the heart by faith.

4:2.

For indeed we have had the good tidings preached to us	we have been evangelized by the apostles
even as they had	by the preaching of Moses
But the word	the word given by Moses
of hearing	the word "hearing" is in the genitive case. It was

preaching of such a kind as
was heard by the ear. This
means that it was a word
that was heard and no
more: it was not a word
received in faith and belief.

did not profit them   In fact, it did them harm
because they took offence at
it

it was not mixed with   it was not joined to
faith   i.e. they put no faith in the
word. But with restraint
and charm he says, The
word in this case was not
joined to faith

in those   the children of Israel
who heard   They heard but they did
not believe. For that reason
it profited them nothing to
have heard when they failed
to believe.

4:3. [**For we which have believed do enter into that rest,
even as he has said, as I sware in my wrath, they shall not
enter into my rest**], although the works were finished from
the foundation of the world.

The Latin translation is obscure here. It would seem, however,
that this verse was written by the Apostle in the first place to
explain what he meant when he said "my peace," and in the
second place to help to discern God's peace from any other. Consequently, if any one should ask, "What is that peace of God which
we shall enter?", he may be told, "The peace of God at the Creation when God had finished all his works." Therefore, Lefèvre
d'Etaples translates thus: "As I swore in my wrath, they will not
enter into my rest, *viz.*, the peace instituted when God's works
were finished at the foundation of the world." The text is best
ordered and understood according to the following interpretation:
we shall enter into his peace, i.e., the peace which is his, instituted
since the time of the foundation of the world when he completed
his work. The phrase "into *my* peace" is to be understood in the
same way also, i.e., the peace which is mine from the foundation
of the world and so on.

Gl. 22:15. **my rest:** He writes his rest, since it is certain that
to have him is to have peace.

We have to read between the lines, however, if we are to understand our translation when it begins the sentences with "And yet . . ." (*Et quidem* . . .); i.e., only to a certain extent do I call my peace that peace which is mine from the foundation of the world. Wherefore, Chrysostom, who has "although" (*quamquam*) should be understood thus: we shall enter into his rest although it has already been instituted from the foundation of the world. In short, though the peace of God has been in existence since the foundation of the world, yet nevertheless we shall enter into it. This is certainly contrary to the peace of men which is prepared after labour, yet this peace is already prepared before any work of ours.

4:4. . . . and God rested. . . .

Augustine[1] expounded the idea of God resting in three ways. First: Just as it is rightly said that God is doing something when we are doing it by the power of God himself working in us, therefore it is rightly said that God rests when we are enjoying God's gift of rest. This is the tropological meaning, of course, because it means the peace of God at work in us. Isaiah refers to this in Chapters 11 and 66: "The spirit of the Lord will rest upon him" (11:2), and "Upon whom my spirit will rest" (66:2).

Secondly, Augustine suggests another interpretation further on and says, God rested from the making of new kinds of creatures, although John declares, "My father worketh hitherto, and I work" (5:17). This is to be understood with respect to the governance of creatures and has nothing to do with the creation of them.

Thirdly, he says, To those who rightly understand, the peace of God is that state in which a man needs nobody else's goods but is blessed in himself. The first and third meaning can be accepted in the case of this text under discussion, "They shall not enter into my rest." The second meaning is rather obscure. Therefore, we may say, we shall then enter his rest (first meaning), when we have begun to have need of no further riches (third meaning). This, however, will come to pass when, according to the Apostle: "God will be all in all" (I Cor. 15:28).

To help towards a clearer understanding of the mode of this rest it is worth noting that as the ark of Noah was constructed in three dimensions, so also man's nature has three aspects, *viz.*, the sensual, the rational and the spiritual. (Man is a microcosm, they say, i.e., a small world.) Each one of these three states, (the sensual, the rational and the spiritual) is either in a state of peace and

---

[1] Augustine, *de Genesi ad litt.*, IV, 9, 16. Migne, 34.302–306.

quiet, or is labouring in a state of disquiet. This happens in two ways, either from within [its own nature] or from without [in relation to external things].

First, let us consider the sensual aspect of man. Man's sensual nature has peace "from without" when it enjoys an object perceptible to the senses. This is to enjoy peace in a positive way. On the other hand, he is troubled and distressed when the perceptible object is thrown into some confusion or withdrawn. But he enjoys peace "from within" when he is quiet in a negative way, i.e., not bothered about public affairs, when he gives up manual labour or sensual experiences on account of his work as a rational being, as is clear in thinking men and in philosophers. On the other hand, this peace "from within" is disturbed when a man is confused on account of some disorder of the mind, as is clear in the morose and in melancholics.

Secondly, let us consider the rational side of man. Man's rational nature enjoys peace "from without" when the subject matter of his thinking and speculating is happy. On the other hand, he is disquieted "from without," if it is sad. He has peace "from within," even if it is a negative sort of peace, as soon as he stops striving and reasoning, and allows his spiritual nature to reflect on faith and the Word of God. He has disquiet "from within," when his spiritual nature becomes troubled because his faith and his trust in the Word of God are put to the test. Such a state is anguish indeed. This distress is the most horrible of all, because it is the most profound and the nearest to hell[1].

Thirdly, let us consider the spiritual side of man. Man's

---

[1] Here occurs, what emerges in all of Luther's writings, a reference to his teaching on *Anfechtung*, approximately translated, "Temptation". *Anfechtung* to Luther is a trial or assault or a temptation which comes from God to try a man,—or from the devil to wreck him—and means all that complex emotional experience of doubt, despair, desolation, uncertainty, fear. It should not be thought of in terms of a subjective experience which comes to men of spiritual worth. To Luther it was the whole work of the universe threatening and condemning a man, an ever present reminder from God to bring man to an awareness of his need of God and the peril of his reliance upon himself. Life provides this unremitting spiritual conflict which never ends till death, the last *Anfechtung*. Rupp (*The Righteousness of God*, pp. 105, 235 ff. *et al.*, see especially the literature on the subject cited as a footnote on p. 106) reminds us of the etymology of the word, and how Luther chooses this word (the basic meaning of which is assault or combat), rather than *Versuchung*, (the basic meaning of which is enticement or allurement). Rupp says that the assault is always an attack on faith.

Vogelsang (*op. cit.*, p. 48) gives the following examples of Luther's discussion of the meaning of temptation: *WA*, 3, 167.18–170.11. *Lectures on the Psalms* 1513–16; *WA*, 1,160.34 ff.; 216.25 ff. The *Confessional Psalms* 1517; *WA*, 1.557 f. *The Resolutions* 1518; 5.622. *Second Lectures on the Psalms* 1521.

spiritual life enjoys "peace from without" when he rests secure in the Word of God and in faith. This is to experience a positive peace. It lasts as long as the object of faith, that is the Word of God, is imprinted on him. But, however, this "peace from without" is broken, as has already been said, when his faith is endangered and the Word of God is no longer there. This takes place when faith, hope and charity are attacked. Now this type is the man who "lives by the Word of God" (Matt. 4:4 and Luke 4:4, "Man does not live by bread alone, but by every word of God"). On the other hand he enjoys a "peace from within," inasmuch as it is peace of a negative kind, when he is sustained by faith and word in the true work of God which is the bringing to birth of the true uncreated Word. Jesus expresses the same truth when he says: "This is life eternal, that they may know thee, the true God, and him whom thou hast sent, Jesus Christ" (John 17:3). (This is the real meaning of the procession of the Son from the Father.) This peace has no disturbance from within. This peace is the seventh day which has no evening to bring it to an end and bring in another day. And from these observations emerges a brief statement of the two kinds of theology, affirmative and negative[1].

4:11. Let us therefore hasten to enter that peace.

This haste is a spiritual haste and is done with spiritual feet. It is an expression of those fervent desires of the kind which burned in the Apostle's breast, when he said. "I desire to depart and to be

[1] As is well known, Aquinas used to teach that as God is a non-sensible reality: he cannot be known to us directly, but only indirectly by what he has done. He believed that we could have a positive knowledge of his existence but only a negative knowledge of his nature. "We can know that God is and what he is not." (John Baillie, Our Knowledge of God, p. 109. See also pp. 109 ff., 168 ff., 252 ff.). We then have to proceed by means of this negative method to know what he is like, e.g. not evil. That is why the names we use to describe God are negative words, e.g. unchangeable, infinite and so on. This method is eked out by the method of analogy. Aquinas was forced into this procedure, according to John Baillie, because of his Aristotelian epistemology and the influence of Neoplatonism. The latter is strongly agnostic and teaches that a knowledge of God is attained less by a progressive enrichment as by a progressive subtraction, so that we gradually discover much that he is not but nothing about what he is. It was Dionysius who transmitted this theology through Erigena, and this theology dominated the Middle Ages. Luther broke through this theologia gloriae into his theologia crucis, and believed all speculation on the nature of God was ultimately a rejection of the Gospel in that it was a belief in works. That what a man was knowing by this sort of intellectual discipline was not God but only himself. Such theology was largely a figment of the mind to Luther. The true knowledge of God was to be found elsewhere: in the incarnation, in the humiliation and in the cross. There we have dealings with God because it was there that God determined to have his dealings with man. The cross is not man's image of God but the image God made of himself for man.

with Christ" (Phil. 1:23). And also Ps. 120:5: "Woe is me that my sojourn is prolonged." These are they for whom this life is weariness and sickness of the kind Augustine described in writing of the death of his mother in Book Nine of his *Confessions*: "Lord, thou knowest, that in that day when we were talking thus, this world with all its delights grew contemptible to us, even while we spake. Then said my mother, 'Son, for myself, I have no longer any pleasure in aught in this life. What I want here further, and why I am here, I know not, now that my hopes in this world were satisfied. There was indeed one thing for which I wished to tarry a little in this life, and that was that I might see thee a Catholic Christian before I died. My God has exceeded this abundantly, so that I see thee despising all earthly felicity, made his servant— what do I here?'[1]." [Luther makes the reference and not the quotation which doubtless he would read or recall in class, and which is necessary for the point of his argument. Tr.] He also once said of himself in a letter, "I wish the last day would come upon me[2]." That is why it is written concerning Abraham, David and many other fathers that they died in "a good old age," "full of days," "rich in days" and "weary of this life." On the contrary it is said of those unbelievers who still have a taste for this life, "Bloody and deceitful men shall not live out half their days" (Ps. 55:23) because they have not wearied of this life. Wherefore, the one and only concern of Christians ought to be, daily more and more to die to this life and in surfeit of it hasten to the life to come. Otherwise, they will be numbered with those of whom it is spoken in Ps. 106:24 And they despised the pleasant land.

4:12. For the word of God is living and powerful

These words are expounded in two ways. First as an exhortation, as Nicholas of Lyra, Lefèvre d'Etaples and some others do. But they are also expounded in a figurative way. So much so that it is hard to believe that the writers understand their own words. However, we shall help them as far as we can. First, God's Word is living. That means that it makes alive those who believe it. Therefore we must rightly hasten to it before we perish and die. Secondly, the Word of God is powerful: because it makes all things possible to those who believe. Thirdly, the Word of God is sharper than any two-edged sword: because it is more penetrating and more real than the actual truth itself. As Jeremiah says: "Thinkest thou that I am a God at hand and not a God far off? Do not I fill heaven and earth?" (Jer. 23:23 f.). Or again: "Hell and perdition is before the Lord, how much more the hearts of the sons of men?"

[1] IX.26 (Pilkington's translation).   [2] *To Boniface;* Migne, 33.1098.

(Prov. 15:11). And the most beautiful of all, Psalm 139 in its entirety: "O Lord thou hast searched me out and known me. . . ." Therefore, if the Lord is present in all places, we must believe in him in complete faith, because he is able to help us at all times, even if we are utterly forsaken. Fourthly, the Word of God pierces even to the dividing asunder of soul and spirit. That means it separates the disposition of the mind from the state of the soul, for faith always purifies the heart, as it says in Acts 15:9: "And he made no distinction between us and them, cleansing their heart by faith." Or again: "The Law of the Lord is right and rejoices the heart," and so on. Fifthly, the Word of the Lord pierces even to the dividing of both joints and marrow: because it separates the limbs and marrow from evil affections, thus purifying not only the heart but also the body. Sixthly, the Word of God is quick to discern the thoughts and intents of the heart: it condemns evil counsels and desires, i.e., self-centredness and self-will, which even in saints have the dominion at one time or another.

Gl. 25:16. (Note on verse 12): As the Word of God makes believers alive, powerful, united and therefore at peace, it makes non-believers on the contrary dead, impotent, disunited and therefore greatly troubled.

Secondly, and better still, these sayings are to be understood as a threat of cruel punishment for the unbelievers. Wherefore Chrysostom says: "The Word is more cruel than any sword, for the Word cuts into their souls and causes terrible plagues and horrible gashes[1]." What kind these are Chrysostom does not explain, but says that he does not think "there was either occasion or necessity to give a definitive list of these things, as he had already provided such a clear account." It is also true that these terrifying plagues are understood by nobody except those who have in some degree experienced them, as David and Hezekiah and many others. For no punishment can ever compare with that which the impious undergo even just to face the angry countenance of God. As it says in Ps. 21:9: "Thou shalt make them as a fiery furnace at the time of thy angry countenance." Also in Wisdom 6:6: "They will appear before you in sudden dread." And again in II Thess. 1:8 and 9: "Those who do not obey the Gospel of our Lord Jesus Christ shall suffer punishment in eternal destruction separated from the face of the Lord and from the glory of his power."

Therefore, since the Word of God is over and above all things, beyond all things and within all things, before all things and behind

---

1 Migne, *loc. cit.*, 285.

all things, and therefore everywhere, it is impossible to escape from it anywhere. Since also it is living and because of that eternal, its power to hurt and cut can never be brought to an end. Since it is also strong and powerful, it is impossible to resist it. And, finally, since it is sharper than a two-edged sword, it is impossible to hide or be hidden from it. This is the way unbelievers will be put to death, by the infinite, eternal, unconquerable thrust of the sword which is the Word of God. Bernard writes beautifully and at length on this topic in his *De Consideratione*, Book V[1]. Because of such punishment, there follows separation of soul and spirit, the cutting of joint and marrow, the disturbance and confusion of all internal and external powers, as expressed in Hebrews 4:12. On a par with this is Eccl. 9:10: "There will be neither work nor reason, neither wisdom nor knowledge in hell." Here also is that fear and confusion about which the Scriptures so frequently write. For the same reason Isaiah counsels: "Enter into the rock and hide in the grave (i.e., believe in Christ crucified), hide from the terrible face of the Lord and from the glory of his majesty, when he arises to shake terribly the earth" (Isa. 2:10, 21). The Apostle says the same thing in this passage under comment. After announcing the punishment, he exhorts the reader to go up to the great high priest.

The word "sharper" (*penetrabilior*) would be better rendered "more penetrating" (*penetrantior*) or "more cutting" (*incidentior*), for a two-edged sword is a sword which cuts both ways and on either edge. The Greek equivalent is *distomos*.

4:12. . . . Piercing even to the dividing of soul and spirit . . .

Philosophy teaches that "form," and this is particularly true of the human form, is the essence of the thing and is indivisible. From this distinction derive those thorny problems, whether in reality the powers of the soul differ in essence or in form. (A habit is formed from oft-repeated acts.) As a matter of fact, as far as we are concerned, we walk in simple faith following the teaching of the Apostle, who describes man as existing in three parts when he says, ". . . that your whole spirit and soul and body be preserved blameless unto the coming of our Lord Jesus Christ" (I Thess. 5:23). Again in I Cor. 14:15 he divides man into mind and spirit saying, "I will sing with the spirit, and I will sing with the under-standing also." But the Blessed Virgin Mary also says: "He scattered the proud in the imagination of their heart" (Luke 1:51). Indeed, Christ himself marks the difference in another way when he said: "Thou shalt love the Lord thy God with all thine heart,

1 Migne, 182.802 ff.

with all thy mind, with all thy soul, with all thy strength or with all thy powers" (Luke 10:27 and parallels). Origen has worked more than anybody else for a better understanding of this problem, and next after him Jerome. Jerome said, commenting on Gal. 5:17: ".... as everybody knows, the body or the flesh is our lowliest part, but the spirit is our highest part, by which we are susceptible to divine truths[1]." The soul, however, lies between these two. If these words are taken to mean that Augustine divided man into a superior and an inferior part, and the soul besides[2], their meaning is clear enough and sufficient has been said about them.

4:12. . . . of both joints and marrow . . .

Some Greek texts have "joints and members[3]," I understand, and certainly that reading is most appropriate. Just as members are related to joints in the body, so also soul and spirit are related to each other in the mind, and "thoughts and intent" in the heart.

4:12. . . . With whom is our speech . . . (or conversation)

Some interpreters want the words *ad quem* "to whom" to mean "him about whom we speak," just as in chapter one *ad angelos* means about or concerning the angels. It could even be said to mean the following: the sermon which we deliver you has this purpose, that we attain to him who is the subject of our sermon. As it says in Ps. 122:6 using the same figure of speech, "Pray for the peace of Jerusalem," i.e., pray for those things which make for and pertain to peace.

---

[1] Migne, 26.411.

[2] H.R. point out, in a valuable footnote (*loc. cit.*, p. 166), that this distinction of man into a higher and lower part is not Augustine's. They also provide some valuable references both to Patristic sources as well as to Luther's writings, which are worth following up by those who wish to pursue the point.

The case is made a little more difficult because their text reads *ac sensu* punctuated to be read with the final phrase "that the things discussed above are clear enough", and therefore interpreted not as a third category of the human mind but adverbially or adjectively. On the other hand, the Weimar text reads *ac sensum* which is punctuated to go with the previous clause in which Augustine is said to have divided man's nature into a higher and a lower *ac sensum*. This would seem clearly to add a third category of the soul. The translator has followed the Weimar text, but he feels (with H.R.) that the terminology is not all-important in this context.

The reader should observe how Luther is turning away from the philosophical distinctions of the schoolmen, and turning towards the terms of Scripture (and the insights of the great Fathers, Augustine in particular).

[3] Luther is here following Erasmus, *Annotations*.

Gl. 25:5.

With whom is our speech   i.e., a reason ought to be
given for our actions

Chrysostom says: "We ourselves are to give a reason for
our actions." This gloss comes from a different meaning of
the word *logos*, since (as Jerome writes in his *ad Paulinum*,
Migne 22.543), *logos* in Greek means "word," "reason," "a
reckoning up," and the like.

CHAPTER FIVE

[Beginning with Heb. 4:14 as Luther did in his September Bible, and as the German Bible still does.]

4:14. Having therefore a great High Priest . . .

Gl. 27:20. To make our faith certain, the Apostle continues the argument he began. He argues that we have Christ himself as our high Priest, not a changeable one nor one of doubtful origin, but one instituted by God himself. Thereafter he shows that he is the true high priest who will declare unto us the unfailing mercy of God (the proper office of all priests).

Having by the most certain decree of God our Father, as is shown in the chapter following

Note this participle *"having"*: After terrifying us, the Apostle now comforts us: after pouring wine into our wound, he now pours in oil.

**Having therefore a
great High Priest** the greatest of all priests most certainly, for he is great and able to save us

who entered heaven, he did not merely penetrate the veil of the Temple as the priests of the old order, because he is the true priest.

Jesus, Son of God, i.e., having power over everything

let us hold fast i.e., let us persevere in acknowledging him, and let us never despair on account

of the sufferings of the
present or because the
Priest is not here with us

**the confession
of our hope.**

this phrase is not in the
Greek.

However, for those who live in fear of his eternal judgment, and
are in dread of being cut up and dismembered by the sharp sword
of the Word of God there is but one refuge left, and that is Christ
our high priest, by whose humanity alone we are protected and
saved from this very condemnation. As it says in Ps. 91:4: "He
shall cover thee with his feathers, and under his wings shalt thou
trust." And Mal. 4:2: "But unto you who fear my name shall the
sun of righteousness arise, and salvation is in his wings." And he
himself said, ". . . how often would I have gathered thy children
together, even as a hen gathereth her chickens under her wing"
(Matt. 23:37). For the same reason there is the frequent cry in the
Psalms: "I will rejoice under the shadow of thy wings" (Ps. 62:8,
et. al.). Or again: "Thou hast hidden me in the innermost recess
of thy tent" (Ps. 27:5). Even the passage from Prov. 30:25 ff.
appertains to this: There are four things on earth which are very
little but are exceedingly wise, The ant—a very weak creature,
yet he stores his food in harvest time. The rabbit—a feeble thing,
yet he builds his house in the rocks. The locust—he has no king,
and yet they all go forth in ordered bands. The lizard—he crawls
on all fours, yet he lives in the palaces of kings. (The rabbit is a
feeble thing yet he makes his nest among the rocks, i.e., we too are
weak but direct our conscience towards Christ.) Thus in Canticles
2:14 the bridegroom says of the bride, "O my dove, thou art in
the clefts of the rocks and in the secret places of affliction." For
these reasons, the Apostle introduces Christ here as high priest
rather than as Lord and Judge, to comfort those who are afraid.

4:15.

Gl. 25:14.

**For we have not a High
Priest who cannot be
touched with the feeling**

Chrysostom says: It is
impossible for him who has
not had the experience of
affliction to know the
afflictions of the afflicted

of our infirmities,	the persecutions and sufferings of this life appointed as by God
but we have a High Priest who has been tempted in all things	this means evil things
like as we are	in passion and compassion
but apart from sin	i.e., tempted just as we are tempted. All the things we suffer he suffered in like manner, except that in his case he was sinless.

Gl. 26:10 ff.: Likeness in this passage signifies the reality of the flesh and the reality of Christ's Passion, not some fantasy as the Manichees imagine. But it must be understood that Christ did not have the same flesh, i.e., the same flesh I have or the flesh you have, but flesh of the same kind, just as we ourselves do not have one and the same flesh but flesh of the same kind. In the same way also Christ did not undergo the *same* passions as we do but like passions. They are truly real passions, but "without sin." We should understand the passage in Phil. 2:7 in the same way: Made in the likeness of men and found in fashion as a man. Therefore it is quite clear that the word "likeness" expresses rather than denies the reality of the flesh of Christ as the heretics try to say.

4:16.

Gl. 26:7.

Let us draw near with confidence	let us not be hindered by scruples of conscience or fear of sins
to the throne of his grace that we may receive mercy and find grace	"his" is not in the Greek
	by which we are urged to redemption and the good life
to help in need	opportune help, or when the need arises.

As it says in Ps. 34:5: "Look to him and be enlightened, and your faces will never be confounded." And in Matt. 11:28 ff.: "Come unto me all ye that labour and are heavy laden, and I will give you rest. Take my yoke upon you, and learn of me; for I am meek and lowly in heart: and ye shall find rest unto your souls. For my yoke is easy, and my burden is light."

5:1. For every High Priest, being taken from among men, is appointed to act on behalf of men in relation to God. . .

The operative phrase in this text is "on behalf of men." It is as if to say: "Behold, let us approach the throne of grace with faith and without fear, because we have a high priest Jesus Christ." If then we have a high priest, then we have someone who is for us and not against us, because "every high priest" "constituted and taken from among men is consecrated on behalf of men." As it is recorded in Ex. 28:38: And Aaron will bear their sins, which the children of Israel shall confess and sanctify in their offerings. This event most clearly prefigures Christ the high priest bearing the sins of all who sacrifice, i.e., of all who believe. For he is not like Moses who only shows sin, but rather like Aaron who bears sin. Aaron did in fact bear the sin of the people. As Ps.77:20 describes it: "Thou hast led the children of Israel by the hand of Moses and Aaron." Not so much by the hand of Moses but rather by the hand of Aaron, because knowledge of sin through Moses i.e., "through the law," leads nobody unto life eternal, unless there be both remission and absolution of sin through Aaron, i.e., unless he find grace. And Num. 18:1 says: "The Lord said to Aaron, Thou and thy sons and thy father's house with thee shall bear the iniquity of the sanctuary, and thou and thy sons with thee shall bear the iniquity of your priesthood." He refers to the "iniquity of the sanctuary" and "the sins of the priesthood," not because the sanctuary or the priesthood have done these things, but because it is the nature and office of a priest to be a bearer and carrier of sins. These sins, therefore, are his own, because he carries them for others and took them from others. In which again Christ is prefigured as the true Aaron and "the Lamb of God who bore the sins of the world."

In this passage, therefore, the Apostle is saying that when Christ cried out for us on the cross, it was then in that atoning work where all human values are reversed, that his priesthood reached its moment of highest perfection. He explains this further in verse 7 saying, ". . . Jesus offered up prayers and supplications, with loud cries and tears" [referring to Matt. 26:36–46; Mark 14:32–42;

Luke 22:40–6]. The same thought finds expression in Isa. 53:4: "Truly it was our grief that he himself bore, and our sins that he himself carried." Which quite clearly he could never have done had he not been high priest for us and not against us. As it says further on in Chapter 12:24: "You have come . . . to Jesus, the mediator of a new covenant, and to the sprinkled blood that speaks more graciously than the blood of Abel." This is because the blood of Abel cries wrath and vengeance, but the blood of Christ cries forgiveness and mercy. This is what Isaiah says: "In that day he will sing to him of a vineyard of pure wine. I the Lord will water it continuously, and guard it in case anybody does it any harm. I guard it day and night, and have no ill-will towards it. Who will give me briars and thorns" [to battle against and destroy] (27:2)? Behold, he himself guards his Church, lest anybody hurt it. For if anybody were to hurt it, it would not then be true to say that he guards it. It would, however, be hurt if it were to experience something of the Wrath (of God), or if he himself were to act in some way as thorns in the vineyard. This matter of God's guarding us is nothing else but the strengthening of our troubled conscience by his appearing.

Every priest, therefore, should follow the example of this high priest, and ought to know that he is a priest not to his own advantage but to serve other men. This service is to bear the sins and iniquities of others, lest they be the chief actors both in their own perdition as well as that of others, as it says in Ezek. 34:2 ff.: "Woe to the shepherds of Israel who have been feeding themselves: should not shepherds feed sheep? Ye eat the fat, clothe yourselves with the wool, and kill the fatlings. The weak ye have not strengthened and the sick ye have not healed. The crippled ye have not bound up, the strayed ye have not brought back again. The lost ye have not sought after but have ruled them with harshness and with force. And thus my sheep are scattered because they have no shepherd." Or again, take the words of Zech. 11:16 f.: "I will raise up a shepherd in the land who will not visit those who are cut off nor seek the lost. A shepherd who will not make the contrite whole nor strengthen such as do stand, but who will devour the flesh of the fatlings, tearing off even their hoofs. O worthless mockery of a shepherd who abandons his flock!" Read further in I Tim. 3:2 and Titus 1:7 ff.: "For a bishop should be without crime," and so on.

Every priest ought to know that he is a priest not to further his own end but to serve others, and should study before all else to be endowed with the tenderest mercy, that he might know how to bear the sins and ignorances of others. Thus it is written over and over again throughout the Book of Judges: "And the Lord raised up for them a saviour." Saviours are therefore portrayed as priests, they are called to be priests, and commanded to behave as priests. Their reputation should be of the kind as was once that of'the kings of Israel when even their enemies trusted in their mercy. For thus in I Kings 20:31 the servants of Benhadad the king of Syria, although Israel had overcome them and cut them to pieces on two previous occasions, said to their Lord: "Behold, we have heard that the kings of Israel are merciful, let us put sackcloth on our loins and let us go out to the king of Israel, and perhaps he will save our souls." And so it happened. In this very event priests are warned that their hands are anointed in preference to those of other Christians, not so much because they are worthy to handle the sacrament of the body of Christ, but rather that they should handle the matter of the sacrament, i.e., the people of Christ[1], gently and kindly. But on the contrary these consecrated hands and anointed fingers are tainted with violent passions more atrocious than any poison. These hands bear arms and haul cannon about. But worse still, they direct them most vindictively against the very matter of the sacrament i.e., against our most gracious Father's dear children in Christ. They rage with anger, and with a piety panting for revenge, hasten to burn a few Jews, who pierce the Host of the sacrament with small lances or cut it with knives[2]. But they themselves destroy not merely the Host, but the very reality [viz., the people of Christ], and not by little lances but by bombardments and every clash and onslaught of arms conceivable. What God has done to the Jews they do not take as a figure and warning to show them that they who destroy the res sacramenti [that means the people of God] so furiously and infernally are seven times more worthy of fire and every kind of death than they who merely destroy the Host. Such priests seem rather to have been selected from the ranks of the demons. One might even say that they

---

1 Augustine describes the fellowship of the people of Christ as "res sacramenti" the matter or stuff of the sacrament, Migne, 35.1614. Peter Lombard describes the matter of the sacrament of the eucharist (res sacramenti eucharistiae) as the unity of the faithful (unitas fidelium), Sent. IV, dist, 8c.3. Luther uses the expression "the people of Christ" (populus Christi) in his exposition of 5:9 and develops the idea in his "Sermon on the worthy sacrament of the Body of Christ" 1519, WA, 2, 742 ff., where he teaches that the purpose of the sacrament is the fellowship of all saints who are one body in Christ. See footnote WA, 57, 168.

2 There is a reference here to the alleged desecration of the Sacrament by the Jews as a ground for persecution. Ficker in a footnote to the text gives some details of these outbreaks and associates them with the dispute over Reuchlin and his persecution. He also provides references to literature on the matter. See WA, 57, 168, footnote.

were appointed to work for the demons and against Christ and the Christians. And Julius tops the lot![1]

Now God promised to his people that the time would come when their priests would deal with them only as beloved children, as Isaiah foretold: "Ye shall be carried at her side and dandled on her knee. As one whom his mother comforteth so will I comfort you. Yes! ye shall be comforted in Jerusalem" (Isa. 66:12 f.) But as long as we neglected these sacred scriptures of God and preferred the mere writings of men, we were deservedly led astray to these insanities and hellish monstrosities. For the Devil himself could not have managed to introduce fury of this sort into the Church unless and until he had first brought about that state of affairs where the flaming sword which turned in every direction had been thrown away and left to rust. This sword is the Word of God, and is more terrifying to him than all Hell. When once the Word of God is set aside, then the Devil may watch us build with the flax and straw and feathers of human reason and human ideas, that is with the unreal enchantment of our own worthless opinions.

5:1. [Every High Priest] . . . is appointed to act on behalf of men.

It must be admitted that it is not enough for a Christian to believe that Christ was instituted High Priest to act on behalf of men, unless he also believes that he himself is one of these men for whom Christ was appointed High Priest. For both the demons and the impious know perfectly well that Christ is a high priest for men, but they do not believe that it is true for them. Thus Bernard in his sermon on the Annunciation[2], (the theme of which is "That glory may dwell in our land," Ps. 85), delivers the following axiom: "It is necessary that thou believest God is able to remit thy sins, confer grace and give eternal glory. But that is not enough if thou dost not most certainly believe that it is thy sins which have been forgiven, it is to thee that grace is offered, and to thee that eternal glory will be given." Now this is the testimony of our conscience which the Spirit of God gives to our spirit, and about which the Apostle writes, Our rejoicing is this, the testimony of our con-

---

[1] This remark is an *obiter dictum* and not in Luther's script! The reference is to Pope Julius II (1503–1513) who was notorious for his wars and campaigns. He ended his days in open conflict with his cardinals who had sided with Louis XII in order to engineer his deposition. He was scathingly attacked by Erasmus in his *Moriae Encomium*. He was also responsible for the re-building of St. Peter's and laid the foundation stone in 1506. It was his Indulgence (designed to draw money to the papal coffers for this expense) which was the occasion later of Luther's Ninety-five Theses.

[2] Not a literal quotation. *Sermo in festo annuntiationis B.V.M.* 1.3, *Opera*, Paris, 1719, I, 978, B. Migne, 183.384.

science, II Cor. 1:12 (cf. Rom. 8:16). The testimony of our conscience of which Bernard speaks, is not to be understood as that self-induced kind, as if we had it from ourselves, for that is Pelagianism and a shameful glory (cf. Phil. 3:19). It is to be understood as meaning that our conscience receives this witness [and does not itself create it] just as it receives both righteousness and truth and all the other gifts bestowed upon it[1].

Therefore, it is a truism that nobody gets grace because he has been through the motions of absolution, or baptism, or communion, or unction. A man receives grace because he believes that in this act of absolution, baptism, communion or anointing, he receives grace. *How true is that widely known and well-proven dictum: It is not the sacrament which justifies but faith in the sacrament, as well as the words of Augustine, The sacrament justifies not because it is performed but because it is believed*[2].

If this is so then it is a most pernicious error to maintain that the sacraments of the new law are efficacious signs of grace of such a kind that they do not require a special disposition in the recipient except that he should offer no "objection," defining "objection" as an actual mortal sin. Such teaching is false through and through!

The truth is the sacrament requires a perfectly pure heart, otherwise a man will receive the sacrament blameworthy, and will bring condemnation upon himself. The heart is not purified except through faith. Read Acts 15: *Philip did not baptize the eunuch until he had discovered that the man believed.* Nor for that matter should any infant be baptized nowadays unless some one answers on his behalf, "I believe." *Therefore, it is not baptism which brings grace, but belief.* By the same token it is a great mistake when people go to the sacrament of the eucharist in the confidence of their having confessed, or *of their not being aware of any mortal sin, or of their having said their prayers beforehand, or of having made their preparation. They all eat and drink condemnation unto themselves.* They do not become worthy

---

1 This distinction is vital to Luther, *viz.*, that Christ, the Gospel, and the entire evangelical dispensation, is *given* at the hands of a merciful God, and ceases to be a Gospel at all if it be conceived as something to which a man may attain. Justification, righteousness, faith, grace . . . and all that goes to make a Christian man are the gift of God and in no sense to be thought of as in any way earned, procured, deserved or even sought after by man. All a man contributes is knowledge of his own sin. Once awakened to this state of affairs, and his natural trust in his own self and his own spiritual works challenged, he is open to receive the gift of faith. Then, and not till then, is he a believer: he is justified by faith.

2 Aug., in *Joann.*, 80, 3; Migne, 35.1840. There are some interesting references to these words both in Luther's writings and in the scholastics to be found in a long footnote in the *WA, ad loc., viz., WA*, 57, 170, as well as in a footnote in Hirsch-Rückert, p. 173.

and pure by performing these acts. On the contrary, through this very confidence in their own purity they become more impure than they were before. But if they believe and trust that at the sacrament they will receive grace, *then this faith alone makes them pure and worthy. Such a faith does not put its trust in these works just described, but puts its trust on the most pure, most holy, most reliable word of Christ, when he says, "Come unto me all who labour and are heavy laden, and I will refresh you"* (Matt. 11:28). Therefore, in confidence in these words they ought to go up to communion, and if they go up in this faith they shall not be confounded.

5:2. He can deal gently

not persecuting sinners and throwing them into confusion

with the ignorant and wayward

so that by such persecution and confusion they forsake the good and follow after evil[1]

since he himself

not less than they who actually sin

is beset with weakness

that means with sin, as well as proneness to sin, and inability to effect the good.

5:3. And because of this

because of this weakness, which is enough to make a priest humble, or even anybody greater than a priest,

he is bound to offer sacrifice for his own sins as well as for those of the people

And in this matter of sacrifice for his own sins, a priest who is chosen from among men differs from him who is sent from heaven. This high priest (Christ) has no need to offer sacrifices for his own sins.

---

[1] Note Luther's continual criticism of the Papacy and therefore the priests for their dismal failure to do, or even attempt, the plain, pastoral demands of their office.

5:4. And no man takes the honour upon himself, but he is called by God, just as Aaron was.

God calls to the priesthood in two ways. In the first way, a man is called who neither seeks nor desires the office: as Aaron was called, and did not know why God had called him of all people; or else, a man is made a priest by the miraculous intervention of God, as in the case of the Apostle Paul; or else he is called by mandate of the Church. In the second way, a man is called by inspiration, as a man is called who desires and seeks after the office. This is proved by the Apostle in I Tim. 3:1: "He who desires the office of a bishop desires a good work." It should be carefully noted in this text that the description "the office of a bishop" sounds the note of service rather than honour and dignity. This is clear by the etymological force of the word, for the Greek word ἐπισκοπεῖν (episkopein) means to superintend or look over, in the sense that a watchman or guard of a town may be called a look-out or an overseer. Therefore Zion, citadel of David and the heights of Jerusalem, is called in Latin "watch-tower" (specula), and signifies the priesthood whose task it is to watch over and superintend Jerusalem i.e., the Church. The same truth is clear from a study of the second half of the text. Paul does not say, ". . . he desires a good *thing*" but ". . . he desires a good *work*." He clearly proves that the office of a bishop is nothing if it be not a work—and, moreoever, "a good work," not a life of idle luxury. The others who climb to the top, and let us be honest about it, in the desire for a life of idleness, and pleasure, and high office—nay rather who lust after these things—these are they who "take the honour upon themselves."

5:6. As he says also in another place, thou art a priest forever, after the order of Melchizedek.

This phrase "after the order of" signifies ordination and priesthood of the type Melchizedek exercised. In other words, priesthood of the kind indicated in the historical narrative of Melchizedek, whose divinely ordered story is recorded in Gen. 14:18 ff. Therefore, this incident ought to mean, not only that Christ offers bread and wine as Melchizedek did, but also, that every detail mentioned in that story ought to be interpreted in the way that the Apostle does with such distinction in chapter seven. Thus, though greater than Abraham he blessed him although Abraham was the father of the Levitical priests and was in possession of the promises of God. Similarly, he accepted tithes from Abraham, although he was without descent, without beginning and without end.

Nevertheless, the word *dabhar* in Hebrew ("word") quite appropriately signifies an event, or an account of an event, or a matter of business, as in Ps. 64:4 when it says, "They bend their bows to shoot arrows, even bitter words" (A.V.). Translated literally, the verse reads. They bend their bow, a bitter thing . . . after which comes the word *"dibrathi."* Translating literally again, the word *"dibrathi"* means "according to order," the root of which is "dabar," "word[1]." But Paul will have more to say on this later!

5:7. Who

> Here he applies the similitude to Christ. He is in fact saying that Christ himself offered sacrifice for men, and that Christ is the priest who could deal gently with the ignorant and wayward, because he had been through the same experience as they.

in the days of his flesh

> that means in the hour of his passion when he was forsaken by the Father and suffered in the flesh[2].

[1] The Massoretic text runs: *dabhar mar*, and Reuchlin's: *"dibrathi"* above, and which Luther used. (The transliteration follows the *WA* text.) Luther's language in this paragraph is virtually in note form, and is too condensed for a simple and clear translation. It needs considerably enlarging. But his meaning is not thereby lost. He seems to be seeking a close identification of the scriptural event with the concrete Word of God realizable in and contained by that recorded event. Luther is right in binding the Word with its historical occasion and in making its meaning embrace history and event.

[2] Whenever Luther refers to the incarnation he always thinks of the humanity in terms of its frailest and weakest. He speaks of the babe at the breast and the child in the manger, of the man forsaken and his dying on a cross. He thinks of the humanity in its hour of impotence, and in its hour of utter humility. The natural man thinks of Christ as the flower and perfection of humanity, but Luther knows that this is a false starting point for man to understand God's redemptive work in the incarnation. The incarnation reveals God but also veils God. Luther does not see the incarnation as a demonstration or proof of God's presence. God cannot be demonstrated or pointed out: he can only be believed.

Luther's continual emphasis in his incarnational theology on the human Christ, the frail Christ, the suffering Christ, the impotent Christ has two important consequences: it safeguards a soul from seeking the false assurance of the way of the *theologia gloriae*, and at the same time gives the soul the true assurance of the *theologia crucis*. Man's way is the way of proofs and demonstration, but God's way is the way of faith: it is the cross which breaks the former and makes the latter. This theological insight into the meaning of the incarnation is paramount in Luther's theology. It receives careful consideration in: Regin Prenter, *Creator Spiritus*, trans, J. M. Jensen, Philadelphia, 1953; Walther von Loewenich, *Luther's Theologia Crucis*, Munich, 1933.

offered prayers and supplications	not calves and goats as they did, but his own self in prayer
to him	the Father
who was able to save him from death	not by saving him from the necessity of dying but by resurrecting him, as is well known from our study of the gospel.
with loud cries and tears	as he said, "Father, forgive them for they know not what they do." Thus he perfected his priesthood. This happened to Christ alone and to no other priest.

Granted the evangelist makes no mention of tears or of a loud cry in this prayer at any rate, yet we must not only firmly believe this to be so, but also that in the words of this most perfect of all prayers he most certainly offered himself for all.

and he was heard for his most godly fear	this means that God loved him because of this, and in this way Christ proved himself to be his obedient and beloved son.

5:7. Who in the days of his flesh . . .

It may seem surprising that the Apostle says "in the days . . ." in the plural, when it would seem that he is referring to that one and only day when Christ did in fact offer himself on the cross. For he was sacrificed only once and on one particular day. It could be said by way of explanation that he expressed himself in an Hebraic thought form and took the part for the whole: i.e., that "days" is taken collectively for the whole of his life, and that he sacrificed himself during some part of it. This manner of speaking is very frequent in the Scriptures, as is clear in the Book of Kings. In his days the king of Syria (?Babylon) came up (II Kings 24:1). In the same way we say that a thing happened in some year or another, or in a particular month, or on a certain day, though it happened only during some part of the month or day or year and not for the duration of the full day, or month, or year. In fact, we ourselves use the idiom that such and such a thing happened "in my days." That means that it happened during my lifetime, but not that it took place on every day of my entire life.

Why then does he refer particularly to "the days *of his flesh*," when the phrase "in his days" would seem enough? The reason is that he was well versed in Scripture. Just as Christ has two natures in his person, a temporal and an eternal, so Scripture attributes to him two kinds of day, temporal and eternal. For it says in Micah 5:2 ". . . whose going forth has been from the beginning, from the days of eternity." There again, "days" is taken as a collective term, and means eternity itself. He describes eternity in plural terms, i.e., "the days of eternity," to differentiate it from his earthly existence "when he began in Bethlehem to go forth as a ruler in Israel." Isaiah clearly distinguishes between the two ages as well. He writes, "Trust in the Lord forever," literally "in the ages of eternity." That means trust in him, he who is the Lord, throughout all eternity. That is why we have the expression in the Psalms "forever," "to all eternity" or "world without end." We find the same idea in Titus 1:2: "Which God promised before the times of this world and this age." For the same reason Paul, in the passage upon which we are commenting, calls "the days of the flesh of Christ" the time of this life here and now to differentiate it from the days of his Godhead.

5:7. . . . He offered up prayers and supplications.

It is not altogether clear in what sense the Apostle uses these two words "prayers" and "supplications," unless perhaps it were the sense in which he uses them in the Epistle to the Philippians where he says, ". . . But in everything by prayer and supplication with thanksgiving let your requests be made known unto God" (Phil. 4:6). When he uses the word "prayers" in this passage he means a request to show want we want, and by the word "supplications" he means to entreat and implore. When we entreat and implore we try to influence the judge and win our case by pleading force of circumstances, our rights, our deserts, the violence of our antagonist and similar pleas, according to the usual rhetorical methods. The text, "Father, forgive them, for they know not what they do" seems to support this interpretation. For by the word "Father" he wins for himself in the shortest but yet the most effective way possible the affection of him to whom he prays, because there is no love more real than that between father and son. By the words "forgive them" he signifies petitions and requests, for in these words he shows that which is sought after, *viz.*, forgiveness of sins. By the words "for they know not what they do" he shows the earnestness of his supplication, because he humbly recognizes and admits their guilt while at the same time extenuating and excusing it. And surely this is the very best way of making supplication.

It should also be noticed that this text sheds a flood of light on the meaning of the sacrifices in the Old Testament. Christ is mystically prefigured by the old "priests who were chosen from among men." In the place of the gifts and sacrifices which used to be offered by these old priests, Paul puts the "prayers and supplications" which Christ offered. Therefore, calves, goats and other sacrifices (apart from the fact that they signify the mortification of the flesh and our earthly members by tropological analogy[1], as Rom. 12:1 and Col. 3:5 teach), mean also offerings of prayers and praises. Thus, Christ made justification by the new law easy so that we could effect by means of our lips what the old priests could scarcely do with the help of everything conceivable, even their earthly possessions. That is the meaning of the passage in Hosea where he says: "Return unto the Lord and say to him: Take away all iniquity and receive the good, and we will render the calves of

[1] According to medieval hermeneutic practice there were four senses in which the meaning of a text could be expounded. There was first the *literal* sense. This is the plain historical meaning of a passage when taken literally. In the passage under discussion it means the sacrifice of animals by the priests of the Old Testament. In the case of prophetic passages, and this would often cover the Psalms, the plain literal meaning was in fact the Christological meaning. Next, there was the *allegorical* sense. By this interpretation the meaning of a passage was drawn out with reference to the Church, the Body of Christ. In this passage, Luther draws out the meaning that in the place of the old animal sacrifices Christians now offer the sacrifices of their lips, i.e., praise and thanksgiving. Then there was the *tropological* sense, by which a passage was expounded in relation to things of the present. In this text Luther interprets the killing of the sacrifices as the killing and mortifying of the flesh and its members. Lastly there was the *anagogical* sense. This referred to the Last Things. Luther goes on in this passage to expound Heaven as the place where we may always offer our sacrifice of praise, and Hell on the contrary, not the place of punishment, but the place where there is no praise of God.

Apart from its own intrinsic worth and interest, the passage shows that Luther is able to expound Scripture freely even in the medieval straitjacket. In the light of his later powers in this direction he is here seen to be breaking through the traditional techniques.

The latin tag ran thus:
Littera gesta docet: quid credas, allegoria.
Moralis, quid agas: quo tendas anagogia.

Luther quotes this in his comment on Gal. 4:24, 1516–17, *WA*, 57 (Section 2), 95, 22 ff., but concludes . . . sed quid speres, anagogia. Vogelsang has an interesting footnote, *op. cit.*, p. 87, where he refers to his *Die Anfänge von Luthers Christologie*, p. 16 ff., for further information. See also Ebeling, *Evangelische Evangelienauslegung*, p. 48 ff., for a most comprehensive handling of the subject.

our lips (14:2)." The Apostle himself approaches this meaning later on the Epistle when he says: "By him therefore let us offer the sacrifice of praise to God continually" (Heb. 13:15), that is the fruit of our lips as they give thanks to his name. The whole of Psalm 50 is written to the same effect: "Hear, O my people, and I will speak, O Israel, and I will testify to thee. I am God, even thy God, (that means, I am no idol, nor a creature made by thee, who is in need of thy sacrifice of calves). I will not reprove thee for thy sacrifices . . . (i.e., when I reprove thee it is not because I want you to offer sacrifices to me), . . . thy burnt offerings are continually in my sight" (i.e., the sacrifices thou offerest are before me already, because "all things are mine"). On that account he concludes later on: "Whoso offereth praise glorifieth me" (verse 23). And again: "Offer unto God the sacrifice of praise," verse 14, (as if to say, when thou offerest thyself, what else but my praise art thou offering?).

Isaiah speaks to the same effect in his first chapter: "To what purpose is the multitude of your sacrifices to me? saith the Lord: I am full of the burnt offerings of rams, and the fat of fed beasts; and I delight not in the blood of bullocks, or of lambs, or of he-goats . . ." (Isa. 1:11), and so on. He says the same thing in his last chapter: "What sort of house is it that you will build for me?" (Isa. 66:1). (To which the Jews would be expected to reply, A house built of wood and stone.) But the Lord says immediately afterwards: "All these things my own hand made, and in fact everything that has been made was made by me, saith the Lord" (Isa. 66:2).

Nevertheless, this expression "the sacrifice of praise" is not to be taken as meaning that brand of faith by which even the impious praise God. It is referred to in Ps. 48:18: "He will praise thee when thou blessest him." On the contrary, it refers to him who praises God out of the midst of his suffering, as Isa. 48:9 proves: "For my name's sake will I turn my anger from thee" (i.e., I will not damn thee), "and will bridle thy mouth with my praise lest thou perish" (viz., in the sufferings and chastisements). This happens when a man, though in the throes of bitter sorrow and in the agonies of death, can yet sing to God with the words: "Righteous art thou, O Lord, and righteous is thy judgment" (Ps. 119:137). As the thief said on the cross: "We indeed [are under judgment] justly, for we are receiving the due reward of our deeds" (Luke 23:41); and as David says in Ps. 119:54: "Songs of praise have thy statutes been to me in the house of my sojourning" (i.e., my tribulations are the commands or judgments of God). The same thought is expressed in Ps. 42:9: (Vulg.) "In the daytime the Lord

commanded his mercy, and in the night he commanded his song."
This means that in the hour of darkness (i.e., tribulation), God
commands men to sing praises and be of good cheer. Wherefore,
Hell is not Hell because punishment is there, but because the
praise of God is not there, as it says in Ps. 6:5: "For there is no
remembrance of thee in death: in the grave who shall give thee
thanks?" God in his righteousness is displeased with such people.
In the same way heaven is not heaven because joy is there, but
because the praise of God is there, as it says in Ps. 84:5: "Blessed
are those who live in thy house, they will be praising thee forever."
God is pleased with them, and on that account they are rejoicing.
Therefore a Christian man as a son of God must always rejoice and
sing and never be afraid: he must at all times be free from care
and anxiety, and continuously pride himself on God.

**5:7. . . . And having been heard on account of his godly
fear . . .**

This word *reverentia* is an ambiguous word and has several
meanings [reverence, fear, awe, respect, regard].

Some[1] understand it in its passive sense as the reverence shown
to Christ, i.e., because he is the son, then since he was called to the
priesthood by God himself, he ought to be revered more than anybody else because of this.

Others[2] go back to the corresponding word in the Greek,
eulabeia. This word means *reverentia* as well as *pietas*, [dutiful con-
duct towards the gods or one's parents, children and relatives,
towards benefactors or towards one's native land; justice sometimes; or even love, pity and compassion.] These people take the
word in this context for the love which a father has for his son.
This meaning seems to me the best. The sense then would be rather
like this: though we thoroughly deserve God's wrath because of
our sin, it is yet natural and in keeping with a father's love that in
spite of our sin he would listen to his Son [pleading] on our behalf.
Consequently, set off against our own sin, which would otherwise
cause God to deny us everything, is the love which he could not
deny his own son. On the strength of this argument the Apostle
draws out for us by this text faith in God, because it is not our
iniquities that God will look at but his own love.

Thirdly,[3] *reverentia* can be understood in its active sense. Thus:
Christ revered the Father, and because there is no man who has
not despised God, he alone of all men could be said to have
revered him, as Isaiah says: "The spirit of the Lord shall fill him."

---

1 Paul of Burgos.
2 Erasmus, and Lefèvre d'Etaples.   3 So *Gl. ord.*, *Gl. interl.*, and *Lyra*.

In fact Psalm 13 could be spoken of us all: "There is no fear of God before their eyes" (Ps. 36:1). Again, it refers to Christ in Ps. 16:8: "I have the Lord always in my sight," as in fact it refers to men in Ps. 54:3: "They have not God before their eyes." For the fear of God is the very highest worship of God, so much so that some say that fear is better than love. For Jacob also calls God "fear" saying "Except the God of my father Abraham and the fear of Isaac had been with me, surely thou hadst now sent me away empty" (Gen. 31:42). Because of this the Hebrews number "fear" among the names of the deity. Isa. 8:13 f. makes a clear allusion to this, "Do not fear his fear" [i.e. of the non-believer], "nor be in dread of it. The Lord of Hosts himself you must sanctify, let him alone be your fear and dread, and he will be a sanctuary to you." For this reason the great fathers of the old covenant are commended for their fear of God. Furthermore, David in his last words praised it in his greatest and final laudation, prophesying that the kingdom of Christ would endure in the fear of God (II Sam. 23:3) saying: "He that ruleth over men shall be a righteous ruler, and shall rule in the fear of God." Therefore, this will be the meaning: Christ is heard, not because we ourselves have been proved worthy. On the contrary, we are most unworthy because of our having none of this virtue named *reverentia*. Christ is heard because his *reverentia* was worthy and of such a kind that he would be heard even on behalf of the most unworthy and the highly irreverent.

5:8. Gl. 29:5.

And if indeed he was the Son of God

as he most certainly was not a slave who owed these duties [as to a master]

he learned obedience by the things he suffered. And having been made perfect

by experience

perfected and restored

he became ... the cause ...

in the way described above where he taught that "Christ was perfected through sufferings," i.e., Christ was made such a person as one who is in every way the proper person to be a high priest, in that he has learnt through his own sufferings to sympathize with our weaknesses.

he became unto all them that obey him the cause

all who believe in him
the author, as it says above, "the author of their

salvation perfect through
sufferings" (Heb. 2:10).

of eternal salvation.

5:9. . . . The author of eternal salvation unto all them that obey him.

The man Christ is the mediator and author of salvation (*causa mediata*), as the saying goes. He is by this token both the sign (*signum*) and the author (*causa*) of our powers of understanding and loving. As it says in Isa. 11:11 ". . . a root of Jesse which shall stand for an ensign (*signum*) of the people," and later: "The Lord shall set up an ensign (*signum*) for the nations, and shall assemble the outcasts of Israel" (Isa. 11:12). Or again, "In those days ten men out of all the languages of the nations shall take hold of the skirt of him that is a Jew, saying, we will go with you" (Zech. 8:23). Again, Jeremiah compares the people of Christ to a girdle which cleaves to the limbs of a man (Jer. 13:11). Again, Christ is compared to a nail on which vessels of every kind are hung (Isa. 22:23). All these similitudes and prophecies signify that power by which the Father draws men to him. As many as are saved are drawn by this power through the revelation of Christ, and cleave to Christ by faith. For this cleaving to Christ is that which is referred to when it speaks of "all that obey him."

5:11. . . . Seeing ye have become dull of hearing.

It is better in the Greek, "since you were slow and lazy", for it fits in better with what follows. For the argument is that they ought to have been masters of the Scriptures for the time they had had to study them, had they been vigilant and eager to understand the Scriptures. Now indeed they had been asleep and had not worked on Holy Scripture, that land of promise flowing with milk and honey. The words of the Book of Proverbs fit their case exactly: "I passed through the field of the lazy man and through the vineyard of the fool, and behold they had filled the whole place with thorns and thistles, and the stone wall was broken down" (Prov. 24:30). This analogy means that Scripture had been neglected and had become nothing but thorny opinions, perplexing questions and fierce contentions, and the whole Bible had taken on a forbidding and neglected look.

5:12. For when after all this time ye ought to have been teachers yourselves, instead of that ye have need to be taught. Taught moreover what are the first principles on which the oracles of God are based.

In the matter of the Word of God[1] the Apostle clearly distinguishes between those who are advanced students and those who are only beginners. On this basis we must permit a third category of improvers who are in course of learning. This distinction is no more difficult than that threefold distinction of theological approach referred to in chapter four, verse 4, *viz.*, the symbolic, the proper and the mystic; or as it is often described the sensual, the rational and the spiritual. Dionysius the Areopagite describes this last approach by the term *alogos*, i.e., non-rational. That means that it cannot be communicated or grasped by word or reason, but only by experience. Symbolic theology is that which teaches that knowledge of God can be given by means of figures and sense images, just as it was taught once before among the Jews that knowledge of God could be found in the Temple, the tabernacle, the ark, sacrifices and such like. These things are tolerated among Christians even today in the ornaments and images in the churches, as well as in their songs, and organs, and the like.

5:13. For every one who is a partaker of milk
of an inferior doctrine based on imagination and picture

has no part in the word of righteousness;
i.e., does not understand the doctrine of justification, for this concerns faith and the spirit;

for he is a babe
his theology is symbolic and perceived by his sense experiences.

But solid food
spiritual doctrine

is for perfect and full grown men
spiritual men

who by reason of use
by long custom

have their senses exercised
their minds and their intelligence stretched

to discern good and evil.
i.e., to discern the letter from the spirit, for the figurative and symbolic meanings are but the letter, and that is death.

[1] Cf. Luther's gloss on 4:1, p. 88.

CHAPTER SIX

Gl. 30:23. Now that the Apostle in these first chapters has
gently chided the Hebrews for their ignorance, one might
even call it dull-wittedness, in this present chapter he now
makes them alive and alert again, and leads them on to a
more perfect understanding.

Gl. 30:18.

6:1. Therefore
so that they could become
masters in the faith. [Luther
carries on the analogy of the
previous chapter, that the
Hebrews should cease to be
babes living on milk and seek
to be men living on solid food.
Judaism is the milk and
Christianity the solid food
for which the milk prepared
the way.]

**let us
put aside**
put elementary instruction
aside, and make a fresh start.

**the first lessons
in Christ**
the rudiments of the faith,
with which their knowledge
of Christ first started.

**and let us be carried
along**
snatched away, or seized or
pulled[1].

[1] There is in this gloss a special interest, in that Bunyan (an unerring interpreter of Luther) uses this same verb. Pilgrim, having got lost in pursuing a
religion of law is again persuaded by Evangelist to proceed to the wicket gate,
which in Bunyan's imagery represents the threshold of Justification by faith.
At this point, Christian is "pulled through." The passage reads, ". . . when
Christian was stepping in, the other gave him a pull."

to full growth i.e., the perfect knowledge of Christ.

In the section under review he expounds the meaning of the phrase "the (elementary) words of Christ." Peter as well teaches us to grow in the knowledge of our Lord Jesus Christ: grow in the grace and knowledge of our Lord and Saviour Jesus Christ (II Peter 3:18).

and not be continually re-laying a foundation of repentance the baptismal rites by which one must confess one's sin

from dead works, but good works. It is by these good works we have to start growing in the knowledge of Christ

and not laying again a foundation

of faith in God,

6:2. or of teaching about baptisms, the laying on of hands, the resurrection of the dead, and the day of judgment. for these are all the doctrines which are no longer preached to established Christians. [Luther does not mean that these doctrines are not important but rather that they are a basis on which to build.]

6:3. And advance we will at once, forthwith
if indeed God permits us to do so.

6:1. Therefore, let us put aside the first lessons in Christ, and let us be carried along to full growth, and not be continually re-laying a foundation of repentance from dead works and of faith in God,

6:2 or of teaching about baptisms, the laying on of hands, the resurrection of the dead, and the day of judgment.

Certain expositors[1] used to maintain that these words are addressed by the Apostle to those who supposed that baptism should be administered frequently and the confession of faith made again and again. They were of this opinion because the terms to which the Apostle refers, *viz.*, belief in God, belief in Christ, belief in the Holy Ghost, belief in one baptism, belief in the remission of sins, belief in eternal life, are the articles of faith delivered to candidates who are about to be catechized for baptism. That is why they are called the *rud*iments of the faith, because the *rude* are instructed in them, as obtains to the present day. This is clear from the Apostles' Creed. In fact at one time, when adults rather than infants used to be baptized, this used to be ceremoniously solemnized. But nowadays, because in most cases it is infants rather than adults who are baptized, these articles of faith are merely read over the candidates for baptism. It is these articles which are "the rudiments of the first principles on which the oracles of God are based" (see above on 5:12), i.e., the teaching on the elementary things of the Christian life. When these things have been done, they have been done once and for all, and it is impossible to do them again.

Wherefore, all theologians hold that the sacraments of baptism and confirmation are not to be repeated. Chrysostom seems to lean to the same opinion. He writes: "Since it is possible that believers may be tempted, perhaps be led away and live wickedly and thoughtlessly, he commands 'Watch'. That is not the same as saying, Because we are living thoughtlessly we will be baptized again, we will be catechized again, and we will receive the Holy Spirit again. If then we fall from faith in the smallest degree, we are able to be baptized again, wash our sins away and take the same benefits we had already received when we were first baptized. People who think this are wrong. The author clearly states, 'It is impossible' (Heb. 6:4). Do not hope for what is impossible. He did not say, it is not expedient, it is not profitable, it is not permitted. He said, 'It is impossible.' Therefore he led them into despair."

When the author speaks of baptisms in the plural (Heb. 6:2), he either makes the plural form do duty for the singular, or, as some would have it[2], he says so on account of those who kept thinking that they could be baptized over and over again.

6:1. . . . let us be carried along to full growth (literally, let us go on to things more perfect).

[1] Chrysostom, Lefèvre d'Etaples.
[2] Lefèvre d'Etaples.

As Chrysostom says, by the words "the things more perfect" he means "the good life." Of what kind that is, James gives expression to it and says: "Let patience come to her perfect end" (James 1:4). Whence Christ also said, ". . . that the good land brings forth fruit in patience" (Luke 8:15). We have the same idea expressed immediately following in the Epistle: "We desire that each one of you may show the same diligence with a view to enjoying the full assurance of hope to the very end" (Heb. 6:11). For patience maintained through tribulation frees the soul from forms and things and from all things visible, and carries it over into a hope in things invisible, as Paul expresses it in the Epistle to the Romans: ". . . suffering and tribulation work patience and fortitude; patience and fortitude bring experience and fullness of character; experience and fullness of character give hope. And this hope never disappoints" (Rom. 5:4).

6:6. [For it is impossible in the case of those who have been enlightened once and for all] and then fall away, to keep bringing them back again to a new repentance, [for they keep crucifying the Son of God afresh to their own undoing, and exposing him to open shame].

Gl. 32:12. **crucifying the Son of God afresh.**

This is in accordance with Rom. 6:6 where it says that our old man was crucified with Christ, and also that as many of us as were baptized were baptized in his name[1]. Therefore, if a re-baptism were necessary, then a re-crucifixion would be necessary as well. The effect of this would be to deprive the first crucifixion of its real value.

To some commentators these words are assumed to have been spoken by the Apostle with regard to those people who in some way or another have lapsed into sin. And, in order to avoid the errors of the Novatians[2], these commentators are forced to change the meaning of the word "impossible" and put the word "difficult"

[1] into his death (Rom. 6:3).
[2] Novatianism was a third-century schism of the Roman Church, and the first in the Church. Its leader, Novatian, set himself the task of making a pure and spiritual Church on earth. The Novatianists were what we later described as Puritans, and actually called themselves such, *viz.*, Cathari. They were orthodox in faith, and their schism found its basis entirely on disciplinary grounds. They disallowed the effectiveness of repentance of grave sin after baptism, which in their particular historical context meant the re-acceptance of those believers who had faltered and lapsed in time of persecution. The schism lasted some considerable period in Rome, and elsewhere in the world, but eventually found its abiding home in kindred Phrygia with her saints, hermits and monks.

in its place. But because it is a highly dangerous expedient to distort the clear words of Scripture into another meaning, we cannot, except in those places where the context demands it, let this happen lightly, lest in the end the whole authority of Scripture is weakened.

In a letter to Jerome, Augustine did not allow the Apostle's words "I lie not" (Gal. 1:20) to be understood as referring to some baleful lie, but rather as a figurative expression (*offitioso et simulatorio*), or, as Jerome expresses it, a matter of good stewardship (*dispensatorio*) [1]. Moreover, with this kind of interpretation, commentators will neither avoid the error of the Novatians nor crush it, for it is just as difficult for God to justify again any sinner at all as it is impossible for man to raise himself above any sin. Therefore, truth is to be affirmed and heresy refuted from other texts as far as possible.

Repentance, however, always remains a possibility for the sinner. That is clear in the first instance from Paul, when he says: "Lest, when I come again, my God should humble me before you, and I should mourn for many of them that have sinned heretofore, and repented not of the uncleanness and fornication and lasciviousness which they have committed" (II Cor. 12:21). And again in I Cor. 5:5 when he delivered the man who had committed fornication with his father's wife to Satan for the destruction of his flesh, so that his soul might be saved (i.e., by repentance). In the same way he advised both Timothy and Titus that the Word of God should be drawn out with gentleness if the impious and the heretics were to be converted to any extent. (See, e.g., I Tim. 3:5, 5:1; II Tim. 2:25; Titus 1:7 f.; Titus 3:10.) In fact, if there were no repentance, the whole Epistle to the Galatians would amount to nothing, because in the epistle it is not actual sins which are discussed, but the greatest of all sins, the sin of unbelief, by which they defected from Christ to a religion of law. Further, one reads in the Old Testament that the most holy David fell three times, and rose again as many times. Similarly, Joseph's brethren too, although they were murderers, were restored by repenting. And lest the (Novatian) heretics cavil that they are basing themselves on the New Testament, let them recall that Peter together with all the disciples fell from faith and fled everyone of them, but they were restored in the end.

In this passage under comment also, the Apostle must be understood as referring to the lapse from belief to unbelief, that is to that opinion by which men think that they can be saved by their

[1] Both Hirsch-Rückert and Vogelsang see fit to emend this sentence to give it meaning. The translator follows the *WA* text, but renders it freely.

own righteous deeds apart from Christ, which is absolutely impossible. For he says in the beginning of this chapter (6:1), that he would omit the teaching of Christ on faith and the beginning of the Christian life. This is another way of saying that for him who has once begun with Christ and then relapses and seeks some other way of salvation, i.e., the self-appointed way of works-righteousness it is "impossible" for him to be renewed by this technique. And that this is his meaning seems to be sufficiently indicated later in Chapter 10:26 where he says, "If we sin wilfully . . . there remaineth no more sacrifice for sins." It was sheer necessity in the primitive Church that compelled the Apostle to speak so severely against the lapsed, for at that time there was not only the danger of changing the morals after the faith had taken root, but worse still, the risk of changing the very faith itself after it had just been planted. The Apostle showed himself most anxious about this in his other epistles, also.

6:7 f. For land which has drunk the rain that often falls upon it, and brings forth vegetation useful to those for whom it is tilled, receives a blessing from God. But if it bears only thorns and thistles, it is worthless and is in danger of being cursed: its end will be destruction by fire.

Gl. 32:15. He illustrates his meaning and makes it clear for the benefit of simpler folk by means of a beautiful parable, like a great teacher or preacher. This may be admitted seeing that among rhetoricians parables are reckoned as being among the best figures of speech and a mark of literary style.

Chrysostom and Augustine prove from Isa. 5:6 that in the Scriptures rain stands for doctrine: "I will command my clouds that they rain no rain upon it." In this context, however, it is clear that he is speaking of the Synagogue, for he goes on to say in the next verse, ". . . the vineyard of the Lord of Hosts is the house of Israel, and the men of Judah his pleasant plant: and he looked for judgment, but behold oppression; for righteousness, but behold a cry." It is this state of things he is describing (in the previous verse) by the phrase, "there shall come up thorns and thistles." He says the same thing in Chapter 45, verse 8: "Drop down, ye heavens, from above, and let the skies pour down righteousness." That is, let them teach the faith of Christ, which is righteousness. Or again, in Ps. 68:9: "Thou wilt give plenteous rain to thine inheritance, O Lord." Also in Micah 2:11; "I will cause wine to drop for thee, and will be for this people the one who causes it to fall." These matters are written in this way so that we may learn the mysteries of Scripture, namely, what Ps. 78:23

means for example: "He opened the doors of heaven and rained upon them." That figure of speech means that the teaching on faith[1] is given from heaven. Thus in Deut. 11:10: "The land whither thou goest in to possess, is not like the land of Egypt from which thou camest out, where, when the seed is sown after the manner of horticulture, water is led on to the land by irrigation. On the contrary, this land is mountainous and hilly, and looks for its rain from heaven." That means[2] that the Church does not teach herself by her own doctrines, but is taught by God. Isaiah says the same thing: "I shall give thee all thy sons taught of the Lord" (Isa. 54:13).

6:9. But, beloved, we are persuaded better things of you

Gl. 33:15. He very kindly mitigates the severity of the threat. He does this so that he may win people of their own volition through the attractiveness of the doctrine of faith, rather than drive those he has invited by fear and despair[3].

He says this because, as Chrysostom puts it: "He who beats a slow man makes him but slower." For that reason Chrysostom adds, ". . . after he has terrified and threatened them, he cared for them again, lest he cast them down all the more and throw them to the ground." For sinners must not be rebuked in such a way that they are only hurt and driven to despair, but they must be cherished again so that they are quickened unto obedience. That will only happen if they are never reproved without the admixture of a little praise and never praised without the admixture of some rebuke. This is what the Apostle does here—he neither persecutes them in all respects nor does he flatter them in all respects. John does the same in Rev. 2:3, where he both praises and censures the

---

[1] *Doctrina fidei:* It is obvious that Luther is referring here to his teaching on justification by faith alone. It is also clear that he is contrasting it with justification by works. The teaching on justification by faith comes from heaven and has heavenly authority. The other comes from man and has human authority only. This contrast between the religion of faith and the religion of works is central to Luther's early theological position and is not a consequence of later controversy.

[2] It is specially interesting in this passage to note how Luther is expressing his new evangelical theology but is not yet emancipated from the scholastic hermeneutic method. (Not all quotations are from the Vulgate.)

[3] Luther is referring here to his teaching on justification by faith alone. He means in this context that when a man has appropriated the free unmerited grace of God by faith, he is no longer under obligation to an external law, but rather that God effects a new creation, which works far beyond that or any law. This is always contrasted with works-righteousness, whereby a man lives under law, and when he fails to keep the law is driven to a better obedience by fear of the consequences of his disobedience and is in a constant state of despair that he cannot in fact keep the law.

seven angels of the churches. Similarly, the Apostle in his Epistle
to the Galatians first reproves and then praises the Galatians.
Indeed in all his letters he observes these two practices. The same
tendency is to be found in the prophets, at one time saying the best
about the people, at another the worst and vice versa. It is for the
same reason that ulcers must not be cut open and then left, but
after lancing must be healed with plasters.

6:10. **For God is not unrighteous that he would forget your
work and love which you have shown toward his name,
you who have ministered and still minister to the saints.**
(Gl. 33:7: apostles and preachers of the word of God.)

Although, in the case of the Apostle (Rom. 15:25), the ministry
to the saints referred to is understood to be the collection or
offering which was at that time being administered to the apostles
and other saints, we should nevertheless accustom ourselves to the
normal manner of speaking found in Scripture. In Scripture, as
many as believe in the name of Christ are called "saints."
Chrysostom also makes the same point in this context. It is an
injury both to Christ and to our neighbour, if we do not call him a
"saint" whom we confess as having been baptized in his name.
For the same reason every service shown to a neighbour in need is
to be understood as a ministry in this sense.

6:11. **But we desire that everyone of you show the same
earnestness so that you may know the fullness of hope to
the very end.**

Again, it is by his example that he teaches those who are to learn.
He does not say, "we want," (as Chrysostom says). "I want"
savours of authority, but the phrase "we desire" savours of the
love of a father or better still a brother. They who have a passion
for correcting act differently: they cast love aside, and dominate
with violence and impatience. And it is generally the case, that
those who do not want a single syllable of their own sermon to
pass unobserved, pay attention to none of it for their own part.

6:12. **. . . so that you may not become half-hearted, but be
imitators of them who by their faith and patience will
inherit the promises.**

How beautifully he joins them both together, faith and patience.
For faith makes the heart hold fast to heavenly things, and allows
itself to be carried away and wheel around in the invisible.
Because of that very fact, patience is necessary. Patience upholds
faith, not only in the hour of temptation, but also when the outside world rages against it. Thus it comes about that the man of

faith hangs between heaven and earth and is, as the Psalm says (Ps. 68:13) "in the midst of the ash heaps" (*inter medios cleros*). "May he sleep!" That means, let him be lifted up in Christ and crucified. [The text is difficult here on account of its brevity and the number of its allusions, and both Hirsch-Rückert and Vogelsang interpret it in slightly different ways. The *WA* text is followed here. The meaning of the passage seems to be that faith brings every man to a cross, and that patience will serve to uphold his faith in his hour of trial. In this experience of being lifted up and crucified, he is between two worlds, and hangs between heaven and earth. Vogelsang points out *ad loc.* that Luther tends to fuse the continual dying of self with the ultimate natural death we all face and the awaiting of the next world, and relates the idea to Luther's exposition here of the man of faith suspended between two worlds. Trans.]

6:13. For when God gave the promise to Abraham. . .

Chrysostom writes: "Just as the Apostle by his preceding words terrified his readers with the threat of punishment, so now by these words he comforts them with the hope of rewards. He thereby shows them the way God works. This way of God is that he does not at once fulfil the things he has promised, but only after a lapse of time[1]." Therefore, he who wants to serve God must know what God's will is, and what his manner of working is. For who can serve any master if he does not know him? Further, it is not sufficient to know God, as a dog knows its master, or as philosophers know his power and write of his nature (Rom. 1:20). This is a natural knowledge of the senses, harmful to those who do not understand it. No, what we ought to know is what God might want, or more accurately, to know the will of God. This he shows in his commands: "He made known his ways unto Moses, and his will to the children of Israel" (Ps. 103:7). But nobody understands his commands rightly, unless he first be illumined from above. As it says in Wisdom 9:13: "For who among men can know the counsel of God, or who can imagine what God might want?" And again: "Who hath known the mind of the Lord, that he may instruct him" (I Cor. 2:16). And again: "The things of God no man knows, only the spirit of God, but God has revealed them to us by his Spirit" (I Cor. 2:11, 10). And that is what he meant in John 14:26 when he said: "The spirit will teach you all things, and will bring to your remembrance all things whatsoever that I told you." As if to say, You are not yet able to bear and understand my words, even though they are the commands and will of

---

[1] Migne, *loc. cit.*, 63.310.

the Father: you will understand them in the end with the help of the teaching of the Holy Spirit. This is beautifully shown in Ex. 20:19 and Deut. 18:15. There, when the Jews were not able to bear God speaking to them, they asked for an interpreter, and God promised them one, who was in fact the Christ who was to come. And for the same reason Ps. 143:8 teaches us how we ought to pray: "Make known to me the way in which I must walk." For that matter the entire one hundred and nineteenth Psalm teaches the same thing: "Teach me . . .," "instruct me . . .," "give me understanding . . .", etc. See verses 12, 26, 64, 68, etc.; 27, 34, 73, 125, etc. and many similar instances, in all of which is commended not so much the nature of God but most of all the will of God. Accordingly, those who presume to comprehend the sacred Scriptures and and the law of God by their own natural capacity, and to understand them by their own efforts, are making a most grievous mistake. It is from this sort of attitude that heresies and impious dogmas arise, the moment men approach the Scriptures not as receptive pupils but as masters and experts[1]. Men ought not to do this since it is written in Ps. 92:13 f.: "They that are planted in the house of the Lord, shall flourish in the courts of our God. . . They shall be full of sap and green, so that they might preach." That is, they will allow themselves to learn, that they might be able to teach.

Therefore, though man cannot of himself understand either the will of God or the laws of God, he must make some attempt to understand them, hard as that is for the inexperienced. First of all, then, in every command his will is that only he is loved and preferred to everything else. For when God begins to effect and fulfil his will, he strips man bare of every work of his own both within and without, and leaves him naked. It is by these acts it can be said that "he bringeth the counsel of the heathen to nought, and maketh the devices of the people of none effect" (Ps. 33:10). Here while in the very depths man says, ". . . thy judgments are a great deep" (Ps. 36:7). It is at this moment a man "comprehends with all the saints what is the breadth and length and height and depth" of the love of Christ (Eph. 3:18). It amounts to this: man is so utterly confounded and troubled, that it is impossible for him to go on and persevere in the will of God, unless "the Holy Spirit

---

1 This point came to be one of the chief gravimina which Luther held against Erasmus and the humanists generally, and is still an issue which the conservative tends to hold against the liberal today. Luther thought that Erasmus sat above Scripture in a superior way and sat in judgment upon it, while in his judgment the proper relation was to be under Scripture and to be judged by it. (See Luther's *Bondage of the Will*, 1525, trans. Johnson and Packer, James Clarke 1957.)

helps his infirmity" (Rom. 8:26). As Isaiah also says, "he will restrain thy mouth with his praise" (Isa. 48:4). At this stage there comes about what Job refers to when he says of man: "Man, whose way is hidden, and whom God will hedge around with darkness" (Job. 3:23). How then, therefore, can he possibly understand God, to say nothing of loving him, when all his judgments and thoughts are disapproved? Therefore, to understand the invisible will of God in such a darkness is nothing else but the work of the Spirit. And certainly, this will of God is tolerable in one way or another until now. At all events it leaves us words of consolation, as in Isa. 54:7: "For a small moment have I forsaken thee, but with great mercies will I gather thee." And there are other similar passages. Indeed, that final will of God, which also brings this word of consolation and promise, makes those words of Christ intelligible: "Except those days should be shortened, there should no flesh be saved" (Matt. 24:22).

6:13. For when God made promise to Abraham . . .

Gl. 33:14. **For when God made promise to Abraham** to encourage his faith and ours as well

33:19. For the greater encouragement of his readers the author provides an instance, rather than leave them with a mere statement of words. He chooses the familiar story of their patriarch Abraham, and comforts their hearts "that they may know that God uses great men also in the same way, so that they may accordingly pass through the trials of this life" [Chrysostom:—trans.]. Of such a kind are the encouragements in the psalm: "I remember the days of old, I recall the works of the Lord" (Ps. 143:5). That means, I console myself in my trials by recalling that the Lord is now working in me in the same way as he worked in our forefathers in the days of old.

God   not content with his promise went as far as to swear on oath.

since he could swear by none greater   in order to make Abraham's faith in God stronger

swore by his own name, I will certainly bless thee, I will certainly multiply thee.

34:17. Note how marvellously the Apostle commends God's loving care towards us. He represents him as anxious to inspire faith in himself, so that, if he could have sworn by a greater than himself, like men do, he would have done so. On that account he was compelled to swear by himself rather than leave us in unbelief.

6:15. And thus, having patiently endured   Abraham endured in faith and patience

he obtained the promise.   the promise of God is a delayed promise. That is to say, the increase will take place in his descendants.

34:21. To say Abraham obtained the promise seems contrary to Heb. 11:39, *infra*: "And these all, having come through the test of faith, received not the promise." Chrysostom reconciles these two points in the following manner: some things he received in the course of time, as for example, the land of Canaan, other things he had not yet received, such as the glory of the resurrection. He is referring to the former in this chapter, and to the other things in Chapter 11.

6:16. For men swear by what is greater than themselves   and so God condescended by swearing for us like a man

and with them an oath   that they might conclude a settlement.

always brings a dispute to an end.   a contradiction or controversy

34:26. Thus unbelief is some kind of controversy of man with God, which God by his oath even condescends to bring to an end.

6:17. In the same way   i.e., he not only made the promises but also swore by them

since it was God's desire to show more fully   (perfectly) of his own good will and not of necessity.

to the heirs of the promise   the promise to his sons,

i.e., you Hebrews

**how unchangeable his
purpose was,**

because he could not fail,
just as any man who
believes in him is perfectly
safe

he added an oath

that is in the form of a
promise

**6:18. that through two unchangeable
things**

namely, the promise and
the oath.

**in which it is
impossible for God to lie**

in either the promise or the
oath, since he is truth itself.

**we might have the very
strongest consolation**

unchangeable, and utterly
trustworthy in the matter of
the promises to come.

35:17. It is as if he means to say that God has no regard for
his own dignity. But on his own volition he makes con-
cessions to our feeble faith, as one man might swear to
another. In fact he leaves nothing undone which might be
conducive to the strengthening of our faith in all the ups
and downs of this troublous and transient life.

**We who have fled
for refuge**

we have left the world
behind, yea, even our own
selves

**to lay hold of the
hope set before us**

the very hope itself, *viz.*,
eternal life, to which we
hold fast, and which up till
now was unseen

**6:19. That hope we have as an
anchor of the soul, both
sure and steadfast**

abiding and enduring

which enters in

going in or penetrating

right up to the inside

i.e., as far as the vision of
the glory of God

of the veil

he interprets the point
figuratively. He is not
referring to the veil of the

tabernacle, but to faith and hope.

6:20. where the fore-runner

the leader of this earthly pilgrimage.

has entered before us

so that we should be quite certain to follow

having become our eternal high priest, after the order of Melchizedek.

CHAPTER SEVEN

Gl. 36:8. Up to this point in the Epistle the Apostle has for the most part tried to explain the difference between the Old Covenant and the New. In the first half of the Epistle his main concern has been to compel the faithless to listen to his argument. Now that he has aroused their attention he turns to the theological explanation of the difference between the Old Covenant and the New.

7:1 ff. It was this Melchizedek, king of Salem and priest of the most high God, who met Abraham and blessed him when Abraham was returning from the defeat of the kings and to whom Abraham gave a tenth part of all the spoils he had taken. Now notice that in the first place his name means king of righteousness and in the second place king of Salem, that is king of peace. This Melchizedek, who is described as being without father, without mother, without ancestry, with no beginning to his days or even an end, has been made the true figure of the Son of God, the true figure of our priest eternal.

Melech in Hebrew means king, as *salem* means peace and *sedech* righteousness. But it has to be recognized that in the Scriptures these words "righteousness" and "peace" are always to be understood as divine righteousness and divine peace. Thus it is obvious that righteousness is the very grace by which a man is justified—which is the same thing as faith, hope and charity. It is to be found in Ps. 31:1: "Deliver me in thy righteousness," and in Ps. 72:1: "Give the king thy judgments, O God, and thy righteousness unto the king's son." And again in Ps. 24:5: "He shall receive the blessing from the Lord, and mercy (righteousness in the Hebrew) from the God of his salvation." Therefore it is as a rule to be carefully watched that the term grace, which the scholastic doctors call "justifying grace" or *fides formata*, is in Scripture called "the righteousness of God," "the mercy of God," "the salvation of

132

God," "the power of God" and similar names. This righteousness, however, is the righteousness from faith, which is referred to in Rom. 1:17, where he says: "In the Gospel the righteousness of God is revealed from faith unto faith." This righteousness is explained wrongly as that righteousness of God by which he himself is righteous, unless it be understood like this, *viz.*, that faith exalts a man's heart and carries him out of himself right over to God, in such a way that man's own heart and God become one spirit[1]. In this way the divine righteousness itself is the righteousness of the heart. The scholastic theologians call the faith which effects this "formative" (*informans*). The righteousness of God and the righteousness of the human heart become one and the same thing, just as the humanity in Christ through union with the divine nature became one and the same person.

Wherefore it follows, that this Melchizedek could not be "a king of righteousness" in any sense other than that he prefigures Christ in type as well as in name. For it is Christ alone who is "the sun of righteousness" and "the king of righteousness" and who justifies all, as many soever as are justified. This is how that passage in Exodus 3 must be explained where it says that even our shoes must be taken off our feet. It means that all human righteousness acquired by elicited works (*actus elicitus*), a fabrication of our own mind, must be removed absolutely and entirely.

We should understand the term "peace" in the same way we have interpreted the term "righteousness." "Peace" is not to be understood as something which can be declared, or written or conceived by man. Neither can it be given by any created being. It is that "which passeth all understanding," it is that which is higher than all reason. It is hidden under the cross and behind the form of death, just like the sun is behind the clouds. Therefore it is written of the ungodly, "The way of peace they have not known" (Ps. 13:3, Vulg., and Rom. 3). It is impossible to know this peace without faith, i.e., the righteousness of God, as it says in Ps. 85:10, "righteousness and peace have kissed each other." Therefore, since God through many tribulations takes away all our goods, even life itself, it is impossible for the soul to be at peace and bear this, unless it cleaves to better things, i.e., unless it is bound to God by faith. It is for this reason the Apostle was wont to begin his letters: "Grace and peace from God our Father and the Lord Jesus Christ . . ." (Rom 1:7; Gal. 1:3, etc.). As Christ said: "My own peace I give to you. It is not as the world gives that I give to you" (John 14:27).

The Author sums up the superiority of Christ and also of his

---

[1] I Cor. 6:17: "He that is joined unto the Lord is one spirit."

priesthood under four categories. First, in the matter of eternity: (*viz.*, "he has neither father, mother, nor ancestry, he was neither beginning of days nor end of life . . ." (Heb. 7:3)). Secondly, in the matter of his blessing: (*viz.*, ". . . he blessed Abraham." (Heb. 7:1, 3) and, "Beyond any dispute it is always the inferior who is blessed by the superior" (Heb. 7:7). Thirdly, in the matter of the everlastingness of his priesthood: (*viz.*, "This man Melchizedek remains a priest for ever" (Heb. 7:3) and, "Here (i.e., in our system of things) mortal men receive tithes, but there (i.e., in the sphere in which Melchizedek acts) however, it is witnessed that he lives" (Heb. 7:8). And fourthly, in the matter of the tenth part: (*viz.*, "To whom also Abraham divided a tenth part of all" (Heb. 7:2); ". . . Abraham, the patriarch, gave a tenth out of the chief spoils. And they indeed of the sons of Levi that receive the priest's office have commandment to take tithes of the people according to the law, that is from their brethren, though these have come out of the loins of Abraham: but he whose genealogy is not counted from them has taken tithes from Abraham, and blessed him who had the promises" (Heb. 7:4 ff.).

Let us explain these four categories. First, there is eternity: Christ is prefigured in Melchizedek, whose beginning is not described. Secondly, there is the matter of the blessing: Abraham was blessed by Melchizedek, and thereby all the sons of Abraham are blessed, with the exception of Christ. Thirdly, there is the tenth part: in that Abraham and Levi gave tithes to Melchizedek as being more worthy than they, but Christ did not. And fourthly, the everlastingness of his priesthood: Abraham and Levi are dead, but Christ however lives in eternity. By these descriptions he excludes the false faith of the Jews who presume on their law and their priesthood, since they, too, like their own patriarch are inferior to the other who blesses them.

The Master of the Sentences[1] expresses himself in a similar way: he says that Christ had not paid tithes in the same way as Levi, because, though he was in the loins of Abraham as Levi was, nevertheless he was not in the loins of Abraham by the same law. For Levi was there by the law of the concupiscence of the flesh, but Christ was there by the law of spiritual love. Therefore, as Augustine says on Genesis[2]: "As Adam sinned, so all who were in his loins sinned: therefore, as Abraham gave a tenth, so all those who were in his loins gave a tenth likewise." That is, they showed

---

[1] Peter Lombard, *Sent.* III, dist., 3.3, Migne, 192.761 f.

[2] Aug., *de Gen. ad litt.*, X 19, 34; Migne, 34.423. *WA* points out that Luther uses this quotation in the sense of Lombard's interpretation and not Augustine's.

themselves as inferior and in need of a blessing. For it was necessary that Christ should be the natural son of Abraham and David and have the real flesh of both, because the Scripture had to be fulfilled which promised Abraham the Blessing and the Kingdom.

Again, it was impossible for him to be the son of Abraham and David by the law and the work of the flesh, i.e., through concupiscence and sin, for in this way he would have been born in sin, and not the blessed One but one needing the blessing. And in this way what was necessary [i.e., that he be born of the seed of Abraham] and what was yet impossible [i.e., that he be born without sin] were set in mutual contradiction (as happens in every work of God), and only the wisdom of God arrived at a solution. Namely this: that without man's co-operation he should be born of a woman only and be superior to both. In this way he would be both the natural son of Abraham and also more worthy and greater than Abraham and all the others, because he was without sin and "full of grace and truth" (John 1:14).

And therefore it is clear that the Blessed Virgin was necessarily a mother of untainted virginity, otherwise "the fruit of her womb" would not have been "blessed" (Luke 1:42). And, therefore, in the course of time, when the truth had been more fully revealed, the same thing is expressed more clearly: "Of the fruit of thy body will I set upon thy throne" (Ps. 132:11). And: "Lo, children are an heritage of the Lord, and the fruit of the womb is (God's) reward" (Ps. 127:3). And Ps. 110:3, according to the Hebrew text, reads: "Thy people shall be free in the day of thy power: in the holy beauty of the womb of the morning will be born the dew of thy infancy." The prophetic vision of Daniel means this very thing, where "a stone torn out of the mountain without hands" (Dan. 2:34) means Christ born of the Virgin without the agency of man. Ps. 22:9 also: "Thou art he who has taken me from my mother's womb," which does not speak like Job who said: "Thou hast poured me out like milk, and curdled me like cheese. Thou hast clothed me with skin and flesh, and hast fenced me with bones and sinews" (Job 10:10 f.). And as the bee collects honey from the flower, so has the Spirit drawn the body of Christ from the most pure blood of the Virgin Mary. And that is the meaning of the reference to the "waters of strife" (Num. 20:13) about which the Jews strive with the Lord even to the present day. It is also prefigured in the Exodus (Ex. 17) that the Jews did not want to believe that Christ would be born a true son of Abraham without the law or the works of the law (i.e., the work of the flesh). But further, this birth of the flesh miraculously created by the operation of the Holy Spirit without the instrumentality of the flesh signifies our own spiritual birth, of which John speaks: "Who were born not of blood nor of the will of the flesh, . . . but of God" (John 1:13).

Heb. 7:11. Gl. 38:13. **Now**

This word introduces the conclusion to which this argument has been leading, *viz.*, that not even the priesthood of Melchizedek much less the priesthood of Levi would have been adequate for salvation—unless we were to say what would be a most unholy thing—that this new priesthood had been ordained in vain.

if there were perfection
i.e., the fulfilment of the law and fullness of righteousness from it

by means of the Levitical priesthood,
whose task it was to teach the law, which issued

for the people
Israel

under it
that they might be taught by the Levitical priesthood or its ministry

received the law,
this clearly means that they received the law and nothing more, for they did not receive grace

what further need was there
this means then that the whole life of Christ would have been lived in vain. For this very reason he argued in the Epistle to the Galatians, "If righteousness were by the law, then Christ has died in vain" (Gal. 2:21).

that another priest should arise after the order of Melchizedek

It is as though the argument might be expressed thus: Wherever another priest is necessary it is evident that the former priest was not adequate. Yet this is how he is described. Because the first priesthood was only a ministry of law, it was but a "ministration of death and sin" (II Cor.

3:7, 9) as the Apostle is bold to describe it. The later ministry, however, is one of grace, life and truth.

and not to be reckoned after the order of Aaron? for this was what was due, if it would have sufficed.

This is the first difference between Christ's priesthood and the Levitical priesthood: (*viz.*, that the priesthood of Christ has an origin other than the tribe of Aaron).

7:12 **For the priesthood being changed** as the prophets clearly foretell

the law had to be changed as well not only with respect to the matter of ordination but in regard to the tribe. Therefore, both the law and its teaching were not enough.

That means, that another priesthood was to come, for thus it had been prophesied. Therefore, with another priesthood there was to be another law. Whence the proverb, "New king, new law." This law, however, is the law of Christ, not written in books, but "shed abroad in our hearts through the Holy Spirit" (Rom. 5:5).

7:12. **When the priesthood changes, a change of law also of necessity takes place.**

In five different ways he extols the priesthood of Christ over the Levitical priesthood. First, because he is of another origin than the tribe of Aaron (Heb. 7:12–14). Secondly, because he is eternal (Heb. 7:15–19), Thirdly, because he was sworn under oath (Heb. 7:20–22). Fourthly, because he is the one and only (Heb. 7:23–25). Fifthly, because he is perfect (Heb. 7:26–28). Wherefore it should be observed in this context that the word law adopted by the Apostles may be taken in two ways.

First[1], taking the lower view, he simply means matters of ceremonial like vestments and the external adornments of the priests. For example, the sacrificial victims and the animal sacrifices; the judgments and teachings in the matter of leprosy, the impurity that came from touching a corpse and the like. According to this view, this is the author's meaning when he says that the law has been changed (Heb. 7:12). He means that ceremonies of this

[1] See page 139 for the second.

kind, once commanded by the law, have been abrogated, and the things which these ceremonies had intended to mean have now been instituted, namely, the spiritual clothing and inward distinction of the priest. Ps. 132:9 refers to this, "Let thy priests be clothed with righteousness," as if he meant also to say, not with the purple and blue of the priests of the law (Ex. 25:4). For in the new law the priest does not differ from the people by a difference of vestments or habit, but rather by a distinction of holiness and righteousness. For the ceremonies and vestments we see have been established by the Church, and in the course of time it has added to them. Thus the oblations and sacrifices of the new law are not goats and calves, but rather the hearts and minds of the faithful and of sinners, as is written in Acts 10:13, where, when the unclean animals were shown to Peter it was said to him, "Arise, Peter, kill and eat." From what follows this is clearly seen to have been spoken of the centurion and the Gentiles who were about to be slain by the word of the Gospel and thus offer themselves to the Lord, as it says in the last chapter of Isaiah: "And they shall bring all your brethren for an offering unto the Lord out of all nations . . . as the children of Israel bring an offering in a clean vessel (into the house of the Lord)" (Isa. 66:20). The same is to be found in Ps. 45:15: "The virgins shall be led to the king after her, her neighbours shall be brought to thee." In such ways the law is certainly changed in judgments and in teaching on the purification of the flesh, because the purity or the impurity which the priest of grace judges and about which he teaches are not matters of leprosy, flesh, hair, clothes, home and so on, but the sins of impurity of the spirit and conscience. For in the new law there is no difference between a leprous Christian and a non-leprous Christian, nor between a menstruant and a parturient woman, nor between a soiled garment and a clean garment. In short, the only thing which distinguishes Christians is sin, which pollutes the conscience. All other things, which are of the flesh and external, granted that once they distinguished Jew from Jew, now count for nothing between Christian and Christian.

COROLLARY

A corollary of this argument is how we are to understand that well-known statement of the Master of the Sentences[1], as well as the commentators who expound him. "The sacraments of the law did not justify, but the sacraments of the new law confer grace unto all who set no obstacle (*obicem*) in their way." This statement is

[1] Peter Lombard, IV dist. 1 c.3. Both *WA* and Hirsch-Rückert provide additional scholastic references *ad loc.*

either not properly understood or is a very great mistake, for the sacraments of grace benefit nobody, in fact they rather hurt everybody, if "they do not approach them in the full assurance of faith." Indeed, faith is already justifying grace (*gratia justificans*). Therefore it is better understood thus, that the sacraments of the law used to justify the flesh only (and not the spirit): that is, they pronounced men pure in the matter of leprous flesh or clean flesh, and between skin and skin, and between vestments and vestments, and between hair and hair. And all these things, clean though they may be, yet because they are external and belong to the flesh contribute nothing towards the cleanliness of the heart. The sacraments of grace, on the other hand, justify the heart by discerning the difference between heart and heart, between conscience and conscience, between faith and faith, between hope and hope, between love and love. If these things are clean, they make the person acceptable to God, even though other things might be unclean. Thus the Apostle boldly declares: "All things are clean to the clean, but to the unclean nothing is clean: even their mind and conscience is defiled." ("All things are clean to the clean, but to those who are defiled and unbelieving nothing is clean, for even their mind and conscience are defiled," Titus 1:15). The reason for all this is because in the sacraments of grace we have the promise of Christ, *viz.*: "Whatsoever ye loose on earth will also be loosed in heaven . . ." etc. (Matt. 18:18). The old law did not have such a promise, because then man was not clean in a heavenly and spiritual sense. He used to be pronounced clean in a human and earthly sense by the priesthood, but he was clean only in this earthly sense. For this reason he calls Christ "a surety of a better testament" (Heb. 7:22), who as such promised remission of sins and purity of heart by the word of his own priesthood. Whosoever believes in him is every whit righteous and pure in the eyes of God.

The second way[1] in which the law may be understood is on a deeper level. The Apostle develops this higher understanding of the law in his epistles to the Romans and the Galatians, where under the term law he understands simply whatever has been commanded from a divine or human standpoint, whether it be a matter of ceremonial or a judicial and moral issue. The meaning of the words then "the law is changed" is this: it is fulfilled in Christ. For Christ "is the end of the law" in the same sense as Matthew means, "I came not to destroy the law but to fulfil the law" (Matt. 5:17). I Tim. 1:9 is to the same effect, "The law is not made for a righteous man," i.e., in so far as he is righteous he has

[1] See page 137 for the first.

all the virtues which the law demands. He is already above the law because he owes nothing to the law: he keeps the law and his life is the very law itself, living and fulfilled. Therefore, it is not properly the office of the priests of the New Testament to teach the law but to declare the grace of Jesus Christ, which is the fulfilment of the law, as Ps. 92:2 declares: "To show forth thy loving kindness in the morning and thy faithfulness every night." And Isaiah also: "Thou hast broken the staff of his shoulder, the yoke of his burden, and the rod of his oppressor"—i.e., the law—"as in the days of Midian" (Isa. 9:4). Therefore John the Baptist, "the voice of one crying in the wilderness" (i.e., the word of the preacher among the sinners), pointed with his finger and said: "Behold the lamb of God which taketh away the sins of the world." But in truth this change (of the law) has not yet been perfected as the first law was, but is being perfected from day to day. Therefore, like John the Baptist, the priest of the New Testament in part teaches the law and in part preaches the grace of Jesus Christ, because the righteous man to whom no law need be given does not exist, for in this life he only makes a beginning to his righteousness.

7:13. Gl. 39:5. **For he of whom these things are said**   Melchizedek, by the prophet David

is of another tribe   the tribe of Judah and not Levi

from which no man has served at the altar

7:13. **He however of whom** (*in quo*) **such things are said belongs to a different tribe . . .**

This phrase "of whom" (*in quo*) could be rendered "in whom" (*in quem*), and is a familiar manner of speech for the Apostle. It occurs in chapter one in the phrase "to the angels however" (*ad angelos*) i.e., *in angelos*. And again in chapter four: "All things are naked in his sight, to whom (*ad quem*) we address our speech," that is *in quem* we address our speech. This illustrates how a word comes into being by a kind of movement of affinity. This is also found in Gal. 3:24., "The law was a schoolmaster to bring us to Christ" (*in Christum*). There are many other instances.

7:14. Gl. 39:7. **For it is evident**   from Gen. 49:10, the sceptre shall not depart from Judah.

that our Lord   Christ
has sprung from Judah

Because the kingdom and the priesthood, which were Reuben's by right of primogeniture, were divided between the tribes of Levi and Judah when he defaulted.

concerning which tribe
Moses said nothing about
priests.

He is now anticipating himself. From Chapter 7 clearly emerges what the true abolition of the priesthood and the law really means.

7:15. And

Now he lays down the second difference between Christ's priesthood and the Levitical priesthood, which is that Christ is the eternal priest.

it is yet more abundantly
clear

that is that the priesthood and the law are to be taken away

if after the likeness of
Melchizedek

It is clear from this text that the phrase "after the likeness of" is the same as "according to the order of." As the Apostle explains himself here, it is permissible (from the Hebrew, at least, it is plausible) for the two words to be interchanged. This may happen with the word *dibhrati*, according to order which seems to come from *dabhar*, word, which means a thing that has happened, or rather the account of a thing that has happened. [See comment on 5:6, page 109 for a fuller treatment of this point. Tr.]

another priest should arise

as ought to happen for it was promised by God.

7:16. Who
was made
not after the law of a
carnal commandment

because he was such a priest was instituted

in which the outward righteousnesses of the flesh

**but after the virtue
of an endless life**
are taught, and which are
therefore temporal
power
i.e., he who is eternal and
immortal is instituted.

It is as if he meant to say: the law, because it is temporal
established what was temporal, but the power which established Christ is eternal. Therefore, he himself is eternal,
too.

7:17. For it is witnessed
by the Spirit, in the one
hundred and tenth Psalm
of David, verse four.

thou art a priest forever
neither a product of the
time process, nor subject
to it

**after the order of
Melchizedek.**

7:18. For there is a disannulling
the use of the word
disannulling means that the
Spirit has been operative.
[Luther means that only
God could disannul what
had been commanded by
him. Tr.]

**of a foregoing
commandment**
i.e., of the old law, by which
the Levitical priesthood was
established.

because of its weakness
as stated above, because it
did not bring man right
through as far as the Holy
Spirit

and its unprofitableness
because that to which it did
lead, namely a righteousness
of the flesh, profited nothing.

7:19. For the law made nothing
that is why I used the word
"weakness" in connection
with the law

perfect
it did not lead to the
righteousness of the Spirit

**but on the other hand we
have the bringing in**

the same word is used (as
was used to introduce the
old law)

of a better hope

of better things to be hoped
for, that is, eternity.

**through which we draw
near to God.**

We draw near to God by means of a New Priest. Since he
is described as being eternal, not only must the good things
set before us and promised to us be understood as eternal,
but the temporal promises of the old priesthood must be
done away with at once, for it is impossible to lay hold of
eternal and temporal things at one and the same time.

7:20. **And**
Here follows the third difference between the priesthood of
Christ and the Levitical priesthood, which is that Christ
was promised under oath.

inasmuch as

i.e., the giving of Christ was
a greater thing by far, and
so much the more to be
pondered

**not without the taking
of an oath**

he was instituted not only
for his excellency but under
oath

**was he instituted,
(yet some**

the priests of the law: the
temporal priests rather than
the eternal

**have been made priests
without an oath;**

7:21. **this priest, however,
with an oath**

Christ
so that his institution should
be shown to be firm and
enduring

through him

i.e., *not by man but by God
himself*

**who said to him, The Lord
swore and will not repent
himself: thou art a priest
forever** (Ps. 110:4).),

7:22. by so much the more a long way better
has Jesus been made the
surety   he has been instituted the
                                               promiser and testator
of a better covenant.

Sch. 193:18. It should be observed, that when it says in the
Holy Scriptures that God gives a testament, there is meant, in
some incomprehensible and obscure fashion, that God will some-
how or another die and arrange the inheritance. As it says further
on in the Epistle: "For where a testament is, there must also of
necessity be the death of the testator" (Heb. 9:16). That is all
fulfilled in Christ. It is for that reason the words "testament,"
"inheritance," "part," "portion," "cup" are found in the Scriptures so frequently. In all these things there is shown the death of
Christ and faith in his resurrection.

7:23 (Gl. 41:15). And
Here follows the fourth difference between the priesthood
of Christ and the Levitical priesthood, which is that Christ
is one and alone.

others indeed   priests of the law
have been made priests,
many in number   as in the books of Exodus
                                               and Leviticus, where not
                                               only was Aaron instituted,
                                               but also his sons with him
                                               and their successors.

for the simple reason that
death prevents them continuing

7:24. But he   Christ the one and only is
                                               named and instituted

because he abides forever
has an eternal priesthood   he fulfils his office of
                                               priesthood in this realm of
                                               eternity.

7:25. Wherefore, he is able to
save for all time   to give eternal salvation
offering himself to God
in his own being   not with the blood of calves
and always living to
intercede for us   that means, living always
                                               for this one purpose, that he

may at all times intercede
on our behalf. That is the
office of a priest.

**7:26. Moreover, we just
needed
such**   it was the most appropriate

This is the fifth difference between the priesthood of Christ
and the Levitical priesthood, *viz.*, that Christ is holy and
perfect, but the others are sinners and imperfect.

**a high priest,
holy,**   born without sin and living
                                         sinless
guileless,   in everything which could
                                         happen, faultless
undefiled,   not stained by alien impurity
separated from sinners   not mixed up as we are
**and made higher than the
heavens.**

"Holy" in scriptural usage means that which is pure and sacred
to God, in distinction to "profane," which is for all uses other than
divine. Therefore in the law it is often written that the people and
the priests are sanctified, and the temple, the tabernacle, the vestments and the vessels sanctified. By this the sanctification of the
Spirit is mystically signified, by which new creatures come into
being.

"Guileless" means blameless, because a holy man cannot properly put his holiness to any use, just as a Christian man cannot
put his baptism and newness of spirit to any use. Guilelessness
(*innocentia*), therefore, means the guileless activity (*usus et opus*) of
the holy man himself. Consequently, the word holy (*sanctus*) refers
to the essential nature of such a high priest, and the word guileless (*innocens*) to the work he does. As it says in Ps. 24:4: "He that
has innocent hands" (i.e., he who is innocent in all he does) "and
a pure heart" (i.e., he who is holy). And again in Ps. 18:26:
"With the pure thou shalt be pure." Wherefore Christ is "the
innocent lamb" (that means he is unblameable and inaccusable):
as Isaiah and Peter express it: "Who did no sin, neither was there
guile found in his mouth" (I Peter 2:22; Isa. 53:9).

"Undefiled" refers to him who could never be polluted by
others. For a priest of the law, even if he were pure and blameless
as far as in him lay, could still be defiled by another person, if, for
instance, he were to touch a corpse or a leper. As Christ, however,

was not defiled by any sin of his own from within, he could not therefore be defiled by any from without.

"Separated from sinners" (and made higher than the heavens) means that Christ is seated in heaven where there are no sinners. The priests on earth, however, being themselves sinners, mix and live with sinners. As Isaiah expresses it, "Woe is me, that I say nothing" (that is, according to the Hebrew idiom, I keep silent from good things) "because I am a man of unclean lips, and live in the midst of a people with unclean lips" (Isa. 6:5). Why does the Apostle say then, "We needed such a high priest . . ." (literally, "such a high priest became us . . ." Heb. 7:26). Or we might ask, of what kind is this appropriateness? What kind of priest is this that becomes us? We needed such a high priest in the first place on account of God, so that this person might be a worthy high priest who would be heard and accepted on our behalf, for "God does not hear sinners" (John 9:31). Or again, "Thou art not a God that hath pleasure in wickedness; neither shall evil dwell with thee" (Ps. 5:4). And there are other texts which might be quoted. And in the second place we needed such a high priest for our own sakes, that he might be able to make us holy, guileless, undefiled, separated from sinners and like unto him in all respects. This happens as long as we cleave to him with a heart of faith, "not attending to the things on the earth but on things above, where Christ is sitting at the right hand of God" (Col. 3:1, 2). This is what it means to be sanctified.

7:27. Who does not need daily, like other priests, to offer up sacrifices first for their own sins,	who are not free from sins
and then for the people;	that means for the sins of the people
for this	that is the offering up of sacrifice for the sins of the people
he did once for all when he offered up himself	he who cannot be equalled as a sacrifice compared with the sacrifice of animals.
7:28. For the law	was given by Moses and mediated through man
appointed men	who are sinners and slaves to sin

When the word man or men is used in Scripture it always
has an undertone of humiliation, for if we are men then we
are children of wrath and sinners. And thus man belongs
not to the category of essence[1], but to Hell and the devil.
For it becomes us to be "sons of the Most High" but it is
grace which makes us so. For nature makes men, but grace
creates sons of God.

The Apostle speaks with reserve and moderation. Though
he could have said that the law made men unholy, guile-
ful, defiled, concoursing with sinners and lower than the
earth (thereby preserving the antithesis of verse twenty-
six), he restrained himself and merely calls them "men,"
and "men having infirmity." But by these words (*viz.*,
"men" and "men having infirmity") is to be understood all
the evil there is in man. As the Psalmist says, "Every man is
a liar" (Ps. 116:11), "Every man living is altogether vanity"
(Ps. 39:5). And Ps. 14:3 also, "They are all gone aside:
they have become worthless. . ."

priests who have infirmity that is they are sinners,
under the influence of which
they are powerless to effect
all good

but the word of the oath in the prophet David

David lived over four hundred years after Moses as
I Kings 6:1 says where it relates Moses and David: "In
the four hundred and eightieth year after the children of
Israel were come out of the land of Egypt, Solomon began
to build a house for the Lord, which was four years after
the death of David and from the beginning of the reign of
Solomon."

which was a word or, if you prefer
it, an oath

came after the law
appointed a son
perfected for evermore always sufficient and
efficacious.

[1] This refers to the first of the ten Aristotelian Categories, which were a frequent
topic for discussion among the scholastics.

CHAPTER EIGHT

Gl. 43:18. *The summary of chapter eight: The Apostle brings together and makes a summary of the things he has said in chapters six and seven where he has shown the differences between the priest of the Old Testament and the Priest of the New Testament, in so far as they relate to the person of the priest. And now in this chapter he will show in addition the differences which arise between the two priests with regard to the office, the sacrifice and the tabernacle.*

Heb. 8:1. Gl. 43:6. Now this is the sum of everything that has been said

i.e., that this chapter (chapter eight) is the sum of all that has been said in chapters six and seven.

We have such a high priest

Jesus Christ

Who sat down on the right hand

and thus has power over all things

of the throne of the majesty in the heavens

and holds all things in his hands.

Sch. 195.7. The "sum" (*capitulum*), which in Greek is *cephalaion*, means in this context the sum and conclusion (*summa*). This was generally referred to as the *summa summarum*. He speaks in this way in Rom. 13:9, where he uses the same manner of speaking: "Every commandment is summed up in this word. . ." In Greek it is "recapitulated," summed up or collected. For instance: Thou shalt love thy neighbour as thyself; as if he wished to say that the summary and abridgement of the whole law is the love of neighbour. Just as "Love is the fulfilling of the law" (Rom. 13:10) means the same thing. He means this when he says using a dif-

148

ferent though equivalent expression, "The whole law is fulfilled in one word: thou shalt love thy neighbour" (Gal. 5:14). And emulating this example Jerome says on Matt. 17:4., The law and the prophets must be brought within the one tabernacle of the Gospel[1], i.e., they are to be gathered together and made into a single abridgement or epitome. Christ also made such a recapitulation (*anacephalaiosin*) or summary (*cephalaion*). "Whatsoever ye wish that men should do unto you, these things then do for them. For this is the law and the prophets" (Matt. 7:12).

8:2. A minister of things holy	because a priest that is of things sacred or spiritual
and of the true tabernacle	in heaven, which tabernacle was pre-figured in the Old Testament
which God pitched	by grace and the gifts of the Spirit as described in I Cor. 12:1 ff.
and not man	not Moses who pitched an earthly tabernacle.

8:3. For every high priest
He now begins to compare and differentiate the sacrifices of both covenants

is ordained either by God or by men
as if he meant to say that the priesthood exists on account of its function

for the purpose of offering gifts	of praise for benefits received
and sacrifices,	expiation for sins:
wherefore it is necessary that this person should also have something to offer.	the high priest Christ

8:4. If therefore he were on earth	this, however, cannot take place on earth, but will be

---

1 Migne, 26.126.

an offering in heaven.

he would not be a priest

For it is possible for him to be both the type prefigured and the realized event at one and the same time.

since there are priests	that is priests in a figurative way of speaking, namely, priests of the law.
who offer gifts	
according to the law.	and so the other priesthood (that of Christ) would be valueless and unnecessary
8:5. Who serve	provide
a copy	a figure and sign

It is a copy in that something other comes to pass. It is also said that their ministry was a copy and a shadow. It is shown by this that the ministry was described in those terms when it was committed to Moses.

and a shadow	by which the truth is veiled
of heavenly things	spiritual and heavenly things
As Moses was admonished of God when he was	
about to make	to perfect
the tabernacle (Ex. 25)	
For see, he said,	look into it
that thou makest all things	all the things of the tabernacle
according to the pattern	the idea or vision
which was shown thee on the mount	Sinai.
8:6. Now however that he has obtained a better ministry	because it is not of earth
by how much also	i.e., it is better than the ministry of priests or the office of a priest by as much as
he is the mediator	namely he receives a better covenant from God and gives it to us

of a better covenant	because he is heavenly and immortal
which has been ordained	established
upon better promises	of eternal life and the purest riches.
8:7. For if that first covenant had been free from imperfection,	the Old Testament had it been unblameable. That is, if it had been worth so much that it could have made men guiltless.

Now he does not find fault with the covenant, but with those who think in terms of the old covenant, as is clearly expressed in what follows: "For finding fault with them . . ." are his words. He does not say, ". . . finding fault with it." For that reason it is their faith he censures, since the law had not been given that it might justify, but to prepare men from the very beginning for justification.

then	because it would be superfluous
no place would have been sought for a second	the New Testament
8:8. For finding fault with	reprehending
them	when they were presuming on the Old Covenant

He says,

In the time of Jeremiah Israel had been scattered abroad and taken captive to Assyria, and Judah alone was left. When therefore he speaks of either of the two, it is clear that he speaks in general terms of the whole congregation as a unity.

"Behold the days will come,"	the day of grace
saith the Lord, "that I will make	will fulfil
a new covenant with the house of Israel and the house of Judah."	

The phrase "new covenant" means that the Apostle introduces the new covenant by means of this Old Testament scripture.

8:9. Not according to the testament which I made with their fathers — when I wrote my laws not on their hearts but on tablets of stone external to them. For that reason they neither understood them nor loved them, but did not know them and hated them.

He adds this to explain his position, lest it appear that he found fault with the covenant God made with Abraham, and in which Christ and the eternal promises are. He means in this context the covenant by which he promised the land of Canaan to the children of Israel.

in the day — at the time
when I took them by the hand to lead them out of the land of Egypt, for these people did not continue — for they neither understood the covenant nor loved it, as explained above

in my covenant, and I disregarded them,

As in the leading into captivity by Assyria and Babylon— or rather more recently by Rome[1]

saith the Lord.

8:10. For this is the covenant — that is, the New Testament
which I will arrange — will prepare
for the house of Israel after those days, — the days of the old law
saith the Lord : I will put — I will give, and that means through the Holy Spirit
my laws into their mind, — not written on tables nor in

---

[1] Luther seems to be making an ironic parallel between the leading away of the congregation of Israel into captivity by Assyria and Babylon and the leading away of the Church by Rome. This later became the theme of one of his three Reformative Writings of 1520, *Concerning the Babylonian Captivity*.

books, but so that they
might understand them.

and on their heart

Because in the former Old Testament it was the case that
the promises were certainly loved but the covenant was
hated. But in the present New Testament, on the other
hand, it is the case that the covenant is loved more even
than the promises.

will I write them

Not in a code of laws, but clearly that they may love them purely and simply.

**and I will be to them
truly God**

if this is done in this way.
For then they shall love me
and me alone, as is my wish.

**and they shall be to me
my people**

because I shall love them
alone before all others

8:10. Sch. 195.22. The grace of the New Testament lies in this
that what is there spoken and written teach the things of the
spirit. They are the words of grace, as it says in Ps. 45:2: "Grace
is poured from thy lips." But not so Moses. He is hesitant in
speech and a poor speaker. As he says in Ex. 4:10 "I am hesitant
in speech, and have a slow tongue." For that reason the
Apostle is bold to say that "the law works wrath" (Rom. 4:15),
and that the law is a "law of sin" (Rom. 7:25, 8:2); even that
Moses is a servant of sin. On that account it may be said that wrath
is poured from thy lips. Wherefore, what happens in the New
Testament is that while outwardly the word of life and grace and
salvation is preached, inwardly and at the same time the Holy
Spirit is teaching. That is the explanation of the two prophetic
texts: "And all thy children will be taught of the Lord" (Isa.
54:13; cf. Heb. 8:10 f.; and Jer. 31:33). "And I will put my law
in their inward parts . . . and they shall all know me" (Jer. 31:33).
For the same reason Christ appeals to these two prophets when he
says: "It is written in the prophets, they shall all be taught of
God" (John 6:45). The same thing is found in the Second Epistle
to the Corinthians: "You are an epistle of Christ ministered by us,
and written not in ink but with the spirit of the living God; not in
tables of stone but in tables that are hearts of flesh" (II Cor. 3:3).
And the same is found again in I John, "His anointing will teach
you all" (I John 2:27), and also in the Gospel, "The Paraclete,

namely, the Holy Spirit will teach you all things" (John 14:26).

Therefore it is in this way that Scripture must be understood when it says that its laws must be written in the mind and on the heart. For Scripture means by the terms mind and heart the seat of the intellect and the seat of the affections (*intellectum* and *affectum*), as we say nowadays[1]. For to be in the mind is to be understood, and to be in the heart is to be loved. And thus, when it says that the law is in the mouth it means to teach the law; when it says that it is in the ear it means to hear it; when it says that it is in the eyes it means to see it. Therefore, it is not sufficient for the law to be in the soul merely as an external idea (*obiective*), but rather in the inmost essence (*formaliter*). That means that the law must be written in the heart out of love for it.

8:11. And there shall be no need for every man to teach his neighbour and his brother

> Because to write that of God is to be taught of God. As it says in John 6:45, "They shall all be taught of God." And also in Matt. 16:17, "Flesh and blood has not revealed it to thee, but my Father..."

saying, know the Lord, for they shall all know me   for I shall be teaching them

> Behold, he says, they shall have knowledge of me, not because of their seeking and working for it, but because I have mercy. For it is neither by our merits and still more not by our efforts we know God, but only by his mercy

from the least to the greatest of them.

8:12. For I will be merciful to their iniquities, and their sins will I remember no more.   If he did regard and remember sins, nobody would be taught anything at all.

8:13. By saying   in what he has said

---

[1] Vogelsang points out *ad loc.* that when Luther makes only the two distinctions *intellectum* and *affectum* according to the prevalent nominalist teaching, he includes under the term *affectum* both feeling and willing.

For purposes of this argument he now quotes the authority
he has introduced

**"A new covenant," he
hath made old   rendered obsolete
the old covenant**

**8:14. But that which is
becoming old**   and at the same time as it
                                       is becoming old is becoming
                                       void and of none effect

**and showing signs of
decay**   for it is old and out-moded
has almost died away   it is vanishing away.

Gl. 47:11. The summary of chapter nine: he pursues the difference of office, as he has done in the previous chapter, between the priesthood of Christ and that of the Levites.

9:1. Gl. 47:5. **Now even the first**   that is the Old Testament
had regulations for divine worship,

> *by observing these the Jews were justified in their worship of God*

The word for divine worship is *cultura* (*latreia* in Greek). That is the cultus by which God is worshipped.

and its sanctuary   sacred place
a sanctuary belonging to this world

As if he meant to say: a sanctuary where not the conscience but only clothes and such things were sanctified.

9:2. **For there was a tabernacle prepared**   the tabernacle of Moses as is clear from Exodus 25 ff.

—the outer one in which were the candlestick,   the seven lights from one candlestick

and the table, and the presentation of the loaves,   the shew bread
which is called the sanctuary   taken as a single entity within the tabernacle.

9:3. **And then, beyond the second veil,**   the other veil which hung

	behind the candlestick and the table
the tabernacle which is called the holy of holies,	was constituted
9:4. having a censer of gold, and the ark of the covenant, overlaid on every part	inside and outside
with gold, in which	i.e., the ark
was a golden urn containing the manna	which as we all know was kept from the time when they were journeying in the desert
and Aaron's rod which budded, and the tables of the covenant	on which the Decalogue was written
9:5. And above it	the ark which we have been discussing
were the cherubim of glory	either angels or winged creatures
overshadowing the mercy-seat, but I cannot talk about these things in detail now.	with their wings which was over the ark.
	Whatever these details might mean, inasmuch as the whole purpose of the comparison of the Old Covenant and the New is to compare the priesthood of the law and its rites and ceremonies with the priesthood of Christ.

Sch. 196:22. The tabernacle of Moses has been expounded in different ways by different expositors. Some[1] are minded to inter-

[1] Jerome, and partly Lefèvre d'Etaples and Nicholas of Lyra. *Vide WA*, 57, 196.22, footnote, and Hirsch-Rückert 208, 15, footnote.

pret it as meaning the universe, i.e., the macrocosm, the whole. They explain its details in some such sort of way as this, that the "Holy of Holies" represents heaven and all things invisible; the "cherubim" the very choir of angels, (which is the reason why in the Scriptures it is often expressed with reference to God, "Who sitteth above the cherubim," Ps. 80:1; Isa. 37:16); "the sanctuary," however, signifies the visible world; and "the second veil" the starry heavens; "the seven candlesticks" the seven planets; the "table of the shewbread" the four elements, and so on . . . But this exposition, whatever truth there might be in it, is rather forced, and does violence to the text.

Others[1] expound it rather in a tropological manner. They understand by "tabernacle" the smaller world, the microcosm, the part, that is man himself, who, in the higher reaches of his mind, is concerned with things invisible and the things that are God's. Thus, as Augustine said time and again, it is God alone who dwells in the higher faculty of man, and only God who satisfies it. And if it is understood in this way, such a man is indeed the ark of the covenant of the Lord, and has the mercy-seat, the Cherubim, the manna and the rod of Aaron. The "sanctuary," however signifies the lower reason which is illuminated by the light of the so-called natural reason, signified by the candlestick. Finally, by the court is understood the mind of the flesh. As a sign of this the court measured five cubits in height, because there are five senses. In short, in this manner of exposition the court represents the mind (sensus), the sanctuary the reason (ratio), the holy of holies the intellect (intellectum)[2]. These divisions correspond to the celebrated threefold division of man by Paul into soul, body and spirit (I Thess. 5:23, et al.). And each of these divisions has its own manner of religious observance, its own theology, its own worship of God. To these divisions the famous threefold demarcation of theology corresponds, namely, the symbolic which appertains to the mind; the proper which appertains to the reason; the mystical which appertains to the intellect or spirit.

Thirdly, others[3], together with the Apostle, understand tabernacle in this place as the spiritual world, which is the Holy Church of God. And accordingly, the Holy of Holies is the Church Triumphant, the sanctuary is the Church militant and the court

1 Gerson. Even Luther himself in his exposition of the *Magnificat*, 1520–1521, *WA*, 7, 551. See also *WA*, 57, 197.6, footnote, and Hirsch-Rückert 209, 8, footnote.
2 Cf. Luther's comments on the same threefold division on 5:12. *supra* p. 117.
3 In the detailed footnote of Hirsch-Rückert, *op. cit.*, 210, 4, it is shown that this exposition comes mainly from the *Glossa Ordinaria*, and also partly from Augustine.

the synagogue. To this, in turn, the height of the court as five cubits fits in, because the synagogue was contained within the writings of the five books of Moses.

The candlestick with its shafts and seven lights signifies either, in the first place, the Word of God, that is the word that is preached (*verbum vocale*) by which the Church is illuminated in this life. As it describes it in II Peter 1:19: "We have also a more sure word of prophecy; whereunto ye do well that ye take heed, as unto a light that shineth in a dark place." The number seven, which is properly the seven-fold spirit, signifies wholeness (i.e., that all the preaching in all the churches shows but one mind and shines by but one light). Or secondly, it signifies the churches all taken together as one Church[1], if it is taken with reference to the seven golden candlesticks as the seven churches[1]. Or thirdly, it may be taken with reference to Zech. 4:10, where it says that the golden candlestick and its seven lights are the seven eyes of the Lord, "which run to and fro through the whole earth." But as we know, the eyes of the Lord are the priests of the churches. For as the eye directs the body, so the priest directs the Church. As it says in Job 29:15, "I was the eye to the blind and the foot to the lame." Or again, in Jer. 15:19, ". . . if thou take the precious from the vile, then shalt thou be as my mouth." Or fourthly, it may be understood in this wise: the lamps are the consciences of individual souls, on a par with that passage in Luke 11:34; "The light of thy body is thine eye."

The table and the shew bread may likewise be taken in two ways. It may mean either the Scriptures, which the faithful receive from the mouth of the preacher just as they receive the bread from the table. An instance of this is to be found in Mal. 2:7: "For the priest's lips should keep knowledge, and they should seek the law at his mouth." Or, it may mean that the table is Christ himself, who is our altar, our sacrifice and our bread as John says in the words "I am the living bread," etc. (John 6:35, 41, 48, 51). He it is whom we receive in the sacrament, and feed on in this life. This is the meaning of the passage in the twenty-third Psalm where it says: "Thou preparest a table before me in the presence of my enemies who trouble me" (Ps. 23:5). This verse may perhaps give the reason why the table was placed on the north side and the candlestick on the south side, because in the Scriptures "north" signifies enemies and oppressors, as Jeremiah says, "From the north shall all evil spread out" (Jer. 1:14). For truly no consolation can

---

1 Luther uses the word church here and further on in two senses. In the first place as the whole Church Universal, the Catholic Church. And secondly, in the sense of an individual member church of the whole Church Universal.

be found nor victory won in any temptation whatsoever, unless we draw near to the sacrament and partake of "the table prepared for us against those who trouble us."

And this ought to be noted as well, that in the Hebrew it says "the Bread of the Countenance" (*panis facierum*) where we have "the Bread of proposition" (*panis propositionis*)[1] which in fact amounts to the same thing. For this bread is so called because Christ ought always to be in our sight and before our faces and set in our memory. This is what the verse already quoted (Ps. 23:5) refers to when it says: "Thou hast prepared before me . . ." i.e., before my face, "a table against those who trouble me." And the same too, when Christ said: "This do in remembrance of me." For the same reason it is also called by another name, i.e., a "memorial" of the passion of our Lord, as in Ps. 111:4, where it says: "The Lord has made a memorial of his wonderful deeds." To other expositors it seems to have been described as "bread of the countenance" because the sacrament is prepared for all and is visible to all, instituted on our behalf and designed for our needs. For Christ does not turn his back on us or leave us forsaken, but rather turns his face to us and comes to us every day in the sacrament. And the word face is written in the plural, because Christ comes in many places at one time.

The ark of the covenant (Ex. 25:10 ff.) made from incorruptible shittim wood and then laid over with gold is at the same time Christ himself, who was born of the most pure and incorrupt flesh of the Virgin, and who was also embellished with the gold of heavenly wisdom and grace "within and without" (Ex. 25:11), i.e., "within" in respect to his inner heart, "without" in respect to his outward deed, especially when he hangs on the cross. At that moment above all he is the ark of the covenant, that is of our reconciliation.

---

[1] Our word "shewbread" is apparently a direct translation, almost a transliteration, of Luther's *Schaubrot*, first adopted by Tindale and found in his New Testament (1526). In the Hebrew the phrase is *lehem panim*. Tindale used different renderings of this phrase in the gospels ("the halowed loaves" Matt. 12:4; Mark 2:26, "the halowed bread" Luke 6:4), and retains a similar inconsistency in his revised edition of 1534. His marginal note on the word *shewbreed* when it first occurs in Ex. 25:30 reads, "Shewbreed, because it was always in the presence and sight of the Lorde."

Wycliffe followed the Vulgate with "breed of proposicioun." The Protestant translators give "shewbred" in the Old Testament, and "shewe loaves," "shewbreads" and "shewbread" in the New Testament.

Nicholas of Lyra in commenting on Ex. 25:30 gives the literal translation, and offers the comment that the loaves were called *panes facierum* because they had the same appearance from whichever angle they were viewed on account of their being a round shape.

He is also **the mercy seat** (*propitiatorium*)[1] on which God is enthroned, and as the Apostle says, in whom "dwelleth all the fullness of the Godhead bodily" (Col. 2:9). This is what is alluded to in Rom. 3:25, where it says: "Whom God has set forth to be a propitiation through faith in his blood."

It also means that **the tables** of the Covenant have their significance in him, for as the Apostle says, in Col. 2:3, "All the treasures of wisdom and knowledge are hid in him." For neither the law nor the wisdom of God can be understood except in Christ, as it is written in I Cor. 1:30, ". . . who of God is made unto us wisdom and righteousness. . ." In the last analysis this means that not even the law can be fulfilled except in Christ. Just because the external word and sacrament (signified under candlestick and table) are common both to the worthy and the unworthy, on that account they are inadequate, unless we discern Christ hidden in these things. As it says in Col. 3:1, ". . . seek those things which are above, where Christ is."

Though **manna** and **the golden urn** were in the ark, they again signify that same Christ in whom alone is the consolation and re-creation of the soul, since manna is called that gift of eternal life which men partake of by taking it and tasting it. This gift of eternal life "nobody knows save him who receives it." As it says in Rev. 2:17: "To him that overcometh will I give to eat of the hidden manna, and I will give him a white stone: and on the stone is a new name written, which nobody knows save him who receives it."

Aaron's rod (*virga*), too, means Christ, who, like as Aaron's rod budded, blossomed from a chaste and pure virgin (*virgo*). It is also referred to in Isa. 11:1: "A rod (*virga*) shall stem forth from the root of Jesse." And also in Num. 24:17; "There shall arise a star out of Jacob, and a sceptre (*virga*) shall rise out of Israel and shall smite the princes of Moab." However, all these allusions are made to apply to the Blessed Virgin by many expositors, and no wonder, when they can refer to any Christian at all on account of his faith in Christ, through which he possesses all things that are Christ's[2].

By **cherubim** many expositors understand the angels in heaven. But there is no general agreement nowadays as to what shape they

1 Cf. Lev. 16:13 ff.
2 In this passage one observes a common principle of Luther's exposition. He seeks to relate all utterances in the first place as teaching Christ. As he said to Erasmus (and frequently elsewhere), "Everything in the Bible has to do with Christ." And then from that position he relates the passage to the believer in Christ. This is important for Luther's Christology.

Note also his reverence for the Virgin but his firm turning away from her to the centralizing of Christ.

were, except that in the Scriptures they are described as having wings (Isa. 10:8). Therefore, some think of them as in the shape of a bird, others as in the form of a winged angel. To choose a less exalted interpretation, cherubim may be understood as the contemplative wisdom of Christ, for as Gregory says[1], contemplation is understood by the term "wing." Thus Ps. 12:11, "He arose and flew upon the wings of the wind" i.e., in spiritual contemplation. But this interpretation hardly does justice to the word, for "Cherubim" are interpreted as meaning "fullness of knowledge[2]." Therefore he also says here "cherubims of glory," showing that the wisdom of Christ glorified is one thing and the wisdom of Christ crucified another. Because by the one the flesh is subdued, through the other the spirit is elevated. Moreover, in contemplating the glory of Christ spiritual wisdom is more necessary than anything else in case we go after the outward appearances of the one and lose the truth of the other, and thereby fall into error and confusion. That usually happens to those who neglect to reconcile in Christ the contradictions in Scripture. They are carried away to a rather one-sided view of things. To give an instance of this: it is said of the Christ that he is the most glorious king of all. Now the Jews are wedded to this idea of Christ and consequently poles apart from the crucified Christ. They pay no regard to the other truth of Isa. 53:2: "He has neither form nor comeliness." The same is true in reconciling in Christ other contradictory and opposed ideas which spring from the difficulty of reconciling his humanity with his divinity. And that is why it is written in the Scriptures (Ex. 25:20) that the faces of the cherubim were turned towards each other and towards the mercy-seat[3]. As the Scripture further says: "In the mouth of two or three witnesses every word shall be established" (Deut. 19:15).

The first **veil**, which used to hang in front of the sanctuary, signified concealment: the veiling of a faith in the Church to come, in the gospel to come, in the sacraments to come, for the synagogue did not see these things as present then. On that account this very curtain was "rent from the top to the bottom" during the passion of Christ, because it was at that moment the Church began and the Synagogue ended. The second veil which hung before the holy of holies, signifies the veiling of our faith in which

---

[1] *Moralia*, 35, 2; Migne, 76.1144.
[2] Peter Lombard, *Sent.* II, dist. 9, cap. 2. Migne, 192.670.
[3] The force of Luther's picture would seem to be that as the faces of the cherubim face different ways yet are focused on the mercy-seat, so the two natures of Christ different as they are, are directed both towards the mercy-seat of the gospel. This he follows up with the support of the two witnesses from Deuteronomy, namely, the witness of the two natures of Christ.

Christ rules as man. This veil shall be removed in like manner when he appears in glory. This is how it may be said that we know Christ according to both his humanity and his divinity: but only through faith. As Paul writes in II Cor. 3:18: "It is given to us all alike to catch the glory of the Lord as in a mirror, with faces unveiled; and so we become transfigured into that same likeness, borrowing glory from glory."

9:4. Having the golden censer

It should be noted that the Apostle says here that there was a golden censer in the holy of holies. This has caused many expositors to come to the opinion that this epistle is not Pauline, since Moses seems to have said nothing about such a censer. In fact the text of the Old Testament itself is not clear, so that it seems doubtful whether the tabernacle had two or three altars. The brazen altar of the burnt offering which stood in the forecourt is described adequately enough in Exodus 27. The other altar, however, the altar of sweet incense covered with gold is assumed by everybody to have stood in the sanctuary between the candlestick and the table. Thus it says in Ex. 30:6: "And thou shalt put it before the veil that is by the ark of the testimony before the mercy-seat . . . and Aaron shall burn sweet incense upon it." It is said in that section of Scripture that incense has to be burned upon it day and night continually. Therefore, the place of the golden censer cannot be understood as the holy of holies, because the high priest used to enter there only once a year. That there was however a third altar in the holy of holies may be suspected in the first instance from Lev. 16:12 f., where the solemn rite of the feast of the atonement is described, and where it says among other things: "The high priest shall take a censer full of burning coals of fire from off the altar (of burnt-offering or incense) and shall take in his hand a mixture of sweet incense and shall enter within the veil in the sanctuary (i.e., into the holy of holies) and he shall put the incense upon the fire that the cloud and vapour of the incense may work over the mercy-seat which is upon the testimony and hide it, for none may see it and live." There is no doubt that it is from this passage that the Apostle has drawn when he says that the tabernacle had a golden censer.

There is a second reason which may justify the assumption that there was a third altar in the holy of holies. At the end of Exodus 30 where the composition of the incense is described, it says: "Thou shalt keep a store of it before the tabernacle of the testimony in the place where I shall appear to thee" (i.e., before the mercy-seat). "The incense shall be to you a holy of holies" (*sanctum sanctorum*) [a holy thing among holy things, set apart for sacred use only]. From this it would seem that there was an altar there in the holy of holies.

A third reason which may justify the assumption that there was a third altar in the holy of holies is that the Greek word for censer *thymiaterion* means in this context not only a censer, but also an altar or a place where incense is burned[1]. As the Apostle says, "in it a golden altar stood."

A fourth reason which may justify the assumption that there was a third altar in the holy of holies is that in the opinion of many, Zacharias, the father of John Baptist, is thought to have been the high priest[2], because it is written that the Angel Gabriel appeared to him standing on the right of the altar of incense. The context of the passage would appear to force one to this conclusion.

But I am not altogether unaware that all these arguments could be easily refuted, for the passages quoted do not actually say that there was an altar or a censer in the holy of holies, but rather that one stood outside, and that the incense with the live coals ought to be taken by the high priest as he entered the holy of holies and kindled inside. Nor is it a decisive argument to say that incense used to be placed on the fire in the holy of holies that its "cloud and vapour" may cover the mercy-seat that is upon the testimony as is explained above. It is indecisive because it refers to the fire which the priest took in the censer from outside, and which he then carried into the holy of holies. Nor is it generally understood to have been a hanging censer, as the Church uses nowadays, but a squat one sitting on a broad base like a cup-shaped vinegar bowl or basin in which the incense was laid. What therefore shall we say to the Apostle who simply says without qualification that there was a golden censer in the holy of holies? It may be said that there was such a censer in the holy of holies since the priest carried one there during the feast of the Atonement. And such is my view until I learn differently.

In support of the argument against Pauline authorship it is usually maintained that it is specifically stated in I Kings 8:9 that

---

[1] Erasmus makes this point in his Annotations to the text. Both Luther and Erasmus spell the word *thymiasterion*.

[2] In the footnote to the text *WA*, 57, 203, the editors remind us that this opinion, coming from Ambrose and Bede, is represented in the *Glossa Ordinaria*. The Hirsch-Rückert footnote on the same text (*op. cit.*, 217) shows in some detail the conclusions of Nicholas of Lyra commenting on Luke 1. Luther thought that not only must he have been high priest but that the altar in question must have been in the holy of holies. Nicholas takes the view that it had nothing to do with the holy of holies and that Zacharias had not been the high priest.

there was nothing in the ark except the two tables of the testimony. Yet the Apostle says there were also in it both the golden urn of manna and also the rod of Aaron. Lefèvre d'Etaples changes the prepositions in the Greek to avoid the discrepancy, and for the phrase "in which" he takes "with which," so that in this way he could aver that the urn and the rod were not actually in the ark but with the ark. Moreover, it is plain enough that it says quite simply in Ex. 16:33 f.: "Take for yourself a pot and put manna into it, and lay it up before the Lord as a treasure for later generations to keep. And Aaron laid it up in the tabernacle." Admittedly, no mention is made of a golden urn in this passage, nor in any other passage of Scripture as far as I remember, though there is mention of a vessel to hold the manna. Granted that it was clearly stated that there was nothing in the ark except the manna, yet it would be wrong to infer from that statement that the manna was put there without a container. In his treatment of the passage the Apostle mentions a vessel and actually calls it "a golden pot." He thus is in agreement with the passage from I Kings 8:9.

In the case of Aaron's rod, however, Num. 17:10 says: "The Lord said to Moses: Bring back again Aaron's rod into the tabernacle of the testimony, that it may be kept there for a token of the rebellious children of Israel. . . ." It cannot be assumed from this text that the rod was actually inside the ark, unless we take the phrase "the tabernacle of the testimony" as meaning the ark, in the way that it must be understood in Ex. 16:34, where it says of the manna: "And Aaron laid it up in the tabernacle" [i.e., the ark], as we said earlier. Others think differently, however. They maintain that it lay outside, by the side of the ark [literally in the side of the ark] and this could be expressed as being in the ark, because the same expression "in the side of the ark" is used in Deut. 31:26: "Take this book of the law, and put it in the side of the ark of the covenant. . . " An alternative suggestion may be offered in explanation of this passage in I Kings 8:9, that when Solomon had constructed the Temple, he took Aaron's rod from the ark to another place. Not that this can be proved from any text of Scripture, but a similar thing could be shown in the case of the discovery of the Book of Deuteronomy where it is said that it was discovered in the reign of King Josiah not "in the side of the ark" but "behind the altar."[1]

9:6 f. Now when these things were thus ordained, the priests always went into the first tabernacle to perform

[1] II Kings 22:8 says that it was found "in the house of the Lord" and gives no such detail. Lyra quotes Rabbi Solomon as saying that it was found in the wall of the Temple (Hirsch-Rückert 220 n.)

their sacrificial office, but into the second, however, only the High Priest went once a year, which he offered for the faults which he and his people had unwittingly committed.

We must understand by this term fault (*ignorantia*) bodily sins against the law, i.e., impurities in the matter of clothing, drink, food and the body. For as the Apostle says further on in Chapter 10:4.: "It is not possible that the blood of bulls and goats should take away sins," that means sins against the conscience. Therefore, the law was a most grievous burden, and in the long run did neither justify nor sanctify except in the matter of carnal or ritual impurity.

9:8 ff. The Holy Ghost signified by this that no entry into the sanctuary lay open to us as long as the first tabernacle maintained its status. And that allegory still holds good at the present time. In such worship gifts and sacrifices are being offered which have no power to bring the worshipper to his full growth as far as his conscience is concerned. They are only about outward observances connected with food and drink and various ceremonial washings, and were obligatory only until the hour of reformation.

From this text, as has already been said earlier, the operative issue between the old and the new law is convincingly differentiated. The sins, righteousnesses, sacrifices, holy things, promises, doctrines and priests of the old law all pertained to the flesh. They did not sanctify as far as the conscience was concerned but only as far as the body was concerned. But now, under the dispensation of the gospel, our sins, righteousnesses, sacrifices, holy things, promises, doctrines and our priest are all operative in the sphere of the spirit, and sanctify in matters of conscience. Nevertheless, both dispensations were given by God, but the old one (as it says here) "was imposed until the time of reformation." Hence, what Peter Lombard writes is to some extent true, although he used to be reproved by everybody. He said that the sacraments of the old law "even though they were performed in faith and love" did not justify. This is absolutely true, for a man is not justified on account of the sacraments and sacrifices he has performed. They do not justify even if they are done in love. It is only love and faith which justify a man. No wonder it says in the New Testament that it is not the sacrament but faith in the sacrament which justifies[1].

[1] Hirsch-Rückert (*op. cit.*, 220 f.) have very full notes on this point, and explain the main scholastic views on the efficacy of the sacraments of the old law. They also draw attention (rightly) to Luther's decisive turning away at this juncture from the general scholastic views to the view which this epistle so unequivocally maintains, namely, the unqualified rejection of the law as a means of salvation.

9:11. But meanwhile Christ

who by this time had come. It was not at all the case that his coming was still in the future, as the Jews wrongly believe.

The Apostle relates the type and figure of the Messiah to the truth now revealed in Christ, and from now on adds to and completes the Jewish view which is a limited view of no further use. This is because the former idea [the Jewish view that the Messiah was still to come] concerned only one race, the Jews; but the latter [that the Christ had already come] concerns every person in the entire world.

has taken his place as our *pontiff*

has already come

i.e., as our high priest, through whom God announces and promises the blessings of eternity, just as God used the high priest of the law to declare the blessings of this life

of blessings which lie in the future. He makes use of a greater tabernacle

greater than the earthly tabernacle

and a more complete tabernacle

because he perfected it. It is much greater than the type which has been abandoned.

not made with hands that is, not of this order of creation

not invented by man

not of wood, or brass, or gold.

He adds this point lest anyone should say that this tabernacle was made by the hand of man as well. It was made by the hand of God, and to that extent he spoke of himself.

9:12. It is not through the blood

i.e., not with the blood, as used to happen in the feast of the Atonement (Lev. 16).

of goats and calves but through his own blood he entered

i.e., with his own blood passed over from this world to the Father.

once into the holy place	the true holy of holies. That is to God who is in heaven
having won eternal redemption	since he achieved it by means of his passion

In the law redemption was temporal and in relation to this world.

9:13. For if
He argues from the lesser to the greater, proving that the redemption in Christ is eternal, for it is a different kind from redemption under the old covenant

the blood of goats	as is described in Lev. 16 on the feast of the Atonement

or bulls
He says "bulls" and not "bull," either to emphasize his point, or because goats and heifers were sacrificed year after year and in that sense many bulls were in fact offered.

and the ashes of a heifer	as is described in Num. 19.
sprinkled over the unclean	those who are defiled, in that they have touched a dead body, or are defiled in the matter of food or clothing.
sanctify to the purification of the flesh	that they might be undefiled as far as the body is concerned and in the sight of men, but not however in the sight of God
9:14. How much more shall the blood of Christ who through the Holy Spirit	for this is that burning love with which Christ sought to offer himself
offered himself	in his cross and passion he was both priest and victim
without spot to God, purge our conscience	by virtue of which we are clean in the sight of God.

He did not do what the priest of the old covenant did, for he was stained with sin and offered a blood that was not his own. The priest of the old covenant did not act in the Holy Spirit but in the spirit of bondage: to be precise, either through fear of losing temporal blessings or in the desire of procuring them.

from dead works   sins

The Apostle carefully says "from dead works" and not "from sins," to stop the mouth of the Jews from boasting of their bodily purity. He uses this expression "dead works" to show not only were those dead works sin, but still more, all works by which God is not served are sin.

[Luther is showing very clearly at this early stage his views on the works-religion of his day which thought in terms of pilgrimages, fastings, penances and the like as works of God.]

**to serve the
living God**   not ourselves or our idols

[By this term "idols" Luther means the ideas of God which man worked out for himself and the ways of worshipping him he devised for himself, all in contradistinction to the revealed God who had declared himself in Christ. It was a rebuttal of the anthropocentrism of contemporary religious thought and practice in favour of a Christocentrism, and played a very important part in Luther's theology.]

Sch. 206:8. It is written in Num. 19:2 ff.: "Speak to the children of Israel that they bring thee a red heifer without spot and free from blemish, one that has never borne the yoke." (The Apostle chooses to call it a calf in this passage, presumably on account of its age.) "This thou shalt give to Eleazar the priest, who will take it forth outside the boundaries of the camp and immolate it there in the sight of all. He will then dip his finger in the blood, with which he will sprinkle the front of the tabernacle door seven times. He will then burn the heifer in the sight of all, all of it, its skin and its flesh, its blood and its dung consigned to the flames. And the priest shall throw into the midst of the flames which consume the heifer cedar wood, and hyssop, and scarlet stuff twice-dyed." And further on: "And a man who is free from defilement shall gather up the ashes of the heifer, and shall pour them out in a place free from defilement outside the camp. And the ashes shall be kept for the congregation of the children of Israel for purposes of sprinkling, because the heifer has been burnt to atone for man's sin." And further on; "And they shall take of the ashes of the heifer burnt for the purification of sin, and shall pour running water over them in a vessel, and a man free from defilement shall take hyssop and dip it into the water and sprinkle it upon the tent and all the vessels, and upon the man defiled by any kind of contagion. And in this manner the man undefiled shall purify the defiled on the third and seventh day" (Num. 19:17 ff.). The same is found in verse 11: "He that toucheth the dead body of a man, and on account of this would be unclean seven days, shall be purified with this water on the third and seventh day, and thus shall be cleansed, But if he has not been purified on the third day, then on the seventh day he shall not be clean." It can now be understood what David means when he said: "Sprinkle me with hyssop and I shall be cleansed," etc. (Ps. 51:7). For all the Church Fathers[1] agree that the Lord's humanity was signified by this red heifer, since the humanity of Christ was sacrificed for us on the seventh day. On the seventh day according to Paul of Burgos[2], because in the whole duration of the law down to the time of Christ, only six heifers were sacrificed in this way. The first by Moses in the desert, as we have in this passage, the ashes of which lasted to the Babylonian Captivity. The second by Ezra for the second temple, and the remaining four by other high priests down to the time of Christ.

9:14. How much more shall the blood of Christ purge our conscience.

He describes beautifully the two different ideas of purity found in the New Testament and the Old Testament and pursues a dialectical argument. He argues that purity in the Old Testament was a matter of purity of flesh, or clothing, or vessels, but purity in the New Testament is a purity of conscience, heart and mind. Uncleanness in the Old Testament is contracted by touching a dead body or an unclean thing, but in the New Testament from dead works or sins. Purity in the Old Testament is directed to the serving of human ideas and wants, but purity in the New Testament is conceived in terms of serving the living God.

Let us run over these items one by one. First, there is purity of conscience, which means that a man is not consumed by the recollection of the sins he has committed nor disquieted by the fear of punishment to come. As Ps. 112:7 says, "The righteous man will not be afraid of evil tidings." For a bad conscience which is troubled about sin in the past and in fear of the vengeance to come

---

[1] On the basis of Augustine, *Quaest. in Hept.*, IV, qu. 33. Migne, 34. 732–37. The exposition of Augustine was carried over into the *Glossa Ordinaria*.

[2] The editors of the *WA* text note that Paul of Burgos is basing his remarks on a rabbinic tradition (*op. cit.*, 207).

is in dire straits; as the prophet says, it is "caught and troubled" (Isa. 8:22, or 30:6?). The Apostle says the same thing in Rom. 2:9: "Tribulation and anguish will be rendered upon the soul of every man that doeth evil." Because, as long as it is not possible to change the sin of the past, and as long as there is no possibility of avoiding vengeance to come, a man must of necessity undergo anxiety and tribulation, no matter which way he turns. Nor can he be freed from these straits except by the blood of Christ, which if a man regards in faith, he believes and understands that his sins have been washed in it and taken away. Thus it is through faith that a man is purified and at the same time given peace of mind, so that in that state not even punishment terrifies him for joy in the remission of sins. No law avails for purity of this kind, no works, nor anything else. Nothing except the blood of Christ. And not even this of itself avails, unless the heart of man believe that it has been shed for the remission of sins. For we are bound to believe the testator when he says, "This is my blood of the new testament, which is shed for you and for many for the remission of sins" (Matt. 26:28; Luke 22:20).

Secondly, there is no doubt that he calls "dead works" sins, because quite unmistakably he calls those activities which defile the conscience "dead works." From "dead works" a man is cleansed through the blood of Christ, for nothing stains the conscience save sin. And it seems to follow from this weightiest of statements that even good works done outside a state of grace are sins, so that they too may be called "dead works." Because if, speaking after the manner of men, the conscience which has not been purified by the blood of Christ is unclean, then it cannot effect other than what it is itself, that is, unclean. The Apostle teaches the same in Titus 1, "To the unclean nothing is clean." It is certain however, that he is not speaking of venial but mortal impurity, for even to the pure and holy nothing is pure in the sense of being without venial sin, since even their righteousnesses are unclean, as Isaiah expresses it: "But we are all as an unclean thing, our righteousnesses are no better than the clouts a menstruant woman casts away" (Isa. 64:6). And thus, the opinion of those who call good works done apart from grace as dead (*mortua*) but not mortal (*mortalia*) [1] is totally demolished because the Apostle clearly makes "dead" and "mortal" mean the same thing in this passage when he says "from dead works." Otherwise, if "dead works" meant the same thing as "non-meritorious" here, as some

---

[1] In this passage "dead" means in relation to works, and mortal in relation to sin. Luther is here referring to Biel and Peter Lombard, and discusses this in his *Disputation at Heidelberg*, 1518, *WA*, 1, 353.27 ff.; 357.19 f. See page 276 f.

say it does, it would follow, that the blood of Christ will cleanse not sinners but those who have done good works "in their kind" (to use their own phrase). Consequently, they would be compelled also to say that "impure," "sin," "trespass" and the like are the same as "non-meritorious," which is nothing else than to turn the whole of Scripture absolutely upside down by a new signification of words. It follows from these thoughts that a good, pure, quiet and joyful conscience is nothing else than faith in the remission of sins, which nobody can have save in the Word of God, which proclaims to us that the blood of Christ is shed for the remission of sins. For we may often see and hear the blood of Christ poured out, yet the conscience is in no way cleansed merely on account of this, unless it is further realized that it is poured out "unto the remission of sins." For the Jews saw it, and all the Gentiles heard about it, but they were not cleansed. Still more, it is not even enough to believe that it was shed for the remission of sins, unless they believe that it was shed for the remission of their own sins. On this showing it is only the blood of Christ poured out [for the remission of sins] which cleanses the conscience through faith in the word of Christ.

For the same reason the Apostle sets out in this passage the phrase ". . . the blood of Christ *who through the eternal spirit offered himself.*" It is found also in Rom. 3:25: "Whom God set forth to be a propitiation through faith in his blood to declare his righteousness for the remission of sins." It should be carefully noted that he does not say merely "through blood" (which amounts to the same thing though it is more obscure admittedly), but he says "through faith in his blood." That means through faith in his blood, and to be precise, faith in the blood that was shed for us, as Christ himself distinctly says in John 6: "For my flesh is meat indeed, and my blood is drink indeed. He that eateth my flesh and drinketh my blood dwelleth in me and I in him." This "eating" and "drinking" Christ means in a spiritual sense, and that means "to believe," just as Augustine expressly expounds the passage, "To what purpose preparest thou thy belly and thy teeth? Believe and thou hast already eaten[1]." Therefore the words "his," "his own," "mine" and the like are to be most carefully noted. Because not all flesh nor all blood cleanses and feeds. Only Christ's blood does that, and that blood was shed for the remission of sins. It follows, therefore, that both those who only meditate on the Passion of Christ and by such activity suffer with him, and also those who arrive at something other than faith, think fruitlessly and as heathen. For who even among the heathen would not sympathize with Christ in his sufferings? But his passion ought to be pondered with such

[1] Augustine, in *Joan. Ev. Tract.*, XXV, 12; Migne, 35.1602.

devotion that faith is increased. To put it plainly, the more often it is meditated on the more fully is it believed that the blood of Christ is shed for a man's own sins. For this is what that expression "spiritual eating and drinking" means. Expressing it in plain words it means to be joined to and incorporated in Christ in a faith of this kind, as it is expressed above.

So utterly true is this, that even the purity of the law was to some extent a matter of faith[1]. For the purificatory rites took no actual impurity away from any body, clothing or vessel which had been polluted by contact with an unclean corpse. It was only a kind of vestigial idea in connection with contacts of this kind. For, in actual fact nothing was unclean about these things except that the law had made them so. How much more is the conscience made clean by faith in Christ, when in this case there was a genuine defilement from sin.

The third point [which the apostle makes in comparing the outward ritual purity of the Old Testament with the inward spiritual purity of the New] is that the blood of Christ sets a man free **"to serve the living God."** It follows from this that apart from Christ a man cannot serve the living God but serves rather creatures or idols, that is, those things "which are nothing in the world" (cf. I Cor. 8:4), even though they seem to do good. Therefore again, that view is demolished which claims that it is possible to serve God and do no sin apart from grace[2]. For if the state of not sinning is the same as not serving the living God, still less of serving something other than God, then the following command would be invalidated: "Thou shalt love the Lord thy God and him only shalt thou serve" (Matt. 4:10; Deut. 6:13). Finally, though the Apostle did write to the Philippians that he had lived in the righteousness of the law without offence (Phil. 3:6), yet on the other hand in Titus 3:3 ff. he confessed that earlier he had served his own desires, "For we ourselves also were sometime foolish, disobedient, deceived, serving divers lusts and pleasures, living in malice and envy, hateful and hating one another. But after the kindness and love of God our Saviour appeared, he saved us not

---

1 When Luther says that the purity of the law was to some extent a matter of faith, he means that the rites of purification prescribed by the law removed no actual impurity as such, for such impurity was a ritual impurity and not an actual defilement. The law had the power to prescribe for a defilement it had defined. Therefore, to believe in the efficacy of this ritual cleansing was to that extent a matter of faith.

2 Luther is referring to the late scholastic view of Biel that the human will can of its own natural powers love God over all things. Biel, in *Sent.* IIId. 27q. un. dub. 2 (lit. Q) gives a detailed exposition of this view. Scotus and Occam held similar views.

Cf. Luther's comment on 9:14, above, p. 168.

by works of righteousness which we have done, but according to his mercy."

9:15. And for this cause

because it was no animal he offered but himself

he is the mediator between man and God
of a new covenant a better covenant of grace

The mediator of a covenant must not be taken to mean that a covenant must have a mediator (unless you take the word "covenant" as equivalent to "people"). On the contrary, the mediator is the author of the covenant by which he himself mediates what pertains to the office of a mediator and an intercessor. And in the New Testament he is the mediator in this sense. The Apostle seeks to give expression to the fact that Christ is both testator and mediator at one and the same time

that by his death intervening

between the time of the Old Covenant and the actual receiving of our redemption

for the redemption of our transgressions

that means that his death so intervened that we were redeemed from our transgressions, for in this way the redemption was declared

under the old covenant

transgressions used to abound under the law

they who were called

through the gospel, nay rather through the spirit of the gospel

might receive the promise

of future life promised in the covenant

of this eternal inheritance

i.e. towards the attainment of their eternal inheritance

When the Apostle uses the expression "for the redemption of their trangressions" he is not to be understood as speaking of trespasses which derive from touching the dead and all the other

defilements he described earlier, "food, drinks and various baptisms (i.e. washings), and righteousnesses of the flesh." For such
trespasses were types and figures of those trespasses which pollute
the heart and conscience, that is those which break the Ten Commandments. These trespasses Christ took away by the New Testament he inaugurated, although he did in fact abrogate those earlier
rites in the process, and brought them utterly to an end by the
same New Testament. The transgressions of the conscience, or
those against the Ten Commandments, he has in truth already
begun to bring to an end as well. But they are not yet finally
ended, for he himself is the end of sins and the beginning of righteousness, as Gabriel expressed it in Dan. 9:24, ". . . to make an
end of sins . . . and bring in everlasting righteousness."

In a similar way he somewhat darkly and rather incidentally
touches upon the giving of the law, when he refers to the transgressions as those "which were under the first covenant" (Heb.
9:15). By this statement he means the same thing as Rom. 5:20
expresses more clearly, "The law entered that offence might
abound." And Gal. 3:19: "The law was added because of transgressions." And again Rom. 4:15: "The law worketh wrath."
This has also been well pre-figured in the ceremonial laws of the
Old Testament. For had there been no law which prohibited
touching the dead, a menstruant woman, a woman in childbed,
the seminal flow, a vessel, clothing, an unclean house, then it
would not have been a sin to have touched any of these. The same
thing applies if the law had not differentiated between clean and
unclean animals. Just as the heathen who lived then did not sin
because they touched some such things and ate others, neither do
the Christians who live now sin because they touch some such
things and eat others. As at that time it was indeed true in the
matter of these ritual laws that "law is the strength of sin" (I Cor.
15:56), and "where there is no law, there is no trespass" (Rom.
4:15), then how much more true is it to say that the real, spiritual
laws embodied in the Ten Commandments are "the strength of
sin." There is however one profound difference. The law of the
Ten Commandments is the strength of sin because it creates
knowledge of oneself. For whether the Ten Commandments are
known or not known, nonetheless there is sin in the human race,
because in that law is necessary it is recognized as existing from
birth. But in truth the ceremonial law sanctioned knowledge only
of such sin as, apart from its own ritual law, never existed.

9:16. **For where there**
is a testament   as the usual custom is

By a rhetorical argument in general use he repeats the reason he had used the analogy of a testament.

of necessity the death of the testator must intervene
between the time of the testament and the receiving of the contents of the testamentation. [In the previous verse Luther thinks of the will or testament as the Old Testament dispensation, and the matter under testamentation, which is man's redemption, as the dispensation of the New Testament. He is pursuing the same line of thought here.]

9:17. **For a testament**
again he offers his grounds of proof on the basis of established custom

He speaks from authority
comes into force after death,
the death of the testator confirms the testament.

it is of no value at all
it is not valid

as long as the person who has given the testament is alive.
the testator

Such an argument of the Apostle clearly opens up the allegorical interpretation of the Mosaic law. From this we see that everything in this law was promised and pre-figured in respect of Christ, and is to be fulfilled in Christ. Therefore, as is seen above, under the name of testament and promise, the death had been determined beforehand, of him who was to be very God and very man. For since he as God could not die but yet had promised that he would die (in that he had made a will and testament), it was necessary that he became man and thus fulfil what he had promised.

Let us therefore follow the argument of Chrysostom[1], who pur-

1 Chrysostom, Migne, 63.123.

sues the symbolic interpretation of both testaments. He says, first, a testament is made round about the last days of one's life. Secondly, such a testimony makes heirs of some and excludes others. Thirdly, a testament has precise conditions laid down which are binding on the testator and the beneficiaries: certain things they receive, certain things they must do. Fourthly, a testament must have witnesses.

The last three points we shall look at in their turn. Chrysostom assumes that the first point is known by everybody, that is that Christ made his testament just before his death. All the evangelists are unanimous in their tradition that at the Last Supper Christ blessed the chalice, gave it to his disciples and said: "This chalice is the New Testament in my blood" (I Cor. 11:25; Luke 22:20; Matt. 26:28; Mark 14:24). But in fact Chrysostom also touches upon, although somewhat briefly, what Christ in his testament meant us to receive, and what really had been the most important thing of all to be transacted. Therefore it should be known that he promised and bequeathed in a most faithful testament inestimable good things, and they were remission of sins and eternal life. For thus he said in Luke 22:20, "This is my blood which is shed for you." Mark adds, ". . . for many," but the clearest of all is Matthew, "For this is my blood of the new covenant, which is shed for many for the remission of sins. But I say unto you, I will not drink henceforth of this fruit of the vine until that day when I drink it new with you in my Father's kingdom" (Matt. 26:28 ff.). With these most precious words he bequeathed to us not the riches or glory of the world, but once for all and at one stroke all good things, that is, as I said, remission of sins and the possession of the future kingdom. As he also says in Luke 22:29, "And I appoint unto you a kingdom" (he says "appoint" not "will appoint," because it is customary to use the present tense in wills and testaments), "as my Father hath allotted a kingdom to me so I allot to you a place to eat and drink at my table in my kingdom." These are those precious and inestimable good things of which Peter speaks, "See how all the gifts that make for life and holiness in us derive from his divine power. They are given through a fuller knowledge of him who calls us by his own glorious perfection. Through him God has bestowed on us precious and wondrous promises, so that through them ye may become partakers of the divine nature leaving the corruption of the world and its passions behind" (II Peter 1:3).

Returning to the other points Chrysostom makes. First: he did not bequeath to all because "he disinherited certain ones." As John 17:9 says, "I pray for them, not for the world." Or the same,

"Neither pray I for these alone, but for them also which shall believe in me through their word" (John 17:20). The same thing, too, in that he did not say that his blood was shed for all but for many (Mark 14:24; Matt. 26:28). Also in this passage under discussion "that . . . they which are called might receive the promise of eternal inheritance" (Heb. 9:15). But this touches upon the subject of predestination, a subject at once too difficult and too unyielding for our feeble intellect to grasp. Speaking most reservedly for that very reason, it can be said that he gave the inheritance only to those who fear his name and believe in him, as John 1:12 says, "He gave them power to become the sons of God, those who believe in his name." And Ps. 25:14, "The Lord is a stay to them that fear him, and he reveals his testament to them," where in the Hebrew it is said to have, "The secret of the Lord is with them that fear him."

Secondly, the matter of witnesses. The witnesses of this testament are the Holy Spirit itself and the apostles. It is expressed in John 15:26 f., "The spirit of truth which proceedeth from the Father, he shall testify of me, and ye also shall bear witness because ye have been with me from the beginning." For that reason the disciples said in Acts 3:15, ". . . whereof we are witnesses." And he himself said in Acts 1:8, ". . . and ye shall be my witnesses in Jerusalem, and in all Judaea, and Samaria, and the uttermost part of the earth."

Thirdly, he also gave expressions to what they who are the beneficiaries of the testament are to do. He said, "This do in remembrance of me" (Luke 22:19; I Cor. 11:24), that is, as the Apostle says, proclaim his death (I Cor. 11:26), and preach penitence and remission of sins and eternal life. Then shall they receive the grace bequeathed in the testament not unprofitably, but shall use it in the struggle against sin. For thus he said, "This is my commandment, that ye love one another," and all the other things he gave them in the most superb discourses of John 12–18 on the bearing of persecution, on love and on peace. Now these are the realities which are signified by the figures and types of the Old Testament, where people were purified by the blood of calves unto the remission of ritual sins, and were thus made clean, and continued worthy possessors of the good things of the promised land.

9:18. **Wherefore neither the first testament**   given by God through Moses

For even the Old Testament was also a testament of God. It was not, however, established by his own death, because he commanded animals to be sacrificed in his place, and in the meantime, "in his forbearance" as the Apostle says in Rom. 3:25, he accepted the death and sacrifice of animals in the stead of his own death.

was dedicated without blood.   established, confirmed

9:19. For when Moses had spoken   as it is written in Ex. 24
every precept of the law to all the people   directed to (*ad*) all the people

he took   Moses took
the blood of calves and goats with water and scarlet wool and hyssop and sprinkled

which was a type of the sprinkling of faith
both the book   of the law of Moses

For he commanded as his testament the observance of ceremonies and the promise of temporal blessings, which were all a type of things to come

and all the people.

9:20. Saying, this is the blood of the covenant which God has commanded you

Here again the Apostle records certain things which are not to be read in the books of Moses. On this basis, the argument of those who would not attribute this epistle to Paul was established. These things are not actually written by Moses in Exodus 24. Only this is found: "And he took the book of the covenant, and read in the audience of the people. And they said, All that the Lord hath said will we do, and we shall be obedient. And Moses took the blood and sprinkled it on the people, and said, This is the blood of the covenant which the Lord hath made with you concerning all these words" (Ex. 24:7 f.). He says nothing about wool, hyssop, water, the blood of goats, the book, the tabernacle and the pot.

9:21. The tabernacle, too, and all the requisites of

the ministry   requisites of worship, and
                                    for the sacrifices.
he sprinkled in the same
way with the blood.

9:22. And almost all things
  He limits his statement by the word "almost," because some
things are purified by fire, and some in water

are cleansed by blood
according to the law,
and without the shedding
of blood   as has been said there were
                                    other sins too, for which
                                    blood was not always shed
there is no remission   of sins
9:23. It was therefore
necessary   the necessity arose from
                                    having to fulfil the
                                    requirements of the law. It
                                    did not arise from the need
                                    for cleansing, for this need
                                    never in fact existed
that the patterns
themselves   the shadows and signs: to
                                    be precise, the very bodies,
                                    clothes and vessels we have
                                    been discussing
of the heavenly world   the spiritual world, the
                                    world of the conscience and
                                    the soul
should be cleansed
with these   by these things, or by these
                                    ritual acts
but the heavenly things
themselves should be
cleansed with better
sacrifices than these   souls had to be purified by
                                    the blood of Christ offered
                                    through the Spirit.

Chrysostom asks[1]: "But what things does he call 'heavenly
things'? Heaven? Angels? Nothing of the kind! Heaven is those
things which are going on all around us. The things therefore

1 Migne, 63.343.

which are ours are in heaven, and the things that we are experiencing now are heavenly, even though they take place on earth." In that these things are possible then it follows, "To be on earth and yet not to be on earth, [i.e., to be in heaven whilst on earth], comes to pass in a certain way and of one's own volition." "If we draw near to God, we are in fact in heaven. For why should I be anxious about heaven, since I behold the God of heaven now, and since I am brought to heaven now?" As Christ said, "We will come unto him and make our abode with him" (John 14:23). So much for Chrysostom.

Therefore, to be heavenly is to have an affection for heavenly things and to know divine things, as it is written in Col. 3:2 f., "Set your affection on things above not on things on the earth. For ye are dead and your life is hid with Christ in God." The same in Phil. 3:20, "Our conversation is in heaven." The same in I Cor. 15:47 ff.: "The first man is of the earth, earthy; the second man is from heaven and is heavenly. The nature of that earth-born man is shared by his earthly sons: the nature of the heaven-born man by his heavenly sons. Therefore, as we have borne the image of the earth-born man, we shall yet bear the image of the heaven-born man." The same is found again in II Cor. 3:18: "But all of us with faces unveiled glimpse the glory of the Lord as in a mirror, and are transfigured into the same likeness taking glory from that glory, as the spirit of the Lord enables us." Throughout the Old Testament the heavens are described in this way, e.g., "The heavens tell the glory of God" (Ps. 19:1), "Drop down ye heavens from above, and let the skies pour down righteousness" (Isa. 45:8).

In brief, to be heavenly is to despise the things that are seen and even the imaginations arising from them, and to cleave to God alone, to the divine good. That means to hold to the will of God in prosperity and adversity, throughout life and unto death. To be earthly means to despise the things not seen, i.e., the divine will, and to cling to the things that are seen having a taste for the prosperity the world affords. Therefore Christ everywhere witnesses that he does the will of his Father, and teaches others the same, "My meat is to do the will of my Father" (John 4:34). To cleave to God is to be deprived of the world and all creaturely blessings, as to carry the image of Christ is to live by the affection and example of Christ. "He who says that he loves God and does not keep his commandments is a liar" (I John 2:4). But all these divine blessings, since they are invisible, incomprehensible and utterly hidden, the natural man cannot attain to or love, unless he is raised to them by the grace of God. For the same reason it also comes about that the spiritual man can be judged, known and seen by nobody, not even himself, because he dwells in the pro-found darkness of God. David taught this thoroughly, and testi-fied in Ps. 31:20, "Thou shalt hide them in the secret of thy presence" (that is, in hidden-ness, in Thy presence). This of course begins in this life, but is perfected in the life to come.

O what a great thing it is to be a Christian man! To have a hidden life! Hidden not in some cell like the hermits, nor in one's own heart, which is an unfathomable abyss, but in the invisible God himself. And thus, while living amidst the things of this world, feed on him who appears only in the despised sign of the word, and even there only as it is heard. As Christ says, "Not by bread alone doth man live, but by every word ... (Matt. 4:4)." The bride in the Canticles says the same thing, "I am asleep (because she is not regarding the things that are seen), yet my heart is awake" (Cant. 5:2).

On the other hand, those who mind earthly things are very much awake, but their heart is asleep. In this sense it is clear why the faithful in Christ are most properly called heavenly, because if the soul is to be found where it loves rather than where it lives[1], and if it is the nature of love to change the one who loves into the one he loves[2], so is it true that those who love heaven and God are, and may rightly be called, heavenly and divine, though not because they are heavenly by nature or in a metaphysical sense. Otherwise, there would be nothing heavenly apart from heavenly bodies, for even the demons would be heavenly, and certainly all the souls of men as well, since they are of a certain heavenly nature, at any rate they are not corporeal.

9:24. **For the sanctuary Jesus has entered is not one made by human hands, it is not some adumbration of the truth; he has entered heaven itself**	sign heavenly truth very divinity, which dwells in a darkness other than the sanctuary, that is, in light inaccessible

[1] Bernard of Clairvaux, *de praecepto et dispensatione*, XX, 60. See the remarks and references Hirsch-Rückert, *ad. loc.*
[2] Augustine, *De Trin.*, VIII, 10, 14; Migne, 42.960, and also *Sermo* 121, 1; Migne, 38.678.
  Similarly Gerson.
  See references Hirsch-Rückert, *ad. loc.*

where he now appears	as the perfect and faithful priest
in God's sight	that means in his unrestricted presence, without the intervention of a veil
on our behalf	for us sinners, but who are nevertheless men of faith

For Christ to have ascended profits us nothing, if he ascended for his own sake. But now our glory and joy is in this, that he went there to our advantage not to our disadvantage. This makes sense of the text in Eccl. 9:1, "A man does not know whether he deserves the hatred or the love of God, because the future is held in uncertainty."

It is commonly said some know Christ speculatively, others practically: the former believe that Christ appears before the face of God for others, the latter that Christ appeared before the face of God for us. That is why a Christian should be certain that it is for him Christ appeared and is a priest before God. For as he believes, so does it happen to him. For this reason it says in Mark 11:23: "Whosoever shall not doubt in his heart but shall believe that those things he saith shall come to pass, shall have whatsoever he saith. Therefore, I say unto you, What things soever ye desire, when ye pray, believe that ye receive them, and ye shall have them." In Matt. 8:13 Jesus says to the centurion: "Go thy way, and as thou hast believed, so be it done unto thee." The same in James 1:6: "But let him ask in faith, nothing wavering. For he that wavereth is like a wave of the sea driven with the wind and tossed. For let not that man think that he shall receive anything of the Lord." That is why the opinion of those who quote Eccl. 9:1 f. must be regarded with the greatest care and caution. They quote, "No man knows whether he is worthy of hate or love," and apply it to the state of the present moment, and in this way make a man uncertain of the mercy of God and the confidence of salvation. This is to turn Christ and our faith in him absolutely upside down. For Ecclesiastes is not speaking of the present time but of our perseverance and that future state of which nobody is certain. As the Apostle says: "Let him that thinketh he standeth take heed lest he fall" (I Cor. 10:12). And in Rom. 11:20; "Thou standest by faith: be not highminded (i.e. do not boast) but fear." This is sufficiently clear even from the text of Ecclesiastes, for the writer says: "The righteous and their works are in the hand of God, and no man knoweth whether he has earned the love or hate of God, but all things are laid up in an uncertain future (Eccl. 9:1 f.)."

Accordingly, those who condemn their own prayers and strivings, and fling them away as of dubious value, do err most grievously. For that is against the Apostle when he says: "I therefore so run not as uncertainly, so fight I (that means fight in battle and strike in conflicts) not as one beating the air." Therefore Bernard advises[1] his brethren in his sermons on the Canticles in no way to despise their own prayers, but to believe before they are fulfilled, that they are written; indeed have been already written in heaven, and that they should certainly expect of their prayers either that they have been heard and will be fulfilled in their own good time, or that it is better for them not to be fulfilled.

There are two questions here, First, in what way the saints under the old law were justified. Here the Apostle denies that these men were holy, righteous and perfect by means of the law. Yet at the same time he is certain that their works done in obedience to the law were meritorious. Indeed many like Zachariah and Elizabeth (Luke 1:6) and others were blameless by reason of these works of the law. The answer to what has just been said is easy. To those who lived by faith, their works were good and meritorious, that is they were keeping the inner meaning of the law spiritually at the same time as they were keeping the letter of the law outwardly. As in Rom. 2:25, "Circumcision verily profiteth, if thou keep the law," yet it is of no profit unless thou keepest the law.

What then does this statement mean: the keeping of the law profits nothing, unless you keep the law and the keeping of the law is of profit if you keep the law? Nothing else than this that the external ceremonies are thus commanded, not because there is salvation in them as such, but only in so far as they provide an occasion to exercise faith and love and also a practical method of bringing pressure on sinners. When however they begin to be cultivated with another end in view, and used with a different intention, as happens in the case of hypocrites, then they are to be abrogated and cleared away without further ado.

It could be very rightly said that the same thing applies in the matter of ecclesiastical ceremonies today. Tonsures, splendid apparel and various ceremonial processions are profitable, I suppose, "if thou keepest the law"; that is, the keeping of the laws of the Church is profitable, if in doing them you keep the law of God. In other words, if it means you fulfil God's law better and sin less. But if you depend on these alone, already "thy circumcision is

---

1 All the editors remind us that it is not in his sermons on the Canticles but in his fifth sermon on Quadragesima when he was preaching on the three modes of prayer, Migne, 183.823.
Hirsch-Rückert provide a long excerpt, ad. loc.

made uncircumcision" (Rom. 2:25), that is, the observing of the law has become the transgression of the law. For the same reason Paul says, "Thou that makest thy boast of the law, wilt thou break the law to God's dishonour?" (Rom. 2:23).

In the light of this we may judge those remarks of the Master of the Sentences for which he is reprehended by everybody, when in Book Four[1] he teaches that the works of the old law were of no profit, even if they were done in faith and charity. If he understood it to mean that they contributed nothing of their own to grace and merit, he understood it perfectly well, because nothing external helps the soul at all. If however he implied that for those who were in faith, their works were meritorious and pleasing to God, which could not possibly be, he failed absolutely, because all things work together for good to the saints (Rom. 8:28), and all the ways of the righteous are mercy and truth[2]. For it is impossible for him who stands in the grace of God to do anything else than a good work. That is exactly what is said in I John 5:18: "He who is born of God does not sin."

The second question is this: How is it that even now our sacrifice does not cease, since we have been perfected and justified by the grace of baptism and repentance? For every day Christ is offered on our behalf. To which Chrysostom replies[3]: "We do indeed sacrifice, but for the remembrance of his death, and this is the one sacrifice and oblation." Which I understand this way: Christ was sacrificed only once, as is maintained in the preceding chapter[4]. What however is offered by us every day is not so much a sacrifice as a memorial of that sacrifice, as he said: "This do in remembrance of me" (Luke 22:19; I Cor. 11:24 f.). For Christ does not suffer as often as it is remembered that he suffered. It is much more necessary, however, that this memorial be repeated than the earlier memorial, when it was commanded that the memorial of the Passover of the Lord and the flight from Egypt must be repeated.

Then, as far as the Head of the Church which is Christ is concerned, this sacrifice of the New Testament has been perfected and absolutely ended. However, the spiritual sacrifice of his body the Church is offered from day to day in that it continually dies with Christ and celebrates its passover mystically. This means that the

---

[1] Peter Lombard, *Sent.*, IV, dist. 1, cap. 4. Cf. remarks on 9:4, p. 157.
[2] The actual text of Ps. 25:10 has "the Lord" and not "the righteous" but in his exposition of the passage in *WA*, 3, 144.8 Luther explains that all the ways of the Lord are those ways in which his own walk. See also *WA*, 3, 529.33.
[3] Migne, 63.349.
[4] Actually the same chapter, on 9:26, but in some editions the section 216.20–218.15 prefaces the Scholia to Chapter X.

Church, mortifying the lusts of the flesh, crosses over out of this world towards its future glory. He makes a beautiful distinction between the two kinds of sacrifice [that is of the Old Testament and the New], when he says that in the sacrifices of the law a remembrance of sins used to be made, but in our sacrifice there was and is made a remembrance of the remission of sins through the word which says, "Father, forgive them" (Luke 23:34). And, "It is finished" (John 19:30). Also, "which was shed for you for the remission of sins" (Matt. 26:28; Luke 22:20). In the former covenant the knowledge of sins abides and increases: in the latter, it passes away and diminishes.

9:25. Nor

that means that Christ did not enter heaven in the same way the high priest enters the sanctuary every year

does he make a repeated offering of himself, as the high priest

the high priest of the law, the figure of the true

when he enters the sanctuary

the one made by hands

makes an offering every year of the blood that is not his own

but Christ offered his own blood. For, says Chrysostom, he himself is priest, sacrifice and victim.

9:26. If that were so

if every year he had to sacrifice himself

he must have suffered again and again from the beginning of the world

For the same person is the priest of all those who are to be saved from the beginning of the world to its end. If, therefore, it were held on the ground of the usage of the law, that he should sacrifice himself every year, then he would have had to have done so in the first year of creation and every year thereafter, and it would have been necessary for Christ to "suffer frequently" (Nicholas of Lyra).

but as it is he has appeared

the priest has gone to God

once for all at the consummation of the age	that is at the moment when the world is beginning to decline towards its end
for the purpose of destroying sin	this work neither the natural man nor the law could bring about, but only the death of Christ by means of faith
by his sacrifice	

All these words commend Christ to us in a most winning manner: that he should be preached to us not as the avenger of sins nor as our judge, but primarily as our priest, as the destroyer of sin, the author of righteousness and salvation. And there is one further point, which consoles troubled consciences still more. He is described not as being present beside us but as standing in the presence of God, the place where our greatest need exists, for it is the place where we stand most gravely accused and guilty.

9:27. And in that it is ordained for men	as any other man dies but once, so ought Christ to die but once
to die once for all	even though they deserve to die many deaths on account of their many sins
and after this there remains only the judgment	eternal judgment
9:28. So Christ as well	though he bore an infinite number of sins
was sacrificed once for all to take away completely	to bring to an end, so that they existed no longer
the sins of many	

This word "many" may be understood in two ways. Either, that he did not take away the sins of all, as Chrysostom says, "Not all believe"; or, in the sense of Rom. 5:18, where "many" means "all," when he says, ". . . through one act of righteousness he brought to all men justification, that is life." In other words "to all men" is the same as "to many."

**for a second time he
shall appear bringing
salvation to all**   even to us
**who are waiting for
his coming**   all who love his appearing
(II Tim. 4:8).

and sin shall be no more.

Chapter Ten

Gl. 54:11.

Contents of chapter ten:

The Apostle again shows the weakness of the old law, repeating the same matter over and over again and hammering it home. He set himself the task of teaching the simple and the uneducated, as well as those who obstinately clung to the righteousnesses of the law.

10:1. What the law contains is but a shadow	Cf. 8:5, "Which serves for a shadow and an example . . ."
of good things to come	remission of sins and grace
and not the full expression of these things.	the full truth.
It can never	the law by means of its sacrifices can never
by means of these sacrifices	repeated and still insufficient
which they offered year by year	never omitting a year
make those who come to them	those who minister and those who sacrifice.
perfect	cleansed and capable of doing good works in the future as a consequence
10:2. If they could	if the sacrifices had made

189

them perfect, for the only
reason for offering them
was to take away sin

**would they not have
ceased being made
by now?**

The worshippers   those making this kind of
sacrifice

**would have no conscience
of guilt left:**   that would in fact be a
contradiction in terms

**they would have been
cleansed once for all**   by some single sacrifice.

10:3. But in those   sacrifices
there is a remembrance   not however an answer to
sin, nor the purging away
of it

**again made of sins
every year.**   as in the feast of the
Atonement

Herein lies the strength of the law. It reminds us that we
are sinners and shows us the nature of sin. The strength of
grace, on the other hand, is to consign sin to oblivion: in
other words, to purge it utterly away.

10:4. For it is impossible   in the first place because
God has ordained it in this
way, and in the second
place because the nature of
sin demands it

that the blood of bulls and goats
for a better sacrifice is
demanded, as it has been
argued in the preceding
chapter 9:12 ff.

should take away sins

**10:5. Wherefore, when he
cometh**   Christ in the incarnation
**into the world he saith
sacrifice**
which was a kind of
perpetual sacrifice

and offering

thou didst not want,

as they were given in response
to a vow and were arbitrary

This word "thou didst not want" signifies something more
than the will: it connotes choice and love. Thus, Isa. 1:11,
"To what purpose is the multitude of your sacrifices unto
me?" And Mic. 6:6, "What shall I offer to the Lord for my
sin? Will he be pleased with thousands of rams?"
The same is clearly expressed in Ps. 50:8, "I will not
reprove thee for thy sacrifices, thy burnt offerings are continually before me."

but a body

**hast thou prepared
for me.**

meaning that instead of all
these sacrifices, a body is
offered in some unique way.

perfected

**10:6. In whole burnt
offerings
and in sacrifices
for sin**

thou hast no pleasure.

that is, in thousands of rams

that is expiatory sacrifices,
which were offered on
account of sin

thou hast not demanded.

**10:7. Then I said,
behold I come:**

**in the chief point of
the book**

that is in the flesh. The
victim intended from the
beginning.

taken rather in the sense as
the theme and purpose of
the book of the law of Moses.
[Luther expounds this idea
below, p. 192.]

it is written concerning me

See John 5:46: "If they believed Moses, then they would
have believed me also. For it was concerning me that he
wrote." On the same: "Ye search the scriptures because ye
think that in them ye have eternal life; and these are they
which bear witness of me" (John 5:39).

to do

thy will, O God.

To yield obedience to God
alone

In performing this obedience

thou willest that I should be
sacrificed for the remission
of sins.

Before we go into details, we shall look at the words in their
proper order in the Hebrew text: "Sacrifice" (*sacrificium*. The
Septuagint has *hostia* and Jerome has *victima*.) "and offering thou
hast not wanted," "ears however hast thou perfected for me."
(The Septuagint has, "but a body hast thou prepared for me,"
and Jerome has, "ears however hast thou opened up for me.") "In
burnt offerings and sacrifices for sin hast thou had no pleasure.
Then said I, Lo, I come, in the volume of the book it is written of
me, I have desired to do thy will, O God, and thy law is deep in
my heart." Emphasis and the raising of the voice must be observed
in the phrase "it is written of me," and also in the word " I wanted
or desired." In fact the whole of the last two verses should be read
with emphasis, so that the meaning is: Away with cattle! It is I, I,
who am written about and desired! It is concerning me that it is
written in the volume of the book! That is the meaning of the
words, "Behold I come!" And while others are contumacious,
loathe to hear and are unwilling to speak, I have thy law in the
depths of my heart, that is in the deepest desire of the heart. In
short, I love thy law perfectly, though it is hateful to others.

To understand this better it is worth reminding ourselves that
in Hebrew certain words are neuter and nominal (they have their
etymological origin in substantives), and that the best way to
understand them is to reduce them to their root word. Take, for
example, this word *volui*, I have wanted, or have willed. It may
mean to will something or to be willing. Or again in Ps. 118:25,
"Give me deliverance, O Lord." In Hebrew this is "Hosannah!",
that is "Save!" In other words, Be the saviour! or, Make salvation! This is beautifully recognized in St. Matthew's gospel where
it says, "Hosannah to the Son of David!", that is, give salvation in
this Christ, the Son of David" (Matt. 21:9). The same in Ps. 22:31
where we read , ". . . (they shall declare his righteousness) unto a
people that shall be born, whom the Lord made." The Hebrew
expresses it by saying "because the Lord made this people." In
short, the Lord is the maker who creates all things in all people,
but we ourselves effect nothing. Thus the Blessed Virgin says in
Luke 1:49: "He has done great things for me, he that is mighty."
This means that he is all-powerful. He worketh all things.

That phrase "in the chief point of the book[1]" (Heb. 10:7 =

---

[1] *In capite libri*. Luther often uses this phrase to mean the central idea or main
purpose of the Bible. This seems to be his meaning here, when he proceeds to
discuss the head of the Bible as Christ and the tail as Moses.

Ps. 40:8), which has been a source of great difficulty to many commentators, is clearly understood if referred to the Hebrew text, which says "in the volume of the book." This text expresses something still more important: the things written in the Scriptures were written about Christ and are to be fulfilled in Christ. Unless anybody were to understand "volume" (*volumen*) in a mystical sense as the veil of the law to harmonize the various translations. He would then take the Septuagint's "chief point of the book " as the mystical sense and the Hebrew text's "volume of the book" in the external, literal sense. This then would make the literal sense the tail of the law, or its hinderparts. For in such a way commentators usually harmonize the different translations. It would seem that it is pre-figured in Ex. 4:4, where Moses is commanded to take up the tail of the rod turned serpent. Likewise in Gen. 47:31, where Jacob prayed on the end of his staff. Or again in Esther 5:2 [where Esther touches the top of the sceptre]. There is no doubt that by the rod the law is signified. If, therefore, "the head of the law," "the end of the law," as the Apostle says, "the summit of the law" is Christ, then indeed the tail of the law, the hinderparts of the law, the letter itself, represents Moses. Thus the Book of Wisdom says, "When thou art twice asked, let thy reply be the pith of the matter." Ecclus 32:7–8 [not literal].

There still remains the problem of how the text "Ears hast thou prepared for me" can be harmonized with "A body hast thou prepared for me." The Hebrew word has many meanings, such as "to fit," "to make ready," "to set in order," even "to dig out" or "to open up," or even "to gain" or "get." Thus the Septuagint, following the first meaning says "body," instead of "ears." (It is the same in the Hebrew text, where the word "body" does not occur.) Wherefore the Apostle follows this reading in this case, and understands "the body that has been prepared" to mean "the body of Christ," and that this body was to be sacrified for sin instead of the bodies of animals. He develops this argument in his Epistle, and takes the meaning of the phrase "the body that has been prepared" to be "the body of Christ," and that this body was to be sacrified for sin instead of the bodies of animals, as is developed in the text. But the Hebrew expression means something different. For "to dig out" or "open up the ears" is nothing else than making a man hear, just as the earth is opened up or dug out. It says the same thing in Mark 7:34 f.: "Ephphatha! Be opened!" And it follows: "And his ears were opened." This phrase "to open," however, means to make a man obedient and believing. For faith is obedience, as it says in Romans 1:5: ". . . for obedience to the faith." Then it would mean that in the New Testament, nay rather at all times, sacrifices of animals are not pleasing to God, only the offering of faith in obedience. As Jeremiah says: "Lord thine eyes regard faith" (Jer. 5:3) (Vulg.). Therefore, the whole interpretation of Scripture leads to but one conclusion, that we hear the voice of God. In other words, that we believe. For he who believes will be saved. (Cf. Mark 16:16.)

The phrase, however: "Thou hast opened up my ears for me" may be taken in an active or a passive sense. Active, in this way: "Thou hast opened up my ears for me," that is, thou hast made me obedient to thee. This sense is rather forced. Passive, in this way: "Thou hast opened up my ears for me," that is, thou hast so worked things that people believe me and have faith in me. Consequently, it is through me and not through animals that remission of sins and salvation is effected to those who believe in me. And this is the sacrifice which is well-pleasing to God, namely, faith in Christ. As it says in Matt. 17:5: "This is my beloved son, in whom I am well pleased. Hear ye him!" Or again in Gen. 49:10 where our text has, "it is he who is the hope of the nations." Others read, "And unto him will the nations listen, and for him will they gather themselves together." As if to say, To him will the ears of the nations be opened, and in him will they believe. For nobody can hear Christ unless the Father digs out and opens up his ears. This is what Christ means when he says, "No man can come to me, except the Father which sent me draw him" (John 6:44). Therefore, what the Septuagint said concerning Christ's real body, this the Hebrew text said concerning the mystical body of Christ by the words: "the opening up of the ears" (of the Church). Therefore, both terms mean the one and the same mystical body, which is continually offered up with Christ. Both interpretations mean the same thing, and so it becomes clear that all three meanings of the Hebrew can have but one sense, and could be combined in the following way: Thou hast made ready, or thou hast dug, or thou hast obtained ears for me; or alternatively: "thou hast made ready, or thou hast dug, or thou hast obtained my mystical body, and this mystical body has been made ready, or dug, or obtained by virtue of our body having been offered to him and prepared for him.

But a peculiar power and emphasis lie in the use of this word "ears." In the new law all those endless ceremonial burdens, which are merely occasions for sin, have been taken away. God no longer requires feet, hands, or any other member, only the ears. To this extent everything is restored to a simple rule of life. For if you ask a Christian what the work is by which he is made worthy of the name of Christian, he can given no other answer than hearing the word of God, which is faith. Thus the ears alone are the organs of a Christian man, because not by the works of any other member but by faith is he justified and judged a Christian.

Gl. 58:15. He has come to the end of his epistle and completed his argument on the exhortation and commendation of faith: he now adds to this his teaching on good works. This is the familiar technique of the Apostle. First he teaches and then he exhorts: first he brings men to faith and then he directs them to ethics.

10:19. Having, therefore, brethren, boldness   freedom, confidence
to enter the
sanctuary   of entering into holy things
by the blood of
Christ   through faith in the blood of Christ

10:20. Which he opened up   consecrated, to be precise by crossing over before us
for us,
by a new

The "old way" is the way of sin, and to that extent is the way of death, as well. The "new way" is the way of righteousness and in the same way therefore is the way of life. For instance, in Rom. 5:17: "For if by the trespass of one man, death began its reign through one man, how much more shall they who receive the abundance of grace, the gift of justification, enjoy a reign of life through one man, Jesus Christ?"

and living way   a way of life and salvation

Romans 6:4 expounds this point more clearly. Just as Christ rose from the dead by the glory of the Father, in the same way we too shall walk in newness of life.

through the veil,
that is his flesh,   In short, he himself went through the experience of the flesh, making a way for us through the same.

10:21. And having a
great high priest   who intercedes on our behalf
over the house of God   from where he began on high
10:22. Let us draw near   for the purpose of entering the holy of holies

with a true heart	that means, in truth because without faith and without the Word of God there is no approach to God
in full assurance	in certainty
of faith	for it is faith which makes "the true heart"
having our hearts sprinkled	not so much our bodies and our clothes
and our bodies washed	baptized
with pure water	sanctified by faith in Christ.

Further, he expounds at the same time the meaning of the figurative types of the old ceremonial cleansings.

By this rather difficult text (10:9 ff.), although in reality it is a very rich text and carries a wealth of meaning, the Apostle only wants us to imitate Christ, who suffered and by dying crossed over to the glory of the Father. He means the same as he wrote in Col. 3:3: "For ye are dead with Christ, and your life is hid with Christ in God." But it must be noticed with what gracious words and with what power the Apostle draws this out. First, the well-known veil of the Temple was figuratively a sign of the flesh of Christ, as the Apostle plainly shows here. The removal of the veil by the priest going through it signifies the death of the flesh of Christ by which he was taken from us and entered the invisible holy of holies. This famous course or entry of the priest after the manner of the ancients was old and dead, and signifies that the way Christ followed and his method of entering through the veil are the "new and living way." And thus Christ has fulfilled the type and put an end to the shadow. In fact all these words show at one and the same time the figure of truth and its fulfilment, for he implies both meanings beautifully at one and the same time, and handles both ideas in the same words by a *double entendre*.

Furthermore, it is a sacramental sign of the *imitatio Christi*. In other words, the flesh which he adopted signifies the weaknesses of our flesh. These we have taken on through sin. By these it comes about that we walk the old and dead road, that is in following the lusts of the flesh. Therefore, a "new and living way" had to be prepared to destroy the lusts of the flesh. In this sense, the passion of Christ's flesh, his death and exaltation are a divine sign (*sacramentum*) of our having to die the same death. And now, Christ's entry into heaven through death is God's sign for us also of a "new and living way," by which we seek and love heavenly things only, having in fact entered into things heavenly with all our heart, so that in line with the Apostle we may say of ourselves, "our citizenship is in heaven" (Phil. 3:20). Throughout almost all his epistles Paul is full of the passion of Christ, which he interprets in a mystical and practical way, e.g., Rom. 6:4, 8:10; Eph. 4:22 f.; Col. 3:3; Phil. 3:10 f. He also teaches everywhere the mortifying of the old man and the renewal of the inward man.

Therefore, a simple statement of what Christ did according to the flesh only, has for us a double significance. For he did not at some time or another pass over from a state of sin in the same way as we do, but he always was in heaven and is there now, as it says in John 3:13: "No one ascended up to heaven except the son of man who is in heaven." As Augustine says, "For we cross in flesh and spirit, but Christ went over in the flesh only[1]." Therefore, he is the prefiguration of the crossing over of our flesh, because we shall be like him (I John 3:2). On the other hand, by the crossing of the flesh is signified, as a kind of sacrament, the crossing over of the spirit. Hence arise those various views of life and death, if I may say so. The life and death we now experience is a vale of testing, in which two different kinds of life and two different kinds of death fight one another, so that if love lives, lust dies, and this is to live to God and die to the world. If lust lives, love dies, and this is to live to the world and die to God. For one or other must die and leave the other living. And these two are called spirit and flesh. For in addition to the life of the body and the death of the body there are two sorts of life and two sorts of death, the death of the flesh and the death of the spirit, the life of the flesh and the life of the spirit, and the Apostle speaks frequently about these.

The Apostle challenges us, however, with a kind of double invitation to enter into this new life. For it is a difficult and desperately hard thing, especially for the inexperienced, to offer everything for Christ and even lay down life itself. Therefore, the Apostle first sets down the example of Christ, our leader who has gone ahead, who, though he himself had no need, yet to give us confidence he was the first of all to cross over, and make this desperate road smooth. But he not only gave us an example, he also reaches out his hand to those following. For that reason he says: "We have boldness to enter" (10:19), because he himself initiated that way for us (10:20) and is at the same time our high priest who having known the feeling of our infirmities (4:15) is able to succour them that are tempted (2:18). And so there is no excuse for anybody holding back, since he cannot do more for us than he is already doing.

[1] Augustine, *De Trin.*; Migne, 42.889 f.

For others as well can teach and exhort a crossing over of such a kind, but in this case it is Christ alone who is not only the companion but is the leader of the way; not only the leader but the helper, nay rather the one who carries us over. As it says in Deut. 32:11: "As an eagle provoking its young to fly, now hovering over them now spreading forth her wings, takes them and carries them on her shoulders." Thus, he who feeds on Christ by faith is carried on the shoulders of Christ. This man will cross over happily to the other side. As it is written of the bride in Cant. 8:5: "She comes up through the desert leaning upon her beloved."

10.24. Let us consider one another to provoke unto love and good works, not forsaking the assembling of ourselves together.

. . .[1] . . . since the Church of the present day consists of believers from all parts of the world, and many who are weak, impotent, imperfect and sinful are mixed up in it, as Christ says in John 12:8: "The poor ye will always have with you, but me ye will not always have."

But the natural man prefers to deal with the good and perfect people rather than with the imperfect and difficult. This fault has the following consequences. Those who are weaker become occasions for insolence, condemnation, judgment and the like at the hands of the more perfect; on the other hand the more perfect become, for those who are weaker, occasions of jealousy and disparagement. Therefore the Apostles studied with all their might to meet this evil, lest schisms and heresies should arise in the Church. These were prevented only by the love they had for one another. Moreover, a love which is shown to equals and betters as the occasion arises is no love at all, neither is it Christian love, as Christ expresses it in Matt. 5:43: "Ye have heard what was said by them of old time: thou shalt love thy neighbour and hate thine enemy. But I say unto you, love your enemies, do good to those who hate you, pray for those who persecute and insult you. . . For if you love those who love you, what reward have you? Do not even the publicans do as much?" Therefore only that is Christian love which is shown to the despised and those unworthy of love; only that is kindness which is proffered to the evil and the ungrateful. For it was in this way that Christ and God showed their love to us and after this same manner of his are we commanded to love. "Be ye therefore perfect, as your father in heaven is perfect" (Matt. 5:48).

[1] The main clause of the sentence seems lacking. Both Hirsch-Rückert and Vogelsang suggest this, and the former that it was possibly a statement comparing the early Church with the Church of the present day.

10:26. **For if we go on sinning wilfully after we have accepted the knowledge of the truth there remaineth no more a sacrifice for sin; there is nothing left but some terrible expectation of judgment, a jealous fire that will destroy everything in its path.**

Chrysostom[1] answers the Novatians[2] here and says: "Here we have again those who deny the chance of a second repentance. To them we say that in this place the Apostle precludes neither repentance nor propitiation which is effected by repentance," "but he does exclude a second baptism. For he did not say there is no further remission but there is no further sacrifice: we cannot have a second cross."

And this refutation made by Chrysostom can be strengthened by the text just discussed, "not forsaking the assembling of ourselves together" in which he seems to speak of those who forsake the Church, apart from which there is without doubt neither repentance nor remission of sins. The same thing is found in the text further on where he says: "Call to remembrance the former days in which after ye were enlightened ye went through a long probation of suffering . . ." (v. 26). Here he is clearly calling even those who had lapsed to repentance. And this is the very thing these people seem to deny. In truth, enough has been already said for men of peace and good-will. More texts from other passages of Scripture would have to be adduced to satisfy the contentious, but such we have adequately done in chapter six. What is quite certain is that all mortal sin is "the despising and treading underfoot of the Son of God," which the Apostle recalls here. The same thing is clearly proved in II Sam. 12:9, where it is said to David: "Why therefore hast thou despised the word of the Lord . . ."[3], for he had not sinned with respect to faith, but with respect to the fifth and sixth commandments.

[In the following paragraph the MS is damaged and the readings are not altogether clear. The last sentence is really an explanatory paraphrase. Ed.]

It can be said quite simply that these words are to be understood in the same way as those in the last chapter of the Epistle of James, (where in advising the congregation on their ministry to the sick and suffering he says: "Is there any one of you sad? Let him pray. Is one of you cheerful? Let him sing a psalm. Is one of you sick? Let him send for the presbyters of the Church, and let them pray

[1] Chrysostom, *loc. cit.*; Migne, 63.361. Not a literal quotation.
[2] Novatians. See comment on 6:6, p. 121 n.
[3] Note that Luther seems here to equate the Word of God and the Son of God.

over him anointing him with oil in the name of the Lord. And the prayer of faith will save him that is sick, and the Lord will relieve him; and if he has committed sins, they will be remitted.")

[Or Luther may be referring to James 5:19 f., where the same idea is developed: "My brethren, if any of you err from the truth" (cf. Heb. 10:26), "and someone brings him back, let him be sure of this, that he who makes a sinner turn back from the error of his way shall save a soul from his death and shall cover a multitude of sins."]

Or again, they may be taken in the same manner as the Apostle speaks of love in I Cor. 13, that it "never ceaseth, beareth all things, believeth all things, hopeth all things, endureth all things. Love never faileth." It is the same in the Apostle John, "He who is born of God, does not sin" (I John 3:9) and the like. It may be expressed the other way round, that apart from Christ a man can never repent. This means that just as a man in grace may do whatever he wants and yet cannot sin but abides in a state of grace, thus a man in a state of sin cannot do well. He may do whatever he likes but yet he still abides in his sins. And in this way is the status of both conditions expressed [the status of being in sin and the status of being in grace]. The author is not referring to the transition from one status to another [i.e., repentance].

10:37. Yet a little
while   left for the exercise of
                               patience
and he who is
to come   either for judgment, or
                               the destruction of the flesh

He quotes the authority of Habakkuk without naming him, because he presumes the prophecy is quite familiar to his readers. He does not alter the words, but changes their order. For Jerome translates Habakkuk in this way: "Though he tarry, wait for him: for he will most certainly come, he will not delay. Behold, he who will not believe, the soul that is in him shall be all wrong: for the just shall live by his faith." The Apostle follows the text of the Septuagint, in fact.

will come
he will not tarry   The negative form of the
                               expression is more powerful
                               than the affirmative.

10:38. But my righteous one
                               he who fulfils the precepts
                               of God
lives   will live

These are words of consolation necessary by reason of those who when they suffer fall by the wayside. For faith, by which I mean the life of a Christian man, is more the work of God than ours: it is in fact our deepest suffering. No man is cleansed save by trials and tribulations. "The more a man suffers and is oppressed, the better Christian he is[1]." The whole life of a Christian man exists in faith, that is in a cross and in suffering. Thus . . . of the law [There is a gap in the MS—Ed.]

by faith	he fulfils the will of God not by doing works but by faith
but if any man draw back	if he grows unbelieving and impatient.
my soul shall have no pleasure in him.	because the soul within him is all wrong.

[1] Luther gives this aphorism in German. *WA* quotes two other German proverbs *ad loc.*: The better the Christian, the greater the trouble and affliction; and also, The devouter the Christian, the heavier the cross.

CHAPTER ELEVEN

Gl. 61:15. The Apostle stirs his readers to faith. Up till now he has taught faith by his words, but he now begins to teach it by the example of the patriarchs. For in every kind of doctrinal matter the clearest way of teaching is, as the famous Varro says, the furnishing of examples. It seems however to certain scholars that "faith" is to be taken in this chapter in the sense of confidence rather than faith. But more about this further on.

11:1. Now faith gives substance to our hopes and gives us conviction on the things we cannot see. It was in this same way, by faith, that our fathers obtained proof.

Modern scholars[1] interpret these words of the Apostle in a number of ways. In the first place, some understand by "substance" (*substantia*) "the cause" (*causa*) or "foundation" (*fundamentum*). And of course it is perfectly true that faith is that foundation of the apostles and prophets upon which the Apostle writes that we are to be built (Eph. 2:20), and the foundation which has been laid (I Cor. 3:11). As even Christ himself said in Matt. 16:18: "Upon this rock I shall build my Church," that is, on the foundation of faith. But whether in fact *substantia* can be taken in this way in this context, we leave to others. They also want *argumentum* to have the connotation of "proof" or "conviction": it would then mean what in dialectics is called "argument," a kind of certainty of "the things we cannot see." I imagine of the kind the patriarchs and other holy men have had.

Now this view does not satisfy me. In the first place because it would follow from this that Adam and Abel had no faith, for they could not have received certainty of faith from others who had believed before them, since they were the first believers. In the

---

[1] By the expression "modern scholars" Luther means the scholars of the medieval period as distinct from the Fathers proper. In particular he is referring to the *Glossa Ordinaria* and to Lefèvre.

second place, because it seems to contain a contradiction within itself. For understood in this way faith would be nothing more nor less than a matter of credulity, the credulity of one persuaded and proved by the credulity of another. And the Apostle thus would not be writing about the faith of every man, but rather on a matter of persuasion, of talking somebody round to a particular view. Faith then is not to be conceived in active terms, in the sense of proving or proof, but in passive terms, in the sense of something proven or accepted. Those who take *argumentum* in the sense of conviction hold the same sort of view. The text: "Which of you convinceth (*arguere*) me of sin?" (John 8:46), they take as if faith should convince unbelief, either one's own or another's. But all these things are more appropriately spoken of the power of faith or its effect. In fact faith, wherever it is present, effects mortification and convinces unbelievers.

In the second place, Chrysostom in fact understands *substantia* as reality (*subsistentia, hypostasis*), even as essence (*essentia*). The Master of the Sentences[1] follows him, except that he takes argument as conviction (*convictio*) which Chrysostom takes as *conjunctio*, a connection of ideas. It could of course be that some manuscript was faulty[2], for *elenchos*, which the Apostle has in the Greek text, signifies argument, comprehension, indication.

If these "things hoped for" are conceived as being without substance, then faith provides them with substance. Or better still, it does not provide them with substance but is their very essence. As an example of this, our resurrection has not happened yet, nor does it exist in actuality (*in substantia*), but hope makes it live in our soul. This is what he means by substance (*substantia*). And again: "O what a wonderful word he used when he said, 'the argument or evidence (*convictio*) of things not seen'." For evidence is evidence only in the case of factual things actually seen. Faith, therefore, is the seeing (*visio*) of what he calls "things not seen."

Thirdly, we follow the general usage in the matter of this noun *substantia*. In the Scriptures it means almost throughout possession, or more properly possibility, as it does in the preceding chapter (Heb. 10:34). Or again in Luke 8:43: ". . . who had spent all her substance on doctors." And also in I John 3:17: "Whosoever hath this world's goods. . ." By the use of this word and by means of the passage under discussion he clearly differentiates "the substance of this world" from the substance not of this world but of another. Therefore, since faith is nothing else than adherence to the Word of God (as it says in Rom. 1:17), it follows that the

1 Peter Lombard, *Sent.* III, dist., 23.
2 The error goes back to *Mutianus Scholasticus*. Chrysostom has *èlenchos*.

possession of the Word of God, that is of eternal goods, is also at the same time a taking away of all present goods (at least in so far as the heart cleaves to them). As it says in Ps. 73:28: "It is good for me to cleave to God." The Hebrews based their substance in the goods of this world. The Apostle quite rightly recalls them, as a wise and faithful steward of his Lord, to that "better substance which is the finding of one's soul," as well as perhaps the goods of this world. He sought to loose them from the love of things temporal and transfer them to things eternal. Jerome follows this interpretation of *substantia* in his commentary on Galatians[1].

11:3. Through faith we understand that the worlds were framed by the Word of God: that it was from things unseen that the things we see originated.

In faith	that means by faith (following Erasmus), and not by reason
we understand	we recognize
that the worlds were framed	perfected
by the Word of God,	through the Word of God
that it was from things unseen	from the divine ideas, for the world was made out of nothing
that the things we see originated.	

In this context "things unseen" do not signify chaos or the primeval abundance of nature, from which commentators believed the world was founded, but rather what is described in Rom. 1:20: ". . . the invisible things of God are clearly understood through the things that are made." In the same way also the Apostle recalls Isa. 64:4 in I Cor. 2:9: "Eye hath not seen, nor ear heard, nor has it entered the heart of man, what things thou hast prepared for them that love thee." And the same in I. Cor. 2:10: ". . . for the Spirit searches all things, yea, the deep things of God." Even as the greatest part may rightly be said to affirm the utter simplicity of the unity of God, it is better by far to have a simple faith and have no knowledge of these things than to scrutinize these matters in a state of inquisitive speculation. Nor must this give the impression that when the Apostle says "from invisible things" (*ex invisibilibus*) that the preposition "*ex*" denotes material stuff out of which the Creation was made, for in this matter we

[1] Jerome, *Comm. Gal.*, Lib. III, cap. 5 on Gal. 5:22; Migne, 26.420.

approach the burning bush of divine Scripture, and like Moses "the shoes are to be taken off the feet" (Ex. 3:5). I leave to others what Wisdom 11:17 means: "Thine almighty hand created the world out of matter without form." The author of Wisdom has gone a long way towards "platonizing." It is said that Philo is the author, and in the nature of the case it is not of much authority.

11:4. **In faith**	by faith (previous verse) and not by works
Abel	
It was not the value of his gift that set him apart from his brethren, as the Jews and many others think, but faith	
offered to God a far superior sacrifice	more sacrifices (following Erasmus)
than Cain's, through which	by faith
he has proved thereby to be righteous	because he pleased God through faith, as it is recorded in the previous chapter (Heb. 10:38)
since God recognized his offering	at the time when God had respect for his offering, and God warmed to Abel
and by it	to the extent that he was shown a man who believed through his sacrifice
though he is dead, he yet speaketh.	Though he is dead, yet because of his sacrifice he still teaches us in the Scriptures.

"He who believeth in me, though he were dead, yet shall he live" (John 11:25).

The Apostle clearly determines here, that the worth and weight of a work are not commensurate with the size of the sacrifice or the total worth of the offering but that faith in the matter in hand is determinative, because God judges the spirit and looks to the motive of the heart. As it says in Ps. 7:9: "He loves the righteous and tries their hearts." And he says to Samuel in I Sam. 16:7: "A man sees what is before his eyes, but God looks on the heart."

Therefore, he requires nothing from a man except the heart. It says in Prov. 23:26: "My son, give me thine heart," not the tongue or the hand. That is why in Ps. 18:20 when he said: "Let him reward me according to the works of my hands . . ." he immediately added to safeguard the spiritual truths, ". . . according to the cleanness of my hands in his sight." (v. 24), lest it seem that he taught the purity of works without purity of heart, since: "in God's sight" the hands cannot be pure unless the heart is pure. Therefore, in Isa. 1:15 he disapproved of so many sacrifices and all the outward works of the law (though in themselves they were good), "because," he said, "your hands are full of blood." For that reason in the psalms the man of faith is described as by some periphrasis or rather idiom as "the upright in heart," for example: ". . . who saves the upright in heart" (Ps. 7:10). And Ps. 11:2; ". . . that secretly they may shoot their arrows at the upright in heart." For uprightness of heart does not deceive, though every person, countenance and name soever deceives, whether he be a priest or a layman, a master or a servant.

Therefore it is quite clear that these words of the Apostle mean the same as those of Gen. 4:4: "And the Lord had respect unto Abel . . ." (The Lord had respect unto Abel essentially because of his faith and not on account of his work, and that is proved by the addition of the words) ". . . and to his offering." Therefore this point, the discerning of the difference between faith and works, is the parting of the ways. Here the real righteous and the hypocrites part company. For those who are really righteous strive after good works by means of faith and grace, but the hypocrites on the contrary in their perverted zeal strive after grace by means of their good works. This is to strive after the impossible. In our days, however, a notorious and endless tradition of human decretals, decrees, statutes and the like has multiplied, and made us into works-ridden hypocrites, like the locusts in the smoke of the bottomless pit (Rev. 9:3). Thus we cannot see the sunlight of faith. Consequently, the Spirit must again groan for the Church in the words of the twelfth Psalm, "Save me, O Lord, for the godly man ceaseth, and thy truths have been outraged by the sons of men."

11:4. . . . through which he obtained witness that he was righteous. . .

The godly Jerome[1] asks here in what way God granted a witness to the offering of Abel, or how it is to be understood that "he had respect to his offerings." And he replies that the translation of

[1] On Gen. 4:4; Migne, 23.944.

Symmachus[1] makes the point clear when he says "and God warmed in his heart (*inflammare*) towards Abel. . . ." For the Apostle seems to have followed him when he says that a witness had been granted by God. In the same way Chrysostom also says in this place: "It is said that a fire descended and consumed his sacrifice." "For the Syriac has 'set fire to' where we have God 'respected' his sacrifice."

11:4. . . . that he was righteous, God testifying of his gifts, and by it he being dead yet speaketh.

By a remarkable example God demonstrates that he cares for the oppressed, in that after the death of Abel he himself speaks on his behalf. By this he gives a very clear indication both of the immortality of the soul and also of eternal life, even if it is rather obscure. For the righteous live, act and speak not for themselves but in God. He shows that Abel lives in God because he also speaks in God. Accordingly, "he being dead yet speaketh" means that he who when he was actually alive could not teach even his only brother by his faith and example, now that he is dead teaches the whole world. This actually means that he is more alive than ever! So great a thing is faith! It is life in God. For this reason it is very appropriate to sing: "The righteous will be in eternal memory[2]." Chrysostom says the same thing. "How does a dead man still speak? Now this is a sign that he lives, because he is on everybody's lips. Had he had a thousand tongues when alive he would never have been held in such high regard as he is now that he is dead."

By these examples, however, all of us are exhorted not only to fear death but even to wish for it, for death was to Abel, as it is to every righteous man, a door; it is a passing over from humanity to divinity, from the world to the father, from misery to glory. For thus at once God showed from the beginning of the world and at the outset of Scripture how he can bring so much good out of a little evil. For Abel had to be slain, that the glory of life be shown in his death, and that the consolation of life found in Abel be greater than the confusion of death brought by Adam.

11:5. By faith Enoch was translated lest he should see death; and he was not found because God had translated him: but before his translation he received the testimony that he had pleased God.

---

1 Hirsch-Rückert point out that this is a lapse of memory on the part of Luther and should read Theodotion not Symmachus.

2 Ps. 112:6. Sung in the Sunday Vesper and in the Gradual on All Souls' Day.

Chrysostom writes: "Many people ask how Enoch was translated and why he was translated and did not die, neither he nor Elijah. And if they are still alive, how they live and in what kind of state. But it is a waste of time to ask questions of this sort. In fact the Scriptures say that one was translated and the other taken up (Gen. 5:24; II Kings 2:11). Where they are, however, and in what circumstances, they did not go on to say. For the Scriptures say nothing more than is necessary." Wherefore, it necessarily follows that whatever may be said about them over and above what the Scriptures themselves say, is only a matter of opinions and suppositions of men who do not know. It is far better to be in a state of ignorance than crammed full of vain curiosity to no purpose. It was for our sakes that God wanted Enoch's translation mentioned in holy writ. And for this reason: "that the human heart might have hope," as Chrysostom says: "that death would be destroyed and the tyranny of the devil be overthrown." For all these things were done so that the faith of the fathers in the future redemption of a saviour be supported and sustained, and that the human race should not see itself utterly deserted and despair of redemption. For consolation was never lacking to the faithful, nor tribulation either. Thus in Abel they saw death but at the same time a better life; in Enoch they did not see death at all, only life.

11:6. But without faith it is impossible to please God. For he that approacheth God must believe that he exists and that he is also a rewarder of them that seek him.

[Editor's note: There is a very valuable note in Hirsch-Rückert, p. 268 f., to which the reader is referred and which explains a few of the scholastic terms in the matter of faith and belief. The editor is largely indebted to these notes.

(*a*) BELIEF: Peter Lombard (*Sent.* III, dist., 23, cat. 4) following Augustine says,

1. *Credere deo* means to believe that the things God says are true, in others words, to believe in God's Word.
2. *Credere deum* means to believe in the existence of God.
3. *Credere in deum* means to love him by faith, to approach him in faith, to cleave to him in faith and be a member of his body.

Only this third sense is belief in any full sense of the word, and when Luther uses the phrase *credere deum* as distinct from *credere in deum* he means belief in the limited sense that God exists.

(*b*) FAITH: Biel (*Sent.* III, dist., 23 qu., art 1, lit) uses the terms *fides acquisita* and *fides infusa*, as the faith which the natural man acquires for himself, and the faith which is created by God in the human soul. The *fides acquisita* is possible for a man to acquire without the operation of divine grace, and Luther called this *fides humana* and dismissed its value out of hand.

(*c*) The text under comment, Heb. 11:6, is frequently quoted in scholastic debates on faith, and Biel uses the text for many purposes. Emphasizing the first half of the text he demonstrates the necessity of *fides infusa*, and then concludes from the second half what articles are to be explicitly believed. Hirsch-Rückert point out that the second use has meaning only if the first be true, and ask in what sense a belief in a mediator arises, and whether this article of belief be explicit (*explicata*) or implicit (*implicata*).

The upshot of Luther's argument is that he leaps over this traditional debate and makes faith a matter of conversion, a personal appropriation. Hirsch-Rückert actually use the adjective "existential" of this kind of faith. Luther denies the validity of the scholastic terms though he still uses the grammatical meanings of *fides de deo* (*credere deum*) and *fides in deum* (*credere in deum*) to convey his thought.

Though not in the context of the above remarks Quick uses a similar argument in the first chapter of his book *Doctrines of the Creed* to clarify the term belief. Ed.]

Now to believe that there is a God (*credere deum*) seems an easy thing to many people, and they attribute this belief both to the poets and the philosophers, as the Apostle also affirms in Rom. 1:20. There are even those who are of the opinion that this knowledge that God exists is arrived at by means of their own thinking.

But in fact in the first place such faith is human, like any other mental activity of man such as art, the cultivation of wisdom, the interpretation of dreams and the like. All these things however tumble to ruins as soon as temptation assails. In that hour neither reason, nor advice, nor human faith can gain the upper hand. "They reel to and fro like a drunken man, and are at their wit's end" Ps. 107:27. For that very reason the apostle James calls faith of such a kind "dead faith" (2:20), and others call it "acquired faith" (*fides acquisita*). Yet in fact there is nothing in man which is not vanity and lies.

In the second place such faith believes nothing in relation to itself but only as it applies to other people. For even if he does believe that God exists and that he rewards them that seek him, yet he is not believing that God exists for him and will reward him. To that extent it is, as the saying goes, faith about God and not faith in God.

Wherefore, the work of faith is a different thing, namely, that we believe that it is we ourselves who are of the number of those for whom God exists and for whom he is their rewarder. (It is far and away more important to believe that God disperses grace because it is in fact only with grace that he rewards men, Gl. 63:15 f.)

But this faith does not come from nature, but from grace. For nature dreads the face of God and flees from it, believing him to be not God but a tyrant and torturer and judge, as in that passage in Deut. 28:65: "But the Lord shall give thee a trembling heart and failing of eyes and sorrow of mind and thy life shall hang in doubt before thee. . . ." As a candle exposed to the wind loses not only its rays but light altogether, but when the sun shines again neither the candle nor its shining can be disturbed by any force of the wind. In circumstances such as these the first kind of faith is extinguished, the second never.

11:7. By faith Noah	Noah commends to us his marvellous faith born of deep and dark experiences. This means, it is plain to see, drawing from the words of sacred Scripture a faith as famous as Noah's, as well as help and instruction.
received an answer	an oracle, a divine command (Gen. 6)
concerning those things	the deluge and the destruction of all flesh. Methuselah died in the year the flood began.
which had not as yet been seen,	this is the glory of faith
he was afraid	because he believed in the flood and in the punishments of God.
and fitted out	prepared
an ark to save his household;	that his family might be preserved from the flood.
through the which	through faith
he proved the whole world wrong	the unbelief of his generation

Chrysostom asks: "By what faith? Because he showed that they who would not repent at his faith in building the ark deserved the punishment they got."

and he was established the heir	because in him all subsequent generations

to the justification
received their inheritance the true, divine justification, not a superstitious human justification

which comes by faith.

Words of Holy Scripture are not to be treated lightly. Since they are the words of the Spirit, it follows that they are bound to carry majesty and authority. Therefore, when the author commends to us the faith of the patriarchs, we must understand that this faith was absolutely perfect, that it was proved in all temptations and made worthy of being described such a glorious example for the whole Church.

And so, first of all, the glory of the faith of Noah was such that he believed and waited for one hundred years, while there are men who cannot believe not even for a moment, as those spoken of in Ps. 106:13: "They soon forgot his works; they waited not for his counsel." Thereafter that thought is frequently repeated in Holy Scripture: "Wait upon the Lord . . ." (Ps. 27:14 *et al.*); ". . . wait for him, if he tarries" (Hab. 2:3). "Wait on the Lord: be of good courage and he shall strengthen thine heart: wait I say on the Lord" (Ps. 27:14), and the like.

The second point is that Noah preached this faith so wholeheartedly and yet no attention was paid him. That he preached at all is certain from II Peter 2:5 where he is called a preacher of righteousness. In fact the more he was tried and afflicted, the less he felt that he was heeded. Events themselves prove that he was not listened to, because in actual fact everybody perished in the Flood. If they had believed, they would not have perished. Therefore, their great sin was their unbelief, just as the righteousness of Noah lay in his supreme faith. On that account the Apostle commends him in such glowing terms, not for his having built the ark but rather because "he built the ark in faith," ascribing faith utterly and completely as the beginning of works and their total content. Then he further commends him for condemning the world on account of its lack of faith, and not because of having failed to do some kind of good work or another. He thus says absolutely clearly that it was not because of some particular sin they were destroyed, but because they had not believed Noah's preaching. As Christ says in John 15:22: "If I had not come and spoken to them, they would have had no sin." For where there is faith even sin is not sin: again, where there is no faith, even righteousness is not righteousness, as Rom. 14:23 says: "Everything which is not of faith, is sin."

Thirdly, the usual consequences follow when faithful teachers teach faithless learners. They are mockery and slander; blasphemy, contempt and ignominy; especially when the evil threatening them is delayed, and the delay gives them new heart and assails the faith of the preacher with obvious and manifest proof. How often was Noah condemned as a fool, how often as a liar, how often as a babbler of utter nonsense, and not just by one person but by everybody, especially during the time that he was carefully building the ark, trusting only his own judgment and standing against the opinion of every man! This he did to such a degree that he discerned the one and only Word of God before everybody else: he used to listen to it, put it to the test, and always and continually preferred it to all else. Saint Peter also extols the patient long-suffering of God with the faithful and the unfaithful in the days of Noah. That the people in the time of Noah were of such a kind can be understood from Luke 17:26 f., where Christ says: "As it was in the days of Noah, so will it be in the days of the Son of Man: they used to eat, they used to drink, they used to take wives and wives were given in marriage until the day Noah entered the ark and then came the Flood and everybody perished." With these words he showed that the faith of this one man was stiffly embattled against the fashion of life of the entire world. For there is hardly any battle greater than this battle, since to know oneself as alone among all men, nay rather as one against all men, is judged by the world as the height of folly. That is why the faith of Noah was not that quiet "quality of soul" that we tend to dream faith is, but it is the inner life of the heart. It is "a lily among thorns" (Cant. 2:2). It is like Jerusalem standing alone in the midst of heathen nations.

11:7. **Noah was alarmed because of his faith.** This means that faith is ceaselessly tried and proven as through fire by many tribulations. On that account the Apostle commends the purity of his heart so highly when he says that Noah was "moved with fear" about those things which could not be seen. For to have faith in things one cannot see is to have a heart surely cleansed and separated from all the things one does see. This purity of heart is perfect righteousness, as it expresses it in Acts 15:9: ". . . purifying their hearts by faith."

11:8. **By faith Abraham**
when he was called   because he believed
to go out into a place   to leave his own country
which he would afterwards
receive as an inheritance   that is the land of Canaan

**went out, not knowing
whither he went.** This was faith: it was not
something he could see.

The first thing to say is that it was hard for Abraham to leave
the land of his birth, for we are all naturally affected by the love
of our fatherland. In fact, love of the fatherland is reckoned among
the highest virtues of the heathen. Then it is a hard thing to leave
friends and their companionship, but greatest of all one's kith and
kin and father's house. By this example Abraham gave a place to
what Ps. 45:10 teaches: "Hearken, O daughter, and consider, and
incline thine ear; forget also thine own people and thy father's
house."

The second thing to say is that he went out not knowing whither
he went, having nothing to follow except the Word of God, and
that was spoken with reference to things he had never seen. For
just as the place where Enoch and Elijah went is situated for us in
darkness, mists and ignorance amidst the invisible things of God,
so also was this place to which Abraham was being called utterly
hidden. But this is the glory of faith, simply not to know: not to
know where you are going, not to know what you are doing, not
to know what you must suffer, and with sense and intellect, virtue
and will, all alike made captive, to follow the naked voice of God,
to be led and driven, rather than to go. And thus it is clear, that
Abraham with this obedience of faith shows the highest example of
the evangelical life, because he left all and followed the Lord,
preferring the Word of God to everything else and loving it above
all things; of his own free will a pilgrim, and subject to the perils
of life and death every hour of the day and night.

Just as every righteous man has the devil for his adversary quite
certainly he will have in addition many to blame him and condemn him in his faith and purpose. They will seek either to convince him of foolishness, or persuade him to some pestilential piety
or another, in case he believes that what has been happening to
him is an experience from God. For of all temptations the greatest
is the temptation of faith. Against faith the devil pits every ounce of
his strength, and uses the power of men and everything else as
well. Thus Abraham's faith was tried "as gold in the furnace"
(Wisdom 3:6), not least in that in the face of so many instances of
others living and asking differently he stood alone and opposed
them all. Although he fights against this way of life very deter-
minedly to serve God, yet on account of his long life as a sojourner,
he is considered an instance contrary to type. So true is this that
the whole of the seventy-third psalm re-echoes the force of a
stumbling block of this kind: "As for me," it reads, "my feet were

almost gone; my steps had wellnigh slipped. For I was envious
of the foolish when I saw the peace of the wicked" (Ps. 73:2 f.).
Or again, Ps. 37:1: "Fret not thyself because of evil doers, neither
be thou envious against the workers of iniquity . . ." and so on,
teems with exhortations and arguments in connection with a
similar mass of stumbling blocks. Jeremiah also seizes on the same
thing, "Wherefore doth the way of the wicked prosper? Wherefore
are all they happy that deal treacherously?" (Jer. 12:1). Moreover, after they entered the promised land, not only was temptation not ended but it was increased, and even a new kind of temptation of faith began. For God gave him "not so much as to set
his foot on" as it says in Acts 7:5, but as a wanderer in that land he
endured to the end many evils and many dangers. Moreover, he
was compelled to wander into Egypt and to come back again
(Gen. 12:15, 20:2). Yet he saw the promises fulfilled neither in
his own seed Isaac nor in his grandson Jacob. Finally, came the
greatest of all trials. He was commanded to sacrifice by his own
hand his own son, doubtless his most beloved son, none other than
him in whom he had accepted the promise of the blessing. For
these reasons he is most justly called and has in fact been established "the father of many nations" (Gen. 17:4; Rom. 4:17 f.),
"the father of our faith" (cf. Rom. 4:16). And therefore, "Abraham's bosom" (Luke 16:22) is doubtless that faith which is
promised in the gospel.

By arguments like these we have to refute those despiritualized
questionings and objections of ignorant men, the Jews in particular,
who with eyes only for the external works of Abraham do not even
consider his faith. They see the obvious for example, that Abraham took a maid to wife (Gen. 16:2 ff.), and another after the
death of Sarah (Gen. 25:1). Or again, the same kind of thing, that
Jacob had two sisters to wife with their maids. They go on discussing these matters getting nowhere, not seeing that it could
have been quite easy for men of such mighty faith who had put
everything aside to have put marriage aside too, had they not
gone into it either in obedience to God or for the sake of the hidden future. For thus, as it is written in Job 41, "God laughs and
scoffs at Behemoth," that is, the hypocrites. But he is also "wonderful to his saints" and shows in the outward life of the saints, the
things by which those hypocrites are altogether offended. Yet he
hides the things he effects within, as it says in Ps. 31:20: "Thou
shalt hide them in the secret of thy presence from the noisy tumult
of men." This is how it comes about that "the spiritual man
judges all things and is judged by no man." That is why it is the
height of rashness to judge one's neighbour, since even the elect of

God are hidden and when all is said are saved through sins most palpable.

11:9. By faith he sojourned in the land of promise as in an alien land   as a foreigner not yet seeing the promise

dwelling

> For thus Stephen said in Acts 7:5: "He gave him no inheritance in it, not so much as to set his foot on." And thus it appeared nothing like what God had promised. And still his faith never failed him.

in tabernacles   in tents like wanderers
with Isaac and Jacob

> Abraham lived one hundred and seventy-five years. When he was one hundred he begat Isaac, who when he was sixty begat Jacob, and so for fifteen years Abraham and Jacob were contemporary.

co-heirs of the same promise.   The promise was that in his seed all the nations of the earth would be blessed.

11:10. For he was looking for a city which hath foundations   the heavenly Jerusalem foundations of rock. Earthly cities are without abiding foundation, for time does not stand still.

whose builder and maker is God.

11:11. By faith also   not works. Otherwise the holy woman would have conceived before this.

Sarah herself though sterile

> Chrysostom comments: "The shutting up of her womb was of two kinds. One owing to her age because she had grown old, the other owing to her nature because she was sterile."

received strength to conceive seed   contrary both to her nature and her age so that she could receive it and retain it

even past her age	because she was ninety. Because "it ceased to be with Sarah after the manner of women."
she believed him	God
that he was faithful	that he was true and a keeper of his promise.
who had promised	Gen. 18:10. "I shall return unto thee at the appointed time, and a son shall be born to Sarah."
11:12. On account of which	the merit of faith
there arose	many sons of Israel
even from one man,	Abraham
and him as good as dead,	that is, too weak to beget of his own nature. "He considered not his own body which was by that time as good as dead" (Rom. 4:19).
descendants as many as the stars of heaven in multitude,	Gen. 15:5: "Look up to heaven and count the stars if thou canst. And he said to him, So shall thy seed be."
and as countless as the sands of the sea	

This simile is frequently quoted in Scripture, even on the occasions that a precise and definite number is intended. As in Judg. 7:12, Midian is likened to the locusts in number and to the sands on the shores of the sea. Yet in chapter eight it is written that there were left one hundred and twenty thousand soldiers who fell.

11:13. In faith	by faith alone, not having obtained the actual thing promised
all these died	Abraham, Isaac and Jacob.

It does not seem to refer to the earlier patriarchs Abel and Enoch, because they had not been given the promises.

Another reason is because it says further on: "If they had been mindful of that country whence they came out . . ." (v. 15) which of course applies to Abraham. Or again where it says: "God was not ashamed to be called their God . . ." (v. 16). It is then quite clear why he is referred to as "the God of Abraham, Isaac and Jacob" and not of Abel, Enoch and the rest.

not having received the promises

that is, the land of Canaan

but they looked forward to them from afar

that means in faith for their descendants who were to come after them

both welcoming and admitting

recognizing and rejoicing, to such an extent were they certain of this

that they were strangers and pilgrims on earth.

The prophet of Ps. 39:12 thought the same thing, too. "Hear my prayer, O Lord, and give ear unto my cry: hold not thy peace from me for I am before thee as a passer-by, a mere wanderer, as all my fathers were."

11:14. For they who say this,

confess that they are sojourners

signify that they seek a country.

It is not only that they have no country but they have given up their own.

11:15. And if indeed they had been mindful

and felt it with feeling. For they remembered perfectly well that they had come from it.

of that land

Syria and Mesopotamia

Mindful in Scriptural usage means in relation to those things which claim the whole affection, as in Num. 11:5: "We remember the fish which we did eat in Egypt freely; the cucumbers, and the melons, and the leeks, and the onions, and the garlick." Or again in Ps. 87:4: "I will make mention of Rahab and Babylon. . ."

**from whence they came,
they would naturally
have had opportunities
of returning.**

because Abraham was a
wanderer from his own
country for ninety-five
years, and yet never once
did he turn back.

**11:16. But now they
desire a better country**

as is proved from the
manner of their
perseverance.

that is an heavenly.

*In that they were strangers and pilgrims on earth, they are now
"fellow citizens with the saints and of the household of God."*

On that account

because of the merit of so
great faith

**God is not
ashamed**

does not feel ashamed; it
does not humiliate him.

**to be called
their God**

Abraham, Isaac and Jacob

**for he hath prepared
for them a city**

in which he will live with
them and be their God
(Rev. 21:2 ff.).

**11:17. By faith
Abraham when he
was tried, offered**

he was ready to offer. In
fact, it could be said that
he had already offered him
in his heart.

**Isaac
his only begotten
son**

his own son

he adds this description for
the sake of emphasis. It is
as if to say that his faith
would have been less had he
offered only one son out of
many

**in whom he
had received**

he had not yet even begun
to doubt

the promises,	and thus there was a clear contradiction to the promise
11:18. Of whom it was said,	it was not spoken to Isaac concerning Abraham, but to Abraham concerning Isaac
in Isaac shall thy seed be called,	Not the children of the flesh but the children of promise are counted for the seed (Rom. 9:8).
11:19. Considering that God was able to raise him even from the dead,	knowing This means that he did not doubt that Isaac was the blessed seed of the future, but only that he did not understand. In this the promise to the seed was fulfilled, just as much as the promise of the blessing.
and in fact in a hidden sense	this means that he was a type and pattern of Christ
he did so recover him.	

Gl. 66:20 ff. The hidden sense is that just as Isaac was led away to be sacrificed but in the end was saved and a ram caught in the thorns was sacrificed in his stead, so the Son of God, since he was both mortal and immortal in one and the same person, was sacrificed, but only his flesh, that is his humanity, was slain.

11:23. By faith Moses when he was born was hidden for three months by his parents when they saw what a fine child he was: and they did not fear the edict of the king. By faith Moses when he was grown up denied that he was the son of Pharaoh's daughter. He preferred ill-usage with the people of God to the brief enjoyment of sinful pleasures. He esteemed the reproach of Christ greater riches than the treasures of Egypt, for he had eyes only for the reward of faith.

First Chrysostom commends the faith of Moses because his

consuming faith caused him to despise the royal court where he was both son and master. That is to say he had the right to live in luxury and honour, and the privilege of spending his life in the court. For this is what the martyr Stephen says (among other things), that Moses had been brought up in all the wisdom of Egypt and was mighty in words and works, and was there till his fortieth year. From this it is clear that he was an important man in the king's court, that he had been educated with great care, and that he was held in the highest regard by everybody. All these things, however, together with all the elegance of the court he held in utter disregard on account of his faith.

Secondly, he looked on all these things as worth nothing, not because he had before his eyes other things which were greater or equal to them, but because of the cross and the experiences belonging to it, which are nothing but adversity and disaster. Even at that early stage he fulfils that famous phrase of the Apostle: "He chose the weak things to confound the strong things, he chose those things which are not that he might destroy the things that are" (I Cor. 1:27 f.). Moses chose the wisdom or rather the foolishness of the cross and rejected the wisdom he had inherited.

Thirdly, and greatest of all, he was rejected even by his own people for whose sakes he had despised these very things and undergone these dangers. They said to him (as it says in Acts 7), "Who made you a ruler over us?" And so he was compelled to flee unto Midian.

[*Editor's note:* At this point the manuscript of the Scholia ends. Most scholars[1] are of the opinion that this is not because scholia on chapters twelve and thirteen have been lost, but that Luther did in fact stop at this point. Many are the conjectures offered in explanation of this alleged abrupt ending. Rupp's discussion of the point[2] is good. He seems to consider it a deliberate closure and a very appropriate ending in the situation which Luther faced, and the present writer views the matter as he does, "a wonderful exit line."

It was a terrifying situation Luther faced. As Rupp says, it was one thing to be a famous young theologian criticizing an outworn scholastic theology, but it was a very different thing to face proceedings for heresy and the almost certain ignominy and disgrace ensuing, even death it self: to have all those who had been admirers and friends grow uncertain, waiting for officialdom to show them how to act and think.

The Archbishop of Mainz had launched a process against him for heresy in Rome. The Dominicans had also done the same and were boldly clamouring for his blood. On his side he had openly spoken against the abuse of excommunication, and his own students at

---

[1] *Vide* Hirsch-Rückert, *op. cit.*, p. 279n.; Vogelsang, *op. cit.*, 176n. f.; Rupp, *op. cit.*, 214 ff.

[2] Rupp, *op. cit.*, 214 ff.

Wittemberg did not improve matters for him by manhandling the colporteur of Tetzel's counter-theses and burning his literature. He was to attend the fateful chapter of his order at Heidelberg in the matter of a few days, and knew perfectly well that he had to journey on foot through enemy territory and might never be seen again.

Rupp rightly says that though history tends to see Luther's great moment in the dramatic hour of the Diet of Worms, it is at this present hour and not at Worms that he stood his greatest trial. At this time, from Easter 1518 to his interview with Cajetan at Augsburg in October 1518, the way lay in front of him, unknown and uncertain, un-nerving and threatening. The issues had not been clearly joined. He knew he would face hostility, he knew it was the way of the cross, he knew he was called to go on. When he had reached this great chapter eleven, and commented on the operative word "faith" beginning as it does in the text every new thought and every fresh patriarch, the students would sense and their master would know that perhaps God was sending another Moses, there was to be another departure from the house of bondage, another freedom of a promised land. How like the role of Moses was Luther's! Like Moses he was threatened by all-powerful enemies and weakened by the fear of being unable to depend on his friends; like Moses by faith he faced his enemies, by faith bore the reproach of his brethren, and counted, by faith, the reproach of Christ greater than all the treasures of Christendom; like Moses he went forward by faith alone.

Be that as it may, nothing comes after the phrase ". . . he was compelled to go into Midian." But the glosses of chapter twelve go on and at greater length, and also the glosses to chapter thirteen. It seems that it was Luther's habit to give his scholia after he had translated and glossed the text under discussion. It is, therefore, feasible that Luther did in fact stop at chapter eleven because he had in fact reached the climax and end of the Epistle and had little further to add on the meaning of the Epistle. Therefore the editor has completed the commentary by translating the glosses Luther does in fact offer. All previous glosses the editor has chosen as further comment on the scholia and are inset in the text. The glosses which follow stand in their own right and are not inset. Footnotes to the glosses are inset. Ed.]

11:27. By faith he forsook Egypt

he fled to the priest of Midian (Ex. 2).

not fearing the wrath of the king

the ferocity, the attack

Exodus records that when Pharaoh heard that Moses had slain and buried the Egyptian, Pharaoh sought to kill Moses, but he fled from his sight and dwelt in Midian.

for he endured

he waited, he was strengthened by faith

For this is the nature of faith, as has been said above: to see what cannot be seen and not to see what can be seen.

as seeing   as if he could see
him who is
invisible   God
11:28. **By faith**
he celebrated   he made them celebrate
                                 throughout Israel

the Passover and
the sprinkling of
the blood   by which the lintels and the
                                 two side posts were
                                 sprinkled
lest he that
destroyed   the destroying angel
the first-born   the first-born of Egypt
should touch them.

For thus it is recorded in Ex. 12:23: "As he passes through the Lord will smite Egypt: when he sees the blood on the lintel and on either post, he will not allow the avenger to enter your homes." The three posts represent the three parts of man's nature, body, soul and spirit, because God himself makes all things clean.

11:29. **By faith**   Ex. 14.
they passed through
the Red Sea as over
dry land

Not by their own strength, nor by their own efforts. For all the works of faith are impossible to the natural man but perfectly easy for the man of faith. For when works of faith are done we experience their being done through us, for it is God alone who works them. As it says in Ex. 14:14: "The Lord will fight for you and you will remain silent." Or again the same in Ps. 37:7, 5: "Rest in the Lord, and he shall bring it to pass." And in Isa. 41:1: "Keep silence before me, O islands, and let the people renew their strength."

whereas the Egyptians,
when they ventured
into it   when they attempted the
                                 crossing in the same way
were drowned   for they had only nature on
                                 their side, and not grace.

11:30. By faith the walls of Jericho fell down after they were compassed about seven days

not by the force of battering rams but by going round them seven times (Josh. 6).

11:31. By faith the harlot Rahab

some describe her as an inn-keeper

In the Hebrew text it is the word *gōnah* which is derived from the word *ganah* to play the harlot. This does not refer to the disgrace of the scouts because they turned into a harlot. That they were in danger of death is sufficient argument that it was not lust but sheer necessity which drove them to her to seek refuge (Josh. 6).

did not perish along with the non-believers because she gave the scouts a welcome

of Jericho

the spies sent by Joshua whom the others were trying to kill (Josh. 2).

and showed no hostility.

11:32. And what more shall I say?

In fact all these works are the works of faith against adversity. They are all of a kind with this Israelitish work, by which I mean the Red Sea crossing. The fact is that all the works mentioned throughout the entire Bible are written up as works of faith.

for time would fail me were I to tell of Gideon,   Judg. 6, 7, 8.
Barach,   Judg. 4, 5.
Samson,   Judg. 13, 14, 15, 16.
Jephthah,   Judg. 12.
David,   I and II Kings.
Samuel and the Prophets.

Kings and Chronicles.

11:33. Who through faith

subdued kingdoms   not by force of arms like
                                    David and Joshua

It is clear, therefore, that at that time wars were fought in faith, and that God did the fighting. On that account they are called "the wars of the Lord" in the Scriptures. It is for this reason that Ps. 60, which was dedicated to the victory over Syria and Edom says: "Who is to lead me into the fortified city, who is to find entry for me into Edom? Is it not thou, O Lord, who hast disowned us and did not march out with our armies? Help us out of our trouble, for vain is the help of man. Only through God can we do battle victoriously: only he shall trample in the dust those that vex us" (Ps. 60:9 ff.).

wrought righteousness,   for righteousness is nothing
                                    else but faith. The
                                    righteous shall live by his
                                    faith (Rom. 1:17).

obtained promises,   because Joshua and David
                                    obtained the law of promise
                                    and extended it

**stopped the mouth
of lions**   as Daniel, David and
                                    Samson.

**11:34. Quenched the
violence of fire**   Dan. 3.
**escaped the edge
of the sword**   as David and Hezekiah.
**were made strong
out of weakness**   were restored to their full
                                    power. Some think that this
                                    is a reference to Hezekiah
                                    (Isa. 37).

Chrysostom thinks that the reference is to the Babylonian Captivity, and this is better. For the Apostle means that those who were weaker prevailed over their oppressors by faith.

**waxed valiant
in battle**   like the thirty strong men
                                    of David (II Sam. 23:8 ff.).

**turned to flight the
armies of the aliens.**

**11:35. Women
received their dead**   mothers

raised to life again   as the widow of Sareptah

others, however,
were tortured

through Elijah (I Kings 17),
and the Shunamite through
Elisha (II Kings 4).

either crucified or fell
in battle

Faith not only effects everything, but also suffers everything. In either eventuality it is invisible. The Greek text reads *etympanisthesan* which has the connotation not only of stretching but rather of crushing or breaking, to signify those who were struck down and beaten to death by cudgels and rods. Ps. 68:25 says: "Before him go the chieftains, and the minstrels with them, while the maids around play on their tympanies." The tympanies represent the holy martyrs who offered themselves as drums to their beaters. For this reason also the holy fathers describe Gideon and these other heroes as praiseworthy vessels and their souls as shining lamps who by their sufferings give light to the Church and vex the sinners. [The text of this sentence is incomplete and the editor has attempted to complete it.]

not accepting
deliverance

as those who had gone
before them had done.
They did not want
deliverance.

that they might obtain
a better resurrection

that means, better than the
deliverance of the body
would have been.

11:36. And others
experiencing mockery and
scourging, even chains
and imprisonment

In this reference the prophet Jeremiah is almost certainly meant. Certainly, Scripture is not sufficiently mindful that the prophets suffered such torments and tortures, except for the words of Christ from which it is certain that all prophets were accustomed to receive hatred, and all prophets were persecuted. Saint Stephen also refers to it: "As were your fathers, so are ye. Which of the prophets have your fathers not persecuted? They have even slain those who announced the coming of this Righteous One (Christ)" (Acts 7:51 f.). Christ said the same thing in Matt. 23:37: "Jerusalem, Jerusalem! Thou that killest the prophets and stonest them which are sent thee . . . !"

11:37. They were stoned

Because the law prescribed that blasphemers were to be stoned. The people in their madness, however, instigated by false prophets, by and large accused the true prophets of blasphemy. Wherefore, it would seem, that many were stoned. In exactly the same way today heretics are wont to be accused of their crime, and even the very worst crimes, by false theologians.

they were sawn asunder	this is spoken of Isaiah, who was sawn in two by Mannasseh with a woodman's saw
were tempted	as Abraham and many others
were slain with the sword	Judith
they wandered about	they wandered without any settled abode like pilgrims

in sheepskins and goatskins, being destitute, afflicted, tormented.

11:38. Of whom the world was not worthy, — the sinners in the world
they wandered in deserts

This is best understood with reference to Elijah and the sons of the prophets, especially in the reign of Ahab and Jezebel.

in mountains, in dens and caves of the earth — because Obadiah, the servant of Ahab, had hidden many of them and fed them secretly. There were forty prophets.

11:39. And all of these having obtained a good report through faith did not receive the promise. — having been found faithful

11:40. God having provided some better thing for us, that they without us should not be consummated — made complete.

CHAPTER TWELVE

Gl. 73:16 ff. Now that Paul has finished the teaching he begins the exhortation. He has laid the foundation of faith and now he begins to build on it "the gold, silver and precious stones" of I Cor. 3:12: in plain words, he now inculcates the finest virtues and dedication to a holy life. The canonical scripture pursues this course most carefully all the time. We on the contrary go about it in the very worst way possible: we begin by laying a foundation of works and then start looking for faith.

12:1. **Wherefore, seeing we also are compassed about**
about us and surrounding us on all sides

with a cloud
an army, a multitude

of witnesses
preachers

let us lay aside all that weighs us down
occasions which impede us

Chrysostom calls the weight that weighs us down the cares and all the other human concerns which choke the Word of God. This is what Christ taught when he spoke of the seed choked among the thorns (Matt. 13:7). And note Chrysostom's evidence. He describes the affairs and business of life as "burdens," just as Christ likens riches to thorns (Matt. 13:22): although men delight in these burdens as if they were highly desirable.

and the sin surrounding us
the sinful habit which clings so closely

Sin: In this place those who believe that holy men have no sin, interpret sin as "occasion for sin," influenced by the word "surrounding." In fact the author prefers to call these occasions "a weight," and sin he quite properly takes as Chrysostom does

227

for that real infirmity and concupiscence of nature, an infirmity which both easily captures us and which also may be easily captured and surrounded. The latter sense satisfies him, but we prefer the former. For this is the meaning it bears in Chapter 3:13, "lest any of you be hardened through the deceitfulness of sin," as if to say that we are surrounded on all sides by the deceits of sin no less than by the witnesses discussed in this verse. Consequently, two different things are going on at one time: the witnesses are helping us and sin is impeding us.

and let us run let us race on with all our might

with endurance for thus it says earlier, "You still need endurance . . ." (Heb. 10:36).

the race for which we entered.

12:2. Looking unto Jesus, the author and finisher of faith for the strengthening of life

as if to say that he is the first and he is the last: he it is who began this life in us, and he it is who will bring it to perfection.

who for the joy set before him the future joy, that is, sustained by hope

As it is written in Ps. 16:8: "I shall keep the Lord in my sight always: for he is at my right hand to make me stand firm. . . ." And further on, ". . . thou shalt make me full of joy at thy countenance" (Ps. 16:11). And in another psalm: ". . . thou shalt give him great joy with thy countenance" (Ps. 21:6).

endured the cross ran his own race as an example to us

despised the shame because his death was very shameful. We, therefore, must not only suffer death, but also despise it.

and now sits on the right of God's throne. he sits above all kingdoms, for they belong to God (Pss. 9:7 f., 20:6).

12:3. For consider think about it, reflect on it

Consider: Nothing is more efficacious against sin and temptations than the thought of Christ, as is illustrated in the incident of the brazen serpent (Num. 21:8 ff.) and at the waters of Marah (Ex. 15:23 ff.). Wherefore Peter made bold to say, "Arm yourselves likewise with the same mind" (I Peter 4:1), preaching that to remember Christ is to arm the soul. As it says in Ps. 45:4: "Thy lips overflow with gracious utterances. Ride on in all thy majesty and beauty." And in Cant. 8:6: "Set me as a seal upon thy heart, as a sign upon thine arm" (The reference to the heart means above thoughts, and to the arm above works). "Because love is as strong as death."

him who endured
such contradiction
greater and worse than yours as much by word, as by thought and deed

from sinners
not from the worthy and the righteous

against himself,
not in the role of a looker-on on another man's injuries.

Gen. 3:15 says, "Thou shalt bruise his heel, and he will bruise thine head." It says "heel" and means by that the blandishments of the senses. It does not say "head," because Christ is the head.

lest ye be
wearied
for unless you recognize Christ you are utterly abandoned and have to do everything left to your own devices. For Christ is our courage, our wisdom and our salvation. Yea, Christ is all things.

and faint in
your minds

The emphasis lies in the words "in your minds." It is as if he meant to say, that you were to keep Christ in your mind, so that in the hour of your temptations no weakness of the body would compel you to desert. For nothing is too difficult for the mind which so considers Christ.

12:4. But ye say that
ye have not yet resisted

unto blood

the shedding of blood. And therefore have not gone as far as Christ and the saints yet.

in your struggle

To fight against sin is to fight against the devil, the world and oneself. The fight against oneself is the worst fight of all. True, he who has begun a good work in you will perform it until the day of Christ. The hatred of evil things and the love of good things are the cause of the whole evil. For we must embrace evil things and flee the good. For strength is perfected in weakness. Sin and occasions of sin keep us from the true Christian life. (What the word "occasion of sin" means is discussed above.) "In the day of good things be thou mindful of the evil things: in the day of evil things be thou mindful of the good" (Wisdom 11:25).

against sin.

The word is "against," because all tribulation fights against us in the interests of sin. For sin has the whole world on its side, and what is worse, it even has our own selves on its side. There is a reference to this in Rom. 6:13, where Paul exhorts us not to make our bodily powers over to sin and make them instruments of harm; and also in Job 41 of the power of the leviathan. Also in Luke 11:22: ". . . and he taketh from him all his armour wherein he trusted."

12:5. And ye have forgotten the words of comfort

divine words of comfort. As it says in Rom. 15:4, "Whatsoever things were written aforetime, were written for our learning."

in which God spoke to you as his sons, saying, my son, do not despise the chastening

do not reject the scourging and the correction

of the Lord, nor faint when thou art rebuked by him

by means of sufferings and temptations

12:6. For whom the Lord loveth he

chasteneth

for he is the perfection
of divine power

It is put in another way in Prov. 13:24: *"He that spareth the rod hateth his son, but the kind father is quick to punish." Ps.* 73 *is a perfect example of this. The Apocalypse says the same thing: "As many as I love, I rebuke and chasten" (Rev.* 3:19). *Also I Peter* 4:17, *"The time is come for judgment to begin at the house of God," which is quoted from Ezek.* 9:6, *"And begin at my sanctuary." Jer.* 25:29 *says: "Behold, in the city in which my name has been invoked, I myself shall begin my work of vengeance. And ye, shall ye be acquitted and go scot-free? No! Ye shall not be let off." Behold, in the days of the martyrs the Church had her finest hour and was most loved: it was then that she was most thoroughly exercised in the discipline of the Lord. Today, however, is the word of Isaiah fulfilled, "Behold in peace is my bitterness bitterest" (Isa.* 38:17). *For in times of peace God is chastising as a judge and not as a father: that means that in times of peace he is allowing all the shameful things to grow strong and virtue to be minished, for he is angry and severe with us. And Isa.* 5:6 *fulfils it: "I will lay the vineyard waste; it shall not be pruned nor dug."*

he even scourgeth
every son he receiveth
(Prov. 3:11**)**

the word "receiveth" is
interpreted rather in the
sense of "he exhorteth."
Our text means the same as
Prov. 3:12; "Whom the
Lord loveth, he corrects: as
a father delights in his son."

12:7. Be patient while
the correction lasts!

endure the chastening

Hezekiah said, O Lord it is thus a man lives, and on such small things the life of my spirit hangs. This being so, thou canst chastise me and make me live. Behold, it is in peace that my bitterness is at its bitterest (Isa. 38:16 f.).

God is offering himself
to you as a Father to his
sons

as to sons who have been
taught by the power of the
discipline he has introduced

for what son is there
his father doth not
chasten?

Foolishness is ingrained in

the heart of a child; but the
rod of correction shall drive
it out of him (Prov. 22:15).

**12:8. But if ye are
without chastisement
of which all of us
have our share**

The highest worship of God is the voluntary renunciation of oneself and of one's own advantage.

then are ye   the sons of God
bastards   illegitimate children
and not sons   and therefore, no longer
          heirs

This is a terrible thing to say. It says the same in Ps. 73:5: "They are not in trouble as other men; neither are they plagued like other men." How is this the case? Because they will be with the demons and in their power.

**12:9. Furthermore, we
have had earthly fathers** mortals, born to a mortal
          life

**who corrected us and
whom we reverenced:
shall we not much
rather**   that is, incomparably more
          so
submit to   be subject to
**the Father of the
world of spirits**   because he educates us for
          eternal life

By gentle co-operation and very effective argument, he pursues his exhortation to bear the chastisements of God.

and live

On either the joy or the chastisement allotted by God.

12:10. For they   our earthly fathers
**chastened us just
as they wanted**   as if to say not always to
          our advantage. On that
          account their instruction is
          often in vain, more than
          that it is often harmful

He gently refers to the unfortunate consequence of the large part of human upbringing, because almost nobody is made better (as far as the heart is concerned) when they are forced to be better for fear of being punished.

and only for a short time, but he for our own good,

because the instruction of God is never unavailing.

that we might be partakers of his holiness

of his sanctifying grace.

12:11. Now no chastening is pleasant while it lasteth; it is, on the contrary, grievous:

it is grievous to the natural man, but it is not so in reality. "We glory in our tribulations"

Frequently in the Scriptures there are two opposite ideas side by side. For example, judgment and righteousness, wrath and grace, death and life, evil and good. This is what is referred to in the phrase, "These are the great works of the Lord."

nevertheless afterwards it yieldeth the most peaceable fruit of righteousness

As in the Psalm: "Righteousness and peace have kissed each other" (Ps. 85:10).

to those who have experienced it

"An alien work is done by him so that he might effect his proper work" (Isa. 28:21)[1]: "The spirit indeed is willing, but the flesh is weak" (Matt. 26:41; Mark 14:38). For in a wonderful way he makes the conscience glad, as it is expressed similarly in Ps. 4:1: "In tribulation thou hast made me greater," that means, thou hast made more of me, improved me. Now this is what infusion of grace means. As it says in Rom. 5:4: "Experience worketh hope and hope maketh not ashamed." Here we find the

---

[1] Cf. the comment on 2:14, p. 58 ff.

Theology of the Cross[1], or, as the Apostle expresses it: "The word of the cross is a stumbling block to the Jews, and foolishness to the Gentiles" (I Cor. 1:18, 23), because it is utterly hidden from their eyes. "It is withdrawn from their eyes and is taught in hiddenness. This means that it is not manifest but is hidden, as in the midst of a tempest. As it says in Ps. 80:8 (Vulg.): "I heard thee in the hidden tempest." And in Ps. 50:8 (Vulg.): "Thou hast made known to me the unknown and hidden things of thy truth."

12:12. Wherefore

since so much of this chastening is of the nature of salvation

lift up
the hands which
hang down

make strong

are tied

and the flagging
knees

are tired

12:13. And make straight
paths for your feet

for they are crooked if they deviate either because of the fear of evil things or for the love of good things

that the lame man
may not falter

This is taken from I Kings 18:21; "How long will ye halt between two opinions?"

but rather regain
his strength.

12:14. Follow peace

that the reproach of restlessness should not appear among you

It is the wish of the Apostle that they do not resist the powers of the world under the pretext of religion (Rom. 13). This is also taught elsewhere, even by Peter quite clearly.

with all men,

Not only with the household of faith, but also with those who are without, as far as

---

[1] On the important theme of the Theology of the Cross readers will find more in the *Heidelberg Disputation* 1518, *WA*1, 362.21 (See p. 291).; *Resolutiones* 1518, *WA*1, 613.22; the *WA* also suggests 1, 33.18 ff; 52.18 ff; 102.40 ff; 141.11; 172.1; and refers readers to Ritschl, *Dogmengeschichte*, II, 1, 48 and von Loewenich, *Luther's Theologia Crucis*, 12 ff.

	in you lies, having peace with all men (Gal. 6:10, with Rom. 12:18).
and holiness	chastity, by which the body is sanctified. I Thess. 4:3, 4, 7
without which no man shall see the Lord	Jesus, "Blessed are the pure in heart for they shall see God" (Matt. 5:8).

He wishes to say what is in Matt. 24:13: "He who endureth to the end, the same shall be saved."

12:15. Looking carefully   having care and thought one for another

The life of suffering is the true way and the direct path to salvation: the life of works and religious activity is regal, but it is a roundabout way. It was because of this the Lord did not want to lead the children of Israel into the promised land through the land of Palestine (Ex. 13), in case they came up against war and wanted to go back to Egypt. There are those now who, having suffered infirmity, or poverty, or some sort of violence, complain that they are not able to serve God: yet God says here that righteousness is made perfect by suffering of this kind.

lest any man fail of	remain backward, be deficient in
the grace of God	but should persevere rather to the end
lest any root of bitterness	anger, or jealousy, or dissension (Rom. 14:1 ff., 10 ff., 15 ff.; Eph. 4:25 ff.)
spring up and trouble you	if anything were to begin to be engendered by any such evil, it would quickly be ended and not allowed to grow. This of course is only what ought to happen. Note the emphatic nature of the word *impediat* (trouble), because jealousy and

dissension are utterly
contrary to the grace of
God.

**and through it
many be defiled**

this means to lapse into
schism and wrong theology.

This text can also be made to mean the impiety of human
ceremonies and human righteousness, on account of which the
people are called in all the prophets, "a bitter and rebellious
house." This is because "their word will eat as doth a canker"
(II Tim. 2:17), and again, "they subvert whole houses"
(Titus 1:11). For nothing is more deceiving or more iniquitous
than a false idea of religion or the outward appearance of
holiness.

More properly "bitterness" is understood as envy, as in
Ps. 10:7 and 14:1 ff.: "Whose mouth is full of cursing and
bitterness."

**12:16. Lest there be
any fornicator or
profane person**

an unclean person, one who
despises things sacred and
desires the trifles of life

**like Esau
who for the sake of
a morsel of meat**

Gen. 25.

he therefore considered the
most sacred thing worthless

**sold
his birthright**

relinquished, resigned

**12:17. For
ye know how that
afterwards when he
wanted to inherit
the blessing**

by the law of primogeniture

receive the inheritance
which carried the headship
of the family and the blessing

he was rejected

in the wisdom of God,
although he had been chosen
by his father

**for he found no place
for repentance**

He grieved not because he had sinned but because he was
damned.

True repentance is a grief less because of one's own damnation but rather because of God's damnation (that means having God as one's enemy). The Apostle is not rejecting repentance by this remark. He is not even discussing sacramental penance. In fact, whenever Scripture speaks of repentance it never means sacramental penance.

although **he pleaded for** **it with tears**	in the end

Because it was so determined by God. For God "does not lie as a man does, nor is he changed in his purpose as a man is" (Num. 23:19). "He does not relent because of sorrow as a man does" (I Sam. 15:29). For Esau sought repentance neither for a true reason nor for a religious reason, but in pursuit of his own interest.

12:18. For

He sets before us and amplifies the difference between the two Testaments: the first, the Old Testament as we call it, was based on fear; the second, the New Testament as we call it, is based on love.

ye have not come to **something that may** **be felt,**	the mountain, discernible to touch, and of which it was said: "Everyone who touches the mountain will die" (Ex. 19:12).
nor to fire that **can be touched,**	something that can be kindled. It had burned up as a flame of fire, and looked like lightning.
nor to a whirlwind	a wind
nor to darkness,	a very dense cloud
nor a tempest.	
12:19. Nor to the **sound of a trumpet,**	because the sound of the trumpet used gradually to increase
nor to that voice,	in which the Ten Commandments were spoken
a voice which they that **heard it entreated**	for they could not bear it, their conscience was guilty

**that they should
hear it no more.**

that it should speak no more

**12:20. For they
could not bear
what was said:**

could not endure
in Greek it is "what was
distinguished." [the word
διαστέλλω (*diastello*) also
means to determine, state
clearly, or command. Ed.]

that even if a beast

it was not only they who
could not bear it, it applied
even to the animals

**were to touch the
mountain,
it had to be stoned**

or thrust through with a
knife (Ex. 19:13)

**12:21. And so terrible
was that which appeared**

the sort of things which
appeared

**Moses said: "I am
overcome with fear
and trembling"**

This statement does not actually occur in the incident in Exodus.
This fact was used as an argument by those who denied the
Pauline authorship of the epistle. Perhaps the author mentions
it here because we read that Moses was terrified in a similar
situation when he lay prostrate before the thorn bush and did
not dare to look at God (Ex. 3). Or again, when about to divide
the Red Sea he heard God say: "Why criest thou to me?" (Ex.
14:15). From this it would appear that he had trembled on this
occasion too, but it is not recorded in the interests of the
priesthood, in case it should ever be said that the giver of the
law had been terrified of the law.

**12:22. Nay! Ye are
come to Mount Zion**

The Church begotten from
Zion, as it says in Ps. 110:2:
"The Lord shall send the
rod of thy strength out of
Zion." As if he meant to
imply that he had sent the
rod of weakness out of Sinai.

and to the city

of the living God	which had to be incorporeal and invisible (Isa. 66:1)
heavenly Jerusalem	the invisible Jerusalem

In actual fact all these things now spoken of are invisible though worthy of our love, just as all the other things were visible and deserving of fear. These must be approached in faith and in the spirit, just as the former were approached in actuality on the feet and in the flesh. And it is a great joy that by faith there is brought to pass for us, nay rather are actually ours, God, Christ, the Church, the angels, the saints and all else.

and to the company of thousands upon thousands of angels,	gathered together countless
12:23. The Church of the first-born,	the patriarchs, those who were called
whose names are written in heaven, and to God the Judge of all,	that means the avenger of his adversaries and our defender
and to the spirits of just men made perfect,	the righteous souls of the faithful
and to Jesus the mediator of the new covenant, and to the sprinkling of his blood	priest and conqueror the blood of sprinkling, with which we are sprinkled in baptism, as it was prefigured in former times by the sprinkling of blood in the law
which has better things to say than Abel's.	

Because the blood of Abel "cries out from the earth" for vengeance (Gen. 4:10). But the blood of Christ has been sprinkled on our hearts, and this blood (which is faith in Christ) calls "Abba," "Father!" (Rom. 8:15; Gal. 4:6).

**12:25. Take heed, do
not refuse to listen
to him who is speaking**   whether he is speaking
                                  through the blood of Christ
                                  or through faith

**for if they did not
escape**   the vengeance, but were
                                  "struck down in the
                                  desert" (Heb. 3:17)

**when they refused
to listen to him**   Moses
who spake on earth   he was setting forth the
                                  oracles of God and the
                                  Word of God

much more we   shall not escape the
                                  vengeance

if we turn away from him   Christ
who speaks from heaven.
12:26. Whose voice   in Mount Sinai
then shook the earth,   it shook the mountain, and
                                  the very men on earth
                                  themselves

**but now he has
promised and said,**   Hag. 2:7.
yet once more   that is in the New
                                  Testament

**and I will shake
not only the earth**

This is understood by interpreters as the movement of the earth, and that means the men on earth. This is a reference to Judea when men registered themselves as a result of the edict of Augustus Caesar (Luke 2:3).

but heaven as well.   This means the angels when
                                  they appeared to the
                                  shepherds and sang "Glory
                                  to God in the highest."

This reference to "the highest" may be understood as referring to the shaking of the universe, and that means all the people in it. This finds frequent mention in the psalms and in the prophets. For example, "The Lord reigneth . . . the world is established that it cannot be moved . . ." (Ps. 93:1). Again, ". . . sing unto the Lord, all the earth" (Ps. 96:1). Again, "The Lord reigneth; let the earth rejoice . . ." (Ps. 97:1). Again, "Let the heavens rejoice, and let the earth be glad . . ." (Ps. 96:11). Heaven is referred to as well. This means the apostles and the Christian saints who are in the world. [Luther gives only the first text and an "etc.": the editor has supplied the last three examples from *WA* in place of the "etc." Ed.]

12:27. The phrase is "yet once more." This means the removal of the things that were intended to be moved,

the abrogation, cessation

those things that were temporal; types

i.e., the things that have been made, that the things which cannot be shaken

made by men

the things spiritual, and not made by man. These things are the things of faith, because they are eternal.

may stand for ever.

12:28. Wherefore, inheriting a kingdom that cannot be shaken

let us inherit

the eternal kingdom of faith

let us receive the grace by which we may serve God acceptably, with fear and reverence

in worship, or as we usually say, with devotion.

12:29 Because our God is a consuming fire.

Deut. 4:24.

CHAPTER THIRTEEN

The Apostle is reaching the end of his epistle, and, as is his usual practice at the close of his letters, establishes by means of a few short precepts, a sound mode of life and the virtues worthy of a Christian.

13:1. Let brotherly love
All the apostles exhort men to love one another under the appeal of the lovely description "brotherly love."
be firmly established among you
Note that among Christians it is not only friendship that is proper, but brotherly friendship. As Christ says, "One is your father in heaven," "and ye are all brothers" (Matt. 23:9, 8). The Lord's Prayer also commands this clearly enough when it says, "Our father . . ." and not "my father . . ."

13:2. Do not forget to show hospitality   as if to say, persevere in it.
for in doing this men have before today entertained angels unawares   they received as guests angels, not knowing they were angels, as in the case of Abraham (Gen. 18:3) and Lot (Gen. 19:2).

"Unawares": "they lay hidden or concealed." The angels lay hidden under the outward appearance of guests. The translation does not give the full meaning of the Greek idiom. Chrysostom interprets it thus[1]: "They lay hidden. What does this word mean? It is this: not knowing it they received angels

[1] *Loc. cit.*; Migne, 63.443.

as guests. It is because of this that the reward is great. But had they known their guests were angels, there would have been nothing wonderful in what they did." It amounts to this: clearly they did not receive their guests because they were angels, but because they were travellers and would do the same for any other travellers. In this way the Apostle disposes of pettifogging humbugs.

13:3. Remember those who are in prison

in compassion. At any rate by feeling with them and praying for them.

as though ye were prisoners also

for both the good things and the evil things are shared by brethren, particularly Christian brethren

and those who endure suffering

at the hands of persecutors and oppressors

for ye also have mortal bodies

and to that extent have been exposed to these same sufferings.

13:4. Marriage must be held in honour by everybody

by those who want to get married, and those who are married

Honourable, not because he orders everybody to get married, but because he wants no one to be a whoremonger, which is exactly what I Cor. 7:9 means when it says, "If they are unable to restrain themselves, let them marry." In other words, marriage must not be a shameful institution but an honourable one, and not to be respected by a certain few but by all of you.

and the marriage-bed kept free from defilement

intercourse will be temperate and restrained, because it will not be contaminated by the passions of lust, as it is among the heathen

but whoremongers

here is the reason "marriage must be held in honour by everybody" because "God will judge the whoremongers"

and adulterers, God will judge

that is through the medium of the earthly power (Rom. 13) or through the medium of the eternal judgment of God.

In the Old Testament under the law, adultery used to be punished by death, but in the Church neither that nor any other sin is punishable by death. On that account he says: "It is God who will judge the whore-mongers."

13:5. Let your life be free from covetousness

let it be characterized by kindness, that means giving to one another and being obliging one to another.

and be content with what you have

with things as they are, or which you now have

for God himself said "I will not leave thee nor forsake thee"

(Josh. 1:5)

Although we may not have to do the same work as Joshua, whom God never forsook, nor be in exactly the same plight, yet certainly we stand in the same faith and trust. Faith may have different tasks to perform, but they are done in the same spirit. As Paul expresses it: "We share the same faith" (II Cor. 4:13). Therefore, though addressed to Joshua only in the first instance, the truth of this statement rightly applies to all of us.

13:6. So that we may confidently say: "The Lord is my champion. I will not fear what man can do to me"

13:7. Remember those who are set over you,

bishops and presbyters

who preach unto you the word of God,

for this is the proper office of one set over you

contemplate   consider
the happy end of
their life,

They are set over you for two purposes: to preach the Word and give an
example.

and imitate their faith.

13:8. What Jesus Christ was
yesterday and is today
he abides for ever   for he is eternal

Therefore, as he championed those who have gone before, he
will not forsake those now living, nor those still to come.

13:9. Do not be led away
by a welter of doctrines   doctrines of no foundation,
                                      as those concerning
                                      ceremonies

As in the other epistles so also in this one, the author contends against the
doctrine of works and the traditions of human righteousness, clearly
declaring that they lead men astray from the truth.

nor by alien doctrines   innovations

This is what Titus is referring to, ". . . commandments of men
that turn from the truth" (Titus 1:14).

for it is the very best
course   that is to say if you are
                                      after good, that is, true
                                      doctrine
for the heart   the conscience
to be established by grace   by faith
and not by observances in
the matter of food,   not by a righteousness
                                      attained by the eating of
                                      certain foods and other
                                      externalities
which have not profited   have not led to a
                                      strengthening of the heart
those who followed them   those who settled their
                                      hopes on them

The beginning of a real despair in one's own works is the
beginning of faith and steadfastness.

13:10. We have an altar   Christ.
                                      And therefore we are neither

and those who carry out

the worship of the tabernacle

harmed nor are we justified by the eating of meat because they are devoid of faith

which is a shadow of external righteousness, a matter of ceremonies of the law

have no right to eat its sacrifices

For it is impossible to feed on Christ apart from faith.

13:11. When the priest takes the blood of beasts into the sanctuary as an offering for sin, their bodies are burned without the camp

As in Num. 19 and elsewhere concerning the red heifer.

13:12. It was on account of this fact

that he might fulfil the type

that Jesus also, when he sought to sanctify the people with his own blood

not the blood of animals but his very own blood

suffered without the gate.

13:13. Let us therefore go out to him outside the camp

let us follow him by faith outside bodily things and apart from all the ceremonials

For it is a waste of time to go in for these things now: a better door has been opened up for us.

bearing the same reproach that he bore

that means through faith, and also our devotion to him.

It means that we must not be ashamed to confess his reproach. We must follow his example and suffer the same sort of things that he suffered.

13:14. For we have here no abiding city, but seek a city that is yet to be

the future life

That is why the old
Jerusalem and the shadowy
relic of the law no longer
suffice.

**13:15. Therefore it is
through him** the mediator and the priest

It is because we are not worthy to stand before him on our own
merits, that we need a mediator and priest. For just because he
himself makes all things and he alone is Lord of all things,
therefore he alone is to be glorified and worshipped. Therefore
the heathen do not rightly discern the truth here when they
worship. On that account, because they offer to God some
worthless, petty work (Luther is doubtless making allusions to
the countless little externalities of his day), they arrogate to
themselves praise and credit derived from their righteousness.
Against such Ps. 9:6 speaks: "Their name hast thou blotted
out." Therefore, as we are nothing and have nothing, then we
ought not to puff ourselves up either with credit or praise of any
kind, but on the contrary, accuse ourselves of every ignominy
and make ourselves nothing in his sight.

**we must continually
offer to God the
sacrifice of praise,** not of calves, nor of
things extraneous

**that is the fruit of
our lips,** for all the benefits of his
mercy and grace which we
have received

**giving thanks to
his name**

For "God to be justified in his words" (Ps. 51:4) means that he
is justified in our hearts. This simply means that the Word of
God is in the heart. However, for God to be praised in our hearts
is to give God the glory, and ourselves the shame of sin. In short,
it comes about that he who is righteous is in us, and that we
confess him as righteous who is in himself externally righteous.

**13:16. Meanwhile do not
forget to do good
and give alms,** do good to one another
"Communicate in all good
things" (Gal. 6:6)

for with such sacrifices as if he meant to say that
these are the true sacrifices

God is pleased.

But he is not pleased by the blood of goats and all the rest. "The fulfilment of the law is love" (Rom. 13:10).

13:17. Obey those set over you and submit yourselves to them: for they watch over your souls

with reverence

if they are worthy of their office

as they that have an account to render,

as Ezek. 3:18 clearly records, "I will require his soul at thine hand."

so that they may perform this task

labour and watch over your souls

with joy

moved by your obedience and humility

and not with sorrow. For that is not to your advantage.

In fact it procures your damnation

13:18. Pray for us. For we trust

because we do not know for certain. It is the Lord who determines: our role is to believe (I Cor. 4:4).

we have a good conscience, in all things, wanting to live honestly. 13:19 But I beseech you the more earnestly to do this that I may be restored to you the sooner

pray for us

This is an argument for the Pauline authorship of the epistle, for this remark sounds like captivity and imprisonment.

13:20. Now God, the author of peace, who brought again from the dead that great shepherd of the sheep, our Lord Jesus Christ

the high priest

**by the blood of an
everlasting covenant**

a covenant is the matter
that has been covenanted.
It is a covenant of an
eternal righteousness fulfilled
by the shedding of his
blood.

**13:21. furnish you
in every good work
to do his will.**

grant you perfect capacity

not your own will, not the
will of the flesh, and not
the will of the world.

**May he carry out in you
what is pleasing in
his sight**

through or by means of you

even if it is displeasing to
you.

For this is the rule, so often proved true, that the things which
please God are not pleasing to us. There are two wills, God's
will and our will, and they run contrary to one another.
Therefore, for God's will to come to pass is nothing other than
that our own will be destroyed, and in this way become more
and more conformed to the divine will. And this is what Paul
means when he says that the old man is crucified with Christ
(Rom. 6:6).

**through Jesus Christ to
whom be the glory for
ever and ever, Amen.**

**13:22. I beseech you
brethren, to bear patiently
with this word of comfort,**

although it may seem to
you to be a word of
chiding. If, however, you
endure rightly, it will turn
out to be a word of
comfort.

**for I have written to you
but a short letter**

and yet I owe you much on
account of my office, and
you by virtue of necessity
are in need.

13:23. Ye must know

receive him affectionately

that our brother Timothy
has been set at liberty,
with whom, if he comes   to me
soon, I will see you.

13:24. Greet all those in
authority, and all the
saints.   the Christians
The brethren from Italy
send you their greetings.

13:25. Grace be with you
all. Amen.

In the year 1517.

Disputation against Scholastic Theology

WA, I, 221–228

INTRODUCTION

IT IS TRUE THAT SCHOLASTICISM CRUMBLED BEFORE the Humanists and the Reformers, but it is right to recall that when the great schoolmen arose in the thirteenth century they proved to be the saviours of the Christian religion. Christianity then faced, to mention but a few of its difficulties, the threats of Manicheeism; apocalyptic communism; the science and philosophy of the Arabs and the Jews; the modernists anxious to forsake the old for the new; mysticism; Augustinianism. Augustinianism is hardly a threat to Christianity, but at this moment it took the form of a traditionalism and conservatism which was a protective mechanism against the responsibility of facing current criticisms and new thought. Further, Christian theology was Platonist and on such a philosophic basis was hardly suited to contain the new modern scientific thinking.

The schoolmen were able to meet the new situation by the rediscovery of Aristotle. But it is only fair to the schoolmen to remind ourselves that these men incurred all the odium that Erasmus earned from his contemporaries when they had made of scholastic theology an authority instead of a temper. Erasmus (as Luther) faced the hot-heads on one side and the die-hards on the other: too few men wanted to claim the new learning for the Church and strengthen her thinking. The schoolmen faced a similar human situation, and they triumphed by the labours of men like Hales, Albertus and Aquinas. These men engaged on a consistent attempt to set up the Christian faith as a ruling principle in all departments of men's activity. They taught men to think, to classify their knowledge and discipline their thought.

They were somewhat hampered by their idea of authority. Theology dominated their studies as "the queen of the sciences."

251

They were right in seeking for a synthesis of all knowledge, but they believed that there could never be a satisfactory explanation of the universe which left God out of account, nor could there be a right grasp of his revelation unless that revelation were interpreted in the scientific light of all the facts. It was not only that they believed in the verbal inspiration of the Bible; the Fathers were authoritative too. Aristotle became to them inerrant, and they were very reluctant to make any real criticism of Augustine. But if their authorities hampered them from our point of view, they helped them from theirs. The schoolman must not be thought of as crippled in his intellectual chains. On his own premises he was a daring rationalist. Before looking at the scholasticism which had no answers to offer to Humanist and Reformer alike we need to recall the daring intellectualism and unquestioning faith by which God gave it birth. If one were to suggest one single failing it would be its very value: men later used its system as an authority rather than an approach, and it failed in the day of trial. But we must recall that the inheritors of the Reformation did the same with the Reformers and gave us another scholasticism as rigid as their fathers had been compelled to demolish.

The brief summary of scholasticism which follows is essentially a selective treatment of the issues with which Luther was concerned and claims in no sense to be complete. There is in this analysis less of the glorious scholasticism of the eleventh and twelfth centuries and more of the pernickety scholasticism in its days of degradation. This lack of balance arises from the nature of this volume. We are here concerned to clarify the antecedents of the issues with which the young Luther was involved, and not to give a full account of the centuries of scholasticism.

Readers are reminded of the other volumes in this series whose purpose it is to meet the need of some comprehensive survey in the field. First there is Volume X, *A Scholastic Miscellany: Anselm to Ockham*, compiled by E. R. Fairweather, which touches the theme of this present volume only at the end with its brief extracts from Scotus (428 ff.) and Ockham (p. 437 ff.), though Fairweather's introduction to his volume (p. 17 ff.), as well as his excellent general bibliography (p. 33 ff.) are germane, and the selections from Richard St. Victor (p. 319 ff.) and Bonaventure (p. 379 ff.) related. Volume XI on *Nature and Grace*, which consists of selections from the *Summa Theologica* made by A. M. Fairweather, shows the thinking of Thomas on the nature of theology, his doctrine of God, sin, predestination and grace, as well as ethics. Volume XIII on *Late Medieval Mysticism*, compiled by Petry, raises issues which are more important for the later Luther than the younger Luther, the period selected for the present volume. Chapter I on Bernard of Clairvaux (p. 47 ff.), Chapter II on the Victorines (p. 79 ff.), Chapter IV on Bonaventure (p. 126 ff.) and Chapter XI on the *Theologia Germanica* (p. 321 ff.) of the late fourteenth century give useful writings of the mystic school of theology which Luther was later to attack with so much vigour as an invalid approach to God.

Let us then engage on a brief historical enquiry as to the nature of scholasticism with a view to understanding the scholasticism with which Luther became involved. We may most conveniently begin with *Thomas Aquinas* (1226–74). Fundamental to the approach of Thomas lay a clear distinction between reason and faith. He believed that by clear thinking a real harmony could be established between faith and knowledge, between natural and revealed religion. Just as philosophy starting from natural fact arrives at truth by reason, so similarly theology starting from revealed fact proceeds to knowledge of God by the light of faith. Philosophy has a different starting point from theology as well as a different sphere of activity, but both philosophy and theology have the same method and the same goal. As a philosopher Thomas was an Aristotelian realist, and as a theologian he had the evangelicalism of Augustinianism with its stress on sin, predestination and grace.

Plato would appear a more suitable philosopher than Aristotle to provide a background to Christian belief since he regards the material universe as created and the spiritual as being above the material. But while this was his strength it was also his danger, for such a view opened the door to all kinds of mystical speculation. It was the very limitation of Aristotle that made him so acceptable, even necessary. Aristotle's philosophy stood for the highest which unaided human reason could of itself attain. It served to emphasize the truths of revelation by showing that these truths were unknown to the Greeks and were not discoverable by natural reason. It was, moreover, the only philosophical basis on which the future experimental science could build: modern science could hardly have been nurtured in a Platonic cradle.

Although Aristotle's influence was paramount in the philosophical formulation of Christian thought the schoolmen should not be thought of as hide-bound Aristotelians. Thomas was highly original in his philosophy of being, and is often clearly Augustinian. Bonaventure was Aristotelian as far as the description of facts was concerned, but his theology was heavily Augustinian and tinged with Platonism. Neither Scotus nor Ockham could be described as thoroughgoing Aristotelianists, and Scotus was certainly more inclined towards Plato and Augustine than was Thomas.

Thomas took the two decisive steps that meant the substitution of Christian Aristotelianism for Augustianism. The first was the separation of faith from reason, the second was to make the senses the source of all human knowledge. Man had two sources of information, Creation and Revelation. Creation could be explored, Revelation had to be accepted, shown to be reasonable and finally, by analogy, related to other knowledge. Reason was man's highest gift. It enabled him to think God's thoughts afresh. He believed in a rational religion. He rejected Anselm's ontological proof, yet, in making his starting point sense experience, from which he argued back to a First Cause, he was assuming the validity of Anselm's argument. All the sciences he related in a hierarchy of dignity, and sought their complete explanation in God. If convinced of the all-pervading power of God he was equally convinced of the freedom of the human will. If man were not free then he could not be virtuous nor God just. Evil he thought of as negative, and sin as concupiscence rather than rebellious will. He thought of man as under a *lex naturalis* valid for his own well-being as well as for the preservation of society; but as also under a supernatural order whose obligations could be fulfilled only with the help of grace. Grace he did not restrict to the fruits of the incarnation, and unlike the Reformers did not feel compelled to regard humanity as a mass of perdition. Grace he always thought of as a gift, and though repudiating any idea of desert certainly made room for merit. In teaching ethics he began with the theological virtues of faith, hope and charity, received only through grace; the cardinal virtues were of the *lex naturalis*. Within this context he incorporated Aristotle's *Ethics*.

If Thomas was an intellectualist and champion of reason, *Bonaventure* (1221–1274) was a mystic and champion of faith[1]. Thomas regarded contemplation of truth as the end of man, Bonaventure love. Thomas was an Aristotelian who incorporated Augustine in his scheme of thinking, Bonaventure an Augustinian who treated Aristotle with caution and had for him a very limited sympathy. He thought all human knowledge but folly when compared with the mystical illumination which God sheds on the faithful Christian.

His most extensive work was his Commentaries on the Sentences of Peter Lombard. His theory of knowledge he set forth in his *Itinerarium mentis ad Deum* a translation of which is to be found in Volume XIII of this series, page 126 ff. In his *Breviloquium*, a handbook of theology, he begins with God and the Trinity, and then goes on to the creation, corruption caused by sin, the incar-

[1] See in this series Vol. X, p. 379 ff.; Vol. XIII, p. 126 ff.

nation, the Holy Spirit, the sacraments and the last four things. In his *Itinerarium* he reverses the process and describes the ascent of the soul to God, the validity of which journey Luther was so strenuously to deny. Bonaventure began with the assumption that man being a sinner could start only by praying for repentance. First, he finds vestiges of God in the world around him; second, by contemplation he seeks and finds the image of God in his own soul; thirdly, he rises to a direct knowledge of God and becomes partaker of the divine nature.

He teaches that the certitudes of faith are prior to and superior to reason, and where Thomas argues from analogy Bonaventure argues from intuition. He believes that man must believe before he can understand. Not that he depreciates reason, for he speaks of the great joy of the soul which understands what it believes. He knew that man cannot know what God is, but must first know that he is. Knowledge of God follows after this. He accepted Anselm's ontological argument. He taught that all enquiry and knowledge start with, and must start with, an enquiry into God.

He differs from Thomas in his attitude to creation. He does not believe that the *materia prima* is potentiality, but rather that it contains *rationes seminales*. It is in their view of creation that a deep difference appears between Thomas and Bonaventure. Bonaventure thinks less of its purpose and more of its beauty. Thomas saw the world as a wonderful machine adapted to certain ends, while Bonaventure (a true son of St. Francis) bowed down in rapture because the world in its beauty spoke to him of God.

Bonaventure understood the nature of man in a way different from Thomas. He believed that body and soul were alike endowed with matter and form, and thereby escaped Thomas's difficulty in accounting for the soul's survival after death. At the same time he rejected the platonizing theory that the soul is related to the body as the boatman to his boat, for the body is much more than the instrument of the soul. He viewed man as a real entity however composite; and this belief was possible for Bonaventure because, unlike Thomas, he recognized the possibility of a plurality of forms. The body to Bonaventure was sacred because the Word had become flesh. The human life of Jesus was the inspiration of all Bonaventure's work.

His views on the sacraments were somewhat different from those of Thomas. He did not share the view of Thomas that the sacraments were the actual physical causes of grace. He formulated the doctrine which came to be known as Occasionalism, and which shows itself again at the time of the Reformation. This was the opinion that the sacrament was of no use apart from its appointed use.

For *Bernard of Clairvaux* (1090–1153) readers are advised to consult the introductory article in Volume XIII of this series, page 47, as well as the twenty-four pages of his writings which the editor of that volume selected.

Bernard is known to have had an influence on the young Luther. He was a saintly, monkish character with a clear grasp of theological problems. He was an eloquent preacher, a master of the text of the Bible, and possessed that sublime faith of the pure mystic. He was a man of deep prayer as well as a faithful and loyal churchman.

He took the view that God should be loved purely and simply because he is God and is there. (See his treatise, *On Loving God*, Volume XIII, p. 54.) Strongly Augustinian, his thinking centred on the two poles of the Love and Grace of God on the one hand with the resultant free response of man on the other. Luther went through all this as a monk, and had not a little of Bernard about him, but he emerged from it all by breaking with most of it and setting the remainder in a quite different perspective.

The great rival school to Thomism was Scotism, founded by the Franciscan *Duns Scotus* (1246–1308). Though Scotism never enjoyed the authority Thomism enjoyed and still enjoys, in Luther's day the evangelical theology of Thomas seemed largely neglected and Scotism dominated the schools.

The differentia of Scotism arose from the grounds on which Scotus criticized the philosophy of Thomas. Scotus was a realist, too, though inclined to Platonism rather than Aristotelianism. Theology he considered not a speculative science but a practical science; faith rested not on reason but authority; and the will is the moving power of the intellect rather than the intellect the moving principle of the will. To these differences many deeper issues were added. The Scotists opposed the Augustinianism of the Thomists by a Pelagianizing tendency: if Thomas approaches Calvin in his predestinarianism, Scotus approaches Pelagius in his libertarianism. By emphasizing love and will over against knowledge and reason he fatally widened the gap between faith and reason, thus tending to make philosophy into a logician's playground, fenced off from the world of actual experience. He opened up the way for his successors to hypostasize any abstract term.

It was Scotus' view on universals that made him concern himself with the meaning of the particular and the individual which in turn gave him his emphasis on the freedom of the will and ultimately its freedom to earn merit and qualify for the *meritum de congruo*. It was his emphasis on the will in his theology that served to cut men free from their old moorings of institutions and beliefs and to prepare the way for revolution.

With regard to the incarnation the minds of Scotus and Thomas ran on different lines. Scotus viewed the incarnation as God's original intention, and this in turn made him think of the cross as determined because of the sin of man. Thomas, on the other hand, viewed the incarnation as a consequence of man's sin.

Scotus came near to denying the sacrifice of the mass, and the centre of gravity of his thinking seems to have moved towards the view of thinking of the mass rather as an activity of the Church with our Lord in a passive role. This thinking would appear to have had two consequences. First, it partly prepared the ground for the Reformer's criticism of the Roman view of the mass as a sacrifice. And secondly, it led to the multiplication of masses and that ghastly abuse of satisfactory masses.

The critical powers inherent in his theology disintegrated medieval theology by widening the gap between faith and reason. He awakened critical faculties but paradoxically stimulated a blind and unquestioning reliance on the Church as "Authority." He allowed Aristotle the field of Physics, but in the realm of the spirit only the Bible (interpreted by the Church and Pope) was the sure guide to ultimate truth.

Of the schoolmen who most influenced Luther Ockham was the chief (1300–1349). Since the days of Bede and the British missionaries, British theology has never had the influence and the respect on the Continent that it had in the days of Scotus and Ockham (Hales notwithstanding): it has certainly enjoyed little since those days, though Wyclif receives some recognition.

When Luther matriculated it was on the roll of Germany's most famous University of Erfurt, already an ancient institution. Its theology was modernist scholastic, which meant Scotist, and its philosophy nominalist. In the convent later, he came under the influence of Ockham's theology as mediated by Gabriel Biel (p. 260 f) and Peter d'Ailly (p. 260). There was in fact a certain measure of secular pressure to encourage Ockhamism in Germany. His popularity in this respect seemed to arise from his attitude to the papacy. He denounced the wealth and temporal power of the papacy, arguing that Christ bequeathed spiritual not temporal power. He placed the plenitude of power with the emperor, a view Luther shared, and which the German princes found agreeable.

Ockham hated the abstractions of the Scotists, and in opposition to their multiplications of entities his logic had a "razor edge." His "razor" was the principle *entia non sunt multiplicanda*. What

Ockham was concerned to attack was the alleged reality of abstract or independent universals as existing in their own right. He denied that the concept "Cause" had any reality outside the human mind. For him only the individual actual thing was real. It had to be observed, analysed, tested, without any preconceptions. Ockham was the prophet of the modern scientific outlook.

Ockham introduced a modified nominalist position, which may be more accurately defined as terminism. For him universals were real in quite a certain, concrete sense. He knew what he meant and what other people meant by a term like "humanity." Ideas like law, cause, purpose and so on were convenient fabrications of the mind. Such universal terms as he did admit were real terms with which to think and argue. What he sought to deny was the notion of independent or abstract universals. He certainly tended in some ways to divorce theology from philosophy because he would not have final causes mixed up with natural events, and he saw nature as contingent on the will of God. In this way he clearly adumbrated the modern world which began to realize that nature could be known only by examining nature. In the end he held that contingent events could only be known through the element of necessity they involved, but he did seek for order in nature through observing and thinking out the order in the empirical series of events, that is in relationships and connections of events and consequences. To the rationalists this appeared like denying the reality of nature, but it was really an adaptation of the reason to a mode of rationality required by natural and contingent events for their knowing. The point of relation of Ockham to the ordered universe of Thomas was that the universe was not ordered in that severely rationalist way through the impregnation of nature with final causes, but it was rational and ordered in another way. Rational may mean logical as understood according to formal logic; if so, then, nature is not rational in that sense. Ockham distinguished between *scientia realis* and *scientia rationalis* where the latter referred to the logical sciences. Thus Ockham represents a change from a more static view of God and creation to a more dynamic outlook. He strongly criticized Aristotelian and contemporary physics as tied up with Aristotelian metaphysics, and this thinking helped to open the way up for new thinking and genuine movement. It loosened the moorings of thought from its ontology of Aristotelian physics, and so indirectly helped to bring about changes and fresh thinking. But this had earlier been made possible in 1277 when the Church condemned the Arabian view that Aristotle has said the last word in physics and metaphysics. Ockham saw that the universally accepted Aristotelian logic was bound with Aristotelian physics, and that when once the physics came under attack, the logical problems were all open, and it became clear that the logical method did not apply to nature or contingent events.

Such thinking meant obviously that it was impossible to *argue* the existence of God. Only observed facts were real, and all argument of necessity *ex supposito*. This meant that man could know nothing of God apart from revelation. After Ockham the ordered universe of Thomas was questioned, the arguments from analogy had lost their cogency, and the whole scheme of natural theology modified. Ockham transferred all the articles of religion to the province of faith, and effected a divorce between religion and science, between faith and reason. Ockham's "agnosticism," if that word may be allowed, contributed not a little to the theological pessimism and restlessness of the late Middle Ages.

Paradoxically, his general agnosticism made for a strong authoritarianism. He insisted on the validity even the infallibility of revelation, by which he meant Scripture and the mind of the Church. True, he believed that popes, councils, fathers, doctors had erred, but he assigned to the whole lot a general aura of authority and infallibility. He accepted the creeds, the doctrine of transubstantiation, the immaculate conception, miracles, the cult of saints. These he thought were deduceable from reason, if not demonstrable by reason. His contention against Thomas was his intellectualism, as well as his subordination of the practical to the theoretical. He sought to make theology less speculative and more practical.

This temper tended to make his dynamic of faith less a matter of pure intellect and more a matter of will. A man could and must prepare the way for God's grace by achieving his own *contritio* and thereby earning his own *meritum de congruo* to which God would grant his *meritum de condigno*. If a man played his part, then Christ played his. It was at this point that Luther was most troubled: he could never be sure that he had done all he should, and therefore could never know God's full mercy in Christ. When Luther resolved this issue evangelical theology was reborn.

If Ockham taught a doctrine of the will in God and man which led to a stress on merit and to Pelagianism, it also opened up the way for the consideration of the Church as a community of believers. The danger of this view was that it led later into independentism, which was followed not by Lutheranism nor Calvinism but by the free churchmen.

The influence of Ockham on Luther is variously estimated. It might be suggested that he took over from him a consubstantialist view of the Holy Communion. It might also be argued that he followed Ockham in his idea of the "godly prince," and with it the corollary that the Church had no authority in secular affairs. There was also the characteristic emphasis of Ockham, shared by Luther, that true theology was born not of speculation but of a rightly directed will. Other emphases of Ockham which may be claimed to have had an influence on Luther were his separation of religion from worldly learning and his making of an antinomy between faith and reason. Faith to Ockham did not follow a train of reasoning, but had its source in the Scriptures and in the Church. Ockham's teaching on merit stirred by contrast a fresh line of thought in Luther. Ockham's critical mind and general agnosticism certainly prepared the ground for Luther's criticism, whilst his emphasis on will and free will called out Luther's powerful emphasis on the servile will. The scientific attack on a problem which was such a characteristic of Ockham and his persistence in looking at a thing in itself apart from any preconceptions, was certainly a mark of Luther's approach to a problem. Some of these influences might be questioned and scholars are not unanimous. Be that as it may, Ockham certainly helped Luther by leaving open at several points medieval rationalism, thus making possible a more dynamic way of thinking, as well as giving a critique of Aristotelian presuppositions which threw faith back on to revelation (which meant the Bible) and challenged the mingling of final causes with nature.

Of the other scholastic theologians criticized by Luther in the disputation against scholastic theology which we are about to translate, little need be said. First there is *Pierre d'Ailly* (1350–1420). He was a French cardinal, and a theologian of Ockhamist outlook. He will be remembered for his work in healing the Western Schism, and for his tractate on the reform of the Church published in 1416 and later used at the Council of Trent. He influenced the Reformers by his view that the authority of clergy derives from Christ and not the pope, as well as by his views that neither pope nor council was infallible. (He was also remarkable for his studies outside the area of theology. In his studies on geography he suggested reaching the Indies by proceeding westwards, studies with which Columbus was acquainted.)

Secondly, there is *Gabriel Biel* (*c.* 1420–1495), one of the last of the great scholastics, and like Luther later, trained at Erfurt. He was one of the founders of the University of Tübingen where he occupied the chair of theology. He is chiefly remembered for his exaggerated views on the sacrifice of the mass and the restricted value he placed on the sacrament of penance, and also (though of less interest for our examination), for his relating theology to commercial life.

For our purposes his theology is Ockhamist, and it was this Ockhamist theology which Biel developed that was, in its theological consequences, a prime factor in the disintegration of scholasticism for it withdrew almost all the data of faith from the realm of reason. The criticism Luther makes of Biel in this disputation could equally well be directed against his master Ockham, and we shall see in the following pages the religious and theological issues Luther selected as the live questions of his day.

Although Luther makes no direct mention of him in this disputation, nevertheless *Nicholas of Cusa* (1400–1464), the German cardinal and philosopher, has a place in this survey. Nicholas was a forerunner of the Renascence. He distrusted both logic and the syllogistic method, and all systems which explained the world. He was more aware of what he did not know than of what he did know. He taught that the proper attitude of man to God was one of wonder; men found God not by reason but by intuition, which God gave to the humble and patient. Truth he conceived of as something infinite, unknowable, absolute and one: man's knowledge was relative, multiple, complex and approximate. He knew that reason could not tolerate contradictions, and yet he saw that knowledge abounded in these contradictions. He believed that these opposites would ultimately find their reconciliation in God. He thought of God as infinitely great yet infinitely small, the maximum yet the minimum, the centre of the world yet its circumference, everywhere yet nowhere, neither one nor three but triune.

He was a great all-rounder, as so many of the scholastic theologians were. He was both mathematician as well as astronomer. He saw that the earth revolved, that it was not the centre of the universe, that the orbit of the heavenly bodies was not circular. (Copernicus was born some nine years after his death.) He showed considerable gifts as an historian rejecting as spurious the False Decretals of Isidore and the Forged Donation of Constantine. He saw the dangers of a neo-paganism on the horizon and tried to win the new learning for Christ. He knew that the degenerate Thomists and Scotists made no appeal to the new scholars and poets, and looked for a new synthesis in neo-Platonism and in Dionysius. He failed in his task, for the humanists had a deeper interest in the world than in metaphysics.

It is not easy for us to appreciate the deplorable degradation of the scholastic method. It deteriorated to the putting of endless *questiones*, not of the kind a modern scientist is continually setting to his hypotheses, but fruitless questions which were divided over and over again into further questions leading nowhere but fizzling out in trivialities and absurdities, into contentiousness and futile curiosity. The Scotist stress on logic emphasized this tendency, though Ockham took advantage of it to expose absurdities. Erasmus and the humanists lampooned these worthless and mischievous intellectual gymnastics: Luther attacked them in the interests of a true theology based on Scripture, Catholic tradition and common sense.

Because the great schoolmen had been too successful in the thirteenth century, the later schoolmen were in bondage to their great predecessors, and in the end, with all freedom of thought sacrificed, they wrangled among themselves and the world ignored them. The Dominicans followed Thomas, the Franciscans Scotus. This sectarianism was disastrous. They followed their master rather than the truth, and when they found themselves in a tight corner they multiplied verbal distinctions. The later schoolmen lived in retirement, and speculated on abstruse problems not caring whether laymen were interested. Even Thomas More said of them that reading the schoolmen was like trying to milk a he-goat into a sieve. Their interest seemed to lie in a barren logic. They loved arguing the absurd, and the common man knew that they were getting nowhere.

By the time that Luther was a young man the world was thrilling at the classics: they found the philosophy of Cicero better than all the subtleties of Scotus. They found the deductive reasoning of the schoolmen faulty because they did not start out with their premises. The schoolmen failed because they could not meet the intellectual demands of the age.

Natural science was born and metaphysics died, and the old learning was first flouted and overthrown by humanism. The age of logic and reason were over. Men fought the controversies of the Reformation over questions of fact not techniques of logic. The scholastic theologians were unable to resist the Reformers: they were pedants who had lost the ear of the people, and became Aunt Sallies for the irreverent scholars of the Renascence.

It is interesting to study the points selected by Luther for discussion on his disputation against scholastic theology. He is engaged not on a negative fault-finding mission but on a positive truth-finding mission. When we study this document, and in fact the more we study the other documents of those tumultuous and troublesome years, the more we need constantly to remind ourselves that in Martin there is nothing of the rebel. He hated revolution and revolt, enthusiasm and excitement: he traced in these the hoof of Satan and not the finger of God. Luther rightly claimed all his life that he held and taught true catholic doctrine, and that he held the true catholic creeds and belonged to the true catholic Church. His criticism of the Roman Church of his day was that over the centuries it had allowed itself to be cluttered up with human theories and traditions and perversions, and it was these he opposed and only these in the interests of a pure Christianity. He appealed to the pope; he pleaded for a General Council representative of all Christendom; he appealed to the laity, that the noble should lead and the peasant heed: and always and only in the interests of the unadulterated gospel. That the pope and emperor opposed him and took with them vast numbers of Christians dismayed Martin but did not deter him. The full truth of the gospel was involved. Martin was like Abraham and all our succeeding great fathers in God whom history will always remember in the company of those who heard God and went out in faith. When we see Martin concerned about perversions of the faith we should remind ourselves that he is concerned for a true faith over against false ideas of faith. True, these perversions can be said to have been started as real genuine efforts to make Christianity comprehensive and acceptable to a developing world, but equally true, they were too often attempts to reduce it to terms low enough to be acceptable to a paganism which was in fact much older than Christianity.

Luther approached this vast intractable spiritual problem of Western Christendom less from the theoretical and intellectual angle and more from the pastoral and spiritual. There was no impetuosity but rather the painful concern and reluctance of a Jeremiah. He saw souls being lost. He saw men in intellectual darkness and uncertainty. He saw Christ being thrust out of the centre of faith. Luther was gravely concerned about this at this time, and his attack on the indulgences scandal should be seen primarily as a concern for men that they come to know God by his mercy in Jesus Christ. It was on this issue that he came eventually to write the Ninety-Five Theses, for scholasticism based on Aristotle was committed to a theory of salvation which was a form of works-righteousness and, therefore, for true Christian theology to be made known, Aristotelian scholasticism had to be dethroned. True, the issue came to a head in the matter of indulgences historically, but it could have come to a head in a dispute on Pelagianism, bondage of the will, faith and works, to mention but a few. The real issue was to find a Christology with all the fullness, freshness, fervour and faith of the apostles: the Christology of Luther's day had been too long encrusted with the follies of the human mind and the foibles of the human spirit.

Medieval theology always admitted in theory that a man's salvation depended ultimately on the prevenient grace of God and on this issue never repudiated Augustine. But in its reverence for Aristotle it had to find a place for the action of man's free will. Scotus taught that the process of justification was an infusion of divine grace which creates a habit of the will towards a love of God and a love of man. This is appropriated by acts of the will which are meritorious, and these gradually change a sinner into a righteous person by setting him on this process. The obvious way to get the initial grace is by means of the sacraments which infuse grace. Grace is infused at Baptism and more and more in the Eucharist. Such is the process. But it is not unimpeded. It is warred against by sin which defeats the life-giving process of justification. Such is the human plight. Penance then, on this analysis, comes to occupy the place of the cardinal doctrine round which all these things hinge. Luther saw that this system had the effect (unintended) of depriving a man of the full meaning of the sacraments of Baptism and Holy Communion. With this doctrine of penance there was involved all the teaching of the distinction between *attritio* and *contritio*; the system of satisfactions imposed by the priestly hierarchy with all its mitigating scheme of indulgences and the revolting pecuniary traffic all too often involved; the treasury of merits; congruent and condign merit; Purgatory, disciplines and punishments.

Luther saw, and knew for himself, that it was possible for a man to range through the whole gamut of the religious process the medieval Church prescribed and yet never know what pardon, sin, repentance, forgiveness and grace really meant as offered in and by Christ. Its whole system was semi-Pelagian at heart and was based on human self-righteousness or works-righteousness. The Church had lost the Augustinian doctrines of grace. She had forgotten to teach the supreme value of faith and of inward righteousness. The whole system taught men to evade the consequences of their sin, while Christianity in its real intent sought to open men to the gravity of sin in order that they may be moved to repent and see and accept God's grace and mercy. In other words, the then Roman conception of salvation deprived man of the mercy of the gospel and the centrality of Christ.

But that was not all. Luther called the whole scholastic theology by the opprobrious name of "sophistry" and its exponents "sophists." Scholastic theology, he alleged, exercised a baleful influence and performed a disservice to true theology: it raised questions life never set and gave answers no man wanted. Its massive intellectual edifice was but a pseudo-structure, for its God was the idolatrous God of Greek and Pagan, Turk and Jew, philosopher and humanist, and certainly not the God and Father of our Lord Jesus Christ. Luther's charge against scholasticism was that it was serving to change Christianity into something quite other than God intended, and that its tendency was towards an anthropology to the loss of its Christology. The schoolmen attempted to reconcile faith and reason by thinking of faith as the sum of the truths extracted from Scripture by the fathers, and reason (given in its highest form in Plato and Aristotle) as the power of human reason to reconcile them. Consequently, to make the Christian revelation fit these thought forms, Christianity had gradually lost almost its entire Biblical realism and dynamism. Not even Aquinas starting with the idea of God as the Absolute and the First Cause can reach Jerusalem from Athens, and certainly his Aristotelian idea of the free will was bound to lead to works-righteousness in some form or another.

Luther wanted to stand alongside the Christians of ancient times when the world was free of all medieval sophistries. He thought the only thing worthy of thought was the doctrine of Christ: His work and our knowledge and experience of that Work. We can only know God in Christ. Anything else, anything more, anything less is idolatry. Christ fills the whole sphere of God for Luther. Christ is *the* revealer, the only revealer we have. Jesus compels us to see God in him—the whole of God. In other words, a God who kept nothing of himself back from man which he could give. With Luther all theology was Christology. His attack on Aristotelian scholasticism was in the interests of a true Christology, so that Christ be allowed to do his proper work.

Some two months before the nailing up of his theses in protest against the scandal of indulgences, Luther raised the standard of revolt in the shape of these following theses directed against scholastic theology in the interests of a Christology, biblical in kind and evangelical in effect.

The subdivisions of the Theses as well as the titles thereof are my own and not Luther's. I put them there, as well as an occasional explanatory note, to make the Theses themselves more easily understandable and less technical to the modern reader.

Disputation against Scholastic Theology

THE TEXT

Master Francis Gunther of Nordhausen
will reply to the theses hereunder
for his baccalaureate in the Bible
under the chairmanship of
the Reverend Father Martin Luther,
Augustinian,
Professor of Theology at Wittenberg.
Dean,
place
and time
to be arranged.

1. On Augustine and the Bondage of Will

1. To say that Augustine wrote at too great length against heretics is to give the lie to almost all Augustine wrote. (This thesis is against the general opinion of Augustine.)

2. This is exactly the same as giving the advantage to the Pelagians and all heretics: in fact of giving them the victory.

3. It is also exactly the same as making the authority of all the doctors of the Church of none effect.

4. And so the truth is that man is created "a corrupt tree," and can neither will nor do anything except evil.

5. It is not true that the desire is free and is able to make one choice as well as another. In actual fact it is not free at all but is in bondage. (This is spoken against the view generally held.)

6. It is not true to say that the will is able of its own volition to conform itself to that which is right (spoken against Scotus and Gabriel Biel).

7. On the contrary, without the grace of God the will produces of necessity an action which is wicked and wrong.

8. Nor does it therefore follow that the will is naturally evil, in other words that the will has the nature of evil, as the Manichees express it.

9. And yet human nature is evil and vitiated naturally and inevitably.

10. It is submitted, that the will is not free to pursue in the light of its own reason any good thing that has been made clear to it (spoken against Scotus and Gabriel Biel).

11. Neither is it in its own power to will or not to will whatever has been made clear.

12. And saying this is not to speak against Augustine when he said: "Nothing is more in the power of the will therefore than the will itself."

2. On Love of God, Love of Creation and Self-Love

13. Therefore it is its quite absurd to argue that because sinful man is able to love creation more than anything else he can on that account also love God (against Scotus and Gabriel Biel).

14. Nor is it to be wondered at that he is able to conform himself to a wrong commandment but not to a right one.

15. In fact such is his real nature: to conform himself only to what is wrong and not to what is right.

16. The conclusion to this argument is rather as follows: man being a sinner is able to love creation, and on that account it is impossible for him to love God.

17. The natural man cannot want God to be God. Rather, he wants himself to be God, and God not to be God.

18. For the natural man to love God above all else is a fictitious figment. It is but a chimera (against almost all accepted opinion).

19. Nor is the view of Scotus valid that the true man of affairs loves the common weal more than himself.

20. An act of love does not come natural to man: it is a result of prevenient grace (against Gabriel Biel).

21. As God sees it there is nothing in the natural man except concupiscence.

22. Every act of concupiscence is evil in the eyes of God, and is a fornication of the spirit.

23. Nor is it true that an act of concupiscence may be directed aright by virtue of hope (against Gabriel Biel).

24. Because hope is not against love, which alone seeks and covets the things that are God's.

25. Hope does not come from earning merits. Hope comes out of sufferings, and sufferings make nonsense of merits (against the generally accepted view).

3. On Grace, Predestination and Total Depravity

26. An act of love is not the best way of doing "what in one lies." Nor is such a deed the best preparation for the grace of God. Nor is it a method of repenting and drawing near to God.

27. But it is an act ensuing from a repentance which has already happened and is complete. It comes in its own good time and proper way, and is a result of grace.

28. In the texts, "Turn ye unto me and I shall turn to you" (Zech. 1:3), or again, "Seek and ye shall find" (Matt. 7:7), or again, "If ye seek me. . . . I shall be found of you" (Jer. 29:13 f.), and statements like these, if they are interpreted as implying that the first half of the activity is man's contribution and the rest is of grace, then what is asserted is only what the Pelagians said.

29. The perfectly infallible preparation for grace, the one and only valid attitude, is the eternal election and predestination of God.

30. The only contribution man makes is to resist it. In actual fact, rebellion against grace precedes any receiving of it.

31. It is the most worthless of fabrications to say: a predestined man can be damned *in sensu diviso* (that is if the notion of predestination is separated from the notion of damnation), but not *in sensu composito* (that is if the notion of predestination and damnation are taken together).

[Thomists have tried to support their theory of efficacious grace by the distinction between *sensus compositus* and *sensus divisus*. Take a rather simple and non-philosophical statement: a blind man cannot see. This is a false statement if taken in the first sense *sensus compositus*, that is if the blindness is taken together (*compositus*) with his alleged seeing. But it may be a true statement if taken in the second sense *sensus divisus*, that is if the notion of blindness is taken apart (*divisus*) from his seeing. In other words that the man was *once* blind but now sees. In this second sense the blindness is separated from (*divisus*) the seeing.

To apply this simple distinction to the ideas under discussion, that a predestined man may be damned in one sense but not in another:—
What is being asserted is that a predestined man could be damned if the predestination and the damnation are separated as blindness was separated from seeing in the example just given. This is manifestly absurd. Luther is challenging such obscurantist sophistry in the interests of a biblical theology. He is arguing that a man cannot be properly described as predestined if he is going to be damned. Ed.]

32. Furthermore, it gets us no further to assert: predestination is necessary for the sake of logical consequences (*consequentia*), but not for the sake of casual consequence (*consequens*).

[The distinction is between consequence in the sense of logical nexus or connection, and consequence in the sense of proposition resulting in the virtue of logical nexus or connection, i.e., the conclusion of a piece of reasoning. The sophists are trying to have it both ways, saying that predestination is a logical consequence of God's decrees, but yet the election itself does not necessarily take place. This is the same sort of absurdity challenged in Thesis 31. Luther is again criticizing the sophistry that seeks to explain away the Biblical theology of predestination and election rather than explain it. Ed.]

33. And that is a false dictum, too, which alleges that to do "all that in one lies" is to remove the obstacles to grace (against certain teachers).

34. In short, the natural man possesses neither a sound reason nor a good will.

4. MORALITY AND ARISTOTELIANISM

35. It just is not true that invincible ignorance (*ignorantia invincibilis*) excuses everything (against all scholastic theologians).

36. Because the natural man's ignorance of God, of himself, and of a good work is always invincible (*invincibilis*).

37. Even a work which to all outward appearances and in actual fact is a good work the natural man in the secret recesses of his heart glories in it and takes a pride in it.

38. There is no moral virtue without pride or pain, that is without sin.

39. We are not masters of our actions from the beginning to the end: we are slaves.

40. We are not made righteous by doing righteous deeds; but when we have been made righteous we effect righteous deeds (against the philosophers).

41. The whole Aristotelian ethic is grace's worst enemy (against the scholastic theologians).

42. It is a wrong thing to hold that the teaching of Aristotle on the highest good (happiness, *de felicitate*) is not repugnant to catholic doctrine (against the moral philosophers).

43. It is a wrong thing to say that a man cannot become a theologian without Aristotle (against the generally accepted opinion).

44. The truth is that a man cannot become a theologian unless he becomes one without Aristotle.

45. To say that a theologian who is not a logician is a monstrous heretic is in its turn to make a monstrous, heretical statement (against the generally accepted opinion).

46. It is a waste of time to work out a logic of faith. The intermediate hypothesis is beyond its terms and categories (against the modern dialecticians).

47. No syllogistic form is valid in reasoning about God (against Peter d'Ailly).

48. But it does not necessarily follow that the truth of the trinitarian formula runs counter to the forms of the syllogism (against certain scholars and also Peter d'Ailly).

49. If the syllogistic form were valid in theological thinking, then the trinitarian formula would be a matter of knowledge and not faith.

50. In short, compared with the study of theology, the whole of Aristotle is as darkness is to light (against the scholastic theologians).

51. It is very much open to doubt whether Aristotle is rightly understood among the latinists.

52. It would have been good for the Church if Porphyry and his universals had never been born into the theological world.

[Porphyry, c. 232–303, a Neoplatonist philosopher whose Introduction to the Categories of Aristotle became a standard work in the medieval schools. Ed.]

53. The well-known definitions of Aristotle seem to beg the question.

5. The Religion of Grace and the Religion of Law

54. For a meritorious work the co-existence of grace is enough, otherwise the co-existence is meaningless (against Gabriel Biel).

55. The grace of God is never co-existent in such a way as to be otiose. Grace is a living, moving and active spirit. It cannot even happen through the absolute power of God for there to be an act of love and the grace of God not to be present (against Gabriel Biel).

56. God cannot accept a man unless the grace of God is there justifying him (against Occam).

57. It is dangerous to believe that the existence of a law implies that it can be obeyed, for the law is fulfilled by the grace of God (against Peter d'Ailly and Gabriel Biel).

58. It follows from this view, that to have the grace of God is already a new demand over and above the law.

59. It further follows from this same view that the works of the law can be done without the grace of God.

60. In like manner it follows that the grace of God has become more otiose than even the law.

61. It does not follow, that the law must be kept and fulfilled in the grace of God (against Gabriel Biel).

62. Therefore he who stands outside the grace of God sins constantly: his sin is not in the actual deed of committing a murder, adultery or theft.

63. But it follows that he sins in not fulfilling the law in its spiritual sense.

64. The man who does not kill, nor commit adultery, nor steal in the spiritual intent of the law is he who neither gets angry nor covetous.

65. It is in this sense just as impossible not to be angry and not to covet as it is to be in a sufficient state of grace to make it possible to keep the law perfectly.

66. It is a righteousness of hypocrites to allege a righteousness of works and of not having committed by overt act murder, adultery and all the rest.

67. It is of the grace of God not being covetous and angry.

68. Therefore it is impossible to fulfil the law in any way without the grace of God.

69. In actual fact, the law is most frequently broken by the natural man living without the grace of God.

70. The law, though a good thing in itself, becomes of necessity an evil thing to the will of the natural man.

71. The law and the will run counter one to another, and without the grace of God are irreconcileable.

72. What the law wants the will never wants, unless out of fear or love it pretends to want it.

73. The law is a tyrant over the will, and is never conquered save by "the little child born for us" (Isa. 9:6).

74. The law makes sin to abound, because it exasperates the will and removes the will from its own service.

75. The grace of God on the other hand makes righteousness to abound through Jesus Christ, because it makes the law a pleasant thing.

76. Every work of the law done without the grace of God appears good outwardly, but inwardly it is sin (against the scholastics).

77. In relation to God's law the will is always perverse and the hand adverse if the grace of God is not there.

78. When the will without the grace of God is favourably disposed to the law it does so to suit its own interests as such.

79. Cursed are all those who work the works of the law.

80. Blessed are all those who work the works of God's grace.

81. *Cap. Falsas de pe.* dis. V confirms that works done apart from grace are not good works, if that passage is not wrongly understood.

82. It is not only that the ceremonial laws are not good law, and that they are precepts in which no man finds life (against many teachers).

83. But even the Decalogue as well, and all that can be taught from it or said about it in either a spiritual sense or a literal sense, cannot give life.

84. The law which is good and by which man lives is the love of God shed abroad in our hearts.

85. If it were possible, the will of every man would prefer a state of affairs where there was no law at all and where it was absolutely free of external constraint.

86. The will of every man hates a law to be laid down to its disadvantage, or alternatively, out of self love desires a law to be laid down to its advantage.

87. Since the law is good the will cannot be, for it is opposed to the law.

88. And from that it is absolutely clear that the entire will of the natural man is wicked and evil.

89. Grace is necessary as the mediator, for grace reconciles the law to the will.

90. The grace of God is given to direct the will, lest it err even in loving God (against Gabriel Biel).

91. Grace is not given so that the deed of love may be elicited the more frequently and easily. Grace is given because without it no deed of love is elicited (against Gabriel Biel).

6. Love of God and Love of Self

92. There is no answer to the argument that love is superfluous if the natural man is able to perform an act of love (against Gabriel Biel).

93. It is evil but thinly veiled to assert that one and the same act can be both the enjoyment of the end itself (*fruitio*) and the means to that end (*usus*).

[Augustine seems to use the word *frui* with respect to heaven and *uti* with respect to earth, or more exactly about our theologizing on earth.

Luther is saying that the same act of love cannot be both a means to an end as well as an enjoyment of the end itself. Ed.]

94. It is also subtle evil to argue that the love of God may exist side by side with a love of the created world, even if that love is intense.

95. To love God is to hate oneself and to know nothing apart from God.

96. We stand convicted of error if we seek to fashion our will to the Divine will at all (against Peter d'Ailly).

97. We ought to want not so much what our will wants us to want but just what God wants.

In these theses we wish to say nothing
nor do we believe we have said anything,
which is not in accordance with the
catholic church and the ancient doctors
of the church.

1517

Disputation held at Heidelberg, April 26th, 1518

WA, I, 350–365

INTRODUCTION

THE INDULGENCES CONTROVERSY FOLLOWED HARD on Luther's attack on scholastic theology (p. 251), and by the time he had reached chapter eleven in his lectures on Hebrews (p. 220), he was summoned to Heidelberg to give an account of his theology.

By now officialdom had shown its hand. Albert of Mainz had forwarded the documents of the indulgences controversy to Rome with the request that Luther be inhibited. In February 1518 this command had been transmitted to Staupitz his superior. In addition to this official movement through the normal channels there was a growing danger astir among the Dominicans who were showing a very hostile mood. In their Saxon chapter of January 1518 Wimpina and Tetzel propounded a series of counter-Theses, and preferred formal charges against Luther on a suspicion of heresy filed at Rome.

But at Heidelberg all went better than Luther ever expected. He received a very sympathetic hearing. Although some of the older men expressed some reserve, seeing the immense potential of this new theological movement but fearing its consequences and developments, yet at the same time he gained many converts among the younger men like Bucer, Brenz and Pellican who were later to achieve fame as Reformers. The meeting also had the effect of giving to Luther a measure of reassurance at a difficult and lonely moment. At Heidelberg the indulgences controversy was set aside and Luther stood before his brethren a theologian among theologians. He had now full ten years of intense theological study behind him which included among other things his close work on Romans, Galatians and Hebrews. He presided at the Disputation, and showed with succinctness and power the meaning of his new theology.

There are forty theses: twenty-eight of them are directed against the scholastic doctrine of salvation and twelve against the scholastic philosophy. The twenty-eight theological themes are followed by some exposition of their meaning but the twelve philosophical theses have none. It is in the explanations following the first twenty-eight theses that the fullness of Luther's new theology is developed, and it is in these explanations that the importance of the document is contained. There is in addition to all this a fairly long *explicatio* which has all the appearances of having been prepared beforehand for the discussion, but which is attached to the Disputation in the nature of an appendix.

I have followed the setting out of the material the Weimar editors adopt. That is the whole series of these theses is set out concurrently without the interspersion of the comments Luther made individually on the first twenty-eight. This was necessary because many of the theses run in paradoxes or in pairs or in such close sequence that to separate them with comment may serve to lose the force of the comparison or sequence. After this Luther's comments are then given in the form of what he calls "Proofs," which are naturally headed in each case with the particular theses he is proving. Following the theses, and then those theses which bear proofs, is the *explicatio* mentioned in the previous paragraph.

Theses of such a kind are difficult for modern man to read and demand a thoughtful, meditative and interpretative kind of study. Here are Luther's great themes of God's righteousness and man's righteousness; of law and gospel; of sin; of justification by works and justification in Christ; of the bondage of the will; of faith inseparably bound up with Christ. Here is developed Luther's momentous theology of the cross in distinction to the theology of glory. Here is, too, his firm attack on Aristotle, an issue raised more fully in the previous Document on Scholastic Theology (p. 251).

Disputation held at Heidelberg
WA, I, 350–365

THE TEXT
THE THESES

Father Martin Luther,
Master of Sacred Theology,
will preside,
Father Leonard Beier,
Master of Arts and Philosophy,
will reply,
before the Augustinians,
of this illustrious city of Heidelberg
in the usual place
on the 26th Day of April, 1518.

THESES FROM THE PROVINCE OF THEOLOGY

With no trust in ourselves whatever, and in the spirit of Prov. 3:5: "Trust in the Lord with all thine heart, and lean not unto thine own understanding," we humbly offer these theological paradoxes to the judgment of all those who care to come. We do this so as to establish clearly whether or no these theses are legitimately expounded from Paul, the peerless and choicest of Christ's chosen instruments and vessels. And also to see whether they are in accordance with Augustine, his most faithful interpreter.

1. The law of God, that most wholesome doctrine of life, cannot bring man to righteousness. It is a hindrance rather than a help.

2. How much less can the works of man bring him to righteousness, done as they are time and time again and aided and abetted by the dictates of the natural man.

3. The works of man, though they always look splendid and

276

have the appearance of being very good, are yet in all probability mortal sins.

4. The works of God, though they may always look evil and have the appearance of being very bad, are yet in fact works of eternal merit.

5. The works of man are not so deadly (we are referring to his good works as they appear good to us), that these same deeds could be called crimes.

6. Neither are the works of God so meritorious (we speak of those deeds which men do), that these same deeds could not be called sins.

7. The works of even the righteous would be mortal sins, if they were to act without a reverent fear of God and were not afraid that their works were mortal sins.

8. How much more are the works of men mortal sins when they are done even without the fear of God and in a spirit of mere self-concerned security.

9. To say that works apart from Christ are in fact dead but not mortal sins seems a highly dangerous relaxation of the fear of God.

10. It is very difficult to understand how a work can be a dead work and yet not be noxious or a mortal sin.

11. Pride cannot be evaded, nor can any real hope be present, unless the fear of judgment and condemnation attends every good work.

12. When men are afraid that their sins are mortal then they are venial in the sight of God.

13. Free will after the Fall exists only in name, and as long as a man "does what in him lies," he is committing mortal sin.

14. The free will after the Fall has the power to do good only when it is in a state of obedience (i.e., when it is a power under subjection to a greater power—*potentia subjectiva*), but in actual fact it is always active in an evil cause.

15. And in the state of innocence man did not exist with the power of doing good (*potentia activa*), but only that good might be done through him (*potentia subjectiva*), much less had he the power to improve.

16. If a man thinks that he will come to a state of grace by doing "what in him lies," he merely piles one sin upon another sin, and is doubly sinful.

17. And to speak in this way is not to give reason for despairing but on the contrary of being humble and seeking to excite a desire for the grace of Christ.

18. It is certain that man ought wholly to despair of himself so that he may become fit to receive the grace of Christ.

19. He is not worth calling a theologian who seeks to interpret "the invisible things of God" on the basis of the things which have been created.

20. But he is worth calling a theologian who understands the visible and hinder parts of God to mean the passion and the cross.

21. The theologian of glory says bad is good and good is bad. The theologian of the cross says what is in fact the truth (i.e., calls them by their proper name).

22. The sort of wisdom which understands the invisible things of God as known from doing good works simply inflates a man, and renders him both blind and hard.

23. The law works wrath: it kills, curses, makes guilty, judges and damns every one who is not in Christ.

24. Yet it is not that this wisdom is evil, nor that we should flee the law, but that the man who has not learnt the theology of the cross puts the finest things to their worst possible use.

25. The righteous man is not the man who does very much in the way of good works, but it is he who apart from any works believes very much in Christ.

26. The law says: "Do this," but it is never done. Grace says: "Believe in him," and everything is already done.

27. The work of Christ may rightly be described as effective in that it effects the good work, and ours as effected. And in this way the good work that has been effected through us may be said to please God by the grace of the work of Christ who is actually effecting the good work [paraphrased. Ed.].

28. The Love of God does not find but creates the object of its love, whereas the love of man is created by the object of its love.

THESES FROM THE PROVINCE OF PHILOSOPHY

[There now follow twelve similar theses from the realm of scholastic philosophy. The editor prefaces these theses from the province of philosophy with a brief explanation of the issues involved so that the reader may appraise the relevance of Luther's terse rebuttals. Where necessary the editor has added brief paraphrases and some explanation to particularly difficult points.

Aristotle's doctrine of Potentiality and Actuality played an important role in philosophy and these terms are discussed here by Luther. Aristotle's teaching is an attempt to answer the question, "How do things come to be what they are?" To solve this problem he directs man's thinking to the process of growth. For example, he sees the acorn as an oak not in actuality but in potentiality. To put this thought into philosophical terminology it would run like this: a thing which has reached its proper Form is the Actuality of which the indeterminate Matter was the Potentiality. The Potentiality becomes Actuality in the end when the process or purpose has been completed and reached its intended end.

It is to be understood that the process is not a process that is unending. The process has a *telos*, an end. Created things were meant to fulfil a purpose. In fact, the end to which things develop is thought of as pre-existing as a purpose or as an idea exerting some pull in the process of fulfilment. This is a very important contribution to man's thinking on the subject of change and time and has exerted a not inconsiderable influence.

Aristotle's teaching on this subject was embraced in his doctrine of the Four Causes. This is an attempt to answer the question, "How does the world order come to be what it is?"

His answer consists of four parts, the holding of each several part of which is essential to the grasping of the truth of the whole. First, there is the material cause of a thing, or in other words Matter. Secondly, there is the formal cause according to which the thing develops, or in other words Form. Thirdly, there is the efficient cause, that is the agent who started off the whole process in the first place. Fourthly, there is the final cause which is the result of the process. This final cause may be expressed in terms of Potentiality and Actuality by saying that the final result we see as an Actuality is the Potentiality of the process which has reached its final expression in the process.

The reader will perceive that in man's actual empirical experience these four causes tend to coalesce. In the last analysis the basic distinction is between the material cause, the very stuff in which the development proceeds, and the final cause which is the end which the development is seeking to achieve.

This explanation is a sketchy and inadequate analysis of the Aristotelian view and is only given to serve to elucidate on the one hand the terminology involved in the twelve theses following and on the other hand to show how Luther's evangelical insights were bound to issue in a sharp anti-Aristotelianism. Luther's concern is that scholastic Aristotelianism is bound to involve a mechanistic self-determinism, which in fact Aristotle develops in his *Ethics*. Here Aristotle teaches that a man is determined not by natural forces nor external environment but rather by tendencies working within him. That a man develops a good character by constantly doing good deeds. But he cannot do good deeds unless he is the sort of man whose nature it is to do them; unless that is he has the good character from which good acts spring. That is a man is impelled from within him and underneath him rather than drawn from outside him and above him. (Modern psychoanalysis endorses this former view very strikingly though within a different framework of ideas.)

Aristotle's view, or perhaps more precisely, what scholasticism had made of it, has doubtless some truth in it as far as it goes. But it is the view of a man looking at man's situation whereas Luther sets the problem on a supra-human level, and acts and thinks in the light of the certainty of what God did and does for us men and for our salvation.

Aristotle's doctrine provides no adequate basis for the doctrine of man's redemption as given in the Gospels, but rather gives room for a doctrine of works-righteousness; a view which thinks in terms of human effort, human endeavour and human righteousness. Luther was actually in conflict with Pelagianism. Luther realized the issues involved at a very early stage and his thinking crystallized out rather sharply because of the bitter waters of polemic with which it was all too soon mixed. The most sympathetic insight into and explanation of his hostility towards the Aristotelian scholasticism of his day may be arrived at by considering Luther's polemic here in the positive sense of a consuming desire of a man saved and elected by God to allow God's work in Christ for us men and for our salvation to be given free expression and unimpeded influence, and to root out any and every human effort or subterfuge to devise or gain salvation. He hated Aristotle because he loved Christ: Aristotle for all his intrinsic worth, turned men's eyes from Christ to a humanist's ethic and a humanist's salvation. Aristotle's hermeneutics did a great deal for the humanists, as it helped them to bring interpretation and study down to earth, but the basically Greek mind mediated by Aristotle did have the effect of developing an ethic whose inspiration was humanism rather than the Gospel and a doctrine of redemption that was man-centred rather than Christ-centred. Ed.]

29. Whoever is minded to apply himself to the Aristotelian philosophy without danger to his soul must first be made truly foolish in Christ.

30. As nobody except a married man can put the passion of the flesh to its natural and proper use, so then nobody can put his mind to philosophy except a fool in Christ, that is a Christian man.

31. It was easy for Aristotle to maintain that the world was eternal as long as he thought that the human soul was mortal.

32. After it has been accepted that there were as many independent universals or Forms as there were things created, it had necessarily to be accepted as well that there were as many material substances of matter.

33. It is not necessary to believe that a thing has been created out of something in the world already. But whatever has been created naturally has however been created out of matter.

34. If Aristotle had known the absolute power of God, to that extent would he have asserted that it is impossible for indeterminate matter [or the material case—see above p. 279. Ed.] to exist pure and simple.

35. In actuality nothing is eternal. Potentiality, however, and Matter exist as constituted in created things, according to Aristotle.

[That is, they cannot exist apart from the Form which gives them shape. Ed.]

36. Aristotle was in the wrong when he reproved and scoffed at Plato's philosophy of ideas which is a better philosophy than his own.

[Luther's point is that Platonism provides a possible philosophical basis for theism which Aristotelianism does not. Ed.]

37. Pythagoras ingeniously maintained the significance of number in life, but Plato far more ingeniously established the participation of Ideas in created things.

38. The disputation of Aristotle with that rare bird Parmenides was (if I may say it to a Christian audience without offence) just shadow boxing.

[Parmenides was a Greek mathematician of about 500 B.C. who argued that the universe was a homogeneous whole and that no part or element of it can change. There can be neither growth nor diminution in respect of any particular quality in the universe. Coming into being and ceasing to be are therefore mere names, and he reached the famous conclusion *ex nihilo nihil fit*, out of nothing there comes nothing. The argument reminds modern readers of Spinoza's monism. Ed.]

39. If, as it seems, Anaxagoras taught that the Infinite is a Form, he was the best of the philosophers, not even Aristotle excepted.

40. In Aristotle it seems that privation, Matter and Form, constancy and inconstancy, Actuality and Potentiality and all the rest of them amount to one and the same thing.

PROOFS OF THE CONCLUSIONS
WHICH WERE DEBATED AT THE CHAPTER OF HEIDELBERG
IN THE YEAR OF OUR SALVATION
FIFTEEN HUNDRED AND EIGHTEEN IN THE MONTH OF MAY

CONCLUSION I

The Law of God, that most wholesome Doctrine of life, cannot bring a man to righteousness. It is a hindrance rather than a help.

This is clear from the Apostle in his Epistle to the Romans: "But now the righteousness of God has been manifested without the law" (Rom. 3:21). Augustine declares the same thing in his book *On the Spirit and the Letter*: "Without the law, that is without any help from the law[1]." It also says in Rom. 5:20: "The law intervened to amplify sin"; and in Rom. 7:9: "When the commandment came, sin revived." That is why he calls the law "the law of sin and death" (Rom. 8:2). In fact in II Cor. 3:6 he actually says:

[1] *de spir. et lit.*, c.9; *Migne*, 44.209.

". . . the letter killeth." This Augustine understands throughout the whole of his book *On the Spirit and the Letter* as referring to the law of God, be it as holy as it may[1].

II

How much less can the works of man bring him to righteousness, done as they are time and again, and aided and abetted by the dictates of the natural man.

Because, since the law of God is holy and pure, true and righteous and so on, and was given to man by God to help him beyond his natural capacities, to illumine his path and impel him towards the good, yet the contrary has actually taken place and man has become worse. How then can man on his own strength and without such help be brought towards the good? A man who does not do good when he is being helped by somebody else must do less good when he relies on himself alone. That is why the Apostle says in Rom. 3:10: "All men are corrupt and there is none who does good. None of them knows God and none of them seeks after him. They have all gone astray."

III

The works of man, though they always look splendid and have every appearance of being very good, are yet in all probability mortal sins.

The works of man appear beautiful, but inwardly they are loathsome, as Christ said with reference to the Pharisees: "Woe unto you, Scribes and Pharisees, hypocrites! for ye are like unto white-washed sepulchres, which outwardly appear beautiful to men but in fact within are full of the bones of the dead and every uncleanness" (Matt. 23:27). For their works seem to be good and beautiful both to themselves and others. But God does not judge according to outward appearances: He looks on the heart of man and to his very inmost being. And without grace and faith it is impossible to have the clean heart referred to in Acts 15:9, where Peter refers to God purifying the hearts of the Gentiles by faith.

Therefore, the argument is proved in the following way: First: If the works of righteous men are sins as the seventh conclusion affirms, much more so are the works of men who are not yet righteous. Now the righteous say of their own work: "Enter not into judgment with thy servant, O Lord, for in thy sight shall no man living be justified" (Ps. 143:2). The Apostle says the same

1 *Ibid.*, c.14; *Migne*, 44.215.

thing: "For as many as are of the works of the law are under the curse" (Gal. 3:10). But, in the second place, the works of the law are the works of men. And the curse is not laid merely on venial sins. Therefore, the works of the law are mortal sins. And thirdly, Paul says: "Thou therefore who teachest another, teachest thou not thyself? Thou that preachest a man shall not steal, dost thou steal?" (Rom. 2:21). This Augustine expounds thus: as far as the will is concerned they are thieves, even if to all appearances they judge and teach that the others are the thieves[1].

IV

The works of God, though they may always look evil and have the appearance of being very bad, are yet in fact works of eternal merit.

It is clear from Isa. 53:2 and I Sam. 2:6 that the works of God are shameful: "He has neither stateliness nor majesty" and "The Lord killeth and maketh alive, he bringeth down to the grave and bringeth back." The way to understand this is thus: The Lord humbles us and absolutely terrifies us with the law and the prospect of our sins so that not only in other men's eyes but even in our own we seem to be nothing, just fools and evil men. The truth of the matter is that this is just what we are in fact. Now when we admit that, and confess that there is nothing stately or comely about us, but on the contrary we live in the hidden God (that is in pure and unqualified trust in his mercy), then we have in ourselves the answer to sin, folly, death and hell. Those words of the Apostle in II Cor. 6:10, 9 mean the same thing: "As sorrowful yet always rejoicing, as dead and behold we live." And this is what Isaiah calls "the strange work of God that he may work his own work" (Isa. 28:21), (that means, that he may humble us in our own eyes and make us despair of ourselves, so that in his mercy he may exalt us and make us men of hope). As it says in Hab. 3:2: ". . . in thy wrath remember thy mercy." Such a man is displeased with himself, therefore, as far as all his works are concerned; he sees nothing comely in himself, but on the contrary has eyes only for his own enormity. In fact, he still goes on doing the very things that seem foolish and horrible to others.

Now this sense of our own deformity arises in us either when God flays us or when we accuse ourselves. This is what I Cor. 11:31 means: "If we would judge ourselves we should not be judged of the Lord." Deut. 32:36 means the same thing: "For the Lord shall judge his people and repent himself for his servants, when he seeth that their power is gone. . . ." In this way, therefore, the

[1] Reference uncertain.

shameful works, that is the humiliations and the anxieties which God works in us, are indeed eternal, for humility and the fear of God make a perfect merit.

V

The works of man are not so deadly (we are referring to his good works as they appear good to us), in the sense that these same deeds could be called crimes.

Crimes are properly speaking those offences which may be charged before men, such as adultery, theft, homicide, slander and so on. But nevertheless the works of man are mortal sins, for they have the appearance of being good but yet at bottom have an evil root and are the fruit of an evil tree.

Augustine shows this in his fourth book *Against Julian*[1].

VI

Neither are the works of God so meritorious (we speak of those deeds which men do), that these same deeds could not be called sins.

"There is not a righteous man on earth who doeth good and yet sinneth not" (Eccl. 7:20). In this instance, however, others say that this means that the righteous man does sin but not when he is doing good. To which I answer, If this authority wanted to say this, why did he use such an excess of words? Is the Holy Spirit pleased with a spate of useless words? For the interpretation they are wanting to give could have been adequately expressed in these words: There is not a righteous man who does not sin. Why then did he add to "a righteous man" the qualification "who doeth good"? As if there were another who was righteous who did evil. For nobody does good unless he is righteous. But elsewhere, when the subject is sins apart from good deeds, it is expressed in this way: "Seven times in a day the righteous man falls" (Prov. 24:16). He does not say here "Seven times in a day the righteous man falls when he is doing good." It is as if a man were chopping with a rusty, indented axe, and though he may be a good craftsman yet it is only with great difficulty he hacks out rough, uneven cuts. This is how God works through us.

VII

The works of even the righteous would be mortal sins if they were to act without a reverent fear of God and were not afraid that their works were mortal sins.

It is clear from the fourth Conclusion that to trust in a work about which one ought to fear is to give the glory to oneself and

---

[1] Augustine, *c. Jul.*, lib. IV, c.22; *Migne*, 44.749.

take it away from God, to whom fear is owed in every work. This, however, is utterly perverse. It means to please oneself and enjoy oneself in one's own works and to worship oneself as an idol. Such is the entire life of a man who feels secure and is without the fear of God. If on the other hand a man is afraid that he is not secure he therefore does not please himself but finds his joy in God.

Secondly, it says in the psalm quoted earlier: "Enter not into judgment with thy servant, O Lord, for in thy sight shall no man living be justified" (Ps. 143:2). And in Ps. 32:5b: "I said, I shall be my own accuser and confess my fault to the Lord: and thou forgavest the iniquity of my sin." It is clear, however, that these sins are not venial because they say that confession and penance are not necessary in the case of venial sins. If, therefore, they are mortal sins, and if all saints pray as the psalmist prays in the next verse, "Let every godly soul then turn to thee in prayer when the time is opportune, for truly, when the floods of adversity overwhelm a man he will not be able to turn to God in the catastrophe," then it is proved that the works of the saints are mortal sins. But the works of the saints are good works, therefore they are not meritorious to them unless they are done in a spirit of godly fear and humble penitence.

Thirdly, a proof from the Lord's Prayer: "Forgive us our trespasses." This is a prayer of saints. Therefore, their good works are sins about which they pray. But further, that they are mortal sins is clear from the words which follow: "If ye do not forgive men their trespasses, neither will your father in heaven forgive ye your trespasses." Behold, of such a kind (i.e., mortal) are those sins which they condemn as unforgiven, when they do not say this prayer truly and forgive others their trespasses.

Fourthly, it says in Rev. 21:27: "Nothing unclean shall enter the kingdom of heaven." But all that prevents entering the kingdom is mortal sin (otherwise mortal sin would be defined in a different way). Yet venial sin prevents entering the kingdom because it corrupts the soul and does not exist in the kingdom of heaven. Therefore . . .

[Luther's conclusion is not drawn. He often leaves his conclusion unstated after stating the premises. His conclusion here is that all sin is mortal sin. Luther implies the abolition of the distinction between mortal and venial and, further, thinks less of sins and more of Sin.]

VIII

How much more are the works of men mortal sins when they are done even without the fear of God and in a spirit of mere self-concerned security.

It is clear that this follows on necessarily from the preceding thesis. For where there is no fear of God there is no humility. Where there is no humility there is pride, and there is the wrath and judgment of God. For God resists the proud. In fact, were pride to cease to exist, there would be no sin at all.

IX

To say that works done apart from Christ are in fact dead but not mortal sins seems a highly dangerous relaxation of the fear of God.

The reason is that men who hold this view tend to feel secure, and in their sense of security feel proud, and here lies the great danger. Because, since the glory that God ought to have is constantly being taken away from him and transferred to oneself, then one should strain with every nerve to give him back the glory that is his as quickly as possible. On this account the Scripture counsels, "Make no tarrying to turn to the Lord . . ." (Eccl. 5:7). For if he who takes the glory away from God does wrong, how much more in the wrong is the man who takes away the glory and by so doing seeks his own security. And he who is not in Christ, or turns away from Christ, takes the glory away from Christ and gives it to himself, as has already been noted.

X

It is very difficult to understand how a work can be a dead work and yet not be noxious nor a mortal sin.

Here is how I prove this statement. It is because Scripture does not have that kind of talk about dead works, that is, that some particular deed or another is not a mortal sin but yet is a dead work. Surely it is not good grammar to say that dead is "more than" mortal. For they say that a work is a mortal sin when it kills, but that a dead work is not one that kills but simply one that is not alive. But what is not alive displeases God, as it is written in the Book of Proverbs: "The sacrifice of the wicked is an abomination to the Lord" (Prov. 15:8).

Secondly, the will has to be involved in one way or another in doing a dead work. Either, it must love to do it, or it must hate to do it. It cannot hate it since the will itself is evil. Therefore, it must love it. This means that the will loves a dead work. It follows then that such a theology elicits an evil act of the will against God, whom it ought to love and glorify both in this and in every work.

XI

Pride cannot be evaded, nor can any real hope be present, unless the fear of judgment and condemnation attends every good work.

This is clear from Conclusion IV, for it is impossible to hope in God unless a man despairs of all created things and unless he knows that without God nothing can work to his advantage. And since no one exists who has this pure hope, as we said earlier, and who does not put his trust in created things, it is clear that on account of our own uncleanness we must fear the judgment of God in all things. Thus pride is avoided not perhaps in the actual deed but yet in the will itself. In other words, we are dissatisfied with ourselves in that our confidence still lies in the things of this world.

XII

When men are afraid that their sins are mortal then they are venial in the sight of God.

It is clear enough from what has been said that the more we accuse ourselves the more God excuses us. As the saying goes: "Tell thine iniquities that thou mightest be justified," and again: "Set a watch, O Lord, before my mouth, and a barrier to fence my lips, That mine heart incline not to words of evil to cover over sins by excuses" (Ps. 141:3-4).

XIII

Free will after the Fall exists only in name, and as long as man "does what in him lies," he is committing mortal sin.

The first half of the statement is quite clear. The will is captive and a slave of sin. Not that free will is nothing, only it is not free, except to do evil. "Whosoever commits sin is the slave of sin" (John 8:34). "If the Son makes you free, indeed ye are free" (John 8:36). Therefore, Augustine says in his book *On the Spirit and the Letter*, "The free will without grace is good for nothing except sin[1]" And in his book *Against Julian*, "You call your will free, but it is in bondage[2]. . ." And in innumerable other places as well.

The second half is clear from what has been said above and also from that famous text in Hos. 13:9: "Thy destruction cometh from thyself, O Israel, but from me only cometh thy help. . ."

[1] Augustine, *De sp. et lit.*, c. 3; *Migne*, 44.203.
[2] Augustine, *Con. Julianum* II, 23; *Migne*, 44.689.

XIV

The free will after the Fall has the power to do good only when it is in a state of obedience (i.e., when it is a power under subjection to a higher power—potentia subjectiva), but in actual fact it is always active in an evil cause.

Because, just as a man without spiritual life (*homo mortuus*) can enter into a spiritual life only by being obedient (*subjective*), he can in fact choose death for himself (*active*) as long as he lives. Yes indeed, the free will is a dead thing. Those dead people whom the Lord raised from the dead are a parable of this fact, as the holy doctors recount. Moreover, Augustine drew the same conclusion over and over again in his writings against the Pelagians.

XV

And in the state of innocence man did not exist with the power of doing good (potentia activa), but only that good might be done through him (potentia subjectiva): much less had he the power to improve.

The Master of the Sentences[1] adduces Augustine in the end as having said, By these evidences it is clearly shown that man received uprightness and a good will in the creation, and furthermore, help by which he could have remained steadfast, otherwise it would seem that it could not have been his fault that he had fallen. He is speaking of the power to do good (*potentia activa*) which is clean contrary to Augustine where he says in his work, *Concerning Grace and the Fall*[2], if he had had the will man would have received the power of doing good, but he did not have the will to make it possible. By the power of doing good (the *posse*) we understand the faculty of good being done through a man (his *potentia subjectiva*), and by "the will to empower him" we understand the power of bringing it off in actual practice (his *potentia activa*).

The second part of the thesis however, that man could not advance in goodness, is clear enough in the Master's writings by the same distinction between the power of doing good (*potentia activa*) and the power of good being done in him (*potentia subjectiva*).

XVI

If a man thinks that he will come to a state of grace by doing "what in him lies," he merely piles one sin upon another sin, and is doubly sinful.

[1] Peter Lombard, *Sent.* II, dist., 24c., I, 12 f.
[2] Augustine, *De corr. et gratia*, XI, 32; *Migne*, 44.935 f.

Because it is clear from what has been said that the position is this: as long as he does "what in him lies" he is sinning, and in all things seeking his own interest. And if by sin he thinks that he can become worthy of grace or fit for grace, he now adds to this a proud presumption, believing that sin is not sin and evil is not evil which is far and away the greatest sin of all. Thus Jeremiah says, "My people have committed two evils: they have forsaken me, the fountain of living water, and have hewn out for themselves cisterns, broken cisterns which cannot hold water" (Jer. 2:13). That means, because of their sin they are far from me, and moreover even presume to do good of themselves.

You say, therefore, what shall we do about it? Shall we lead an idle life because all we can do is sin? I reply, No! When you hear these words fall prostrate and pray for grace, and transfer your hope to Christ, in whom is our salvation, our life and our resurrection. Therefore, to the extent we are taught these things, to that extent the law makes sin known, so that when sin is recognized grace is sought and obtained[1]. Thus, to those who are humble after this fashion God gives grace, and he who is humbled is exalted. The law humbles us, grace exalts us. The law works fear and wrath, grace works hope and mercy. Through the law comes knowledge of sin. Through the knowledge of sin comes humility, and through humility grace is acquired. In this way, when God makes a man a sinner that he may make him righteous, God is bringing in his strange work that he may in the end bring in his proper work.

XVII

And to speak in this way is not to give reason for despairing, but on the contrary, of being humble and seeking to excite a desire for the grace of Christ.

It is clear from what has been said that according to the gospel the kingdom of heaven is given to children and those who are humble, and that Christ loves these. The humble, however, cannot be those who do not understand that they are sinners, damnable and loathsome. Sin, however, is not known except through the law. It is clear that not despair, but rather hope is preached, when it is preached that we are sinners. For that kind of preaching about sin is the preparation for grace, or rather, it is the

---

1 *WA* and Clemen give the following marginal note, and both think that it was added in 1545: This is indeed the true humility which is in utter despair of itself and hastens back to Christ in complete trust. This is the faith which saves. This embraces and precedes all merit. This faith is the humility which turns its back on its own reason and its own strength.

acknowledgement of sin and faith in such preaching[1]. For the desire for grace surges up the moment a knowledge of sin has arisen. The sick man seeks a cure the moment he realizes the seriousness of his illness. Therefore, just as the danger of his illness is told to a sick man not to give him cause for despair or death but rather to provoke him to the trouble of seeking a cure, so then to say that we are nothing and sin continuously when we do "what in us lies" is not to make men despair (unless they are fools) but to make them anxious for the grace of our Lord Jesus Christ.

XVIII

It is certain that man ought utterly to despair of himself so that he may become fit to receive the grace of Christ.

The purpose of the law is that a man should despair of himself as it leads him to hell and humbles him, showing him that he is a sinner in all his works, as the Apostle does in Rom. 2 and 3: "We have all been proved to be under sin" (Rom. 3:9). However, he who does "what in him lies" and believes that he is doing something good, is not making himself absolutely nothing, nor is he despairing of his own powers. On the contrary, he is presuming to such an extent that he is striving after grace on his own strength.

XIX

He is not worth calling a theologian who seeks to interpret the invisible things of God on the basis of the things that have been created.

This is clear from those who were theologians of such a kind, who were in fact described as fools by the Apostle in Rom. 1:22: "Professing themselves to be wise they were made fools." Furthermore the invisible things of God are his strength, his divinity, wisdom, righteousness, goodness and the like. Knowledge of all these things does not make a man worthy or wise.

XX

But he is worth calling a theologian who understands the visible and hinder parts of God to mean the passion and the cross.

The visible and hinder parts of God are set over against those which are visible. These invisible parts mean the humanity of God, his weakness, his foolishness. Paul calls these "the weakness and foolishness of God" (I Cor. 1:25). For because men put to wrong

[1] The *WA* editors note that the rest of this passage was inserted in 1545.

use their knowledge of God which they had gained from his works God determined on the contrary to be known from sufferings. He sought to condemn that sort of knowledge of the things invisible which was based on a wisdom from things visible. So that in this way those who did not worship God as made known in his works, might worship him hidden behind his sufferings. For thus he says in I Cor. 1:21: "For seeing that in the wisdom of God the world did not know God by means of its wisdom, it was God's good pleasure to save those who believe by the foolishness of the preaching" so that from now on it could never be enough for a man, nor could it benefit him to know God in his glory and majesty unless he knows him at the same time in the humility and shame of the cross. In this way he destroys the wisdom of the wise and brings to nought the understanding of the prudent. As Isaiah says, "Verily thou art a hidden God" (Isa. 45:15).

Thus in John 14 when Philip asks in the spirit of the theology of glory, "Show us the Father," Christ immediately pulled him up sharp. He took him with his high-flying ideas of seeking God somewhere else and led Philip right back to himself, saying, "Philip, whosoever sees me sees my Father as well." Therefore in Christ crucified is the true theology and the knowledge of God. He says elsewhere also, "No man comes to the Father except through me" (John 14:6). And again, "I am the door: by me if any man enter in, he shall be saved" (John 10:9).

XXI

The theologian of glory says bad is good and good is bad.
The theologian of the cross calls them by their proper name.

This is really quite clear, for as long as a man does not know Christ he does not know God as hidden in sufferings. Such a man, therefore, prefers works to sufferings, and glory to a cross: he prefers powers to weakness, wisdom to foolishness, and at all times good for evil. These are they the Apostle calls enemies of the cross of Christ. Quite clearly, because they hate the cross and sufferings they certainly love works and the glory that goes with them. And thus they say that the good of the cross is evil, and call the evil of works good. But God is not to be found except in sufferings and in the cross as has been stated already. Thus the friends of the cross say that the cross is good and that works are evil, because through the cross works are destroyed and the old Adam, who is rather inclined to be made stronger by good works, is crucified. For it is impossible for a man not to be inflated by his own good works unless the experience of suffering and evil, having previously taken

all the spirit out of him and broken him, has taught him that he is
nothing and his works are not his own but God's.

XXII

*The sort of wisdom which sees the invisible things of God
in known good works simply inflates a man, and renders him
both blind and hard.*

This has been said already. For since it is clear that they know
nothing about the cross and even hate it, then of necessity they
love the opposite, that is wisdom, glory, power and the like.
Therefore by such a love they become more and more blind and
hardened. For it is impossible for cupidity to be satisfied with the
things it desires when it has acquired them. For just as the love
of money grows as fast as the wealth increases, so it is with the
thirst of the soul, the more it drinks the more it thirsts. As the poet
said, "The more the waters are drunk the more they dry up." The
book of Ecclesiastes says the same: "The eye is never satisfied with
what it sees nor the ear with what it hears" (Eccl. 1:8). The same
is true of all longings and desires.

For the same reason, too, the curiosity of knowing is not satisfied
with wisdom when it has been acquired, but it is more and
more aroused. Thus the desire for glory is not satisfied by glory
when it has been achieved. Nor is the desire to conquer satisfied by
the power and might gained. Nor is the desire for praise satisfied
with the praise given. And so we could go on. Christ gave expression to the same thought, too, "He who drinks of this water shall
thirst again" (John 4:13).

The remedy remains the same. It is not cured by satisfying it
but by destroying it. That is, that he who wishes to become wise
should not go forward and seek wisdom but should become a fool,
go back and seek foolishness. Thus, he who wants to become powerful and famous, to have a good time and enjoy all the good things
of life, let him flee from power, fame, enjoyment and a sufficiency
of everything and not seek after them. This is the wisdom we are
talking about, the wisdom which is foolishness to the world.

XXIII

*The law works wrath: it kills, curses, makes guilty,
judges and damns every one who is not in Christ.*

Thus in Gal. 3:13: "Christ has freed us from the curse of the
law," and similarly in Gal. 3:10: "As many as are of the works of
the law are under the curse." Rom. 4:15, also: "The law works
wrath." And Rom. 7:10: "What was intended to bring to life was

found to bring me to death." Rom. 2:12, also: "As many as have sinned in the law shall be judged by the law." Therefore, whosoever glories in the law as being wise and learned glories in his own shame: he is glorying in being cursed, he is glorying in the wrath of God, he is glorying in death. He is like those Jews Paul addressed in Rom. 2:23: "Thou who boasteth in the law, dishonoureth thou God in breaking the law?"

XXIV

Yet it is not that this wisdom is evil, nor that we should flee the law, but that the man who has not learnt the theology of the cross puts the finest things to their worst possible use.

For the law is holy (Rom. 7:12) and every gift of God is good (I Tim. 4:4). All creation is perfectly good (Gen. 1:31). But as was said earlier, he who has not yet been broken and brought to nothing through the cross and suffering assigns to himself works and devises his own idea of wisdom. But these works are not the works God wants nor is the wisdom God's. In this way such a man abuses the gifts of God and renders them odious.

The truth of the matter is that whosoever has been brought to nought by sufferings does not thereby do good works. On the contrary he simply knows that God is working in him and effecting everything. Therefore whether he is doing good works or whether he is not doing good works is all the same to him: he neither boasts if he does a good work nor is he ashamed when God is not working anything in him. Thus he knows that it is enough if he suffers and is broken through the cross, nay rather is utterly brought to nought. But this is exactly what Christ says in John 3:7: "Ye must be born again." If we are to be born again we must first die and be exalted with the Son of Man. I said, "Die," and that means to find death ever present in all experiences.

XXV

The righteous man is not the man who does very much in the way of good works, but it is he who apart from any works believes very much in Christ.

Because the righteousness of God is not acquired by acts frequently repeated, as Aristotle taught, but is infused by faith. For the righteous man lives by faith (Rom. 1:17), and as it says in Rom. 10:10: "With the heart man believeth unto righteousness." Wherefore I want that phrase "apart from works" to be understood in the following way: not that the righteous man does no good work, but rather that the good works he does do not create his righteousness. Or still better, that his righteousness is effecting the good works. For without any work of ours grace and righteousness are infused, and when they are infused the works follow at once. Thus it says, in Rom. 3:20: "By the works of the law shall no man be justified in his sight." And Rom. 3:28: "We conclude therefore, that a man is justified by faith apart from the works of the law." That means, quite simply, that works do absolutely nothing towards salvation. Then because a man knows that the good works he is doing are the outcome of such a faith and are not his own at all but God's, he therefore does not seek to be justified or glorified by these. On the contrary, he seeks God: the righteousness which comes from faith in Christ is sufficient for him. Christ is his wisdom, his righteousness and all, as it says in I Cor. 1:30; the justified man is surely the work and instrument of Christ.

XXVI

The law says "Do this," but it is never done. Grace says: "Believe in him," and everything is done already.

The first statement is clear from the many references in the Apostle and in his interpreter, Augustine. Further, it is clearly established earlier in the Disputation (Thesis XXIII) that the law rather works wrath and holds everybody under its curse.

The second statement is also clear on the same authorities, Paul and Augustine, because it is faith that justifies. As Augustine says: "The law commands what faith achieves." In such a way is Christ in us by faith. Nay rather than in us he is one with us. Now Christ is righteous and fulfils all the commands of God, therefore we also through him fulfil all things when he is made ours through faith.

XXVII

The work of Christ may rightly be described as effective in that it effects the good work, and ours as effected. And in this way the good work that has been effected through us may be said to please God by the grace of the work of Christ who is in fact effecting the good work.

Because while Christ is dwelling in us by faith he then moves us to do good works by this living faith in his works. For the works which he does are the fulfilments of the commands of God given to us by faith: when we behold them we are moved to imitate them. For that reason the Apostle says, "Be ye imitators of God, as dearly beloved sons" (Eph. 5:1). Wherefore works of mercy are called forth by the works he did and by which he saved us. As Gregory says, "Everything Christ did is for our instruction, nay rather our inspiration." If he is active in us then he is alive through faith. He draws us to himself most powerfully. It says something like this in the Song of Solomon, "Draw me after thee: we will run into the odour of thy perfumes" (Cant. 1:4). "Thy perfumes" means in this connection "thy works."

XXVIII

The love of God does not find but creates the object of its love, whereas the love of man is created by the object of its love.

The second half is obvious and is common to all philosophers and theologians, for, following Aristotle[1], they lay down that the object of love is the cause of the love, that all power of the soul is passive, that it is of the category of matter, and that it effects things in that it is a receiving agent. And thus he actually testifies that his philosophy is at cross-purposes with theology, in that it seeks its own in all things and receives rather than confers the good.

The first half is clear, too, because the love of God living in a man loves sinners, evil men, foolish men, weak men, so that the love of God makes them righteous, good, wise and strong. In this way it flows forth rather and confers good. Thus sinners are lovely because they are loved: they are not loved because they are lovely. That is why human love shuns sinners and evil men. As Christ said, "I came not to call the righteous, but sinners" (Matt. 9:13). And that is what love of the cross means. It is a love born of the cross, which betakes itself not to where it can find something good to enjoy, but where it may confer good to the wicked and the needy. For "it is more blessed to give than to receive," says the Apostle (Acts 20:35). Whence Ps. 41:1: "Blessed is he that considereth the poor and the needy." Yet since the mind of man naturally cannot have as an object of its understanding or love something that is nothing, (I mean by that the poor and the needy), but can only have that which has being and is true and good, therefore it judges according to the outward appearance. It looks to the person of men and judges only by externals.

EXPLANATION OF THE SIXTH CONCLUSION

WA, 1, 365–74.

Whether the will of man when it is not under grace is free, or whether it is enslaved and captive.

[1] *Eth. Nic.*, VIII, 2, (1155), b, 18.

Conclusion [i.e., Discussion of the question. Ed.]

The will of man when it is not under grace, granted that it is free of all compulsion, is nevertheless not a free agent but is of necessity enslaved and captive. This is true whether the acts of the will are contrary one to another or contradictory (terms explained in next paragraph).

For proof of this conclusion it must first be explained that acts of the will which are contrary one to another (*actus contrarii*) are activities such as to want (*velle*) and not to want (*nolle*), one of which is positive. Acts of the will which are contradictory one to another (*actus contradictorii*) are to will (*velle*) and not to will (*non velle*), or what amounts to the same thing, to be unwilling (*nolle*) and not to be unwilling (*non nolle*). That means sometimes the will wants and yet sometimes it neither wants nor wants not, but remains uncommitted and does neither one thing nor yet another.

The second thing to be noted is that when we are discussing the freedom of the will we mean the freedom of the will only with respect to its claim to earn merit or demerit. For in the matter of its own lesser concerns I do not deny that it is free. At least it seems free as far as its own interests are concerned both to do things that are sometimes contrary to one another and things that are sometimes contradictory one to another.

If these statements are taken as established I now turn to the proof of the first part of my thesis, that the will is not free in those matters which are "contradictory" to one another. Thus if the will (*velle*) is free to choose not to pursue its own interests, it follows then that it would be free to avoid all future sin. But this is manifestly false! In fact it is heretical and contradicts the saying of Gregory, "Sin which is not washed away by repentance, by its sheer weight soon drags the sinner to further sin[1]." But if the will is free it is possible for it to refuse to be dragged away to further sin. Or if it cannot resist the pull, then it is not free. I prove this also from the general saying that apart from grace the will cannot long stand without mortal sin. Therefore, it cannot long stand without its freedom being made captive.

Finally, I prove it from the saying of the Apostle, ". . . that they may recover themselves from the snare of the devil, by whom they are taken captive at his will" (II Tim. 2:26). But the will of the devil is that they should will and do evil.

Second part of the Conclusion

---

[1] *Moral*, 25, 9, 22; *Migne*, 76.334. Quoted Aquinas, *Summa Theologica*, I, II, qu. 109a, 8.

I prove the statement that the will is not free in matters that are "contrary" one to another from Gen. 8:21: "All the thoughts and imaginations of the human heart are bent towards evil all the time." If the will is inclined towards evil continuously, it follows then that it can never be bent towards the good which is the term contrary to evil. That this however happens both freely and necessarily I prove in the following way: The natural will has its own power to will or not to will just as any other creature has its power of self-determination and is no more deprived of its freedom to act than anything else is. But it is impossible that wanting (*velle*) should be under compulsion and not free: therefore of necessity it is free, and of necessity freely wills.

Therefore the two propositions which follow are true.

(*a*) A falling man can do nothing but fall if he relies on his own strength to save him.

(*b*) A falling man can prevent his fall if he relies on an external power to save him.

By the same token the will apart from grace is not free. Or to express it in terms of our analogy it is so created as to be in a state of falling, and can do nothing but fall if it relies on its own powers. It wills evil left to itself. By the grace of God, however, it is able not to fall, or at any rate stop falling. Thus with these few words I leave the conclusion proved.

Corollary

I draw a corollary of this kind: Since there is no righteous man in the world who in doing good does not sin, how much more does an unrighteous man sin while he is doing good.

Proved by Scriptural authorities

First by the text of Isa. 64:6: "Unclean are we all, and all our righteousnesses are but a menstruant's clout." If our righteousnesses are unclean, what will our unrighteousnesses be? Also Eccl. 7:20: "There is not a righteous man on earth who doeth good and sinneth not." Also James. 3:2: "In many things we all offend." Also in Rom. 7:22: "I delight in the law of the Lord according to the inward man, but I see another law in my members warring against the law of my mind and bringing me into captivity to the law of sin." And Ps. 32:2: "Blessed is the man to whom the Lord imputes no sin."

Corollary

It is clear that a righteous man sins even when he is doing good.

First, I prove this from the text of Eccl. 7:20: "There is not a righteous man on earth who doeth good and sinneth not." Now some say that this text means that every righteous man is a sinner most certainly but that he is not sinning when he is doing good. The answer to that is, if this authority wanted to say that why waste so many words? Does the Holy Spirit delight in loquacity and inanity? For that meaning could have been made abundantly clear simply by saying this: "There is not a righteous man on earth who sinneth not." Why then add that qualifying phrase ". . . who doeth good"? As if there were another righteous man who did evil. For nobody does good unless he is righteous. Moreover, when the authority discusses sins and not in the context of good deeds, he expresses himself in these words, "Seven times a day the righteous man falls" (Prov. 24:16). In this context he does not say, "Seven times a day the righteous man falls, when he is doing good." It iş like a man chopping wood with a rusty indented axe: though he is a good workman, yet it is only with great difficulty that he hacks out rough, uneven cuts. God works through us in like manner.

In the second place I prove it from the text of Rom. 7:19: "The evil I do not want to do, I do. The good I want to do, I do not." And further on: "I delight in the Law of the Lord according to the inward man, but I see another law in my members warring against the law of my mind." Now look! At one and the same time he delights in the law of God and yet is displeased with the law of God. At one and the same time he wants to do good according to the spirit, and yet he does not do this but does the opposite. This opposite, however, is a distinct "non-willing" which is always there when there is a "willing." By the latter he does well, and by the former ill. The state of not being willing (the *nolle*) is of the flesh, but the state of willing (the *velle*) is of the spirit. In so far as there is unwillingness, difficulty, compulsion, resistance, sin is there: in so far as there is willingness, agreeableness, freedom, joy, virtue is there. These two are mixed in all our life and in all we do. And if the unwillingness be total and complete, then mortal sin is already there, and also a turning away from God. In this life, however, the will whole and entire does not exist. We are in fact always sinning even while doing good, admittedly sometimes more and sometimes less. This is the reason why there is on earth no righteous man who doeth good and sinneth not. There is however such a righteous man but he is in heaven. As therefore no man exists without this perversity of will, no man is without it whatever he is doing. And because of this a man is never without sin. If a man can neither live without it nor even exist without it, how then can he do a good work and be free from it? For thus saith the Scripture, "Who can boast that he hath a pure heart?" (Prov. 20:9). Again in Gal. 5:17: "The flesh lusteth against the spirit and the spirit against the flesh. These two are contrary one to another, so that ye cannot do the things ye would," etc.

In the third place I prove it from Ps. 143:2: "Enter not into judgment with thy servant, O Lord, for in thy sight shall no man living be justified." Here I ask myself, if that righteous man (the man we have imagined for the sake of argument) were actually here in the full splendour of his merit, would he nevertheless be numbered among "the living"? If he is not excepted from this category of ordinary mortals, then he is not justified. Then how can this be, unless he has sinned in his very merit and work-righteousness?

I prove now by argumentation and reason

Whoever does less than he ought, sins. But every righteous man even while he is doing good does less than he ought. Therefore every righteous man is a sinner.

I now prove the minor premise: Whosoever does good but not out of a full and perfect love of God, does less than he ought. But every righteous man is of such a kind. (Therefore every righteous man even while doing good does less than he ought.)

I prove the major premise by that precept, "Thou shalt love the Lord thy God with all thine heart and with all thy strength" (Deut. 6:5). Concerning this command our Lord said, "Not one jot or tittle shall pass from this law till all be fulfilled" (Matt. 5:18). Therefore we must love God with all our strength, or sin. But the minor premise that we do not love with all our strength has been proved above. The perversity of will in our flesh and in our members prevents this totality, so that we do not love God with all our members and all our strength. The perversity of our will resists the inner will in the love of God.

But some people say, "God does not expect his command to be perfectly obeyed by us." I then ask, "Of whom then is it required? Stone and wood? Or sinners?" This is a mistake. As Rom. 3:19 says, "We know that whatsoever things the law speaks, it speaks to those who are under the law." Therefore, to us it is commanded and from us it is demanded. Because of this completely false interpretation of the saying, "God does not demand perfection," has come about a state of affairs when people say that whatever is done that is less than perfect love is not sin because God does not demand such a standard of perfection. It is not that it is not sin because it is allowed. It is no longer counted as sin because it is forgiven.

I now turn to argue the objections

First John says in his epistle, "Whosoever is born of God does not sin" (I John 3:9). Again, in Gen. 20:6: "God gave testimony to Abimelech that he had acted in the integrity of his heart, and therefore had not sinned." And also Ps. 86:2: "Preserve my soul for I am holy." And all the others that could be adduced as well.

My answer is this: both statements are true. "Whosoever is born of God does not sin," and "Whosoever is born of God does sin" unless perhaps we say that Paul had not been born of God (Rom. 7), and that even John had lied when he said, "If we say that we have no sin, we are liars" (I John 1:8). The man born of God sins in fact while he is doing the good work on account of the will of the flesh; he does not sin because of a perverse will of the spirit.

You will then ask, How therefore shall we fulfil the law of God? I answer, we do not fulfil it, for we are sinners and disobey God. This is no venial sin of some kind or another, because nothing wicked shall enter the kingdom of heaven (Rev. 21:27). On that account condemnation is demanded of every sin, since Christ said that not one jot or tittle of the law shall pass away till all be fulfilled. Augustine spoke very rightly in Book I, 19 of his *Tractates*. All divine commands are fulfilled when forgiveness precedes consequences. Therefore the commands of God are fulfilled more when God of his mercy forgives than when man of his righteousness does good works. The mercy of God is greater than the righteousness of man.

What the others are saying is this, that God does not demand perfection, when they ought to be saying that God forgives. But whom does he forgive? The secure? Those who think they are not guilty of this kind of sin? Not for a moment! It is those who say, Forgive us our sins: people who know their sin and hate it because their heart is true. As Ezek. 20:43 says: "Ye shall loathe yourselves in your own sight for all the evils ye have committed."

This is what Ps. 32:6 says: "For this shall every one that is holy pray unto thee." If a man is holy he has no unholiness, save that which has been remitted in the forgiveness of his sins. For what then does he pray? He prays of course for the sins that are to be remitted not those which have been remitted, for in the case of those that have been forgiven it is more appropriate to give thanks than to seek forgiveness. In that case he would not have said,

"Every one that is holy shall pray for this," but "Every sinner shall pray for this," if he wanted to speak of the forgiveness that is past. For a man is holy if his sins have been forgiven, and yet a holy man prays for the remission of sin. This is a wonderful sentence. It cannot be refuted by their foolish human gloss, that the holy man is praying about past forgivenesses. Because the prophet is speaking not about himself but about those saints whom he saw sanctified and their sins forgiven. And yet he says that they pray for forgiveness. Unless perchance the prophet is lying, or flattering, or calling them saints whose sins had not been forgiven. But then he ought to say that they are praying "that they might be forgiven," or "for the remission of sins."

Therefore

This is the sweetest mercy of God that it is not imaginary sinners he saves but real sinners, upholding us in our sins and receiving our works and our life, worthy as they are of total rejection, until he perfects and consummates us. Meanwhile, we live in the protection and shadow of his wings. We escape his condemnation because of his mercy and not because of our righteousness.

They try to pile up flimsy and insubstantial arguments: One and the same act cannot be accepted and rejected by God. For it follows that it is good and not good at one and the same time. I reply: Is it not then conceivable that a man may fear the judgment and yet hope for mercy at one and the same time? I say, therefore, that every good act is both acceptable and unacceptable. And the opposite is true: every good act is both unacceptable yet acceptable. It is accepted because it is forgiven, and in this way accepted by God. In his mercy he forgives what is less worthy of acceptance. Yet the same thing is unacceptable, that is it is sin, inasmuch as it is an act out of the wildness of the flesh. But yet God forgives this sin at the present time, though the standards he demands are as high at the moment as they will be in the future. For there is nothing we do which God simply accepts as it is. (These ideas are just conjured up by the brain of man.) Every single thing we do he pardons and forbears. People who spin these ideas out of their brain presume that there is someone whom he accepts without the need for forgiveness, but this is not true. When therefore God forgives he is neither accepting nor rejecting, but forgiving, and in this way he is accepting his own mercy in our works. It is like the case of Job whose beauty God found acceptable on behalf of his comforters (Job 42:8): this means that the righteousness of Christ on our behalf is found acceptable to God. For this is the propitiation of God who forgives us our deeds and offers pardon so that we fill up our own deficiency with his fullness. For he himself is our sole righteousness until we are conformed to his likeness.

Further Proofs

1. "In me, that is in my flesh, there is nothing good" (Rom. 7:18). Much less will there be anything good in those who are nothing else than flesh and blood. For the Apostle is speaking of himself and all the righteous. Therefore if these righteous people, in doing what is beyond them and working under grace, still cannot do what they ought though they labour manfully, how much more true is it of those who in comparison with them are not labouring manfully and are not under grace, that they cannot do what they ought by doing what "in them lies." Yet here again they say, It is true that they are deficient, but this kind of deficiency is not sin. I reply, sin comes from a sinful nature, but God does not impute sin to the broken heart.

2. Through that text of Gen. 6:5 (and Gen. 8:21): "The entire imagination of the human heart is inclined towards evil from its youth up." It does not say in this passage "the imagination" but "the entire imagination." Whatever man imagines is evil because he seeks the things which are his own and cannot do otherwise without the grace of God.

3. It is said of charity alone that it does not seek the things which are its own (I Cor. 13:5). Without it, the Apostle declared, "They all seek their own and not the things which are Jesus Christ's" (Phil. 2:21). But to seek the things that are one's own is mortal sin.

4. Hos. 13:9: "Thy perdition, O Israel, thy perdition is in thyself. But in me is thy help." He does not say, "Thy righteousness is in thyself" but "Thy perdition is in thyself." From thyself thou effectest nothing but perdition.

5. "A bad tree cannot bring forth good fruit" (Matt. 7:18).

6. "He who is not with me is against me" (Luke 11:23). But to be against Christ is mortal sin. And not to be with him is to be outside grace.

7. "If a man abide not in me he is cast forth as a branch and withers away. And men gather it up, cast it into the fire and burn it" (John 15:6). Behold, to be outside Christ is to be worthy of fire and wither continually. Of course, doing whatever can be done cannot be understood as referring to venial sins.

8. The foolish virgins were rejected, were they not, not because they had not served but because they had served without oil (Matt. 25:1 ff.)? They had done good on their own resources and

not by virtue of grace. They sought their own glory, and it is impossible for man to be without this fault.

9. God sends his rain on the good and the ungrateful alike (Matt. 5:45). The ungrateful man is he who does not offer back the gifts of God which he has received from God, and this is mortal sin. And thus of necessity his works are done outside grace.

10. He who sins is the slave of sin (John 8:34). How can a man who is a servant of the devil and a slave of sin do anything else than sin, whose servant he is? How can he who is in darkness do a work of light? How can he who is sick do the work of a healthy man? Many more examples of this kind could be given. Therefore, all the things he does are works of the devil, works of sin, works of darkness, works of folly.

11. If it pertains to man to be under the power of darkness how then does it not pertain to his works as well? The tree is under the dominion of the devil, yet they deny that its fruit is under the same power.

12. The text which the Apostle adduces, "The Lord knoweth the thoughts of men that they are vanity" (Ps. 94:11). And, "The Lord scatters the intentions of the heathen, he rejects the imaginations of the people, and condemns the deliberations of the princes" (Ps. 33:10). Here I ask: Do you understand the imaginations of men to be those which man works out on his own devices? If so, you have heard that such imaginations are not merely dead but condemned, displeasing in the sight of God. If however there are thoughts which man produces not from himself but from an evil bent, one ought not to call them imaginations of men. It is certain that what he understands as the counsels and deliberations of men are those thoughts where men are led by the dictates of natural reason. Otherwise he would have called them the foolishness of men. See now! God condemns man's wisdom, how much more his foolishness.

13. The proverb, "Lean not on thine own understanding" (Prov. 3:5). This may be taken as a statement of universal application or of particular application. If universally, then there is no view emanating from the natural reason of man which is not rejected or condemned. If particularly, as many think, then whenever one allows oneself to rely upon oneself and one's own wisdom, one acts against this text expressly.

14. If a man could do any good thing on his own strength without sinning then he could properly give himself the glory for the measure of goodness done by him. Let him therefore say that he is good, wise, strong and let him boast as a man before God, against

the Apostle who expressly says, "He that glorieth, let him glory in the Lord" (I Cor. 1:31).

15. "I gave them up unto their own heart's lust" (Ps. 81:12). Behold, punishment pertains to sin: I have left man to the devices of his own heart, therefore have I left him to mortal sin. And man's heart is just the same as his will the world over: it is not under grace. Otherwise he would have said: "I gave them up to the desires of their enemy, and they will submit to the devices of their enemy and not to their own."

16. "Everything which is not of faith is sin" (Rom. 14:23). Augustine understands this phrase "of faith" as meaning "of Christ." Admittedly, some interpret it as conscience. But nevertheless faith in Christ is a good conscience, as Peter says, "The answer of a good conscience before God" (I Peter 3:21), that is to have full trust in God. Therefore, if a good work done apart from faith is not mortal sin, it would follow that Paul is here referring to venial sin. This is wrong, since no man living is without venial sin. Therefore everything that is not of faith is mortal sin and to be condemned, because it is also against the conscience. I weigh my words, a good conscience towards God means the consciousness of faith in Christ because its confidence is not in works. Such faith does not believe that it pleases God to earn merit nor does it lead to faithlessness and a bad conscience of the kind under discussion.

17. The state of the sinner would be better than that of the righteous, for the righteous man even while he is doing his good work sins venially, yet the unrighteous man does not sin at all. Wherefore it must be conceded that it is better to sin than to sin venially. Or again, the righteous fear their own works, yet how much more ought the works of the unrighteous to be feared? Or to put it in another way, the state of the unrighteous is better than the righteous, for the latter is afraid but the former believes himself secure.

18. If grace is given to a man who is doing "what in him lies" then a man can know that he is in grace. It is proved in this way: A man either knows or does not know that he is doing "what in him lies." If he knows, then he knows that he has grace also, for they say that grace is certainly given to him who is doing "what in him lies." If he does not know, then this sort of teaching serves no purpose and he loses all comfort, because no matter what good work he has done he still does not know whether he has done "what in him lies." Therefore he is in a continual state of doubt.

19. It is asked, what kind of good work is it that a man does when he does "what in him lies." If none can be given, why then is he taught to do something he knows not what? If this kind of

good work exists then let it be stated. Now it is given by some people as the work of loving God above all else.

If I may be allowed a digression at this point, I would say in the first place that such experts in the grace of God attribute nothing to our works except that they deck somebody out in spiritual honours. Grace was not given to heal the spiritually sick but to decorate spiritual heroes! The ordinary everyday good works we are able to do, but not anything special! And so grace is the most despised of all things. It has come to be regarded not as a gift of absolute necessity to us, but as arising from the arbitrary will of the lawgiver as an additional demand, as they say! And what Christian man is going to put up with this outrage? It means that Christ's death for us was pointless: his passion because God willed it. Not that it is a matter of our need but the arbitrary will of the lawgiver[1]. It is as though we could fulfil the law on our own resources but that God was not quite satisfied with what we did and so exacts the demands of his grace over and above the demands of the law[2]. And so it is not Pelagius who has returned but a worse blasphemer than Pelagius. Thus we find that they say that they in their own natural capacities love God more than anything and everything else, and they are not ashamed to say "more than anything or everything else." But in the last resort my answer is, If the crowning achievement of loving God is that a man should do "what in him lies," the position will remain as it has always been: that is, a man will not know when he is loving God, and because of this will not know when he is doing "what in him lies." There remain two alternatives. Either, he will not know how he is doing or what he is doing so that he can do "what in him lies." Or, he will be certain of grace—which they all deny.

If you say that a man ought to try and do "what in him lies" then this is my answer. I ask again: Does he know when he is trying? Does he know how he ought to try? Does he know what he has to do in order to try? If he does know, then on the one hand he is certain: if he does not know, then on the other hand there is nothing in it. In fact to attempt this is the same thing as doing what is in oneself, and the same question crops up. Besides there is something more to say. It means that a man by not doing "what in him lies," but trying to do something of the same kind, is doing what is in him. Therefore by doing what is in him he is not yet doing "what in him lies."

---

1 Luther is attacking the Ockhamist view which thought of God as arbitrary will and that man's morality had no justification beyond the divine fiat.

2 The view of grace as enabling man to do a little more than demanded Luther deals with at greater length in *Contra Latomum*, (*WA*, 8, 54.1 ff.). See this volume, p. 308.

20. Stop talking rot and let us look at life as we experience it! Let any man do what is in him when he is angry, or when he is exasperated, or when he is tempted! Still better, let him aspire to the illumination of his dark ignorance, and let us see how far he gets! Let him get on with it and make a start for heaven's sake, and then we shall see what he does and what comes of it all.

21. If a man obtains grace by doing "what in him lies," it seems impossible to avoid the conclusion that if not all then at least the greater part of mankind would be saved. I put this question then: when a man is proud, or when he commits a sin, or does anything wrong, is that man himself doing such a work or is another doing it? Himself of course. From himself and his own resources, or from another and from outside resources? From himself and from his own resources. Therefore, when man sins he is doing "what in him lies." And therefore, contrariwise, when he does "what in him lies," he sins.

But an objection is raised at this point: "I am talking of man and his virtues as naturally good and not as they are in their abuse." To which I reply, The natural virtues are always in abuse because they are corrupted. For creation is good but it is corrupted. Nor does it carry on its activities apart from its disease, but it goes about its work infected by disease. Therefore it cannot carry on except as diseased, even if it be good. It is rather like an axe allowed to go rusty. It is iron, but it functions only as a rusty axe, be it ever such good iron.

22. Why then do we admit that lust is unconquerable? Do what in you lies and do not lust. But you cannot! Therefore the natural man does not fulfil the law. If you do not fulfil this commandment how much less can you fulfil the commandment to love? The same argument holds in the matter of all the commandments. For example, do what in you lies and be not angry with him who strikes you. But you cannot! Do what in you lies and do not fear danger. But you cannot!

23. Do what in you lies and you will not fear death. I put the question: What man is there who does not fear death? What man is there who is not nervous in the hour of his death? And yet from the fact that God wills us to go through the gates of death, it is clear from our natural fear of it that we love our own will more than God's will. For if we loved the will of God more than our own we would accept death with joy. In fact we would think it profitable and to our advantage as we think when our will is expressed. Therefore these are figments of which we speak. He who hates death (which is the will of God), or at any rate does not love it, loves God a long way less than himself. In fact he hates

God. And we are all alike in this matter. Where now is the love of God above all things? The truth is we love God but not more than our life and our own way. What then shall I say of hell? Who does not hate this?

24. The very Lord's Prayer in itself is abundant witness that we are workers of iniquity in every department of life. Just imagine the man who does "what in him lies." Ought he to pray "Thy name be hallowed, Thy will be done"? or rather "Thy name has been hallowed, thy will has been done." If his name is to be hallowed then he is admitting that he is sinful: if his will is to be done then he is admitting that he is disobedient. If this happens in the case of sons and saints, how much more in the case of the ungodly!

In the year 1518

Answer to Latomus *1521*
(Contra Latomum)
WA, 8, 36–128

INTRODUCTION

AS EARLY AS MARCH 1520 LUTHER HAD ANSWERED A combined attack on his theology from the universities of Cologne and Louvain (*WA*, 6, 170 ff.). Louvain sought to carry the attack further. They suspected that Erasmus was behind Luther's writings, and were very anxious for Erasmus to show clearly where he stood either by helping them to frame the best method of attacking Luther, or at least by having the support of his signature to the attack they were to frame. Erasmus would oblige in neither way but rather goaded the Louvainian theologians to embark on an academic refutation of the Lutheran theology with a view to publication of the debate. Already, one of their number, Jacobus Latomus, had conceived a plan of attack by seeking to answer Luther's resolutions of the Leipzig Disputation with John Eck (*WA*, 2, 388 ff.). It is known that on November 7th, 1519, Latomus, after having attacked Mosellan and Erasmus, was planning a third book against Luther in defence of scholastic theology. Another colleague of Latomus, Turenholtius by name, was engaged on a series of disputations against Lutheran theology. Erasmus knew of these two protagonists but accused both of them of not having the courage of their convictions to publish their thoughts. Eventually, Latomus did so, and published his work on May 8th, 1521.

Luther knew of the impending threat of Latomus' attack before his journey to Worms and received a copy of the document on May 26th, 1521, when he realized the unwelcome necessity of having to answer it. Luther was at a great disadvantage imprisoned in the Wartburg without a library of any sort, and it is remarkable that there are so few errors in the work. He completed his answer within a month, June 20th, 1521, a work of some forty thousand words in the Latin.

On a few occasions the work suffers in the eyes of a modern reader from being slightly prolix, and sometimes a little personal and controversial. I have taken the liberty (of which other and famous translators have sometimes availed themselves) of omitting these few passages as now serving no purpose to the argument of the book proper nor even of being of much interest to the modern reader. Wherever I have done this I have indicated it: where the omission is brief, by a few dots; where somewhat longer and a link was necessary, by a few summarizing sentences (clearly indicated as a summary by being set back a little from the Luther text). None of these minor omissions have any theological significance and can be neglected without any loss of any kind: they only add up to some few pages in all. Each paragraph of the translation is numbered with the page and line of the Weimar text, Volume 8.

The work falls into three clear parts. Part one contains Luther's defence of the propositions Latomus condemns in the form of four theses. First that God commands the impossible. Secondly, that sin remains after baptism. Thirdly, that not every mortal sin need be confessed to a priest. And, fourthly, every good work of the saints is nevertheless sin. Part two turns to the articles of doctrine Latomus attacks under the form of two articles on the nature of sin. First, that every good work is sin. Secondly, that there is not a righteous man on earth who does good and sins not. Part three discusses the authority of Scripture and tradition with reference to law and gospel.

The work marks a convenient halting place in Luther's life. It makes in fact a kind of watershed. Luther has developed into a great university teacher and Church Reformer with consequences for society a few feared but the many awaited in hopeful expectancy. The pope had excommunicated him, the Emperor had outlawed him. He now stood in the Wartburg in lay protective custody, and it was at this moment he wrote the last and perhaps most important work of the collection in this volume. In the four years covered by these four works, we have watched him grow from an unknown university lecturer to the great Reformer who, under God and in his cause, successfully challenged on the one hand the authority of the pope (supported by canon law, theologians and jurists, scholastic theology and philosophy), by an appeal to Scripture, tradition and reason; and on the other hand the emperor (upholding these same ecclesiastical authorities), on the grounds of the same appeal, though now somewhat strengthened by the responsible lay opinion he had himself awakened.

And in the ominous and pregnant silence of that Thuringian summer of 1521 we leave Martin the exile working and waiting.

Answer to Latomus

THE TEXT

To the most honourable Justus Jonas,
Dean of the Clergy at Wittenberg,
his superior in the Lord,
Martin Luther
sends greetings in the Lord.

After beginning with a short preface to Justus Jonas, Professor of Canon Law at Wittenberg, a supporter of the evangelical cause and Luther's companion at Worms, Luther addresses himself to the preface of Latomus, closing with the words, "In the place of my exile. June 8th, 1521."

45.16. ON THE PREFACE OF LATOMUS

Luther writes that Latomus advises moderation, prayer and patience, but objects that this means in effect the toleration of the pope and his court. Luther dismisses this as pious talk, and argues that his alleged harshness has in actual fact hurt no one and deceived no one. He calls for a clear understanding of the gospel and the life of freedom this guarantees. It is never right to go against the Word of God even if it means setting a man in opposition to the pope. The hierarchy he asserts can neither teach the Bible nor proclaim Christian doctrine, and far from condemning himself for opposing the pope he condemns himself for being too sparing hitherto to him and his bishops when he thinks of the thousands of souls destroyed by them. When Latomus raises the objection of sedition, Luther counters that it was the same matter raised against Christ and that nothing can take precedence of the eternal salvation of souls. It is not that the Word will bring trouble but that godlessness has already created it.

Latomus also objects that Luther's approach is not in the

true academic tradition: under the pretext of academic discussion Latomus alleges that Luther hides heresy, and is not concerned to elicit truth but to attack the Church. Luther asks did not Christ engage in dispute and answer back. Latomus, Luther argues, identifies the opinions of the University of Louvain with truth and considers its theologians at once both teachers and judges, unerring on both counts. But Luther argues that Latomus' position is itself a very controversial one and indicates bold arrogance: Latomus' claim that the Fathers are on his side is built on sand. Not only did orthodoxy until Luther's day pay little heed to and show slight knowledge of the patristic tradition, but they are wrong in treating them as infallible for they can be readily shown to be human and erring.

Latomus argues that some of Luther's statements are opposed to the principal articles of the faith, so Luther begins his refutation by defending his condemned propositions.

PART ONE

The first of my theses which he attacks is: God commands the impossible

(See Art. 68, *Contra Scholasticam Theologiam*, p. 251.)

8.53.11. This honest upright man pulls this thesis about so as to take my breath away, he even disregards the qualifications "for us" and "without the grace of God," which he does not deny are in my writings. We want to know what this rigid and unchanging role of faith is which says that commands of God are not impossible for us, that is, in our own strength apart from the grace of God. Did Paul say so? Or Christ? Or did Moses lay it down? No, it is just some human decretal, taken from Jerome, which runs: "Whoever says that God commands the impossible, let him be anathema." This ambiguous and obscure statement of a mere man is so vaunted by the sophists as to close their minds completely and make them shout nothing but Anathema! Anathema! Anathema! so that you would consider them out of their mind on their own admission. A man has to say nothing and give in to this purely human judgment, no matter how many obvious and clear passages of Scripture there are to the contrary in case this so tender decretal permits as much as a syllable of an explanatory gloss. And yet at the same time it is so unequivocal that it rings out loud and clear, is boasted about, dinned into everybody's ears and pushed down their throats to the greater peril of faith and knowledge of the grace of God. And all for no other reason than that it is a statute promulgated by man, and because our theological masters are in the habit of considering it infallible. This is the explanation why the idea of the freedom of the will has gained not a little strength from this decretal.

8.53.29. This rule of faith is like the ambitious and insolent Romulus who would not allow his twin brother Remus to rule jointly with him. For there is another decree which is holy enough found alongside this scandalous one, which runs, "Whoever says we are able to fulfil the commands of God apart from the grace of God, let him be anathema" (Synod of Orange 529). This unhappy decree has nobody to vaunt, extol, inculcate and insist on it but has been forced to yield the kingdom to its brother. This statement is not a principal article of faith: our theological masters judge and condemn nothing by it. Why is this so? Because it is far too godly a decree, and almost all the writings of our masters run contrary to it.

8.54.1. Moreover, look at the wonderful fairmindedness of our masters. It is not enough to hide the decree but they must add something to it. Consequently, they emasculate it and take away its whole effect with this doltish gloss: "The commandments of God may be fulfilled in two ways. In one way according to the actuality of the deed, in another way according to the intention of him who commands." In lighting upon this way of escape how beautifully they have played off the truth. From this they have deduced that grace is not needed to fulfil the commandments of God but only to fulfil God's intention exacted over and above the commandments. In this way they make God into a wicked taskmaster who is not satisfied when his commands are fulfilled but demands that they be fulfilled in grace. Consequently, grace is no longer grace: it is an exaction of some sort. This means that free will has satisfied God's law but God is not content with this! This is the most godless and blasphemous opinion of them all! But, as I said earlier, this is what happens when this decree is neglected.

8.54.12. Now if as a result of devout study a man seeks to modify this first decree that God commands the impossible to the effect that the word "impossible" may be understood in two ways, that is, either in a state of grace or not in a state of grace, at once they are up in arms. They fight with tooth and nail, fire and sword. They will not let you touch it at all. Unless you profess it exactly as it is, they cry out, "Heretic! heretic! heretic! he is denying the decrees of the fathers, he does not believe Holy Church and he does not hold the principal articles of the faith!" I ask you, what else can you do except let this generation of vipers prepare its own "fire that dieth not." Can you any longer doubt that monstrous sophistry of this kind is the synagogue of Satan? Look how this inflated Latomus brazenly uses a decretal of one kind against me, and how magisterially and ignorantly he keeps quiet about the other. Doubtless he sought to charm the world's ears so that they would never find out how godlessly the Louvainians had behaved.

8.54.22. What is still worse, look at the importance they attach to their godless and blasphemous gloss. They teach that so much can be effected by good works actually done, provided they are done with all one's power, that God of necessity and without fail hands out grace to them. This is what it means for a man "to do what in him lies" (Thesis 26, *Contra scholasticam theologiam*, p. 268). Yet Paul, and Augustine after him, thundered unceasingly that a man without grace only grows worse through the law. For the law works wrath (Rom. 4:15), and was introduced to make man aware of his sin (Rom. 5:20; Gal. 3:19). And the consequences of this blasphemous theology are that they have emptied the New Testament of all its content, and by it have led away us unfortunate people to such an extent that we are Christian only in name. We have reached the stage where Christ serves no purpose at all except to provide us with an ethic.

8.54.30. Now as they talk nonsense in this connection about informed faith, acquired faith, general faith and special faith, or for that matter about their principal articles of faith, what necessity is there to repeat it? It amounts to this: that even if it is impossible without grace to fulfil the commands of God as he intended them, yet it is within your power and on very easy terms to acquire grace from good works performed. As a result free will is in ultimate control not only in the matter of doing good works but even in fulfilling the intention of the Lawgiver. To put this into plain words the very grace of God is subject to free will, for whether grace is given or withheld rests in our hands. From this they work out good things that are moral, good things that are neutral, and what else shall I say? These fellows hold as many articles of the faith as there are sayings of the fathers, decrees of councils, ordinances of the pope and opinions of professors. Consequently you see that on the issue of faith the world has perished in this flood of doctrines. Then what do you think will be the sequel and where will it end? And although this teaching is that seven times accursed theology of the modernists (Scotus, Occam, Biel) as nobody can deny, yet this man of Louvain dares to push his impudent and impious face in front of everybody and sing his lullaby to the effect that these modernists are teaching the same doctrines as the ancient fathers. He still goes on harmonizing the sayings and doctrines of one with the other, so that he holds Christ and Belial in common and confuses light and darkness.

8.55.7. Let us take a look and see how many passages of Scripture have been forced to give place to this scandalous doctrine by and large. . .

Luther then discusses the loss of the following instances: "For what was impossible by the law in that it was weak through the flesh God effected. He sent his own son in the likeness of sinful flesh, and in the matter of sin condemned it, so that the righteousness of the law might be fulfilled in us . . ." (Rom. 8:3 f.). ". . . through this man is preached unto you remission of sins, from all of which you could not be acquitted by the law of Moses. Every one who believes in this man is justified" (Acts 13:38 f.). Had the Apostle not enough skill in the Greek language to say "it was difficult to be acquitted of them" that he had to say it was impossible? The same thing is said by Peter, "This is the burden which neither we nor our fathers were able to bear" (Acts 15:10). . . Yet Latomus tries to say here, "Peter is talking about circumcision as is clear from the beginning of the chapter." Was it circumcision they could not bear? In fact he is talking about the Law of Moses. For a little earlier it is written: "There arose certain of the sect of the Pharisees who had believed. They said, It is necessary to circumcise them and make them keep the Law of Moses also" (Acts 15:5). That is the burden which Peter says is impossible. How does he define it eventually? "But we believe," he said, "that we shall be saved through the grace of our Lord Jesus Christ just the same as they" (Acts 15:11). I omit the references in the Epistle to the Hebrews concerning this alleged impossibility, and they are not just in one place.

Christ also said: "It is easier for a camel to go through the eye of a needle than for a rich man to enter the kingdom of heaven" (Matt. 19:24). His disciples were stupefied that salvation was impossible and said, "Then who can be saved?" He was unaware of this principal article of faith. He did not deny the impossibility of salvation but rather affirmed it. Nor did he change it into something difficult, but actually said: "It is impossible as far as men are concerned, but as far as God is concerned all things are possible." Now he did not say this so much in the matter of riches but in reply to the specific question, "Who can be saved?". . .

8.56.6. Therefore since in the New Testament the ministry of the spirit ought to prevail, and this means according to the Apostle the preaching of grace (II Cor. 3:6), one could wish either that Jerome had never said what he did, or that it had remained in oblivion. For Christians should preach nothing but the glory of God, that is confess the impossibility of it all to us but the possibility of it all to God, just as Christ says (Matt. 19:24–6). All the scandals, of which this decretal is among the worst, which may have the effect of encouraging belief in the freedom of the will or of puffing it up, must be utterly abolished, so that the knowledge of the pure grace of God and our own miserable plight may be preserved.

8.56.15. It rather bothered Latomus when I said that even in a state of grace not all the commandments of God could be properly fulfilled in this mortal life. But that is not just my opinion: it is the opinion of Augustine in Chapter XIX of his *Retractions*[1]. We shall look at this further on. Now when I said this does not happen I did not mean that it could not happen. This braggart of a sophist has not learned his own game of logic well enough to know that "does not happen" is one thing and "cannot happen" another. I said "does not happen" but he infers that I said "cannot happen." Yet who doubts that God could give enough grace to anybody to fulfil the law perfectly (as we feel he did in the case of the Blessed Virgin) granted that he does not do it for everybody? If this is objectionable, as far as the decretal goes then let the decretal go to blazes and be anathema.

8.56.23. Latomus labours under another handicap from which sophists are never free. And that is *petitio principii*, begging the question.

This is the most pernicious form of disputation, and his whole book is steeped in this sophistry. The perpetual foolishness of the sophists is that they seize upon and presuppose as an infallible principle of faith the very point which has to be proved and demonstrated as true in the first place. This is the case here. In the first instance Latomus ought to have proved that "to fulfil the commands of God perfectly" means the same thing as "to satisfy the commands of God in every detail so that there is no need of forgiveness." Now this is what Augustine desires, as I do, and Scripture as well. But he stops at nothing and rushes on as if he were in secure possession of an article of faith needing no proof. He thinks he is devastating the enemy with the sword of the Spirit whereas in fact he is quite ridiculous, playing about in front of us with the "hay and stubble" of his own opinion. Not even this decretal of his supports his views, for we say that the commandments of God are all fulfilled not by our doing them completely

[1] Migne, 32.615.

but by the abundant grace of a forgiving God. In our argument it is not a matter of something impossible but rather that all things are fulfilled. Thus I am saying something very much better than if I were to assert that every commandment could be fulfilled by our own good works alone without the forgiveness and mercy of God. As I say, he has to prove that his "impossible" signifies what he thinks it signifies. But these folk admit that grace is never fully given in this life and is always growing. Since then grace is not given except to fulfil God's commandments, it follows then that to the extent that the commandments are not fulfilled, then to that extent is grace imperfect. But because our dear friends the Louvainian masters say so, then on that account it is not to be condemned. Had Luther said so, it would have been all wrong.

8.57.3. The second thesis: Sin remains after baptism

This proposition Latomus condemns on the authority of Gregory[1] but I have proved it on the authority of Paul (Rom. 7)[2]. Latomus patently begs the question and says that in this passage sin is not sin but weakness. He talks as if he had successfully carried his point that the passage must be expounded in such a way as if Paul did not know what words he ought to use, or as if I were not allowed to use Paul's words.

8.57.8. Let us look at Gregory's proof. He says, "Christ says: He that is washed is clean every whit. Therefore nothing remains of the contagion of a man's sin when he that redeemed him pronounces him totally clean." I overlook the stupidity of Latomus who promised not to count but weigh his witnesses. But this means that he is speaking with sophist artifice and wanted not to weigh them but number them. I take Gregory up. Tell me, Gregory, where does Christ say what you say? Ought you not to have quoted the words of Christ literally? You say, He that is washed is clean every whit. But in actual fact Christ said this: "He that is washed has no need to wash save for his feet but is clean every whit." Whence is this soiling of the feet after bathing? Does he not assert complete cleansing in such a way that nevertheless the feet have need of washing? What else can this mean except that sin is completely forgiven in baptism and yet remains, as Paul also says in Rom. 7:18 f. The feet are washed all through life even in the case of those who are utterly cleansed: as Christ says, "Ye ought to wash one another's feet."

8.57.20. Now does this text not speak in support of me but against Latomus? All sins are washed away but there is still

1 Epistles, 9, 45; Migne, 77.1162.
2 Cf. Leipzig Debate 1519, Thesis 2; WA, 2, 410 ff.

something left that needs washing. The meaning is absolutely clear. How could all sins be washed away unless they were remitted and pardoned by grace? How could cleansing still be necessary unless in fact sin actually remained? We shall say more about this later. For the moment the self-confidence of this fellow Latomus must be shaken so that in the first place he can see that the fathers are but men, and in the second place so that he can recognize his mischievous method of disputation, which is, as I have said, a *petitio principii*. He ought first to have proved that "to be clean every whit" means the same as "no sin remains after baptism." The words of Gregory do not compel this interpretation, or if they do, they should be denied. And now our opponents having foisted their own views on to the words of the fathers sally forth like asses in lions' skins. These crafty fellows seek to manufacture principal articles of faith for us, not derived from the views of the fathers but from their own opinions which they foist on to the words of the fathers.

8.57.32. The third thesis: Not every mortal sin need be confessed to a priest

Latomus says that this thesis was condemned by a general council and consequently it is simply an opinion that has been condemned. According to his lights Latomus holds this as a necessary inference. But what Scripture supports this Council? If the decrees of a council were authoritative without the support of Scripture, then it is enough merely to gather a few cardinals' caps and monks' tonsures together. Why not gather together some wooden and stone statues from the churches, put mitres and cardinals' caps on their heads, and say now we have a general council? Is it not a most pernicious thing for a council to meet and reach decisions apart from the Word of God? In fact I now say more precisely what I wrote in a book of mine written in German[1] and which I shall publish in Latin when I find time. I wholly deny that confession must be demanded. The traditions of men must be banished from the Church. Latomus agrees in his *Dialogue* that they can be repealed by men. This horrid rule of confession is nothing but a tyrannical exaction of the popes without any support in Scripture.

8.58.7. The fourth thesis: Every good work of the saints while pilgrims in this world is sin[2]

Aha! How absurd he makes this thesis look! In fact, in the opinion of this very great man, it seems in direct contradiction to

[1] *On Confession*, 1521. *WA*, 8.129–85. Luther never actually found time to put it into Latin.
[2] Cf. *Heidelberg Disputation Theses* 6 and 7, p. 284 f.

the statement in the Athanasian Creed, "They who have done good will go into life everlasting." Here he is triumphant in real earnest, so much so that he throws his weight about asserting that it would be a shameful thing to seek to obtain proof out of them in a matter of this sort. In a word this fierce man adopts even a threatening attitude in case anybody makes common cause with me. This is exactly what the Jews did before Pilate. "If this man had not been a malefactor we would not have handed him over to you" (John 18:30). What stupid and shocking people not to believe at the mere nod of our dear Louvainian theologians! To imagine that they were like other men who could want to do wrong or who could make a mistake! Especially since their work has been approved by the Bishop of Bulls. Bulls? Better bubbles! [Luther plays on the Latin word *bulla* which means both a bull and a bubble. Ed.]

8.58.16. Take note of the utter worthlessness of the man. I for my part insist that sin is present in any good work, but he invariably interprets sin as what they call "that which is worthy of damnation." He does so on the ground that this sin is the only kind of sin rebutted by the credal statement, "Those who have done good shall go into life everlasting." Now they themselves admit that a good work in which venial sin may be present is not contrary to the Creed. They go so far as to maintain what Gerson said, "No venial sin is venial by nature, and God's grace is more often a taking away than a giving to, so that it is only by the mercy of God that sin is venial[1]." And what surprises you is that Latomus does not at once proceed to admit the possibility of venial sin (negligence for instance) in every good work. And as a result of such reasoning it would not have been absurd if they had thus allowed sin to be present in a good work, nor would it be against the Creed. And for no other reason than it was not I who said it but they!

8.58.26. But further on in the argument I shall even compel them to admit that it is uncertain whether any good work of any man, no matter how good it is, is without sin. The chances are they might even be inclined to agree for they compel nobody to affirm this of his good works. And note, what is uncertain may in certain circumstances obtain, and this may even be their view. But if this is expressed by somebody else it is absurd and runs contrary to the Creed, and as a consequence they want it thought that nothing more absurd could be said. Yet this uncertainty stops them from asserting its opposite. And that is why my thesis is neither denied nor condemned. In all the quotations he makes

[1] Gerson, *Opera Omnia*, ed. Du Pin (Antwerp 1706), III, 10.

from the Fathers he begs the question in every instance. He does not prove that his quotations are pertinent to the issue at stake, that is that there is no sin in a good work. No matter how many of the Fathers say their works are good they do not condemn my thesis. . .

PART TWO

A. Article One

The first article attacked by Latomus is the one which runs: Every good work is sin[1]

8.59.3. In the first place Latomus makes inferences that do not follow from his premises. In the second place he sets up contrary views. In the third place he refutes my basic premises. This is the way he divides his work. As far as I am concerned I shall drive this Sennacherib back to his own country. I shall begin with his third division and defend my own views first.

8.59.6. In order to deprive me of that most wonderful passage in Isa. 64:6 which runs, "And all of us have become unclean, and all our righteousnesses are as a menstruant's clout" he pulls it about in such a way that it can save neither him nor me. He does it by making it uncertain of whom it should be understood. He quotes some who refer it to the Assyrian captivity, others to the Babylonian captivity and others to the Roman occupation. He himself takes the last view along with Jerome and Lyra. But finally as a fourth possibility, even if he admits it refers to the faithful, he takes refuge in synecdoche, a common figure of speech in Scripture, and by this figure wants "all our righteousnesses" to mean the same thing as "some righteousnesses." And so, in that he affirms nothing for certain and also in that the authority of Jerome is not sufficient, for as he wrote to Augustine it was his habit merely to quote the opinions of others in his commentaries, we are all left hanging in mid air.

8.59.16. Now let this be the first thing to say in reply to all those beliefs he builds, or establishes on, or infers from this opinion: You must fight with certainties. Therefore, if this authority is uncertain in the opinion of Latomus, it is useless to use it against me. As far as my task goes I must find an authority that is certain and effective when directed against him.

8.59.19. First of all I agree, and shall later prove, that this text refers to the captivity of the Jews and was spoken about the captives. It does not refer to the Assyrian captivity for at that time the city of Jerusalem was not destroyed nor the tribe of Judah taken captive. Yet it is precisely this situation that the prophet is lament-

[1] Cf. *Thesis* 58. *WA,* 1, 605. Conclusion 2 in *Leipzig Debate, WA,* 2, 410.

ing. Now if I can show that it must not be understood of the Roman occupation either, I shall then have shown that it must of necessity refer to the Babylonian captivity. But first of all let us examine the text proper (Isa. 64:5-12).

8.59.24. "Thou runnest forth to meet him that rejoiceth and worketh righteousness: they will remember thee in thy ways. Behold thou art angry with us because we have sinned: we have always been in these sins yet we shall be saved. And we have been so created that we are all unclean, and all our righteousnesses are but a menstruant's clout. We fall like the leaves of autumn and are whisked along in the wind of our own iniquities. There is none left who calls on thy name, who bestirs himself to take hold of thee. Thou hast hidden thy face from us and hast delivered us into the power of our own wickedness. Yet, O Lord, thou art our father still: we are the clay, thou art the potter who fashions us: we are all the work of thy hands. Be not angry with us as we deserve, and remember not our iniquity for ever. Behold! look down on us! We are all thy people. The city of thy chosen servant is deserted. Zion has been made a desert, Jerusalem a desolation. The house of our sanctification and our glory, where our fathers praised thee, has been destroyed by fire, and all our pleasant places have been turned into ruins—Wilt thou hold thyself back in these circumstances, O Lord? Wilt thou keep silence and overwhelm us with disaster?"

8.60.3. Latomus like a star performer takes a flying leap over the hurdle which stands in the way of his interpretation. The hurdle he leaps over is the words: "... and we shall be saved." These words cannot be spoken of reprobate Jews, but without a shadow of doubt are spoken of the elect and the faithful. Now in relation to the words "Thou runnest forth to meet him that rejoiceth" he asks, "Who is this man that rejoiceth and doeth righteousness whom the Lord runs forth to meet?" But he offers no answer. He has bitten off more than he can chew. And as a result you do not know what he is asking. Perhaps he is afraid of turning out to be a poor expositor. But I want it understood of any believer at any time.

> Luther then argues the case that this passage of Scripture refers to the Babylonian captivity, but that God speaks through these words today, for the words were meant not for the faithless Jews of the time but for the People of God he intended to create in Christ. He shows how Latomus will not take the plain, full meaning of Scripture but makes certain passages bear a figurative meaning only and is arbitrarily selective.

Luther then turns to his own argument. He dismisses in the first place all argument from figures of speech on the plain authority of common sense, adducing further the dictum of Augustine that metaphor is no proof.

8.64.17. Therefore, in the case under discussion, it is simply not good enough for my dear friend Latomus to say that "this can be understood figuratively, and the word 'all' taken as equivalent to the word 'some.'" I refuse to tolerate figurative interpretation. It is permissible as long as it does not teach anything absurd, or make a necessity of the imagery. No! I urge upon him that he *must* understand the meaning of the words, "All our righteousnesses are unclean," in their simple, true and primary meaning. As I was saying he must do this because in this text there is nothing absurd which runs contrary to Scripture. And thus the authority of this text still holds good and laughs at Latomus' efforts and his premature boasting. It proves that all our righteousness is unclean and that every good work is sin. What surprises me is that he has forgotten those evading tactics he uses in all other instances. He could have said equally in this case that "uncleanness" is nothing other than "imperfection," as he does in the case of "fault" and "sin," on the ground that these theologians normally put names to things and meanings to words just as it suits them. But our great hero was hoping to become famous by some rather more spectacular victory than he has actually earned by the only way of escape left to him.

8.64.30. There is also a further reason why a figurative interpretation is out of place in this context. As a general rule, when a universal statement is made clearly and without qualification, that is to say without letting the part stand for the whole or a particular truth stand for a universal truth, Scripture is not content to lay down the mere universal affirmative statement but adds to it the same statement expressed in its universal negative form.

Luther then instances Rom. 3:11, 12; Ps. 14:3; Rom. 4:7, 8; Ps. 32:1, 2; Lam. 2:2; Ps. 28:5 and shows that the text under discussion, Isa. 64:6 ff., is a combination of affirmations confirmed by negations, so as to leave the meaning of the text in no doubt whatsoever.

Luther further argues that there is no case known to him in Scripture where a universal expression stands for the particular. Luther instances Isa. 1:5, 6 ". . . the whole head is sick and the whole heart faint. From the sole of the foot even unto the head there is no soundness in it . . .," and points out that synecdoche cannot apply in this instance for in the first place it is expressed as a universal affirmative and in the second expressed in its negative form.

8.66.24. There still remains the problem of how these statements can refer to the faithful. I do not believe that it is necessary to prove that these captives were faithful and pious, since at the call of Jeremiah and in obedience to God they surrendered themselves to captivity, some willingly and some compulsorily. Inasmuch as the flesh of Christ and his apostles would one day issue from them, because of this fact alone we could say that they were godly and faithful since it is properly believed that the line of Christ's descent according to the flesh may be traced as a holy and elect seed right down to the Virgin Mother. I shall speak therefore at first summarily and later to the text.

8.66.31. I have taught[1] that our good works are of such a kind as cannot bear the judgment of God, in accordance with Ps. 143:2: "Enter not into judgment with thy servant, O Lord, for in thy sight shall no man living be justified." Now since his judgment is true and just he does not condemn works which are entirely unblameworthy, for he wrongs nobody, but as it is written, "He renders to every man according to his works" (Rom. 2:6), it therefore follows that our good works are not good unless his mercy is reigning over us and offering forgiveness. And it also follows that our works are in fact evil if his judgment is hanging over our heads, for he renders to every man according to his works. This is the way to teach the fear of God and hope in God. Yet this godly wisdom my calumniators condemn, and bombastically teach their own ideas of good works. They rob men of the fear of God and of hope in him, and make them proud with their pestilential doctrines. They have fashioned for themselves their own idea of good works that deserve praise, reward and honour and are talking rot just like Latomus.

8.67.4. This teaching I have also established by the passage of Isaiah under discussion: and rightly so as far as I can see. In fact this doctrine is now more firmly established for me than it was before Latomus set himself up as a laughing stock. Isaiah means that God was angry with his people and thrust them from him into captivity and utter ruin: that God no longer dealt with them in mercy but in judgment, nay not judgment but rather wrath. And if there were godly and righteous men there whose righteousness (the judgment apart) could, under a rule of mercy, be described as pure, they too would have been under the same condemnation. In such circumstances so little does their righteousness profit them that they are just like the most extreme and

1 *Leipzig Debate*, Thesis II; *WA*, 2, 410.

impurest of sinners. When wrath of this kind breaks God does not acknowledge them as his own but treats just and unjust alike. God does not restrain himself. What else is he doing then than holding those who are righteous as if they were not righteous? He holds them so and makes them appear so. Nevertheless, because his judgment is righteous and true it must necessarily mean that these people are righteous and yet impure at one and the same time. And thus he shows that no one ought to rely on his righteousness but only on the mercy of God.

8.67.16. This is also the meaning of Job 9:22, "I say one thing: innocent and wicked he consumes alike." He is not talking about someone who thinks he is innocent, but who is eventually consumed by God, and not unjustly. In the same way Isaiah also understands in this passage those who are truly righteous and pure. For the Holy Spirit does not speak as the pious do about the hypothetical righteous nor about the hypothetical idea of righteous persons. Their righteousness, most genuine as it is, is yet as uncleanness because they suffer all the things the ungodly suffer. However, they cannot suffer innocently at the hands of a righteous God, even though they suffer innocently in men's judgment and in the judgment of our conscience.

8.67.23. This is the meaning of Psalm 44:17 f. as well, where it is said of those who had suffered many evils, "All these things have come upon us though we have not been untrue to thy covenant. Our heart has not turned back nor have our steps departed from thy way." This is the same thing he says in Jer. 49:12, "Lo, they whose judgment it was not to drink the cup have drunk it to the dregs: wilt thou because thou art innocent set aside the cup? There is no acquittal for thee. Thou shalt surely drain it to the last drop." How was it that they were not under condemnation and yet had to drink the cup? It was because they were not under condemnation in their own conscience and in the judgment of men, as it was in the case of Job whom the Lord testified as innocent in like manner, and yet the same man speaks far differently in Chapter 9. Otherwise a righteous God could not have afflicted them.

Again he says in Jer. 30:11, "I shall chastise thee in just measure lest thou seemest altogether blameless in thine own eyes." Therefore when God judges we are all sinners in his sight, and when he is angry we all perish. Yet if his mercy is working in us we are innocent and godly both in his sight as well as in the judgment of our fellow men. This is what Isaiah means here.

8.67.35. It should be understood that this reference to "him that worketh righteousness" (Isa. 64:6) does not mean him who does justly as it does in Ps. 15:2, where we read "him who does righteousness." In our text Isaiah calls all righteousness of this second kind unclean and is referring to him who is a doer of righteousness, that is its author, that righteousness might prevail in his days. As it says in Jer. 23:5, "He will reign as king and show himself wise, and will execute justice and righteousness in the land." Also in Ps. 119:121, "I have done justice and made righteousness." Prosperous and joyous are those times when there are doers of righteousness who necessarily are workers of righteousness. The whole passage of Scripture bewails the fact that even were there good and righteous men yet in a time of wrath like this they could not raise up a righteousness by which the wrath of God might be appeased and held in check, but they too would be consumed along with the ungodly, their righteousness held as nothing because the wrath of God would not allow them to make any claims on him. You can now expound this passage at greater length on these lines. I am prepared to take the risk.

8.68.7. "Thou runnest forth to meet him that rejoiceth . . . (Isa. 64:5). When times are happy and righteousness which is thy rule of grace prospers, thou also art favourable and runnest out to men and receiveth them with open arms. They call on thy name and thou hearest them, they arise and find thee, they cleave to thee and thou carest for all as in the days of Moses in the desert. At such a time is there a walking in thy ways, and remembrance and praise and thanks are offered to thee for the benefits thou hast showered upon them. But now when thine anger rages and the times are sad, we are nothing but sinners: thou dost not run forth to meet us, thou dost not find us, thou dost not take us in thine arms. And if there were any good and righteous men yet there is not a single one of them who would stand up and cleave to thee, or who would call on thy name for us, because he dare not. In this situation there is no praise to thee for thy benefits, only so much lamentation in our miseries. And just as in the days when righteousness flourished the sins even of the others were made as white as snow and thou didst not punish them, in fact thou didst account them as no sins, so now in these days of wrath when righteousness is collapsing on every side, thou dost reckon even all our righteousnesses as unclean and dost punish our righteousnesses along with the sins of others: thou dost overwhelm them with evil, dashing us against the power of our own iniquity, allowing us to become what our sins have merited, as if we were unclean every one of us. Thus, if the mercy of God be taken away our iniquities carry us away like the wind, and in the face of that all our righteousnesses are nothing worth. . . . If ever there were a time that this text could be offered as a prayer it could find expression today when though there are many godly men yet the Antichrist pope so prevails that he drags the elect not only into the evils of penances but even into error as well, and there is no man who will rise up, stand his ground and call upon the name of God on behalf of us wretched men. . . Therefore judgment in all her fury and severity ravages righteous and unrighteous alike at one and the same time, and mercy alone saves those who are saved. . . . The principle stands firm, I repeat, that a good work in itself is unclean if the covering cloud of grace is removed, and only if God's forgiving mercy is there may it be considered pure, worthy of praise and honour.

8.69.7. Therefore this text not only supports my argument but even furnishes at the same time an instance of the doctrine it teaches. For apart from his forgiving mercy God deals with good works in the very way that Isaiah bewails. And yet unless they were actually impure and evil, a just judge would not deal thus with them. From this we learn how rich the grace of God is to us-ward, how he cares for those who do not deserve his care so that we may be grateful from the bottom of our hearts, and love and praise these wonderful riches of the glory of God and of his grace. This kind of worship of God and this kind of knowledge of the truth these sophists with their reasonings and qualifications hasten to destroy for they alone claim to be the sole interpreters of Scripture, and yet they do nothing else with it except tear it into tiny fragments, and render them ambiguous and obscure.

8.69.16. At the same time these remarks are an answer to Latomus' pompous scoffing. He ridicules Luther in very strong language for saying that this passage applied not only to the Jews but to the saints of all ages, though I know perfectly well that it refers to the Jews in the first instance. The same Spirit Isaiah possessed in the hour of his trial in his own day and generation was also in Job. He was in Abraham. He was in Adam. He is in every member of the whole body of Christ until now, from the beginning of the world to the end of time. He is with each and every one of us in our day and generation and throughout our temptations. Unless you want to say that Paul should not have said, "And so we believed and therefore have we spoken" (II Cor. 4:13), on the grounds that he did not experience the same rapture as David and at the same time. Times change, so do things, so do our bodies, so do tribulations, but the same spirit, the same meaning of things, the same food and drink abide in and through everything. If this is unacceptable then let the Louvainian arsonists[1] burn the Psalter of David and put together a new one to celebrate their triumphs over Reuchlin and Luther, for that old thing commemorates the doings of the Jews and these do not suit us modern folk! Blind old moles that we are! Thus you study the divine Scripture on the surface and judge according to works and not according to the Spirit. You are like the Jews in the wilderness who stood every man at his tent door and saw nothing more than Moses' back as he went into the tabernacle of the tent of the Lord (Ex. 33:8).

8.69.34. *Let us now turn to the points that remain.*

[Luther reasserts that the passage does not refer only to the legal righteousness of the Jews contemporary with Isaiah but to the righteousness of all men everywhere at all times.]

8.70.9. When I said that in itself the righteousness of the law was not a bad thing and further only condemned the use made of it as blameworthy, Latomus again showed how learned he was in Holy Writ. He quoted that passage in II Cor. 3:10: "What once had been glorified has no glory at all because of the glory that excelleth it." Then he believes that I have not noticed that passage in Ezek. 20:25: "I gave them statutes which were not good." If he were to say this to my face and was nice about it I would say that he was joking, or if he was horrid about it that he was mocking. But for the sake of others we shall say a few words. Many are persuaded that in this passage Paul is discussing the ceremonial righteousness which has now been abolished. Yet the fact is that Paul is speaking of the law as a whole, and is comparing law and grace not law and law. The error creeps in because they consider the gospel as a teaching of laws.

8.70.18. Let us briefly explain the position. There are two ministries of preaching, the one of the letter and the other of the spirit. The letter is the preaching of the law, the spirit is the preaching of grace. The former pertains to the Old Testament, the latter to the New Testament. The distinguishing feature of the law is the knowledge of sin: the distinguishing feature of the spirit is the revelation of grace, or the knowledge of grace, which is faith. Therefore the law was not able to make righteous. In fact, since human frailty was not able to bear it, in these circumstances grace has been veiled on Mount Tabor right down to the present time. For no one can withstand the power of the law unless he is protected by grace. This is why Moses was compelled to veil his face.

---

[1] The word "arsonist" is not merely abusive. It refers to the fact that when the pope threatened to excommunicate Luther in his bull *Exsurge, Domine*, he issued a demand for Luther's books to be burned. The Louvainian theologians complied and burned Luther's works, and so he quips them as being arsonists.

It is because of this that the Jews do not understand the law even to this day. They seek to establish their own righteousness and do not want their own righteousness to be made sin as a means of subjecting them to the righteousness of God. Now this is the glory of the law: it was given to convict everybody of sin. As it says in Rom. 3:9, "It includes everybody under sin." Thus the law is the strength of sin, and works wrath and death. The Spirit, on the other hand, makes alive. Therefore, when Ezekiel says, "I gave them precepts which were not good, and ordinances by which they could not live" it applies to the law as a whole and not to the ceremonial law as such. The same is true of Paul's statement, "It is no longer glorified what had once shone brilliant in this respect": it pertains to the same law taken as an entire whole. For the whole law was holy, righteous and good, as Paul said in Rom. 7:12. But as far as it affects us, that which is good cannot be good to us nor give us life because of our sin: it kills us. For even God himself, and he is the highest good, is not good for the ungodly but is the greatest cause of their fear and trembling. As Hos. 5:12, 14, says, "I am like a moth to Ephraim, like dry rot in the house of Judah. And I will be as a lion to Ephraim, and as a young lion in the house of Judah."

8.71.1. Therefore, the trouble with our Louvainian theologians is that they know nothing about the Scriptures. They never understand what law is and what grace is, nor what is a matter of ceremony and what is a matter of law. Therefore their thinking is so confused in this matter that they follow the one when they ought to follow the other. I repeat, therefore, that just as the law of the Ten Commandments is good if it be observed, that is if you have faith, which is the fulfilment of the law and its righteousness, so on the contrary, it is death and wrath and no good to you if you do not observe it, that is if you do not have faith, no matter how many of its works you might do. (For the righteousness of the law, even that of the Ten Commandments, is unclean, and has been done away through Christ, even more than is the case with ritual righteousness. Now this righteousness of the law is properly the veil over the face of Moses which the glory of faith removed.) Therefore, ceremonial law of any kind is good if you observe it, not in the spirit of works but in faith, that is if you keep the ceremonial in such a way as to know that justification is not in these observances but in faith. Contrariwise, it is not a good thing but it is death and wrath if you keep it apart from faith. It is the same as not keeping it. It is clear, therefore, that the entire law is the letter that killeth, but grace by faith in Christ is the spirit that giveth life.

8.71.13. Since therefore God gave to the Jews by the hand of Moses the law of the letter but not the law of faith, he rightly says (Ezek. 20:25) that he had given statutes which were not good and not life-giving, because these statutes were not able to make men good and give them life. Grace, however, is the law of life turning men good, giving them life and making them righteous. And thus Paul wants the ministers of the New Testament to be ministers of grace and not of law, because their office is not that of Moses (for this work had been done already) but of Christ, that is to preach the splendour of grace. Moreover, I would like to learn from our Louvainian experts just how they know that Ezekiel (Ezek. 20:25) and Paul (II Cor. 3:6 f.) are speaking of the ritual law. Are they not maintaining but their own views, or those of other men? This is the way of these men: they rush at the words of Scripture like filthy swine to the trough. They seize on passages without any sense of judgment and find in them whatever they want. They even dare to do battle for the faith before considering their weapons whether they are worthy or worthless.

8.71.25. When in fact I so handled the passage in Isaiah as to urge that the words "all our righteous deeds" and "we are all unclean" are universal statements because it says "all we" and "all our," this very smart dialectician turns the argument round and says, "Now this is the way to reason. The prophet does not say 'all' but 'all we'; neither does he say 'all righteousnesses' but 'all our righteousnesses' wanting these statements to apply to those ungodly Jews, but not to the faithful and not universally." But this has been utterly refuted already, for it is based on the capricious opinion of Latomus. I have proved, however, that this text applies to the faithful themselves and in particular to the finest of them.

8.71.32. But this wondrously resourceful theologian has another way out. He argues, "Granted the prophet said quite simply 'all righteousnesses' and 'all are unclean,' yet it must be restricted to the part and not the whole, i.e., to some Jews but not to all Jews." He again calls his patron saint to his rescue, St. Hyperbole or St. Synecdoche! Now were you to ask him, "How do you prove that this is a figure of speech and that it must be limited to a part and not to the whole?" he would reply, "It is found in this way in other parts of Scripture (as shown above), for instance, The whole head is sick. . ." Here again you see that provided Latomus is master any one is free to allegorize and play about with Scripture just as he pleases. And this is what is called at Louvain the weighing of the testimonies of Scripture by the theologians, authoritative teaching and a jolly victory over the heretics! . . .

[Luther then argues that by this reasoning the text could be made to apply to one Jew and therefore not to the Jews as a whole, and this makes nonsense of the text.]

8.72.14. Note carefully therefore the methods of study and the ways of thinking of the sophists. By these techniques all they do is make everything untrustworthy and a matter of caprice. They prescribe that petty little decretal of theirs ("Let him be anathema who says that the commandments of God are impossible") with such inflexibility and determination and in its literal meaning, that not one syllable of godly interpretation is allowed. They pronounce the whole world heretical if it so much as murmurs anything against it. Why do they go on like this? Because the decretal was promulgated by themselves, spun out of the mind of man, a mere human idea. Yet when you use the Scriptures of God against them they then break out into countless subterfuges, and then everything they think up is at once an authoritative article of faith. And they never think of anything that is simple, invariable and the same thing for everybody. . . . If to be a Christian man meant I had to sweat over opinions, parallels, and variations, I would not want to be a Christian. How could I ever hope to find the rock of truth in such storm and flood? What then remains? Without any doubt, since Latomus is unable to prove that this passage is to be interpreted figuratively he will be compelled to put aside the figurative talk and accept the authority of the proper and simple interpretation. In plain words, apart from the mercy of God all the righteousnesses of all men are sinful and all men are unclean.

B. Article Two
Another text, Eccl. 7:20

There is not a righteous man on earth who does good and sins not.

[Luther argues quite briefly that to glory in one's works is precisely the idolatry against which Isaiah and Jeremiah used to warn the Israelites (Isa. 2:8; Jer. 9:23).]

8.73.30. It is very easy to say that the statement "There is not a righteous man on earth who does good and sins not" is the equivalent of "There is not a man who does not sin" (I Kings 8:46). But on this point when Latomus equates "man" with "righteous man" and "doing good" with "not sinning" he gets out of his difficulty, for in the Book of Kings it does say quite simply "man" and "does not sin." He runs away from the consequences of the text and its context as well, which were the very things he professed to study above all else. On the other hand, I watch these points and abide by their consequences, and understand it is not for me to assert that "man" means the same as "righteous man" nor that "to sin and do good" is the same as "not to sin." Yet I freely admit that had Latomus been the advocate of my view and set this verse before me and contended that in the Scriptures man is almost always taken in a bad sense for sinner he would certainly have put me into a tight corner. For example, "My spirit shall not always abide in man for he is but mortal flesh" (Gen. 6:3), "the imagination of man's heart is evil from his youth" (Gen. 8:21); and Paul, "Are ye not but men?"; or again more frequently still, "I speak as a man" (Rom. 3:5 *et al.*), or again, "the day of man" (I Cor. 3:4), or again in Ps. 82:7, "Ye shall die like men"; and others.

8.74.7. This text Latomus quotes (I Kings 8:46) must be refuted by most certain warrant of Scripture to prove that it does not bear this meaning; or it must be admitted, as long as it bears the same meaning as most of the other passages. There is only one proof, but it is made more certain if it is supported by two or three witnesses. . . . It so happens that in the Hebrew the phrase rendered "he who is doing good" (*faciens bonum*) means he who is responsible for the good deeds that are actually done. It is not so much a personal righteousness which is claimed but rather a goodness that is effectively directed to the benefit of others. And yet it says of such a man that he sins. How much more then does it make the doer of good works a sinner? Nevertheless, if any Hebrew can be trusted, I would maintain that this is the meaning of the original Hebrew, for it runs, "There is not a righteous man on earth who does good and sins not. . ."

8.75.2. I do not ask myself what Bede says, or what any man says. I ask what they ought to say. One must look at God's Scripture only, and not simply what is said but who says it. . . He cannot simply set down texts in juxtaposition, he must reason his case. . . I ask, how often must he be told not to set down passages that are parallel but passages that are contrary, as I have set out passages that are not parallel and similar, but contrary? . . . This is the most thick-headed kind of sophistry and is disquieting to the natural common sense and good judgment of the world.

[Luther then argues that Latomus is shaky on his logic, his dialectic and his grammar; that he argues from propositions he ought first to have established; that he cannot differentiate between predication that is essential and predication that is accidental; that he argues from similarities. Evidence from life of the saints may be illustrative, but cannot be conclusive. The struggle in which we are engaged is one where we need the support of testimonies which have the authority of God, and where human witnesses are clear and without any doubt.]

8.80.9. And what about that passage from the Psalter, "Enter not into judgment with thy servant, O Lord, for in thy sight shall no man living be justified" (Ps. 143:2). Do we have synecdoche here also so that "no man living" stands for "many" or "some"? But Paul further says, "I am not aware of anything against myself" (what about the good works?) "yet am I not thereby justified" (I Cor. 4:4). Certainly, thou hast preached the gospel with all thy strength, thou hast organized (as Latomus mentions) a collection with every attendant virtue on the Aristotelian list. Surely thou canst not deny that this was a good work? How then art thou still a sinner in the light of all this? Or perhaps thou art not a sinner and art not justified in what thou sayest? Or perhaps thou liest in calling thyself justified when thou art not justified? . . .

8.80.29. But you refer to Jer. 17:16, "Thou knowest that what came forth from my lips was right in thy sight. I have not desired the day of man. Thou knowest I follow thee my Shepherd." And also to II Kings 20:3 where Hezekiah says, "I beseech thee, O Lord, remember I pray thee how I have walked before thee in truth and with a perfect heart, and how that I have done what was pleasing to thee." My reply to that is this: he does not say at all that he has not sinned in doing these things he mentions, he is in fact saying the same as the Apostle, "I am not aware of anything against myself, I have done the things that please thee and whatever has been commanded, yet am I not justified by that." He speaks only of what he knows. Finally, in the psalms and in many other places, the saints invoke the judgment of God in their cause against their enemies. But they who are blameless in man's judgment and in their own are not justified before God on account of this but on account of someone else, and that some one is Christ. If therefore the Apostle is bold enough to declare that he is not aware of anything against himself and yet is not justified on that account, how much more are Ezekiel and Jeremiah not justified by the things they recount, for it is a far greater and more perfect spirituality to know nothing against oneself than claim to walk in truth and do things pleasing to God. For these could be well aware of something against them and at the same time say these things, as even Latomus proves from Jerome. . .

8.82.3. On this account God has been wondrously mindful of us. He assures us of two facts. First, he teaches us that good works are plain to see. "The fruits of the Spirit are love, joy, peace, longsuffering, gentleness, goodness" (Gal. 5:22); and "By their fruits ye shall know them" (Matt. 7:20). Secondly, he makes us absolutely certain that these good works are not without taint of sin in case we put our trust in them, so that we are able without doubt or mistake to confess that in every good work we do we are sinners and men whom mercy has found. And what is more, to ensure we enjoy a peace that never faileth, he has given us his word in Christ on which we may rely in confidence, secure from all evil. Even the gates of hell and all the sins within shall never prevail against the word of God. This is the rock of our refuge where like Jacob we can wrestle with God, and if I may say so, dare to urge upon him his promises, his truth and his very own word. Who will judge God? Who will judge his Word? Therefore, let these men and all our Latomuses stop bringing discredit to the glory of God! Let them restrain their blasphemous talk, and stop setting up for us idols of our own uncertain and faithless works (Rom. 1:23), lest we also change our glory into the likeness of a calf that eateth hay.

8.82.19. Finally, he is indignant because the Louvainians are accused of not understanding what sin is according to the usage of the Scriptures. Let us see, he says, what sin is in Scripture, and then takes it in four ways. First, as the cause of sin; secondly, as its effect or punishment; thirdly, as the sacrifice for sin; fourthly, as the guilt by which the soul stands accused. I even marvel that they did not accept a fifth meaning as well, i.e., the reward of sin, and then, so that we might have the whole bang lot of Aristotle these men of fertile imagination could distinguish between essential sin (*peccatum per se*) and accidental sin (*peccatum per accidens*). If I were to ask at this juncture which scripture it is where this quartet of sins has been noticed by Latomus, he replies: "Origen and Ambrose call the devil sin. Also, according to Augustine[1], concupiscence remains after baptism, or the tendency to concupiscence." From these remarks I conclude that Origen, Ambrose and Augustine are holy writ. Accordingly, not only are their gods multiplied by their belief in good works, but also the scriptures of their gods by their teaching on sin. For what is the point in having gods if they do not give us holy scriptures? Latomus says in addition that the man who has the sort of sin described secondly, that is concupiscence or the tendency to concupiscence after baptism, is not to be called a sinner.

But let us pass over these extravagant fictions and come to the point. At this juncture, dear reader, I entreat thee be a free Christian man. Swear no allegiance to the words of any man. Stand loyally by the word of Holy Scripture. If Scripture calls anything sin take great heed lest you are persuaded by the words of any of those men who in seeking to express it better deny sin itself. At one

---

[1] *Against two letters of the Pelagians*, 1.13; Migne, 44.562.

time they want to call it imperfection; at another time penalty, at another time fault. In this way they water down Scripture and play about with the word of God for not a single one of these terms is to be found in Scripture.

You may take it for granted that the Holy Spirit was quite capable of expressing these matters in his own words so that we have no need of the figments of men. It is beyond belief how Paul must put these sophists on the rack when they read Rom. 6–8, for there he calls the concupiscence which remains after baptism plain sin and not penalty. They would pay the highest price to rid themselves of this word but they cannot.

. . . 8.83.14. It is not only that they cannot teach that sin means penalty in this passage of Scripture. There is more to it than that. Not even the Louvainian technique of theologizing can make this passage mean that sin is the same as penalty. Nor can it do anything to produce one single instance in Scripture where sin is the same as their idea of penalty. This still holds good even if the text itself did not compel us to take the passage as referring to sin in this precise sense. Since, however, this is the cardinal point on which the whole question hinges, and since that great lout of a Latomus has brought complete chaos and is proud of his performance and equivocations on the doctrine of sin, we shall have so to go about our business as to assert the truth in such a manner that our adversary has no occasion to make game of us. The laugh will be on us, however, if we cannot prove that distinctions and equivocations of this sort are not made about sin in the Scriptures, as in actual fact neither they nor ourselves can prove that they are. For which reason we must stand firm in the simple, consistent meaning of the term, and never depart from it until a clear authority compels us to move from our position. So the things we said earlier must be gone into again.

8.83.26. In the first place, have no doubt in the matter that in the Scriptures sin is taken not in many senses but in one very simple sense, and you must not allow this to be wrested away from you by these loquacious sophists. In truth sin is nothing but what is not in accordance with the will of God. The meaning of Rom. 7:7 stands unchallenged, "Through the law is the knowledge of sin" (and Rom. 3:20), just as on the other hand through sin comes ignorance of the law. For sin is darkness, which the law shines on and reveals, so that it may be recognized as sin. Now we admit freely and gladly that the Scriptures use philological figures of speech, as for example, synecdoche, ellipsis, metaphor, hyperbole and in fact in no other literature are figures of speech more frequent. . .

8.86.29. These examples, [here omitted] have been considered to show that Scripture is crammed with figures of speech, not for us to make as many meanings and technical words as there are figures, for otherwise what is the point in using figures of speech? Let us then come to the point of the discussion. When Christ was offered for us, he was made sin in a metaphorical way of speaking, for he became like a sinner in every detail. He was condemned, forsaken, put to shame, so that in no respect was he any different from a real sinner, except that he was not responsible for the sin and guilt he bore. . . Now in this interchange of ideas there is a metaphor not only in the words but in the actual realities concerned. For in actual fact our sins have been taken from us and placed on him. As a consequence every one who believes this has in actual fact no sins at all, because they have been taken away, placed on Christ and swallowed up in him, and no longer condemn him any more. Then just as figurative language is sweeter and more effective than plain, straightforward talk, real sin is grievous and intolerable to us, but sin which has been taken from us is (to speak metaphorically) happy sin and a matter of our salvation.

8.87.13. Just as in I Cor. 10:4, therefore, Christ is actually called a "rock" where the Apostle says, "And that rock was Christ," so Christ is actually called "sin." In the same way Christ is the brazen serpent, the paschal lamb and all the other things said of him. But we do not go as far as saying that the brazen serpent must bear two designations, nor for that matter the rock. No one ever said that the paschal lamb means a sheep at one time and Christ another time. No one ever said that David is the son of Jesse at one time and Christ another time. Or that Solomon is the son of David at one time but Christ another time. Yet we say quite truly that David is a type of Christ, as are Solomon, Aaron and all the other figures of the Old Testament. And further, on account of this Christ having been made sin, he is by analogy even called "sin," that is the offering of the Old Testament. Consequently, it is not the differences but the similarity which holds good in this treatment of sin, and it is the resemblance which gives occasion for metaphors and which gives expression to the meaning common to them all. But these Louvainians so pull the word "sin" about, as if these four kinds of sin were as different as heaven and earth. Because of this dissimilarity the mind is dulled, the soul confused and all idea of grace destroyed, not only as a word but in actuality. When Paul discussed sin in this way, he said, And in the matter of sin he condemned sin (Rom. 8:3). Paul is referring to that sin which he made Christ be when he had taken away our sin unto himself and condemned our sin. Let us now have a look at this.

8.87.31. We therefore say that the sophists do not really know what sin means as the term is used in Scripture. When they call sin "penalty," they are dreaming of something utterly different from sin. Scripture does not do this. Because, as I said, Christ was like sin in every respect except that he did no sin. For every single evil which comes to us after an act of sin, for instance the fear of death and hell, Christ both felt and bore. But these sophists have not the ghost of an idea what their teaching on guilt and the attribution of punishment really means.

For Christ felt this imputation of sin and was like him to whom sin is imputed, guilt excepted of course. What, in truth's name, is an imputation you do not experience? It is absolutely meaningless! . . . It is a thing to be experienced rather than discussed and defined in words. We would go so far as to say that the sophists have some idea of what the essence of sin is (that is an offence against God and a transgression of his law), but they know absolutely nothing at all of what nature it is in the "categories" of quantity, quality, relation, action and passion. Wherefore, I shall deal with this now in such a way as to reply once and for all to all the arguments Latomus has produced. The reader must be spared, otherwise the book would grow to an inordinate length if I were to argue the case point by point.

. . . 8.88.25. Of course, as I have already said, the sophists are not without some understanding of the substance of sin. But after baptism and the infusion of the power of God, sin is such that one can hardly say that it has ceased to exist, yet it is so ground down and brought to heel that it can no longer do what it once could. But what is this power it once had? It used to make us feel guilty in the presence of God, it used to plague our conscience tyrannically, it used to drag us day by day from one evil to a worse, it used to be supreme in quantity, quality and activity, it used to have the mastery in place and time, for it prevailed everywhere at all time in all our faculties and at every hour. The category of suffering did not apply, for it would not allow the law to accuse it nor allow itself to be affected by it. It then used to establish its place in the heart, set its face on the downward path and rush headlong to hell. What is more it was the bringing back of all that was worst, because it was opposed to grace, and subject to the wrath and anger of God. Thus it used to reign, and thus we ourselves used to serve it.

8.88.37. Now when the kingdom of God appeared this kingdom of sin was divided and the prince of this world cast out; the head of the serpent was trodden to pulp and what remains of it is our responsibility to destroy in the end. It is rather like the children of Israel when they entered the land of Canaan. They slew all the kings, and when their power was destroyed there still remained some of the Jebusites, Canaanites and Amorites (as is written in Judges 1:27), a true and real part of the peoples who had been destroyed. They did not however exercise rule nor were they the equals of the children of Israel, but remained as subordinates and slaves until David eventually destroyed them when he established the kingdom. We are in a like position. We have been called into the kingdom of faith by the grace of baptism and gained the mastery of sin, for all its strength has been broken. Only the remnants remain in the members harking back to the nature and type of the kind destroyed. This residue we ought to destroy by our own exertions, but this will come about only when Our David has established his kingdom and is seated on his throne in majesty. The question at issue between the sophists and me is this matter of residual sin, whether it should be considered real sin or not.

Now, as has been said, they cannot deny (as they would like to) that it is called sin by the Apostle, and so they flee to the glosses and distinctions of the Fathers. They have prevailed to such an extent that the voice of Paul is silenced throughout the world and there is nobody left who calls it sin, the name Paul calls it. They want to make that an absurd and dangerous view. As if the Holy Spirit were not sufficiently far-seeing, or did not know the right words to use in his own concerns—as well as teach us to speak! Therefore, to bring back again the use of the Pauline word we here reject once and for all everything the Fathers or anybody else have ever said who call this residue concupiscence, weakness, penalty, imperfection, vice or whatever else they want to describe it. We set Paul up against them: Paul, our own Apostle, that is the Apostle of the Gentiles, that most sufficient of sureties. He calls it sin, not only in one place but every time: never penalty, never imperfection, never weakness. Not even Augustine, though he is the greatest of all the Fathers, allowed himself to alter Paul's expression and find another.

. . . 8.89.29. I can exonerate the Fathers for they were driven by necessity and duress. They stoutly denied that sin remained after baptism because they were fighting those who simply denied grace. Therefore to commend grace worthily they asserted all sin was taken away. Further, their words were beautifully appropriate to the subject matter for their opponents were disputing about the reign of sin which they said was not taken away. But this is shocking! For the truth is all sin is destroyed so that it no longer reigns supreme. Nevertheless, Augustine himself in many places calls the residue quite plainly both fault and sin. For example in a letter to Jerome[1] where he says that in this life no man has so much love that it need not be increased, he says: "In that it is inadequate it is a fault." He goes on to say, "because of this fault shall no man living be justified in the sight of God. On account of this fault if we say that we have no sin we deceive ourselves and the truth is not in us. Because of this fault there is not a righteous man on earth that does good and sins not." So much for Augustine. Here you see that Augustine had also understood this text in such a way that a person in doing good sins because he is working with a love which has not yet grown great enough. He calls this a fault, explaining that there is nothing lacking in that work except that the love is not complete. Is that not clear enough? . . . I ask you, dear reader, who wonders at my making game of these sophists, whether my indignation is not justified at such unheard-of temerities and such brazen sycophants. May I not sport with them who are not only not content to mock the Scriptures of God, the sayings of the Fathers and plain rational evidence, but in addition go on to gag everybody and treat us all like brute beasts, as if we did not understand our own language? . . .

8.91.1. Therefore we condemn this meretricious insolence and bring Augustine and Paul together. What Paul calls "sin" (*peccatum*) Augustine calls "fault" (*vitium*). But we know that a fault is something which has guilt and blame attached to it and is worthy of reproof, even in matters pertaining to the things of the flesh. This is the universal usage of the Latin language. Wherefore, let us hear what Paul says about sin in Rom. 8:3, 4: "God sent his son in the likeness of sinful flesh, and because of sin condemned sin in the flesh that the righteousness of the law might be fulfilled in us, who walk not according to the flesh but according to the spirit." What does this mean "sin is condemned because of sin"? We have said that Christ was made sin for us, as it says in II Cor. 5:21: "Him who had known no sin he made sin for us that in him we might become the righteousness of God." Here he uses the one word sin in both places. Whether it is used metaphorically or allegorically it is still Christ whom as sin he condemned for our own real sin. For how else could we have our sin taken away unless Christ had been made sin for us? It certainly was not taken away on account of our virtues or merits but it was taken away by the sin of God, that is, him whom God made sin. The question I want to put to these people is this: why did Paul not say, "he abolished

[1] *Ad Hieronym*; Migne, 33.739.

sin" but most carefully states that "he condemned sin." We do not share the view of our Louvainian sophists that words failed Paul. Paul was a chosen vessel, fore-ordained to speak in the proper chosen terms. Now what does the word "condemned" mean? He proceeds to add to the word "condemned" the words "in the flesh," clearly stating that sin is in the flesh, though it has been condemned. Now a man is really condemned when he is not only prevented from committing a robbery or any other crime, not only caught and locked up, but when the verdict has been given, the sentence passed and he is led out to execution, so that nothing further can possibly happen to him except to be taken from our midst, if he has not yet already been carted off. Where then lies the power of a robber in this plight?

8.91.24. In the same way the sin in us is caught through baptism, condemned and rendered wholly incapacitated so that it has no power at all. It is scheduled for total abolition. He who conspires with what is condemned incurs the condemnation mentioned in John 16:8: "The Spirit will convince the world of judgment, because the prince of this world has been judged already." We ought to believe that sin has been condemned, that this judgment is right and that we ought to carry it out.

8.91.28. But what are the chains of this kind of captivity? In Isa. 11:5 it reads: "And faith will be the girdle of his loins, and righteousness the girdle of his waist." So also in Ps. 68:18, "Thou didst ascend on high, thou hast led captivity captive, thou hast received gifts among men." Now who does not know already that a robber at large is no less a robber when he is caught? But his capacity to rob has been destroyed so that nobody could be weaker than him who faces death, for he cannot do even what being a robber he wants to do. Therefore, he is to be pitied. But he is still a robber, and if you were to let him go, he would behave as a robber. By analogy, sin in us after baptism is truly speaking sin. But it is sin in essence, not sin in the categories of quantity, quality and action: it finds its completion in suffering. For the prompting of wrath or lust is the same in the godly man as it is in the godless. It is the same before grace as it is after grace, as it is the same flesh before and after grace. But in a state of grace it has no power; apart from grace it prevails. This is what Paul means when he says in Rom. 8:2, "The law of the spirit of life in Christ has set me free from the law of sin and death." Why did he not say ". . . freed me from sin and death"? Has not Christ set us free from sin and death once and for all? But Paul is speaking of the proper work of the law of the Spirit which does what Christ achieved. In actual fact Christ once and for all absolved and freed everybody from sin and death when he achieved for us the law of the spirit of life. Then what did that spirit of life effect? He has not freed us from death yet, nor yet from sin, but he will however free us in the end, for we have still to die and still to labour in sin. But he has freed us from the law of sin and death, that is from the reign and tyranny of sin and death. As a result sin is certainly present but it has lost its power to tyrannize and can do nothing. Death faces us all, of course, but its sting has been drawn and it can neither hurt nor terrify. Here then are two instances where Paul calls the evil that remains after baptism "sin."

8.92.12. For this reason Paul in Rom. 8:13 and Col. 3:5 orders the putting to death of our members that are on the earth, wrath, lust, covetousness and the like using very plain language. He does not just say sin but uses the proper appellations, wrath, lust and covetousness. But these words are not the names of faults or sins our new linguistic authorities will persuade us. For in fact the Apostle is writing to saints and believers. They therefore persuade themselves as follows: passion in this context is not a vice but the penalty of sin, some imperfection, which is not against the law of God. Was there not already a penalty for sin before baptism? Why then was it sin? Did the mere fact that it was imputed to Christ change the nature of sin and its reality? If this were so they will of necessity have to take out all of Paul's original words and make them good with new ones. Thus Rom. 6:12 says: "Let not sin reign in your mortal body to make you obey its lusts." Could anything have been said more clearly? Sin is in the body and also its lusts, but care must be taken lest it get the mastery. That is a third text for you. Here is a fourth: "Sin will not have the dominion over you, for ye are not under the law but under grace" (Rom. 6:14).

Notice he is writing to those living in grace and he tells them not to let sin get dominion over them. And this must be understood as applying not to other people but to ourselves. For who can resist another's sin or stop another sinning? Here is a fifth text saying the same thing, "Our old man was crucified with him that the body of sin might be destroyed" (Rom. 6:6). It is our old man he is saying was crucified, and even in us self-same people the body of sin has to be destroyed. Never for a moment does he attempt to say that the body of imperfection might be destroyed, or the body of penalty. Now look, we have five clear passages in which Paul describes sin, apart from those we have not counted where he uses particular descriptions of faults. And yet these insignificant smoke merchants[1] compel all these thunderous pronouncements

1 See note, p. 327.

from heaven to give way to them for some worthless little gloss devised out of their own head and unconfirmed by a single passage of Scripture. Later on in this refutation we shall look at Rom. 7 which pertains to all this.

8.92.38. What then? Are we sinners? Nay rather we are justified, but by grace. Righteousness is not situated in those qualitative forms but in the mercy of God. In fact, if you take mercy away from the faithful they are sinners, and really have genuine sin, but in that they believe and live under the reign of mercy, and sin has been condemned in them and is being continuously put to death in them, it is on those grounds not imputed to them. That is the nature of that most glorious pardon which comes through baptism. In fact, if you were to study the matter closely, it is almost a greater thing to hold him righteous who until now has been tainted with sin than him who is thoroughly pure. It ought not to be said, therefore, that baptism does not remove all sin: it does actually take away all sin, but not the essence (*substantia*) of it. It does take away the essence (*substantia*) of most sin as well as the power of all. And at the same time it gradually takes away the essence (*substantia*) day by day, so that it will eventually be taken away utterly. And I am not the first or the only man to say these things since the time of the apostles. Augustine's words are: "All sin is remitted in baptism, not so that it no longer exists, but that it be imputed no more[1]." Do you really hear this? There is sin even after remission, but it is not imputed. Does this unspeakable mercy of God, which justifies you completely from all sin, still not suffice thee? A mercy which accepts you as though you were without sin, so much so that you go on further to mortify what has been already condemned by him and brought to its final hour. This demonstrates the absurdity of the argument of Latomus, and consequently he urges that the Apostle must not be understood properly speaking as referring to real sin. Do you still say that what is not imputed is in such a circumstance not sin? But this is exactly what I want, that it be attributed not to a kind of good work but to the mercy of him who does not impute it. Latomus, however, sets mercy and forgiveness to one side, and does not want sin to be there as a natural thing. But this is to rob God of his role.

8.93.17. From the foregoing arguments I think that my thesis has now been defended, that is that every good work is sin unless it is forgiven by the mercy of God. Even the Louvainians cannot say that fruit is not related to its tree. Now it has been shown that the tree is not without its fruit, in other words sin, even if the sin

[1] *Retractions*, 1, 19; Migne, 32.614.

has been condemned and forgiven. On this point, no less a person than Augustine concludes (in the place where he is discussing whether the commands of God can be fulfilled in this life), "All the commandments of God are fulfilled when whatever is not done is forgiven[1]." Does he not say here quite clearly that the commandments of God are fulfilled, not when good works have been performed but when the mercy of God forgives? But what is forgiven if not sin? . . .

8.93.35. And while we are on the subject of sin I would like to forewarn the reader and provide him with material for a concise answer to all the arguments brought up by Latomus. Note this first of all: Latomus proceeds unwaveringly through all his arguments as if sin which I insist on amounted to nothing, and as if it had been long overcome, as it is the habit of these sophists to celebrate the victory before the battle and beg the question cruelly. Therefore, whatever bits and pieces of the Scriptures or from the Fathers he is able to scrape together where it says the faithful do not sin he believes relevant to this argument to refute me. All you have to do against arguments like these is to use the text of Paul in Rom. 6:12, "Let not sin therefore reign in your mortal bodies," so that you can tell that for "sin to rule" is one thing and "sin being ruled" is another. Now do you understand?

. . . 8.96.8. Now we believe that the remission of all sins has been accomplished, and we have no doubt about it all. But we go about our daily task in the expectation even yet of the abolition of all sin and freedom from it in every way. And it is those who work in this faith who do the good works. You see, this is my faith since it is the catholic faith. In fact, the sophists who attack these views do so to make our faith into a work and so make less of God's mercy than his work in judgment. As it says of those matters in Ps. 10:5: "The judgments of God are far away out of sight of the wicked man." And so they undermine both the fear of God and our faith. Apart from this we could put up with them if they did not threaten to destroy and lay waste this our inheritance allotted by God and the main bulwark of our salvation, and if they would not lose all sense of judgment in playing around with trivialities.

. . . 8.96.27. As far as I am concerned I ask nothing more than to be allowed, as I have argued, to call that which remains after baptism by the name "sin" (as they themselves call it "venial sin"), and therefore in need of the mercy of God, as well as being evil and vicious by nature. If you consent to this argument you have then made sin to reign, you have been a slave to it, and have sinned mortally. In support of this I have recalled Rom. 6 often

---

1 *Retractions*, 1, 19; Migne, 32.614.

enough already and am not going to allow myself to be dragged away from this position. I say that they cannot deny that there are two evils which survive baptism, sin and the lust to sin. The words of Paul are plain enough: sin, the very tinder, is natural evil, and lust is its impulse. He says the latter must not be obeyed and the former destroyed, "that the body of sin might be destroyed" (Rom. 6:6). Let them call these things what they like, they cannot thereby get rid of the fact that these things were said by Paul . . . 8.97.10. Who will be convinced by my words if he will not accept Paul's? . . . Even if the Fathers were to seem to speak in support of their views, even so we must stick to Paul rather than to them, for even if they said things that are true they write much more obscurely and ineffectively than Paul. The words of Paul are much too clear to need any gloss: in actual fact they tend to be obscured when glossed. Although, as I have said, even if the Fathers sometimes call what has been left over after baptism "sin" and "fault," nevertheless they speak more often of the sin which reigns. . . The sum total of Luther's refutation of Latomus amounts to this: If it can be proved that sin in those passages of Paul the Apostle which I have quoted is not sin in the true and proper sense of the word, then Luther collapses headlong in ruin. If this cannot be proved then Latomus collapses headlong in ruin. . .

8.98.27. Now you will say, "Do you not believe then what the Fathers have said?" My answer is, "Ought I to believe? Who has decreed that they must be believed? Where is the command of God in respect of that article of faith? Why do they themselves not believe their Fathers? Especially Augustine who wanted to be free himself and ordered all men to be free in the matter of all human writings[1]. Or is it because these sophists have forced upon us this tyranny and deprived us of our liberty to such an extent that they have forced us into the position where we dare not oppose Aristotle (curse him!) but must submit to him. Shall we therefore be kept in this bondage for ever and never breathe in Christian liberty again? In this Babylon shall we not sigh out for our Scriptures and the right to return home again?" "But," you say, "they were holy men and elucidated the Scriptures." But who has ever proved that the Scriptures have been elucidated by them? Suppose they obscured them? . . . I am not commanded to believe their fancies but the Word of God. One is our Master, Christ, and the Fathers are to be estimated in the light of the divine Scriptures to know who has elucidated them and who obscured them. . . "But Scripture that is obscure needs clarification?" Put it on one side where it is obscure, hold fast to it where it is clear. And who has proved that

1 *Letter to Vincent*; Migne, 33.338 ff.

the Fathers are not obscure? We are going to be brought back to the position of having your opinion in the form "it seems to me . . ." or their opinion in the form "the Fathers say. . ." But what did even the Fathers do except seek out the clearest and simplest testimonies of Scripture and offer them to men. O wretched Christians, whose Scripture and faith still depend on the glosses of men, and await their clarification! These things are worthless and blasphemous. The Scriptures are common to us all. They are clear enough in all things necessary for salvation, and at the same time difficult enough for enquiring minds. Let every man strive for his own portion in that most abundant, universal Word of God! Let us either reject the word of man or read it with caution. . .

8.99.25. Part Three

[Luther argues that Latomus must face up to the significance of Paul. Christian theology cannot hold Latomus and Paul: either Latomus kills Paul or Paul Latomus. The distinction between mortal and venial sin is human and not scriptural, and is postulated to uphold a position held on human and not scriptural authority. The difference between Luther and Latomus is that Luther follows the Scriptures but Latomus the Fathers.]

8.101.33. And so we come to the meaning of this word sin. Paul calls that which remains after baptism, sin: the Fathers do not call it sin but rather weakness and imperfection. Here we stand at the parting of the ways. I follow Paul, you the Fathers. I make an exception of Augustine, however, because he almost always calls it quite definitely vice or iniquity (*vitium* or *iniquitas*).

8.101.38. We then come to the nub of our difference. Is it only by the forgiving mercy of God, or is it by its own nature, that this sin (infirmity as you want to call it) is not contrary to the will of God and against his law. Is not this the sum total of our disputation? . . .

8.103.16. There are two things that concern me. First, I want to have the pure unadulterated Scriptures in all their glory, undefiled by the comment of any man even the saints, and not hashed up with any earthly seasonings. But you are the very people who have not avoided profane and vain babblings (to use Paul's words, I Tim. 6:20), and have wanted to cover these holy and divine delicacies with human glosses and pep them up with earthly spices. And like Ezekiel (Ezek. 4:12) my soul is nauseated at having to eat bread baked with human dung. Do you know what this means?

8.103.23. Secondly, I am concerned that you are no longer able to handle the full mystery of grace and sin genuinely, and consequently are not able to understand it. Eventually you are not able to love it. And thus you have become cold, pallid, disconsolate, lax in the praise and love of God. The word of man when added to the Word of God serves as a veil to the pure truth. Nay, worse, as I have said, it is the human dung with which the bread is baked, as the Lord figuratively expresses it in Ezekiel. The Word of God is the manna which God wished to be preserved in the golden urn and not to be tossed about and turned over by hands of men. . .

8.103.35. The divine Scriptures deal with our sin in two ways: in one way by the law of God, and in the other by the gospel of God. These are the two testaments of God ordained for our salvation that we may be freed from sin. The law does not deal with sin except to reveal it, as Paul says in Rom. 3:20, "through the law is the knowledge of sin." This knowledge teaches us two things: the corruption of our nature and the wrath of God. Rom. 7:7 speaks of the former, "I should not have known that lust is sin if the law had not said, 'Thou shalt not covet.'" For nature did not call this wanton itch sin but rather when this itch or wantonness was put to an evil use on the body of somebody else, as in debauchery, adultery and fornication. Similarly, it does not describe wrath or avarice as sin but rather their expression in theft, fraud, slander, murder. It does the same for the other expressions of sin as well. I do not believe that sin is ever taken in Scripture for those activities we call sin. It seems almost to speak of sin as that deep-seated ferment which bears fruit in evil deeds and words. It is the law which really reveals that what was before the dispensation of law an unknown and non-existing idea (as Rom. 5:13 and 7:8 say), is properly speaking sin; that it is in fact very much alive, and lies hidden in the splendid good works of the hypocrites. But Paul says that the Scripture hath concluded all men under this very idea of sin (Gal. 3:22). Yet sin can never remain hidden to such an extent that it does not produce its fruits in one way or another in every one of us. But you cannot give a single evil work under which all men may be included, as you can include them under the single category of sin, though more about this some other time.

8.104.12. Concerning the second thing the law teaches: Rom. 4:15 expresses it, "The law works the wrath," because as it says in Gal. 3:10, "Cursed is every one who does not abide by all the things written in this book and do them." Rom. 5:12 refers, too, to "death through sin," and Rom. 6:23 to "the wages of sin is death." So far then the light of the law instructs us, teaching us that we are under corruption and wrath, and concluding that every man is a liar and the child of wrath. Perhaps we might have disregarded the fact of our corruption and been quite pleased with ourselves in our evil plight had the second evil, the Wrath, not refused to indulge our madness and resisted it with the terror and threat of death and hell so that we might have precious little peace in our former evil plight. And quite certainly, Wrath is a worse evil than corruption, for we hate the experience of punishment more than the knowledge of guilt.

8.104.22. This being the case, the law reveals a two-fold evil: an internal one and an external one. The internal one we impose upon each other, that is sin, or the corruption of our nature. The external one, God ordains, that is wrath, death and the curse. If you want to call these two evils guilt and penalty, that is all right by me, but we have long been in the habit of handling these two ideas of guilt and penalty in such a way as to take all body and fire out of them, and have invented all sorts of alien thoughts and ideas. As far as we are concerned we call sin (or guilt or the evil within) that universal corruption of nature following the plain sense of Scripture: a corruption found in every part of us, evil and inclined to evil from our youth up (as Gen. 6:5 and 8:21 writes). And so great is this wrath that those things which seem good, as for instance, the arts, talents, prudence, fortitude, chastity and all the other natural, moral and respectable decencies, profit us nothing. The common sense of every man can see no harm in these, so that today, even our theologians number them among the good things of life. They attribute nothing evil to them, for although apart from grace the good deeds do not merit the kingdom of heaven, yet on the other hand neither do they deserve hell or punishment. They would be prepared to assert quite openly that these good deeds can merit even heaven, but for the fact that they have heard something about the need for grace. They think that these things lack nothing the law requires, but only what grace demands. They teach that the claims of law have been met but not those of the gospel. They then go further and say that these works are so good that they certainly merit congruent grace[1], and so they become wholly good if not by their own merit at least on account of their own merit. It must be conceded to these men that God himself does not say that these things are not good, as in fact it cannot be

---

[1] Luther is referring to the scholastic teaching whereby a man may earn by his own efforts a *meritum de congruo*. This state of merit God takes and makes into condign merit (*meritum de condigno*). It is true that the scholastics taught that it is only this God-given *meritum de condigno* which actually makes a man acceptable in God's sight, but Luther's point is that to reach that stage of congruent merit by which a man is acceptable to God as a candidate for *meritum de condigno* a man is depending entirely on his own efforts. It resolves itself simply into salvation by works.

denied, but he rewards them and adorns them with temporal benefits such as power, wealth, glory, fame, dignity, honour, happiness and the like. Consequently a cloak which is not only beautiful in itself but is distinguished by divine rewards befalls this natural blindness, a blindness which does not know the truly good so that it contends with confidence and stubbornness against the things that are good. On this matter prophecy laboured mightily, and all the prophets were slain because they attacked these good things and demanded those that were really good. For prophecy is nothing else than the polishing up of the law, and if I may say so, it was the practice and application of the law: or, as it is described in logic the "subsumption," which declares whether any particular kind of good work is truly good or falsely good. Hence we are astounded at the many things we read were condemned in the ancient books. This is the reason God warned them not to follow their own understanding but to listen to his voice. Therefore he always provided them with prophets who put the law into effect in the matter of these things that are truly good, so that, if I may so express it, they could demonstrate by examples what the law really is.

8.105.13. Therefore, it is the law alone which shows that these things are bad, not of course in themselves since they are God's gifts, but because they are used and understood in the wrong way. They serve this wrong purpose on account of that radical deep-seated sin which makes men trust in these good works, makes them pleased about them, and makes them rejoice in the evil to which they are blind. Now as always the law makes this the deepest and worst sin, for a man must have faith only in God, rejoice only in God and glorify God alone, as Jer. 9:23 says, "Let not the wise man glory in his wisdom, nor the strong man in his strength, nor the rich man in his riches." Now all these things are good but they are freely distributed to evil men more frequently than they are to good men, so much so that Psalm 73:2 f. complains that the righteous man is in danger on account of this very thing, as he expresses it "his steps had well nigh slipped." But as I said, all things are concluded under the wrath and the curse, and serve to nobody's salvation. And therefore, on that account they do not afford congruent merit to prepare a man for the reception of grace, but serve rather to fatten his heart in case he should desire grace or feel the need of it, as Ps. 119:70 says, "Their heart is curdled like milk." The Hebrew text expresses it better, "Gross is their heart like fat." This people is quite properly accused in the Scriptures of ungodliness, and unbelief, and of being stiff-necked, for they cannot control their ungovernable inclination towards these specious goods: they can recognize in them neither the significance of the law nor the fact of their own sin. They always think that because of their good works they are superior to everybody else, even the truly righteous, in the matter of obedience to God. You preach to them in vain: they are bloodthirsty, deceitful men (Ps. 5:6). To sum up: the law has been fulfilled by these men, and they have no need of grace, as I said, except to fulfil some extra demand or other from God. For them Moses is veiled: they cannot bear his horned face. It is not their desire to be evil, engaged in such great wisdom, goodness, righteousness and religion: they cannot see that they are evil because they do not hear the Word of God. You see, therefore, how incomparably the law exceeds natural reason and how profound is the sin of which the law gives knowledge. Therefore, all these men are under the Wrath, because they are all in sin. The gospel, on the other hand, deals with sin so as to remove it, and thus follows the law most appropriately.

8.105.37. Now the law introduced us to sin and overwhelmed us in the acknowledgment of its reality, so that we would seek to be freed from it and long for grace. Now the gospel as well as the law preaches a two-fold truth, and teaches both the righteousness and the grace of God. Through the righteousness of God it heals the corruption of human nature. This righteousness is, of course, the gift of God, that is faith in Christ as Rom. 3:21 says: "Now, however, the righteousness of God has been revealed apart from the law." And again in Rom. 5:1: "Since we are justified freely by faith we have peace with God through our Lord Jesus Christ." And again Rom. 3:28: "We conclude that a man is justified by faith without the works of the law." Further, this righteousness, which in the Scriptures is almost always set over against sin, is understood as of the nature of a deep root whose fruit is good works. The concomitant of this faith and righteousness is grace or mercy, the favourable attitude of God towards us. It is set against the Wrath which is the concomitant of sin, so that everybody who believes in Christ knows a merciful God. Now we would not be happy and content in this righteousness, good though it is, nor would we be able to praise this gift of God sufficiently, if righteousness were all there was to it, and if it did not gain for us the grace of God. Here I quite properly understand grace as the favourable disposition of God towards us, as ought to be the case, and not as a quality of the soul as our modernists have taught[1]. This grace effects a true peace of mind eventually so that a man is healed of his disease and knows in addition that he has a gracious God. This is what puts marrow into the bones. This brings back a

---

[1] Aquinas, *Summa Theologica*, II, I, qu. 112, art. 2.

conscience that knows joy and security and stands without fear. There is nothing it will not dare, nothing it cannot do, and in such trust in God's grace laughs even at death. So that just as wrath is a greater evil than the corruption of sin, grace is a greater good than the health of righteousness, which we have said comes from faith. For no one (if such a thing were possible) would not prefer to be without the health of righteousness than be without the grace of God. For remission of sins and peace of mind are properly attributed to the grace of God, but the healing of the corruption is attributed to faith. Because faith is the gift and the inner good which is opposed to sin and which purges it: it is that leaven of the gospels thoroughly hidden in the three measures of meal (Matt. 13:33). But on the other hand the grace of God is an outward good, it is God's favour towards us, the opposite of wrath. These two things are distinguished in this way in Rom. 5:17: "For if many died through the trespass of one man's sin, much more have the grace of God and the gift in grace of one man Jesus Christ abounded for many." He calls faith in Christ the gift in grace of one man (and more often calls it the gift) for it was a gift to us through the grace of Christ. That means, that because he alone among all men is pleasing and acceptable to God he has a gracious and merciful God, and consequently merits for us this gift and this grace besides.

8.106.29. John expresses it this way in the first chapter of his gospel. "The law was given by Moses. But grace and truth came through Jesus Christ" (John 1:17). And further on ". . . full of grace and truth" (John 1:14). The truth flowing into us from Christ is faith, and grace accompanies faith on account of the grace of Christ. As the same author indicated earlier ". . . of his fullness have we all received, grace for grace" (John 1:16). What does he mean by this phrase "grace for grace"? What grace, and "for" what grace? The first grace is our grace in the way God favours us; the second, "for" or "on behalf of" the grace of Christ, is the grace by which God favours Christ. "Because," it says, "the law was given through Moses, but grace and truth came through Jesus Christ." We have, therefore, two goods of the gospel set against the two evils of the law: the gift over against sin and grace over against wrath.

8.106.37. Then surely it follows that these two realities, wrath and grace, are so constituted (since they both act from outside us) that they are poured out upon the person in his entirety. Consequently, he who is under wrath has the whole of him under the whole dispensation of wrath, and he who is under grace has the whole of him under the whole dispensation of grace, because grace and wrath have to do with persons. It is man in his entirety God receives when God receives a man in grace; it is to man in his entirety God shows his favour when God shows favour to a man. And in the same way, it is with the whole man God is angry when he shows his anger to a man. For he does not portion out this grace as he portions out gifts: he does not love the head and hate the feet, nor favour the soul and hate the body. Yet he gives to the soul what he does not give to the body, he gives to the head what he does not give to the feet. It is the same as well throughout the whole Church which stands under the same grace of God, as Rom. 5:2 says, "Through whom we have obtained access to this grace wherein we stand." His gifts he portions out in many ways and in many different forms. And so, to express it in the opposite way he is unfavourable to the whole of man when he is unfavourable, but yet he does not punish the whole man. Indeed, to express it at greater length, he to whom God does not show his favour abides wholly under wrath by the sin of one man (Adam) but he to whom God does show his favour abides wholly under grace by the one gift of one work (Christ). As I said, grace must be utterly dissociated from a man's other gifts, since it is grace alone that is life eternal (Rom. 6:23) and wrath alone that is death eternal.

8.107.13. We now come to the point of the disputation. The righteous and faithful man has without any doubt both grace and the gift. Grace which makes the whole man pleasing so that as a person he is wholly acceptable and there is no place for wrath in him any more. The gift, which heals him from sin and total corruption of soul and body. It is therefore highly irreligious to say that a baptized person is still in sin, or that all his sins are not fully remitted. For what sin is there in the person to whom God shows his favour, in whom he wills not to know any sin, and where he wholly accepts and sanctifies the entire man. But this must not be attributed to our purity, as you see, but only to the grace of a God showing his favour. Everything has been forgiven by grace, but everything has not yet been made whole by the gift. The gift has been infused, the leaven has been added: it is working to purge away the sin for which the person has been already forgiven and to drive away the wicked intruder for whom permission to throw out has been already given. In the meantime while these things are going on it is still called sin, as that is what it is in fact. But now it is sin without the wrath and without the law: it is sin that is dead, sin that is harmless, as long as you persevere in grace and in his gift. There is no difference as far as its real nature is concerned between sin before grace and sin after grace. The difference lies in the way it is handled. It is now dealt with otherwise than before. How did it use to be treated before? As existing in its own right, as being recognized as such, and as overwhelming us. Now, however, it is handled as if it did not exist and as if it had been driven out. Yet nonetheless in spite of this it is real sin and true to type. Indeed it is ingratitude and a disservice to the grace of God and to his gift to say that this is not real sin. Certainly, when grace is there there is no sin, because the whole person pleases; when however the gift is there there is sin, because the gift is purging it away and driving it off. But also a person neither pleases God nor has grace except on account of the gift which is working to purge away his sin in this way. God saves not imaginary but real sinners, and teaches us to mortify not imaginary but real sin.

8.107.37. Now notice that in dealing with sin and grace I am seeking and want also to preserve the simple Pauline way of understanding them and speaking about them. This teaching is unadulterated and unspoiled, and is grasped with no difficulty at all. It needs no nice distinctions and is wonderfully attractive and clear. It opens up the whole of Scripture. There is no need in this case to say that in Paul sin is taken for weakness. Nay rather sin has to be taken for real sin, so that the grace and the gift of God may be truly and purely praised. And if anybody says that this is not real sin this man blasphemes the gift of God and is ungrateful to him. And so I declare, and this is also my teaching, so that every man should know that in every good work he does there is as much sin as he has in him not yet cast out. As is the tree so is the fruit. This I teach lest he boast to God of the purity that is in him rather than glory in the grace and gift of God: that he should know that he has a God who feels graciously towards him, a God who does not impute his sin, and more than that has given him the gift by which it may be purged. That man therefore confesses the truth who admits that if he were to be judged according to the nature of his works apart from grace, he would not be able to stand before his face. Now that he relies on grace there is nothing which can accuse him. Now are these truths as difficult as those immense tomes of the sophists packed full of teachings on sin and grace? Do they not all run together in perfect accord, the word of Paul, the duty of faith and the argument which seemed to compel us to take sin for penalty? What could be easier than saying that sin must be dealt with either according to law or according to gospel? If you deal with it in terms of law alone it is death and wrath, but if in terms of gospel alone it is grace and life, though of course it is still sin really and truly, whichever way it is treated. All the quotations from the Fathers which say that there is no sin in a righteous man must be understood in terms of grace and not in terms of law or the nature of sin. For Christ has made us free, so that we are no longer under law but under grace. . .

8.109.11. Let us now see how Scripture agrees with this interpretation. Christ says in the last chapter of Luke (Luke 24:47) that repentance and remission of sins are to be preached in his name. Why was it not enough to say simply remission of sins? Does not the following statement meet the difficulty: repentance is the interchange of corruption by incorruption and the continual renewal from sin which faith the gift of God works; remission of sins is the gift of grace so that in these circumstances sin and wrath should no longer be operative? For Christ does not teach us to preach that fictitious repentance of the sophists, which is still being preached up to this very moment. Repentance and renewal must be preached as long as there is preaching and as long as anybody is alive so that sin may be driven out. You could never make these two terms repentance and remission the same as weakness and penalty, could you? Who would do penance for a weakness? Who would renew himself on account of a penalty? The word of John Baptist says the same thing and was repeated by Christ, "Repent, the kingdom of heaven is at hand" (Matt. 3:2, 4:17). What does this mean if not to change one's life? This is what faith does when it purges our sins away. What does this mean if not being under the rule of God? This is what grace does when it remits sin. For example John calls these "fruits worthy of repentance" (Matt. 3:8) when sin is purged and outward works are not simulated. The parable of the leaven hid in three measures of meal (Matt. 13:33) is so exquisitely appropriate however, if you call sin "weakness" and "penalty." In fact you have already spread such darkness by using these words that you can neither see nor understand the parable. The parable of the man left half-dead and cared for by the Samaritan (Luke 10:30 ff.) pertains to this point through and through as well as in its first intent. This man was not only healed but he was at the same time picked up and cared for, while the Levite and the priest, ministers of the law, saw him but did not help him. To revert to what I said, the law makes sin known, but Christ heals through faith and restores a man to the grace of God. That text of John 13:10 supports this view, "He who is bathed is clean every whit," and that means through grace. And yet he washes the feet, that is the sin that still remains in a man, by the faith working in him. A further illustration: We are the branches in Christ who is the Vine, since we bear fruit as if we were thoroughly cleansed. Yet the heavenly husbandman prunes us to bear more fruit (John 15:2). You cannot make one of these passages fit ideas such as "penalties" or "weaknesses," for you lose at once the whole idea of cleansing, and purging, and healing. You would have to drag in vague talk of venialities. But that is a superficial meaning: it is like plucking off the leaves instead of plucking out the root. Or to use a simile of Latomus, this method of curing is like shaving the hair where it will only grow again. Not thus is the gift of God! The gift of God works at killing the root, and by cleansing not the act but the person doing it. Consequently, these venial faults cease or at least are markedly checked. It is a waste of time to resist venial sins, unless you damp down the tinder of sin which sparks them off. Sin is always covetous, but you resist its power if you do not so much resist its promptings as throttle the sin itself. This comes about by the gift of faith which kills and crucifies the old man of sin, as Paul expresses it, and wears him down with various kinds of suffering. . .

8.110.13. To bring it all to some conclusion. Paul in Romans 6 speaks of "sin in our mortal body" (v. 6), of "sin not having the dominion over you" (vv. 12, 14), of "our body in sin which must be destroyed" (v. 6); and in Romans 8 of "being set free from the law of sin and death" (v. 2); and in Romans 7 of "sin working death" (v. 13), of "sin warring against the law of our mind" and of "sin making captive and compelling us to serve the law of sin" (v. 23); and in I Cor. 7:5 of "incontinence"; in I Cor. 5 of "the old leaven of malice and wickedness" (v. 8); in Eph. 4 of "putting off the old man which is corrupt" (v. 22); in Col. 3 of "mortifying and putting off our wrath, our lust, our avarice . . ." (vv. 5, 8); and in Heb. 12:1 of "the sin which so easily besets us." In short, Paul never calls it anything else but sin and vice. Had he called it sin only once, I would not yield to an angel from heaven who tried to call it by some other name. But since he repeatedly asserts the same thing in so many places, who are these men to compel me to blot out Paul's words and put their glosses on the text in their place? I want to have nothing to do with their opinions. I say that sin is in us and in all our works alongside faith, as long as we are on this earth.

8.110.23. If, therefore, my Louvainian friends had listened to me earlier, and applied themselves more to the Word of God than to man's opinions, they would certainly have known the truth more clearly, and truth would have saved them from such outrageous blasphemy, sacrilege, crime and offence. And quite certainly they would not have burned the Word of God so rashly. However, I still offer them the chance of repenting, of admitting their error, of giving the glory to God and of confessing their foolish ways which they cannot support with a single reason. If they were to do this all would be forgiven. Most gladly will I unite with them. I will never think of their sins as I hope God will not think of mine. But if they persist in what I hate, I will most certainly consider them anathema. God will know whether my excommunication is nothing more or less than a result of that bungling, bloody, blasphemous bull, so typical of the pope and of Rome. Amen!

8.110.33. It is my belief that by these statements I have now adequately stated, defended and strengthened all those things which I adduced in reference to this point of doctrine in my original resolution and which Latomus attacks; and that all the arguments which Latomus brings forward amount to nothing but ignorance of Scripture, mere presumption and *petitio principii*.

8.110.37. I shall add one further consideration. . . I merely ask whether the sophists dare admit that there is any man who could say of one single work of his, "This is without sin," even in the sense in which they speak of sin. For my part I cannot believe that even they or any other man would have the audacity to say this of his good work. . .

8.111.24. But let us be done with considerations of this sort. It is plain to see that there is not a single instance in this life of the rule that "a good work is without sin." Paul, as we have said, did not dare to assert this of his own works. As he expressed it, "I am aware of nothing against myself, but I am not justified because of that." (I Cor. 4:4). However, we have to be certain, and so God in his grace has provided us with a Man in whom we must trust and not in our own good works. For although he has justified us by the gift of faith, and although he has shown himself favourable to us through his grace, nevertheless it is his will that we put our trust in Christ lest we grow unsettled in ourselves and uncertain about his gifts. It is also his will that we put our trust in Christ, so that the righteousness which has begun in us may be considered inadequate unless it is a righteousness which cleaves to Christ and flows from him. This is in case a man is so foolish as to think that once he has accepted the gift he has done all that is necessary and feels himself secure. But it is his will that we be caught up into Christ more and more from day to day and not stand still in the truths we have accepted but rather be wholly transformed into Christ. His righteousness is certain and it is everlasting. There is no change there, no lack of anything, for he himself is Lord of all. Therefore, whenever Paul preaches faith in Christ he so preaches it as to make clear with wondrous care that righteousness is not so much through him or from him, but rather in him. This he does to lead us back into him, to transform us, and set us as it were in hiding until the wrath passes over us. It is thus in Rom. 5:1: "We are justified by faith, we have peace with God through our Lord Jesus Christ." Note that faith in itself is not enough: he is thinking of a faith which hides itself under the wings of Christ and glories in his righteousness. Or again, "Through whom we have access to God by faith in this grace" (Rom. 5:2), a further example where he teaches faith in such a way as to leave it under the wings of Christ. There is Col. 1:20 also, "And he was pleased through him to reconcile all things in him." Note the words "through him" and "in him." And further, in the same verse, "Making peace by the blood of his cross through him." What does the Apostle mean by these remarks except that this uncertain faith of the sophists, which thinks that once the gift is accepted it simply carries on on its own, is not enough? But faith is just precisely that sort of relationship of you to Christ as that of the chickens to the mother hen, so that you may have hope under his wing. For Malachi speaks of salvation in his wings (Mal. 4:2), so that you will not rely on a faith once accepted for such belief is fornication. The intention of such imagery is for you to know that faith is when you cleave to him and take him unto yourself for he is your holiness and your righteousness. Look! this faith is the gift of God, and this faith obtains the grace of God for us and purges away our sin: it makes us saved and certain of our salvation, not because of our good works but because of Christ's work. Consequently we can stand firm and abide forever, as it is written, "His righteousness abides forever" (Ps. 112:3).

. . . 8.114.16. Now God has provided two of the strongest and safest of supports so that the sin that is in us should not lead us unto damnation. The first is this, that it is none other than Christ who is our propitiation (Rom. 3:25). As a result we are safe in this grace, not because we believe or because we possess the gift, but because we have these things in the grace of Christ. No man's faith will endure unless he relies on Christ's own righteousness and is preserved under his protection. For as I have already said this is true faith, not some quality of the soul that is absolute (better obsolete!) as they make it out to be. This faith will not allow itself to be separated from the grace of Christ, and relies only on him who it knows stands in God's grace. Christ can never be condemned, nor can anybody who utterly throws himself upon him. Now this really means that the sin which remains is such a serious matter, and that God's judgment is so unbearable, that unless you plead on your behalf him who you know is without sin, you will never be able to stand firm. This is precisely what true faith does.

8.114.28. The other support is that when they have received the gift they do not walk according to the flesh nor are they obedient to sin. But the first support is the principal one as well as being the stronger. Of course, the second has its place, but it is there only by virtue of the first. For God has concluded a covenant with them who are in Christ in this way, so that if they fight against themselves and their sin, there will be no damnation for them. Now there is no condemnation to them not because they do not sin, nor because there is no sin in a good work. When Latomus says this he is on the wrong tack altogether. This talk the sophist invents out of his own head. It is utterly other than and in opposition to the plain text of Paul. There is no condemnation, the Apostle says, because they are in Christ Jesus and do not walk according to the flesh, quite clearly referring to mortal sin. The sole concern of the sophists is to minimize the sin which God is so concerned to maximize with the purpose of setting his Son over against it. In fact, by means of his consuming condemnation, he proposes to urge all men to come to Christ and compel them to come to him, that trembling, breathless and in utter despair, they may betake themselves to the shadow of his wings. Now those theologians who say that this residual sin is no sin make men negligent, and make men feel secure because they have accepted the gift. By doing so they both make Christ's grace cheap and God's mercy of little worth. The result of this inevitably is love that is cold, praise that is tardy and gratitude that is luke-warm. These men know precisely nothing about Christ. You for your part must watch these most pestilential of theologians, and learn that the works of God are great, wonderful and glorious. Know therefore as far as you are concerned you cannot make this sin great enough. For no man was ever able to discover or comprehend his wickedness, since it is without end or limit. This is so that you in your turn may know that the works of God done for you in Christ are immeasurable in that he has fore-ordained such effective grace for you in Christ. This grace will not suffer you to be overwhelmed by an evil so great as your sin, and though you deserve this evil, yet because of the grace of this one man not only will you not perish under it but will even be liberated from it eventually. The glory of grace must be magnified: it is not possible to magnify it sufficiently. That is why Paul cries, "Thanks be to God for his unspeakable gift" (II Cor. 9:15). Therefore, pay no regard to those cold half-hearted murmurings of the sophists with their lisping talk of good works without sin, infused faith, acquired faith and free will. It is just stuff and nonsense: stage play in what is a very serious matter. It is unto Christ you must be caught up, as Isa. 2:10 says, "Enter into the rock and hide in the dust from the

face of the Lord in his wrath and from the glory of his majesty."
In the Canticles, too "O my dove in the clefts of the rock in the
holes on the cliff" (2:14). Make no mistake. The greatness of the
protection indicates sufficiently how great that sin is, as long as
you do not think of Christ as some wooden idol or another. All the
saints tremble under this judgment, and unless they have Christ as
a refuge, they perish. And yet we still go on playing about and
arguing whether there is sin in good works! And you know as well
as I do this is the way we understand the fearful and awful majesty
of God, as if we were discussing some fellow or another, when we
were discussing it.

[Luther now argues, as he has already done in this disputation, that the
Louvainians introduce new-fangled words and notions into the plain
meaning of Scripture. He concedes that the Nicene fathers introduced a
non-scriptural word in *homoousios* (*of the same substance* as the Father), but
denies Latomus this precedent as an excuse for the medieval tendency
to proliferate their notions and fancies in interpreting Scripture. Luther
claims that he could refuse to subscribe to the non-Scriptural Nicene
word *homoousios* and not on that account be heretical provided he held
on a basis of Scripture the theological truth the Nicene fathers sought
to define and preserve.]

8.118.12. Let the Fathers say what they think fit. I want the
words of this man Paul to mean exactly what they mean in their
original context (Rom. 6–8). The figments of the sophists about
offences (*reatus*) and obligations (*debitum*) and all that kind of
foolish talk serve to cloud the mind rather than help it. The words
of the Apostle are easy to understand, open for all to see, and may
be depended upon. They do not need trimming up by men: they
burn and shine in their own right like the brightest of suns. . . .
Are not these things so clear and so easy that there is none so dull
that he cannot understand it quite easily? At present we have to
put up with scholastic subtleties about offences, obligations, form,
matter, sin, privation, habit, act, expulsion, infusion, qualities,
forms, subjects, intrinsic and extrinsic good, intrinsic and extrinsic
evil, congruent merit, the different kinds of good, acceptation and
de-acceptation. Who can name much less recount all the terms of
these pestilential creations (lit. frogs and flies)? Even they themselves are not agreed as to who the authoritative teachers are.
It has come to such a pass that before the wretched man in the
street can get from them any real knowledge of sin and grace he
has to swallow wholesale the dregs of philosophy (increased
enormously in recent times!). Let these absurd, revolting views of
the sophists be banished from our midst!

[Finally, Luther now turns to examine Rom. 7:14–25.]

8.119.8. Truly, therefore, Paul says, "But I am carnal" (Rom. 7:14). He does not say, "I was carnal, sold under sin." Now then, prove to me that to be "carnal" in Scripture means subject to penalties and weaknesses. He quite truly calls himself carnal, not because he is completely carnal, for he is spiritual as far as his mind is concerned and carnal as far as his flesh is concerned. In the same way a man is free from sin as far as his mind is concerned but sold under sin as far as his flesh is concerned: as he says, "I serve the Law of God with my mind but the law of sin with my flesh" (v. 25). Do not allow Latomus to deceive you in this matter by positing two wills. Paul is but one single person who confesses that he lives under two dispensations: under grace he is spiritual but under law carnal. But it is one and the same Paul in both instances. The effect of the gift is that he is spiritual and under grace, the grace of the one man Jesus Christ. The effect of sin is that he is carnal but not under wrath, for grace and wrath cannot be present at one and the same time; they neither fight one another nor does one dominate the other as the gift does in relation to sin. And so, "That which I do, as a carnal man I do not understand" (v. 15), but I so understand as a spiritual man, otherwise how could he say of himself that he did not understand what he was doing? In what follows he calls what he does evil. Therefore, he understands what he does as evil, but he does not understand in the flesh what he understands in the spirit. The truth is that he thinks that the sin raging in his flesh is the good which he desires, and so it appears to the man who does not see that it is evil. "For the good that I want I do not, but the evil which I hate, that I do" (Rom. 7:19). You see he does understand good and evil, but it is the spiritual Paul who thus understands, and wills, and hates. In fact the carnal man does not understand the good but perpetrates the evil instead of the good, and loves it. . .

8.120.31. Let us therefore follow Paul. "If then I do that which I do not want to, I consent to the law that it is good" (Rom. 7:16). This is a remarkable combination. He consents to the law that it is good, but not with his whole being, for he does not do as a whole man what he does not will as a whole man. In this matter it is not the whole man who agrees, acts and shows himself unwilling; but yet it is the same man who consents to the law that it is good and who does what he does not want. This action is contrary to the law which he knows to be good and which also he wants. And he goes on to say, "So then it is no longer I that do it" (Rom. 7:17). Who is that "I" who now does not do what it has just been said to do? You must know that this "I" is the "I" which I spiritually am, because according to this "I" I am now reckoned in a state of grace, which does not permit me to be reckoned in accordance with sin, by which I am carnal. All sins have been washed away, and there is another "I" now different from the one before grace was given, when I was reckoned as wholly carnal in accordance with sin. "It is no more I that do it but sin that dwelleth in me": does this mean that you do not do it but that which is in you does it? Your hand strikes me and yet it is not you who is striking me? Quite true, for in such circumstances the hand does it against my will, and it is in accordance with that I am reckoned. Yet nevertheless, I truly do it because a part of me does it. But now I am not reckoned in accordance with that part of me. My hand does evil and it is imputed to me unless my soul is innocent. But it is not for that reason that what the hand does is not evil, but because it is not imputed. It is not imputed because the soul is innocent. So sin is truly sin, but because the gift and the grace are in me, it is not imputed: not because it does not matter as though it were not harmful, but because grace and the gift reign within me.

8.121.9. "For I know that in me, that is in my flesh, dwelleth no good thing . . ." (Rom. 7:18): It is my flesh not somebody else's. Therefore, what dwells in it is said to dwell in me. . . Truly therefore sin dwells in the flesh, and equally truly it is sin. . . Therefore there is nothing good in the flesh, nothing good at all. It is not just a penalty, but sin. "For to will is present with me, but how to achieve it I cannot discover" (Rom. 7:18). Paul explains himself more clearly how in sinning the spiritual man does not do evil but rather wills the good, and yet on account of sin dwelling in the flesh cannot accomplish what he wills. Nevertheless, this will to do good is not to be discounted because he does not carry it out. In the same way the opposite is true. The evil which dwells in the flesh is not to be discounted even though it may not be I myself who works it but rather sin. I am saying two contrary things: evil happens and does not happen. It happens in that sin does it. It does not happen in that the mind neither does it nor wants to do it, though the will does not succeed on account of the activity of sin. I ask you, would Paul ever describe such a mighty battle with such meticulous care, if it were waged between penalty and spirit. Here again is another instance which contradicts the sophists. . . Their glosses as well as their text, their subject matter as well as their vocabulary are alien to the entire usage of Scripture and the judgment of all godly men. Consequently the absurdity which dogs them in their glosses is no less than the one they try to avoid in the text. It is most absurd to maintain what you can nowhere find and never prove; but worse still, you are just compelled to listen to a mass of contradictions.

8.122.1. "For the good that I would, I do not; but the evil I would not, then it is no more I that do it, but sin that dwelleth in me" (Rom. 7:19–20). . . . No one could understand this text except as referring to the spiritual man, nor could they take it as referring to those who perpetrate evil deeds. In this passage Paul says that the one is hampered by the other, but in such a way that the spirit prevails, so that it is attributed to the spirit that he neither effects nor wills the evil. Now he does not turn the sentence round to say, "For it is not the evil I will which I do, but the good I do not will which I do. Now if I do the good I would not, then it is no longer I that do it, but grace which dwells within me." This is the way the flesh would speak if it reigned over the spirit rebelling against it. Now since it is the spirit which complains and accuses the flesh, it is clear that it is not the flesh which is lord and master. The flesh is the rebel and is troublesome to the spirit which is the ruler. None of this is spoken in the interests of the flesh but rather against the flesh. A carnal man constituted outside the grace of God would not do this. Therefore, the grace of God does not allow this work of sin to be imputed to the man, for in actual fact he does not do it. And yet nevertheless it is in him, and in actual fact it is he who does it into the bargain, as has been adequately stated already.

8.122.22. "I find then that when I want to do good, evil is very close to me" (Rom. 7:21). Now it is not one person who wills to do good and another to whom evil lies close at hand. The spiritual man wants to do good as a whole and entire person, but the carnal man is close at hand and it is he who is evil and is less than the whole and entire person. "For I delight in the law of God according to the inner man, but I see another law in my members warring against the law of my mind and making me captive to the law of sin which is in my members" (Rom. 7:22 f.). Here Paul explains himself with perfect clarity, for to delight in the law of God is only in the nature of a pious and righteous man. The man who is not righteous does not resist the law in his members, and does not want to either. Now Paul does not call the law of the mind "natural law" as the scholastics do. He sets the law of the mind against the law in the members. He names it, therefore, the will of the spirit which delights in the law of God, and opposes it to the law in the members which delights in the law of sin. Consequently, the law in the members is at the same time the will which works contrary to the will of the spirit. Paul's actual words are "it is warring against," and he certainly means the evil not of penalty but of guilt. For it is an evil thing to war against the law of God. Now he says not only "does not obey" but "wars against," and this is a much weightier matter. He uses this word to guard against your considering the sin left after baptism too lightly. This sin is considerable, but at the same time it is taken away by a gift of God that is considerable and by grace that is considerable, for the sake of the spirit which does not war against the law of God but delights in it. And what is more, that last phrase, "making me captive" is very disturbing. I beg you to look most carefully at the impressive number of strong words he piles up to emphasize what sin is, the very thing our opponents extenuate and remove. He says not only that it exists, not only that it is alive, not only that it has a will of its own, not only that it is active and working, not only that it wars against, but even that it is a raging power and makes captive. I ask you, are these light words? And who does not feel that this is exactly his own experience? Who does not undergo at some time or another the furious onslaughts of lust, angry thoughts and outbursts, no matter how much he does not want to? Its fury is untamed: as a matter of fact, what is rather surprising, it does not rage in this way in the ungodly because they do not resist its onslaught. They give way to it and obey it, and therefore never experience how much struggle and vexation is needed to resist sin and master it. Onslaught of such a kind demands a strenuous warfare, and so Christ is called "the Lord of Hosts," and "the King mighty in battle," (Ps. 24: 10, 8), because it is through his gift that a man not only sustains these heavy onslaughts, but conquers them.

8.123.7. See therefore the greatness of the gift and the grace of God that evil so great does not damn the godly. Evil thoughts are stronger in the godly than in the ungodly, but yet the evil thoughts of the godly do not corrupt or damn them, while the evil thoughts of the godly though they are less evil, do corrupt and condemn them. Why is this? Is it not the same sin in both? Of course it is the same sin, but the godly have an antidote while the ungodly have none. On account of this the godly do not sin under an onslaught of sin that is relatively greater while the ungodly do sin under an onslaught that is relatively weaker. Not because it is not sin in both cases, but because this triumph is owing to the grace of God and not to its evil nature. If grace is not present sin truly damns. But now grace restrains its evil nature lest it bring to condemnation. Therefore we say, "Not unto us, O Lord, but unto thy name give the glory!" (Ps. 115:1). The sophists plough a crooked furrow in this matter. It is not, as they allege, that such great fury against the law of God is not sin. Neither is it penalty nor weakness. It is great sin of the kind the psalmist speaks when he says: "I shall be thoroughly cleansed of the very great offence" (Ps. 19:13). Let our glorying in this our innocence be utterly banished. Paul says, however, "to make captive," not because the spiritual man is taken captive, but because from the side of sin nothing is omitted by which the spiritual man may be captured. The same kind of expression occurs in Gal. 1:13 where Paul says, "And I used to lay waste the Church of God." It is impossible to lay the Church of God waste, but he left nothing undone and did all he could to destroy it. For that reason he does not say here, "it makes war and I have been captured": he says "it makes captive," but I am not captured. Even if he had said he was captured, the meaning would compel us to take it as far as the flesh is concerned. Just as he said that he was sold, and that he was carnal according to the flesh, so in this context he means that he is captive according to the flesh. This is the meaning as far as I see it, as it is the simplest and the most acceptable.

8.123.28. "O wretched man that I am! Who shall deliver me from the body of this death?" (Rom. 7:24). Here he calls sin death, using it figuratively of the worst possible harm. He does the same as Pharaoh did when he besought the locusts to be taken away, "Pray for me to the Lord that he take away this death from me" (Ex. 10:17). As Pharaoh did with reference to the locusts Paul calls sin by the most hateful of names on account of its restless and distressing ragings which never cease and are never tamed. Because of these ragings of sin we cannot have any peace in this life but are compelled to stand in battle array continuously. Paul is not expressing in this context a dread of those dominant and quiescent inclinations to which Latomus refers[1]. Nor does Augustine mean what Latomus attributes to him[2]. . .

8.124.17. "Thanks be to God through Jesus Christ our Lord!" (Rom. 7:25). Paul gives thanks not for his own righteousness, but to the God of mercy, and he does this through Jesus Christ our Lord. For it is always he whom he presents to God: it is under his wings he hides and in his grace he revels when he rejoices and glories in the grace and gift of God. Nevertheless, he longs to be freed from this dreadful body. For he does not say, "Who will free me from the death of this body?", but "Who will free me from the body of this death?" (Rom. 7:24). Because he sees that in this life the purity of the Louvainian saints is not possible, but yet he still wants to be pure, it is on that account he wants to die. Such a sentiment the ungodly man never expresses, or if he does, he does not say it for the same reason. Paul does not cry out and invoke

[1] Latomus refers to lust in disposition or inclination rather than in actual fact (*in habitu* rather than *in actu*).
[2] Latomus quotes *Contra Julianum*, VI, 8; Migne, 44.666.

death in this way because of punishment but because sin troubles him exceedingly. You see therefore that this passage applies to the holiest of people and that they suffer from a wild and raging sin. This is so that we might learn not to lessen the grace of God in making light of our sins by calling human glosses to our aid and saying that they are not sins. On the contrary we magnify and emphasize sin as much as we can, so that it becomes clear that the confession and emphasis of sin is the work of God who is wonderful in his saints and who performs his entire will with them, even though we still seem to have sins in ourselves (and do in actual fact have them). Because his will for us is not the sin which is in us, but our sanctification from that very sin. Paul therefore concludes his discussion on the state of the godly man in this world and says, "Therefore I myself serve with my mind the law of God, but with my flesh the law of sin" (Rom. 7:25), the "I myself" meaning one and the same man. . . These words are much too clear in their meaning to be made to come to terms with the subterfuge of the sophists. He says "I myself" and not somebody else. And then he says "I serve": he does not say "I have sin" but rather "I serve sin" or what amounts to the same thing, my flesh serves it. But what does it mean "to serve sin"? Does it not mean to do its will? Does it not mean to act contrary to the law of God? But the flesh is doing this as long as it is warring, as long as it is in bondage, as long as it rages, for in these ways it is serving sin. Yet because the spirit is not consenting to sin nor being conquered by its ragings, on that account it is not damned. The service of sin is made unprofitable and all its efforts frustrated. Nevertheless that does not necessarily mean that such servitude is nothing nor that the flesh does not sin under its evil bondage. Although it serves its master in vain and its master sin does not prevail, yet because of this it has to be crucified and killed so that it may cease to serve in this way. "For there is no condemnation to those who are in Christ Jesus and who do not live according to the flesh" (Rom. 8:1). No condemnation, of course, but not no sin, for sin is obviously there. And not that sort of sin which only Latomus imagines he knows, and by which the spirit apart from grace serves sin, but that sort which would happen if the grace and the gift of this One Man had not prevailed. The essence of sin is still in them, of course, but it is not now in a position to do what once it could.

. . . 8.125.27. If the words are taken just as they stand we have established that "to serve sin" or its law is the same thing as "to sin," no matter who says it or where. As Christ said, "Everyone who commits sin is the slave of sin" (John 8:34). And Peter, too, "What a man is conquered by, to that is he now the slave" (II

Peter 2:19). And Paul himself also, "Ye were the slaves of sin, but now ye have been freed from sin and have become slaves of righteousness" (Rom. 6:17). And so in the passage of Scripture under discussion Paul himself is a slave of sin, but because he adds "in the flesh" he clearly distinguishes between serving sin purely and simply (which is all that Latomus wants, and believes he understands), and serving sin in the flesh. What Latomus teaches, that there are occasions when a man does not serve sin, is simply not true. It is neither true of the state of serving sin, purely and simply, nor of the state of serving sin in the flesh. If a man is the slave of sin then everything he does is sin. For he is given over to sin, and slavery describes a condition rather than a deed, and covers the whole activity of life. Conversely, it is one thing to serve God purely and simply but quite another to serve him carnally. The righteous serve God purely and simply for such service has regard to the person, but hypocrites serve him in the flesh in that they serve him only by works and not by a true faith. And as the latter are damnable hypocrites, then the former are really saved hypocrites, if I may be excused the expression. They are saved hypocrites because though they serve sin in their flesh and have every appearance of evil, yet in truth they are good men. And as the external works of the hypocrites are not without worth but are in fact useful and good because they are useful creatures of God, in the same way the sins of the righteous are in actual fact evil and harmful because they are works of sin. And as their good works do the hypocrites no good, so their sins do the righteous no harm.

[Luther now brings his refutation to a close by saying that the case has been adequately argued. He recapitulates the errors of Latomus as they strike him. He accuses Latomus of always starting out with a premise which is really a question which needs arguing. Latomus continually refuses to take the word "sin" in its plain grammatical scriptural sense, and insists on interpreting it always in the sense that scholasticism has come to give it. He will not recognize what grace and sin, law and gospel, Christ and man are. He refuses to submit to the plain meaning of Scripture, distorts both the patristic evidence as well as Luther's writing, and argues divine truths on a basis of human opinions and writings. Luther makes a plea for the replacement of the study of scholastic theology in the universities by a study of the Bible, and invites his Wittenberg colleagues to take up the battle, for he is in exile without his books except for his Bible.] He closes with the words

Farewell from my Patmos. 20th June 1521.

BIBLIOGRAPHY

SOURCES

All references to the Luther text are made to the Weimar text, volume, page, line, and where significant to the title and date of the work cited.

All references to Patristic texts are made to Migne's *Patrology*.

References to the text of the Bible are made to the Vulgate, but where Luther quotes, it is his quotation that is translated not the Vulgate text (where possible, chapter and verse references are to the A.V.).

1. SCHOLASTIC AND PRE-REFORMATION BACKGROUND

Consult the full bibliographies in the companion volumes in this series. Especially:

Vol. X   p. 33–43
          p. 232–237
          p. 375–378
Vol. XI   p. 369–374
Vol. XIV p. 380–382

Carré, M. H., *Realists and Nominalists*, 1946.
Curtis, S. J., *Short History of Western Philosophy in the Middle Ages*, 1950.
Hägglund, B., *Theologie und Philosophie bei Luther in der Occamistischen Tradition*, Lund, 1955.
Jetter, Werner, *Die Taufe beim jungen Luther*, Tübingen, 1954.
Leff, Gordon, *Medieval Thought*, Pelican, 1958.
Lohse, Bernard, *Ratio et Fides*, Göttingen, 1958.
Lohse, Bernard, Art. in *SJT*, Dec., 1960.
McKeon, R., *Selections from Medieval Philosophers*, 1931.
Mellone, S. H., *Western Christian Thought in the Middle Ages*, 1935.
Meyer, Hans, *Philosophy of Thomas Aquinas*, Bonn, 1938. English trans., 1944.
Smith, H. Maynard, *Pre-Reformation England*, 1938 (excellent bibliography).
Walker, G.S.M., *Church History A.D. 600–A.D. 1300*, 1961 (useful bibliography).

2. LUTHER

A. *editions*

Werke, *Weimarer Ausgabe*, 1883 (90 vols.). Cited *WA*, vol., page, line.

Clemen, *Clemen's Edition*, Berlin 1950 (8 vols.). Cited Clemen, vol., page, line.
(This text is in many instances superior to the definitive Weimar edition.)

B. *translations*

Luther's Works, Philadelphia and St. Louis, 1955– (55 vols.). General Editors: Pelikan and Lehmann. Cited *LW*. vol., page, line.
Works, Works of Martin Luther, Philadelphia (6 vols.). 1932 ff. Cited *WML*. vol., page.
Reformation Writings, Lee Woolf (vols. 1, 2), Lutterworth 1952, 1956.
Watson, P., *Epistle to Galatians*, Edin., 1953.
Packer and Johnston, *Bondage of the Will*, 1957.
Kerr, *Compendium of Luther's Theology*, 1943.

C. *secondary works*

Aland, Kurt, *Hilfsbuch zum Lutherstudium*, 1956.
Bainton, R., *Here I stand*, 1950.
Beard, Charles, *The Reformation of the Sixteenth Century*, 1883, 1927.
Boehmer, Heinrich, *Luther and the Reformation*, 1930.
Boehmer, Heinrich, *Martin Luther*, 1946.
Bouyer, Louis, *The Spirit and Forms of Protestantism*, 1956.
Carlsen, E. M., *Re-interpretation of Luther*, 1948 (Philadelphia 1948).
Denifle, Heinrich, *Luther und Luthertum*, Mainz, 1904.
Grisar, Hartmann, *Luther* (Six volumes) 1913–17.
Holl, Karl, *Gesammelte Aufsätze*, I, Tübingen 1932.
Harnack, Theodosius, *Luther's Theologie*, Munich, 1926–1927.
Koestlin, Julius, *Luthers Theology*, Eng. trans. 1883.
Koestlin, Julius, *Life of Luther*, 1883.
Lindsay, T. M., *History of the Reformation*, Edin., 1906
MacKinnon, James, *Luther and the Reformation* (4 vols.), London, 1925 ff.
Rupp, Gordon, *Luther Studies*, 1953.
Rupp, Gordon, *Luther's Progress to the Diet of Worms*, 1951.
Schaff, L., *History of the Church* (2 vols.), 1888.
Smith Preserved, *Life and Letters of Luther*, 1911.
Watson, Philip, *Let God be God*, 1947.
Whitney, J. P., *History of the Reformation*, 1940.

INDEXES

GENERAL INDEX

368 GENERAL INDEX

Catholicism *(continued)*
Luther's catholicism evangelical and
ancient, 65 n., 265, 273, 342
Christ
faith in, 62, 76, 229
as priest, 66, 133–4
as mediator, 174
contrasted with Moses, 67
priesthood compared with Levitical,
137–46
with respect to office, sacrifice and
tabernacle, 148–55, with respect to
Levites, 156–66
as interpreter of Scripture, 127
power over sin and death, 63, 339–
40
as fruit of resurrection, 61
as sacrament, 159
his sacrifice, 185–6
in Old Testament, 193
Christology, 23, 30–43
Person and work of Christ, 23
Christ's work, 48–66, 116, 161, 162–3,
187, 197–8
Chrysostom
on Hebr. 3:15, 86
on Hebr. 4:1, 2, 88–9
on Hebr. 4:15, 100
on Hebr. 6:1, 121
on Hebr. 9:28, 187
on Hebr. 11:1, 203
on Hebr. 12:1, 227
on Hebr. 13:2, 242
on Abel, 207
on Abraham, 128
on death, 54, 60–2, 64–5
on death and eternal life, 207–8
on Enoch, 208
on faith, 72, 124, 210
on faith of Moses, 219–20
on frequent baptism, 120
on the incarnation, 65
on knowledge of God, 126
on promise of God, 129
on man, 48
on second repentance, 199
on sacrifice of Christ, 185
on saints, 125
on sin, 227–8
on *substantia*, 85
on meaning of testaments, 176–7
on Word of God, 95
Church
Augustine and Lombard on Church,
104 n.
on forsaking church, 199
as people of God, 321, 323
nature of people of God, 38
ruled by Word of God, 39
in the world, 198

Commandments of God
as impossible, 312
Synod of Orange on, 313
Conscience, 172
Councils
authority of, 318
Creation
out of nothing, 204
Cross, 23, 102
accepting, 72
foolishness of, 291–2
theology of, 234–5, 291–2, 293
meaning of, 53
reveals God, 290
as a sacrament, 196–7
as destruction of will, 249
as worship, 232
Cusa, Nicholas of, 261
Cyprian
on immortality, 62

Death
on fearing death, 207
the Devil and death, 58–9
Dionysius
on angels, 42
Dominicans
opposition to Luther, 22, 274
Wimpina and Tetzel propound
counter-theses, 274

Eck
and Leipzig Debate, 14, 151
Erasmus
on Hebr. 2:4, 49–50
on Hebr. 4:2, 89
on Hebr. 5:7, 114
on Hebr. 11:3, 204
on the censer, 164
support against Luther sought by
Louvain, 308
Etaples, Lefevre d', (Faber Stapulensis)
on Hebr. 4:1, 2, 88–9
on Hebr. 5:7, 114
on Hebr. 9:4, 165
on frequent baptism, 120
on nature of Christ, 49
on *substantia*, 202
on the tabernacle, 157
Eternal life, 177–8, 207
Eusebius
on man, 51
Exodus
meaning of, 86–7

Faith, 38, 84–5, 172–3, 239, 244
Biel on faith, 208–9
Chrysostom on faith, 72, 124, 210
Jerome on faith, 85
Lombard on faith, 208

BIBLICAL REFERENCES

OLD TESTAMENT